# THE GREAT

AN ILLUSTRATED TRIBUTE TO LEGENDS OF THE BOOK

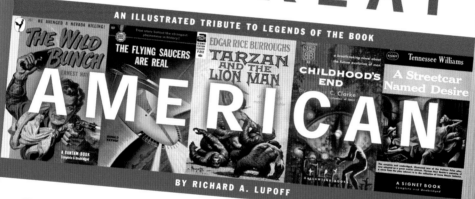

# AMERICAN

BY RICHARD A. LUPOFF

# PAPERBACK

Book Design  Drive Communications, New York
Copy Editing  Lori Stephens

Printed in Hong Kong

First American Edition

9 8 7 6 5 4 3 2 1

Collectors Press books are available at special discounts for bulk purchases, premiums, and promotions. Special editions, including personalized inserts or covers, and corporate logos, can be printed in quantity for special purposes. For further information contact: Special Sales, Collectors Press, Inc., P.O. Box 230986, Portland, OR 97281 Toll-free: 1 800 423 1848

*For a free catalog write to*: Collectors Press, Inc. P.O. Box 230986, Portland, OR 97281 Toll-free: 1 800 423 1848 or visit our website at: www.collectorspress.com

Library of Congress Cataloging–in–Publication Data

Lupoff, Richard A., 1935-
      The great American paperback :
      an illustrated tribute to legends of the book/
   by Richard A. Lupoff. — 1st American ed.
         p.   cm.
      Includes bibliographical references and index
      ISBN 1-888054-50-6 (alk. paper). —
      1. Paperbacks—Publishing—United States—History.
      2. Paperbacks—Publishing—United States—Pictorial works.
      3. Book covers—United States—History.
      4. Publishers and publishing—United States—History.
      5. Popular literature—United States—History and criticism.
   I. Title.
   Z479 .L86 2001
   070.5'73—dc21                                      00-065904

CIP

# THE GREAT

AN ILLUSTRATED TRIBUTE TO LEGENDS OF THE BOOK

# AMERICAN

BY RICHARD A. LUPOFF

# PAPERBACK

PORTLAND, OREGON

# CONTENTS

THE GREAT AMERICAN PAPERBACK

This is a simple story, isn't it? In 1939 Pocket Books made its debut with *Lost Horizon* by James Hilton, and it's been full speed ahead ever since.

Right?

Wrong.

Although *Lost Horizon* was Pocket Book Number One, it wasn't really the first Pocket Book, nor did the first Pocket Book appear in 1938. Read on, read on, and all will be revealed.

The story isn't that simple.

It's a fascinating yarn, and it starts in 1837, almost exactly a century before Pocket Books issued its historic first ten titles.

There was a prosperous publishing industry in the United States in the 1830s (and even earlier). In colonial times books had been imported from England and the Continent, but once the colonists had presses they started creating newspapers and books of their own. After the Revolution the Americans, as they now were, they were able to print their own books.

The books were printed on high quality paper and were elaborately bound in leather, cloth, or "boards" (actually heavy cardboard), and they were appropriately expensive.

In fact, the young country was prospering, but in 1837 the economy took a severe downturn. In the nineteenth century they called these events panics, in 1929 and well into the 1930s they called it a depression, and since then we've called them recessions.

Factories closed. Workers lost their jobs. People had to struggle to acquire the bare necessities of life, and book sales plunged. But there was still an audience for books when they were produced cheaply enough.

Enter two sharpies named Rufus Griswold and Park Benjamin. Griswold and Benjamin knew that newspaper distribution was subsidized by the Post Office Department. They also knew that newsprint was cheaper paper than the superior rag-content paper normally used for books. They devised a method of publishing books on newspaper presses by printing them on large sheets of newsprint and folding the resulting pages into pamphlets.

They began a weekly series called *Brother Jonathan*. It was printed, folded, and distributed like a newspaper but *Brother Jonathan* was certainly not a newspaper. Was it the first fiction magazine published in the United States, or was it the first paperback book series?

Decide for yourself.

In any event, *Brother Jonathan* was successful and was soon imitated by other pioneering publishers of paperback books, including some legitimate newspaper publishers who fought the Griswolds and Benjamins of their day by issuing fiction supplements. Some of these little books had brightly colored covers. Prices started at fifty cents. That was a lot of money in those days, but competition steadily drove prices down until they bottomed out at five cents.

The nickel novel was born.

In 1856 the first major nickel or dime novel publisher, Beadle and Adams, came into being. The company struggled initially but within four years had a bestseller. This was *Malaeska, the Indian Wife of the White Hunter* by Mrs. Ann S. Stephens. The novel offered the lure of the wild frontier, the thrills of weaponry, and the titillation of miscegenation. It sold 65,000 copies — not bad for a mass-market paperback today. In its day, the success of the book was phenomenal, and its formula still works. If you doubt that, check out the paperback racks at your local bookstore.

Soldiers carried nickel and dime novels in their rucksacks in the Civil War. They read them in their encampments, using them to while away the boring hours between terrifying moments of gunfire and carnage. Soldiers have done the same ever since.

Westerns were the mainstay of those proto-paperback publishers until 1883. Detectives had been creeping into the literature as town sheriffs, U.S. marshals, and private eyes pursued criminals on the wild frontier. The most prominent private detective firm of the era had been founded by Alan Pinkerton, who promoted himself and his company with a series of self-glorifying books. The slogan of these detectives-for-hire was, "We never sleep." Their symbol was a wide-awake eye — very likely the origin of the expression "private eye."

In 1883, Beadle and Adams' chief printer, George Munro, broke away to start his own company. Two years later he introduced Old Sleuth, an urban detective, and once again, everything changed.

Old Sleuth wasn't the first series detective in fiction; that title is disputed. Most likely it belongs to Edgar Allan Poe's C. August Dupin. But Old Sleuth was the first mass-marketed, popular fiction detective to appear in a long series of adventures. Within a few years he was joined by such mainstays as Old Cap Collier, Diamond Dick, and Old King Brady. Old King Brady had a couple of assistants, Young King Brady and Alice Montgomery (Alice was apparently the first female detective in fiction).

But the most popular and enduring of dime novel detectives was Nick Carter. He made his debut in 1886 and survived in a series of dime novels, pulp magazines, comic books, motion pictures, radio shows, and modern paperback books until at least the 1970s. Uncounted authors contributed to his saga. The character evolved from a master of disguise and escapes to a tough, sexy, James Bond-like Cold War agent. He seems to be out of print these days but don't count the old boy out. He might pop up again at any moment, on the printed page or computer screen.

You've probably never heard of Irvin S. Cobb (1876-1944), but in his day he was one of the nation's literary leading lights. A native Kentuckian, he started out as a journalist and then went on to become an immensely popular short story writer. His most successful creation was Old Judge Priest, a Confederate veteran turned small-town solon.

In the essay, *A Plea for Old Cap Collier*, Cobb reminisced about his favorite boyhood reading:

"Looking back on my juvenile years it seems to me that, generally speaking, when spanked I deserved it. But always there were two punishable things against which — being disciplined — my youthful spirit revolted with a sort of inarticulate sense of injustice. One was for violation of the Sunday code, which struck me as wrong — the code, I mean, not the violation — without knowing exactly why it was wrong; and the other, repeated times without number, was when I had been caught reading nickul libruries, erroneously referred to by our elders as dime novels.

"I read them at every chance; so did every normal boy of my acquaintance. We traded lesser treasures for them; we swapped them on the basis of two old volumes for one new one; we maintained a clandestine circulating-library system which had its branch offices in every stable loft in our part of town. The more daring among us read them in school behind the shelter of an open geography propped on the desk.

"Shall you ever forget the horror of the moment when, carried away on the wings of adventure with Nick Carter or Big-Foot Wallace

DEATH IN FANCY DRESS

35¢

JEFFERSON FARJEON

AMERICAN LIBRARY

JOHN STEPHEN STRANGE

SILENT WITNESSES

*A Note About Images And Captions*

The images in *The Great American Paperback* come from many sources, most of them private collections. It would be impossible to cite the donor of each image in the book; the owners are listed in the acknowledgement. When possible, first printings are used, but in some cases later editions were substituted for reason of condition or availability. When possible I have cited title, author, publisher, year of publication, and cover artist. When a given item is unknown I have omitted it, and readers who furnish missing information or correct any errors will earn my gratitude. Where an artist is not credited and a legible signature is not visible on the painting, I have at times made an attribution based on the artist's style, the expert opinions of collectors, or citations in earlier works. Each book is evaluated on a scale of one to five "books" for collectibility. In general this corresponds to dollar value, but this may not always be the case. I have refrained from placing specific dollar values on books as the increase in interest in the hobby, variations in taste, and general inflation affect these factors constantly. In the broadest terms, a one star book is not considered a significant collectible and should be available for a nominal price. The value of a five star book may reach several thousand dollars. Priority of edition is important, the law of supply and demand is of paramount importance, and I cannot overemphasize the impact of condition, condition, condition.

*Richard A. Lupoff*

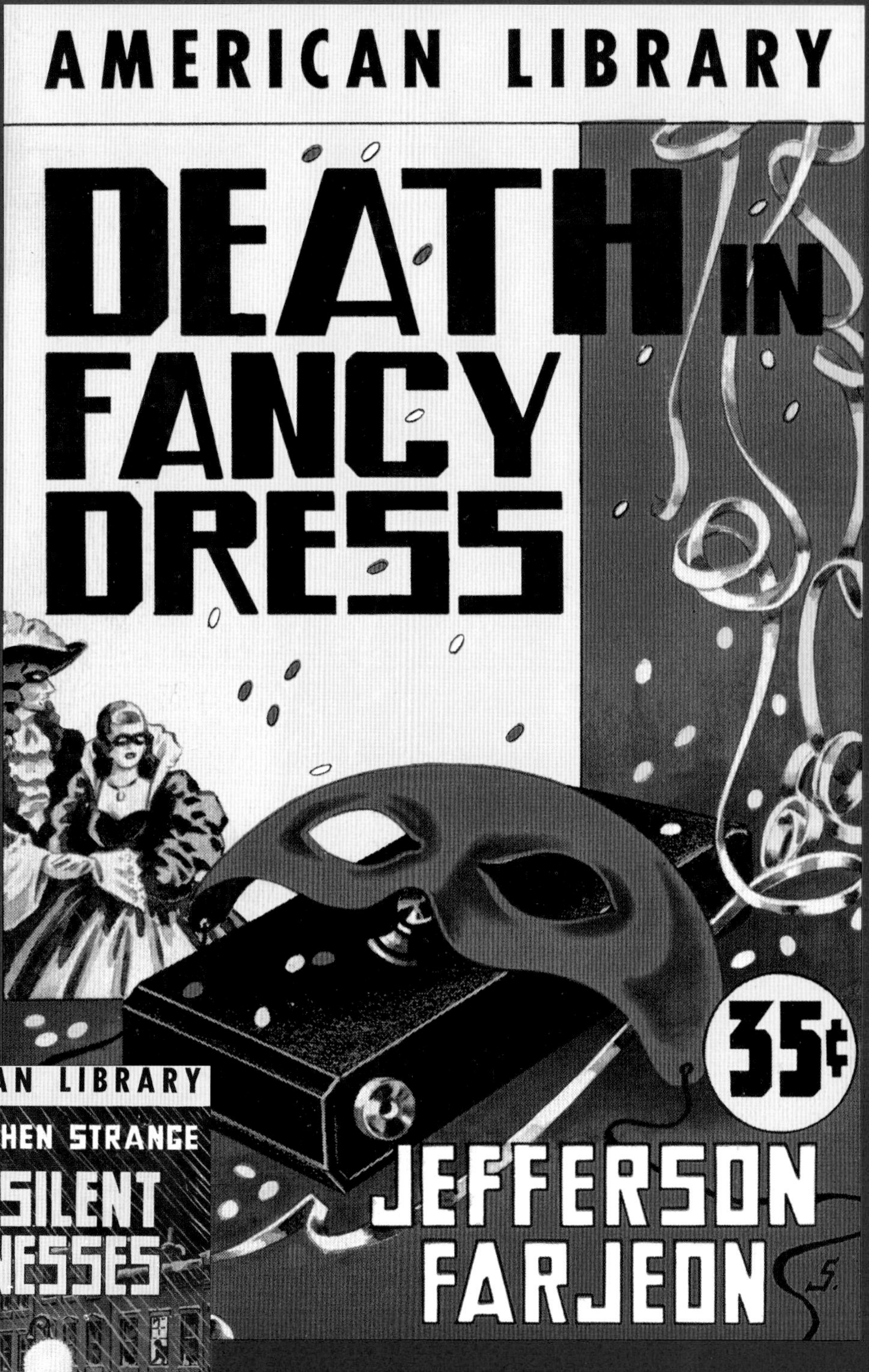

**SILENT WITNESS**
JOHN STEPHEN STRANGE
AMERICAN LIBRARY, 1930's

A wonderfully evocative scene — you feel as if you could step into that snowstorm. Note distributor's sticker over the publisher's price.

**DEATH IN FANCY DRESS**
JEFFERSON FARJEON
AMERICAN LIBRARY, 1930's

Bright colors and bold design — American Library books should have succeeded but somehow they did not. Was the 35¢ price too much for consumers in the era?

or Frank Reade or bully Old Cap, you forgot to flash occasional glances of cautious inquiry forward in order to make sure the teacher was where she properly should be, at her desk up in front, and read on and on until that subtle sixth sense which comes to you when a lot of people begin staring at you warned you something was amiss, and you looked up and round you and found yourself all surrounded by a ring of cruel, gloating eyes?

"...What, also, we might have pointed out was that in a five-cent story the villain was absolutely sure of receiving suitable and adequate punishment for his misdeeds. Right then and there, on the spot, he got his. And the heroine was always so pluperfectly pure. And the hero always was a hero to his fingertips, never doing anything unmanly or wrong or cowardly, and always using the most respectful language in the presence of the opposite sex. There was never any sex problem in a nickul librury. There were never any smutty words or questionable phrases. If a villain said "Curse you!" he was going pretty far. Any one of us might whet up our natural instincts for cruelty on Foxe's *Book of Martyrs*, or read of all manner of unmentionable horrors in the Old Testament, but except surreptitiously we couldn't walk with Nick Carter, whose motives were ever pure and who never used the naughty word even in the passion of the death grapple with the top-booted forces of sinister evil."

❦❦❦❦❦

Those nickel novels and dime novels came in two formats. The larger numbers were roughly 7" X 10", about the size of a "Golden Age" (1940s) comic book or a modern news weekly. The smaller ones were approximately 5" X 7", so-called "digest size."

In addition to several generations of homegrown American authors, the early paperback houses had access to foreign literature. Copyright protection was sketchy or nonexistent for foreign authors, and popular novels published in England and other countries were pirated by American publishers. Sometimes, especially when magazine serialization preceded book publication, an American paperback house would rush a first book edition into print even before the first British edition had appeared.

In 1891 U.S. copyright law was amended to provide protection for foreign authors, and British publishers were quick to go after American "pirates." A major source of first-rate, royalty-free material was no longer available to American publishers. They either had to stand in line and pay for publication rights or forgo the works of foreign authors.

Even so, publishers would surely have adjusted to the new reality and these paperbacks might have continued to appear, but instead there was a hiatus in paperback book publishing. As the nineteenth century waned and the twentieth century burgeoned, nickel and dime novels were crowded out of popular favor by the new pulp magazines. Beginning with Frank A. Munsey's *Argosy* in 1896, the pulps were themselves a marriage between the so-called "family magazines" then flourishing and the dime novel.

Month after month (in some cases week after week) the pulps flooded the nation's newsstands with unmeasured miles of adventure stories, westerns, love tales, science fiction, sports stories, horror stories, jungle stories, murder mysteries, heroes and heroines in every conceivable setting.

Once again, one can only wonder why the public turned away from books and to magazines. Perhaps as the new century raced ahead with its ever faster pace set by the automobile and the airplane, the radio and the motion picture, readers lost interest in the time-consuming novel format and in its place welcomed the pulps (and slicks as well) with their diet of short stories and serial segments.

At any rate, the first incarnation of paperbacks faded away and the age of magazines took shape.

This is not to say that no paperback books were published between, say, 1900 and 1939. There were any number of efforts to publish paperbound books, either in digest size or in the smaller format that swept the publishing scene after 1939.

One prolific publisher was Emanuel Haldeman-Julius. He was a socialist, a student of psychology, and a believer in "trial marriage" and other ideas considered radical in his day. A confidant of pioneer science fiction publisher Hugo Gernsback, Haldeman-Julius published a series of Little Blue Books starting in 1919.

These books lived up to (or down to) their name. The page size was considerably *smaller* than that of modern paperbacks. The covers were typically printed on plain blue stock without adornment. The typography was crude. The books were unattractive, but they were very economical; they were widely promoted through advertisements, and they covered an astonishing array of topics, including a relatively small percentage of fiction.

Ten years after Haldeman-Julius started publishing his Little Blue Books, Charles Boni inaugurated his own, Boni Paper Books. Charles Boni was a distinguished publisher who had operated the firm of Boni and Liveright and had been co-founder of the immensely successful Modern Library. Boni paperbacks were published in the larger digest size and had pictorial covers by distinguished artists including Rockwell Kent and Vera Bock. Boni paperbacks were solidly made, durable books, and surviving examples are often in remarkably good condition. However, the company suffered from distribution problems, and its timing could hardly have been worse. The Great Depression began in the same year, and two years later, Boni was out of business.

In 1932 the National Home Library Foundation, headquartered in Washington, D.C., inaugurated its Jacket Library. The format of Jacket Library books was identical to that of modern paperbacks. An example was *Green Mansions* by W. H. Hudson, published "Complete and Unabridged." Keep that phrase in mind — it was to become a watchword for paperback publishers a decade later.

The series was edited by Sherman F. Mittell, and the book had a plain green cover broken only by type. As many paperbacks were to do in later years, *Green Mansions* carried a self-congratulatory message from the publisher to the reader:

"THE JACKET LIBRARY extends its greetings to the American public. Its birth comes timely with a nation's need. It is the desire of its sponsors to meet this need by making available to all American homes and schools the best works of the world's literary masters, at a price within the reach of all.

"The Library is dedicated to the memory of those great Americans who devoted their lives and their efforts towards widening the educational facilities of our land.

"The aim of JACKET LIBRARY will be to further their work: to see to it that all sections of the nation are adequately provided with books that give joy and charm and knowledge. And at a price well within their means.

"The Library can grow into a vital cultural institution by bringing to the many in this land the best that has been thought and said. It is our hope that the homes of America will respond heartily to a program that must in the course of years make of this nation a happier one."

∎ ∎ ∎ ∎ ∎

Alas, such was not to be the case. The Jacket Library managed to get fifteen titles into print. Most were classics, solid, respectable, and not especially exciting. But the list did include Mark Twain's *Adventures of Tom Sawyer* and a highly collectible edition of Conan Doyle's *Tales of Sherlock Holmes*, an unusual selection of Holmesian cases. Despite its noble ideals and promising initial list, Jacket Library soon sank, leaving behind hardly a ripple.

### AGAINST THE GRAIN
**J. K. HUYSMANS**
**BONI, EARLY 1930's**

Boni Books brought more than a touch of class to early paperback publishing. Sold by subscription rather than on newsstands, they failed to reach a large market.

### PRIZE POEMS 1913-1929
**BONI, CIRCA 1930**

Obviously, Boni was uncompromising in presenting serious literature to the readers, whether the readers wanted it or not. Hard to fault Charles Boni's idealism—but his business sense was another matter.

### GREEN MANSIONS
**W. H. HUDSON**
**JACKET LIBRARY, 1932**

Shown is the actual book cover. A true forerunner of the modern paperback, Jacket Library expired after issuing fifteen titles.

### HER SECOND LOVE
**BERTHA M. CLAY**
**ARTHUR WESTBROOK COMPANY,**
**CIRCA 1900**

Bertha M. Clay was an immensely
popular author. Her romances might
seem mild after a century, but at the
time they were considered daring if
not downright risqué.

### HER HUSBAND'S GHOST
**MARY E. BRYAN**
**ARTHUR WESTBROOK COMPANY,**
**CIRCA 1900**

Colorful illustrative covers gave
turn-of-the-century paperbacks a
remarkably modern appearance.
Love stories and ghost stories
were popular, especially among
female readers.

"Once a reader, always a reader"

NEW MAGNET LIBRARY No. 1212

# A Double Handed Game

By NICHOLAS CARTER

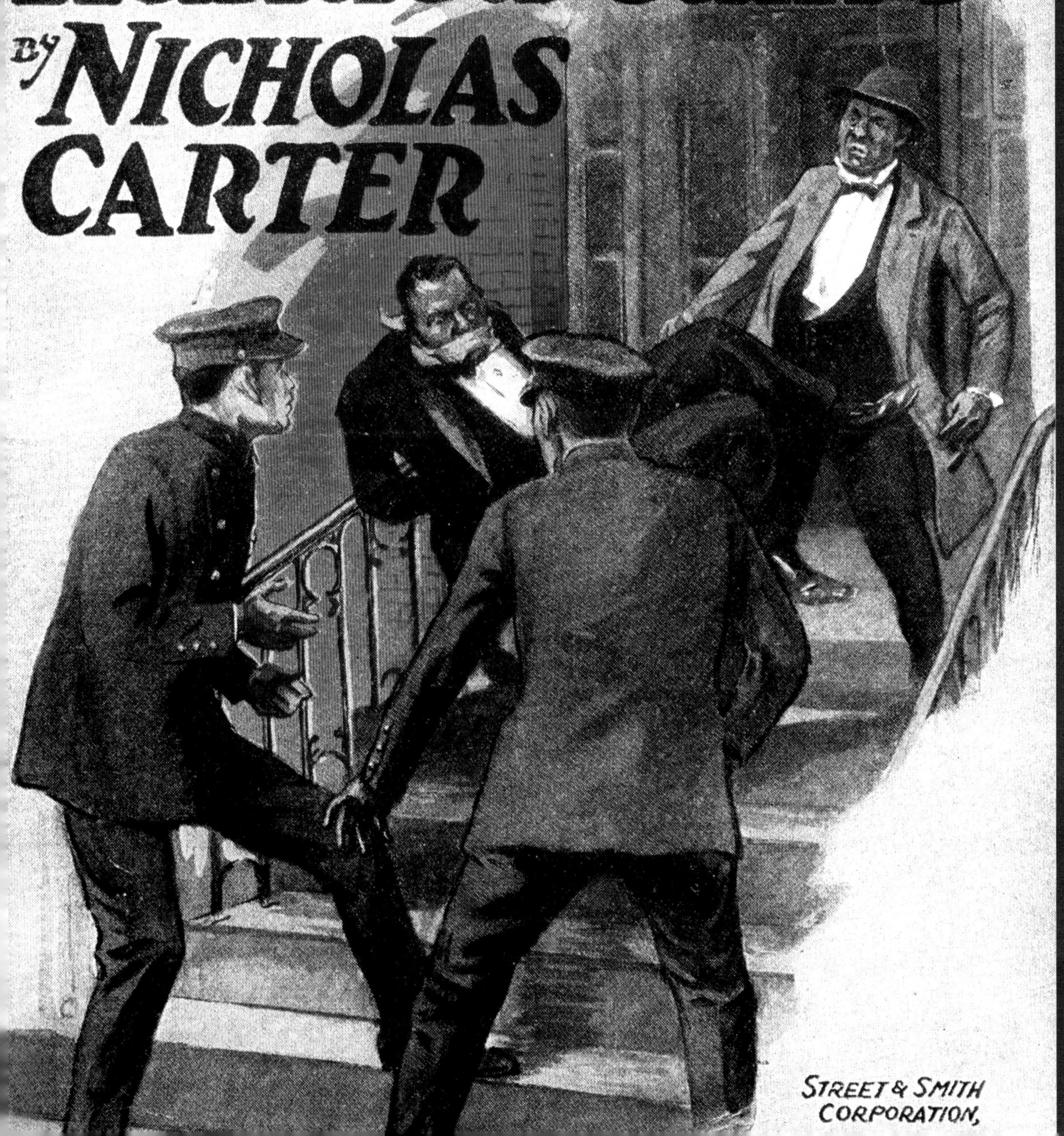

STREET & SMITH CORPORATION,

But paperback publishing had enjoyed a long and successful history on the other side of the Atlantic Ocean, and even though this book is concerned with American paperbacks, European publishers cannot be ignored.

One of the first of these was Tauchnitz Editions, founded by Bernard von Tauchnitz. He created his company, coincidentally, in 1837, the year of the financial panic that led to the first wave of American paperback publishing. Headquartered in Leipzig, Germany, Tauchnitz Editions' "Collection of British and American Authors" offered cheap paperbound editions of English-language books.

Tauchnitz Editions were sold chiefly to English-speaking visitors to the Continent (British or American business travelers and tourists). British copyright law prevented their sale in the United Kingdom, but for businessmen riding between cities in railroad cars or honeymoon couples taking the Grand Tour, they became a byword.

A number of other companies published English-language paperbacks in Europe. By far the most significant of these was Albatross, and again, the timing was intriguingly coincidental. In the United States, the National Home Library Foundation initiated its ill-fated Jacket Library with *Green Mansions*. In Europe, the new Albatross Modern Continental Library made its debut with *Dubliners* by James Joyce.

The format was still conservative, although not quite as conservative as that of the Tauchnitz editions. Albatross books had a "cleaner," more modern look than those issued by Tachnitz. There was even an illustration on the cover—

a drawing of an albatross, the far-venturing bird considered an omen of good fortune by sailors. The typography was more up-to-date than Tauchnitz's, and Albatross introduced another design feature that would have important impact within a few years. The book covers still lacked pictorial content (except for the symbolic albatross itself) but they were color-coded to designate the type of book: red for detective and adventure stories, green for historical novels and biographies, and so on.

Albatross concentrated on British and American fiction, for the most part of a serious, mainstream nature. The lists included works by Aldous Huxley, Sinclair Lewis, Compton Mackenzie, Joseph Hergesheimer, and Ludwig Lewisohn. Albatross ventured into non-fiction with *The Magic Island*, by W. B. Seabrook, an account of voodoo practices in Haiti.

But Albatross showed a populist bent with *The Love of Julie Borel*, a tear-jerker by American romance writer Kathleen Norris. Even more notable were *The Man at the Carlton* by Edgar Wallace, *The Bishop Murder Case* by S. S. Van Dine, and *The Maltese Falcon* by Dashiell Hammett.

In these four books, Albatross addressed four segments of the mass-oriented, popular readership: the "women's novel," the pulp-style thriller, the traditional "cerebral" mystery, and the hard-boiled private detective tale.

Albatross was up against long odds. By 1932 Tauchnitz was almost a century old and deeply entrenched in the English-language European market. The economic crash of 1929 had spread from Wall Street and the effects were felt worldwide. Germany was in a state of political turmoil; Communist and Nazi mobs battled in the streets of major cities; and Adolf Hitler was less than a year from coming to power.

## A DOUBLE HANDED GAME
**NICHOLAS CARTER**
**STREET & SMITH, 1902**

Nick Carter lived in story papers, dime novels, pulp magazines, and mass paperbacks. Not to mention comics, radio dramas, and movies! With updated costumes, the illustration on this novel is, regrettably, timeless.

▐ ▐ ▐

The new company was the creation of three partners, and it was truly international in scope from its beginning. They were John Holroyd-Reece, whose background was in British publishing; Max Christian Wegner, a German who had worked for Tauchnitz as an editor; and Kurt Enoch.

Kurt Enoch was the scion of a German-Jewish family that had been involved in book publishing and distribution since the nineteenth century. Young Kurt would surely have been the pride and joy of the Enoch family. He had served in the Kaiser's Army in World War I, was decorated repeatedly, and rose through the ranks to become an officer. Mustered out of the Army after the armistice of 1918, he returned to university in Hamburg where, in 1922, he earned a doctorate in political economics.

After a decade in the family business, he teamed up with Holroyd-Reece and Wegner to create Albatross. Even though Albatross did not distribute in England, the company's financial backing came from England, and from Albatross's London office, Holroyd-Reece maintained a liaison with the English-language literary community. Wegner ran Albatross's Paris office, where the company's editorial work was done. Enoch remained in Hamburg, in charge of production and distribution.

Tauchnitz was by now an old and tired company. Albatross was young and energetic, and within two years a merger between the two was proposed. The new Nazi government, suspicious of Albatross's international and Jewish connections, attempted to stymie the deal, but Albatross used a "blind" buyer and succeeded in taking over Tauchnitz.

Enoch could not remain in Nazi Germany for long, and he shortly moved his office to Paris. At this point Kurt Enoch leaves our story—but not for long!

While Albatross was winging its way to success on the Continent, another bird was about to crack its way out of its shell on the other side

of the English Channel. This was the odd, flightless bird that gave its name to Penguin Books.

Penguin was the creation of Allen Lane, and once more we encounter the scion of an established publishing family. Lane's cousin John operated a company called the Bodley Head. John Lane had been a successful and highly regarded publisher for many years, and Allen had worked for the company since he was a teenager. In 1924 John Lane died and young Allen ascended to the leadership of the company. Allen and his two brothers, Richard Lane and (another) John Lane, were soon firmly in control.

As the worldwide depression reached England, the Bodley Head faced economic ruin. Allen Lane would certainly have been aware of the popularity of paperback books in Europe, including the activities of Tauchnitz and Albatross. The three Lane brothers, led by Allen, sought to imitate Albatross's success. Thus Penguin Books was born.

By July 1935 the first Penguin release was ready for market, and the very first Penguin was a biography of Shelley, *Ariel*, by André Maurois. Other books on the list were similarly respectable, including *A Farewell to Arms* by Ernest Hemingway, *Carnival* by Compton Mackenzie, and *South Wind* by Norman Douglas.

The list also included two mysteries. One was *The Unpleasantness at the Bellona Club*; the other was supposed to be *Murder on the Links* by Agatha Christie, but instead this book was postponed and replaced in Penguin's initial release by *The Mysterious Affair at Styles*. Penguin copied Albatross's practice of color-coding its books. And the Lanes succeeded in getting distribution through the Woolworth chain of stores, thereby gaining exposure to millions of potential customers around the world.

Penguin Books was an immediate success, the parent company was saved from imminent ruin, and Allen Lane was the shining star of English publishing. He was also an ambitious man, and when he surveyed his company's market penetration of the English-reading world he found a glaring gap: the United States. He wanted desperately to distribute Penguin Books in the U.S., and he had the wisdom to hire an American to run his American office.

He soon met someone who fit his specifications. This was a brilliant young man, a recent college graduate doing advanced work at the London School of Economics. Like Lane and Enoch before him, he had family connections in the publishing industry. He was the nephew of Saxe Cummins, a Random House executive in charge of Modern Library which Random House had taken over from the failing Boni and Liveright. The young man was fascinated by publishing and eager to promote paperbacks.

His name was Ian Keith Ballantine.

Allen Lane and Ian Ballantine struck a bargain. Ballantine would return to the United States and establish an American office for Penguin; Lane would provide "product." Initially, American Penguin would function solely as a marketing arm for British Penguin. Ballantine himself would be more than an employee: he would also be part owner of American Penguin.

By the time Ian Ballantine returned to New York to set up American Penguin, another experiment was being prepared in paperback publishing in the U.S. As we've already seen, there had been many others, some more successful than others, but none would have the impact of this one. The creation of Robert de Graff, it was called Pocket Books.

De Graff knew about Allen Lane's Penguin Books and he was aware of Lane's intention to expand his operation into the U.S. The result was a race between Pocket and American Penguin to become the leading paperback publisher in this country.

Ian Ballantine returned to the United States from England and set up American Penguin with a staff of three: himself, his wife Betty (born and raised in India of English parents), and Ian's one-time college buddy, Walter Pitkin, Jr. In his book

*Two-Bit Culture: The Paperbacking of America,* Kenneth C. Davis describes an hilarious scene of the three partners working away in a cramped New York office, scissors in hand, industriously clipping the British price off books that Allen Lane sent them from England.

That was how British Penguins became American Penguins.

The arrangement didn't last long. On Sept. 1, 1939, Adolf Hitler's invasion of Poland plunged Europe into war. Penguin was subject to paper restrictions, as were all civilian publishers in England. Transatlantic shipping became difficult and dangerous as German U-boats roved the ocean, sinking British ships at will.

If American Penguin was to survive, Ian Ballantine and his partners had to do something drastic. They did. They began publishing books of their own, but they didn't do it entirely *on* their own.

As Hitler's forces rolled across more and more of the European Continent, Enoch had to flee. He traveled from France to Spain, then to Portugal, and from there, aboard a Greek ship, to the United States. Miraculously, he even managed to bring his family with him.

In 1941 Allen Lane risked a Transatlantic voyage to the United States which was still technically a neutral power. He met with Kurt Enoch and arranged to bring him into American Penguin as another minority stockholder. Enoch would be Lane's eyes, ears, and voice in dealing with the obstreperous Ballantine.

The unhappy team struggled along through the war years. From time to time Lane would send emissaries in less than successful attempts to assert his absentee authority over American Penguin. In 1946 he added Victor Weybright to the team. Weybright has previously been involved in publishing and had served in the American Embassy in London during the war. He had also become close friends with Lane.

Weybright's arrival at American Penguin may have been the final straw. Battle lines were now drawn.

On one side was the Ballantine camp with its independent attitude and its freewheeling method of operation. By American standards, the Ballantines were relatively conservative. Their choice of authors and titles and their packages positively reeked of class and restraint when compared to such newcomers as Avon Books and Popular Library, but to Allen Lane's perception they had lost their bearings and plunged into the depths of pandering.

On the other side was the team of Enoch, Weybright, the English Eunice Frost, and other Lane loyalists.

The first completely American Penguin titles had not appeared until 1942. By this yardstick, de Graff and Pocket Books won their race with Penguin by a healthy margin. But if we count the books that Ballantine imported as early as 1939, the race would have to be declared a dead heat.

What about that first true-blue American Penguin? It was a mystery: *Murder by an Aristocrat* by Mignon G. Eberhart. Ballantine saw fit to start the numbering of the true American Penguins with 501, and any collector who manages to turn up an American Penguin with a lower number must clearly have been shopping in an alternate universe.

The early American Penguins, like their British predecessors, were color-coded but otherwise lacking in cover art. This situation would not last long; soon American Penguins were appearing with colorful cover illustrations.

The two artists most identified with American Penguin and its eventual successor, Signet Books, were Robert Jonas and James Avati. An interesting early pictorial-cover Penguin was *Cimarron* by Edna Ferber (Penguin 605, 1946).

The color coding is still there and the friendly little Penguin logo proudly tops the cover. The painting by Jonas is stylized, almost abstract, far from the lurid sensationalism that many paperback houses would be accused of—and with justification—in later years, especially in the 1950s.

But even though the pictorial-cover Penguins were restrained and dignified in appearance, Lane considered pictorial covers *per se* to be cheaply commercial. He wanted to publish *literature*, not trash, and to him the presence of a cover painting on a paperback book was the sign of trash.

Ian Ballantine showed his initiative and aggressiveness in other ways. He signed up co-publishing deals with other organizations, most notably the Military Services Publishing Company. In short order, Allen Lane found himself the absentee sponsor of such odd hybrids as books with double logos—a tough-looking, rifle-toting, helmeted GI, a fat, cheerful little aquatic bird, and the slug line, *Infantry Journal–Penguin Books.*

By 1946-47, American Penguin was thriving under Ballantine's guidance. But Allen Lane and his allies found Ballantine's policies—and his insistence on having his way—intolerable. In retrospect, it is astonishing that the Lane-Ballantine partnership lasted as long as it did. It could go on no longer. Ian Ballantine walked out.

Kurt Enoch and Victor Weybright remained at American Penguin, which was swiftly transformed into the New American Library. In earlier years, Lane had established several other imprints within the Penguin family. The most important of these was Pelican Books, a line devoted to serious literature, often nonfiction. Under the aegis of NAL, American Penguin was transformed into Signet Books and American Pelican became Mentor.

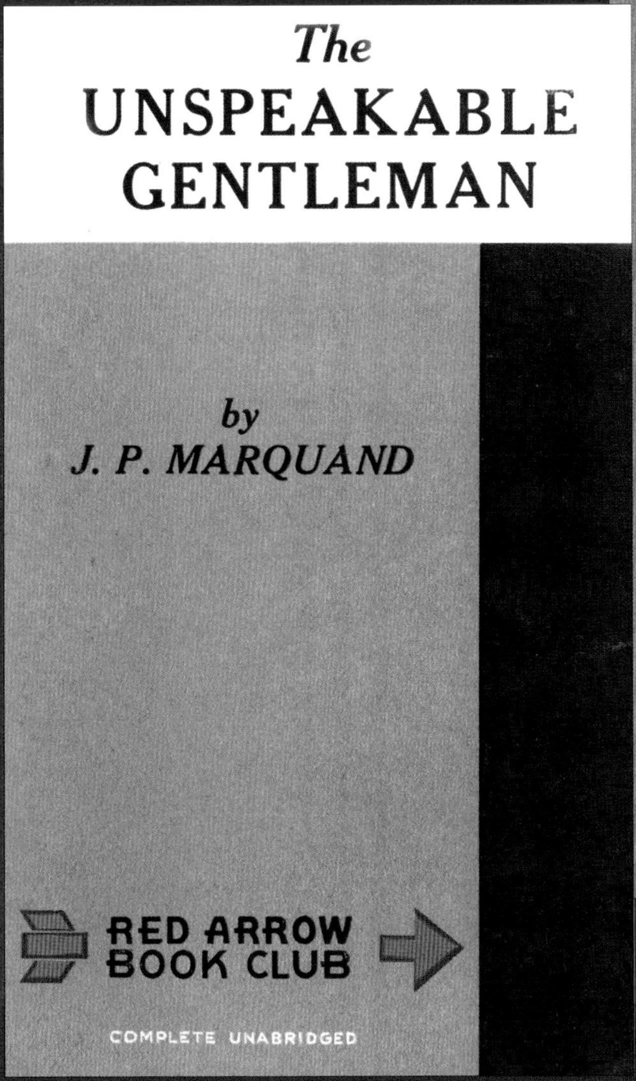

## The
## UNSPEAKABLE
## GENTLEMAN

by
J. P. MARQUAND

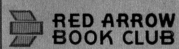  RED ARROW
BOOK CLUB

COMPLETE UNABRIDGED

**13 AT DINNER**

RED
ARROW
THRILLER

POISON

WILL

## AGATHA
## CHRISTIE

### THE UNSPEAKABLE GENTLEMAN
J. P. MARQUAND
RED ARROW, 1939

Note the book club indicia and plain cover. Little is
known of Red Arrow. It may have been a subscription
publisher, which might have led to its demise.

### 13 AT DINNER
AGATHA CHRISTIE
RED ARROW, 1939

Christie has been a favorite of paperback readers for
more than sixty years, with no end in sight. This Red
Arrow book is one of her scarcest editions.

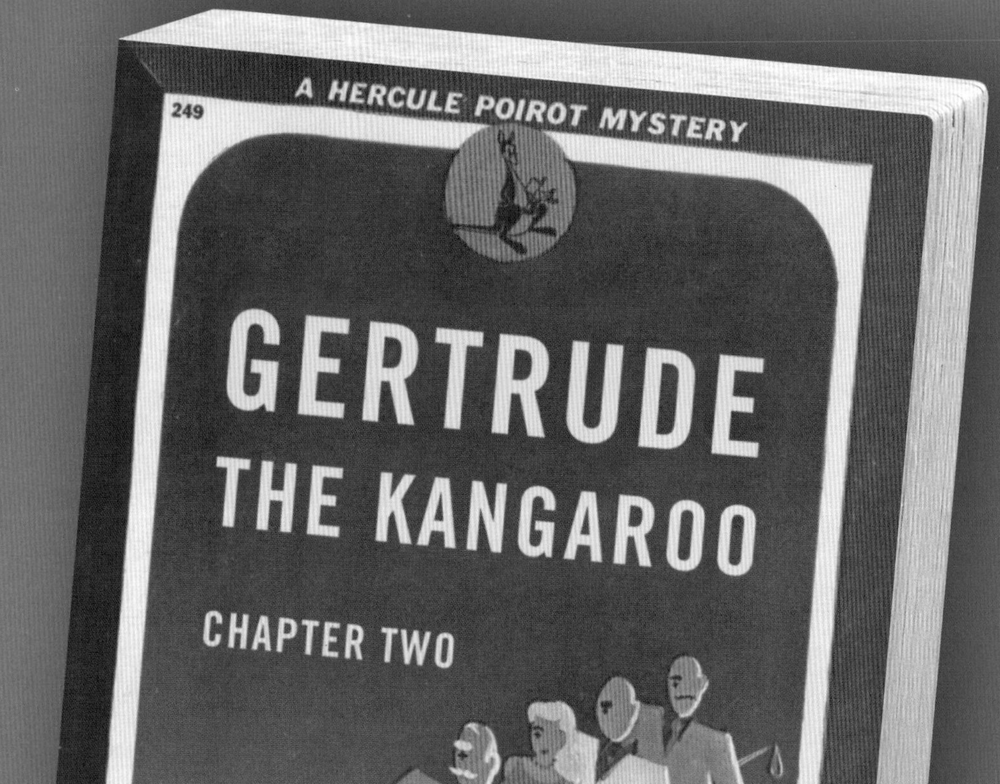
249
A HERCULE POIROT MYSTERY
GERTRUDE
THE KANGAROO
CHAPTER TWO
AGATHA CHRISTIE
POCKET BOOK EDITION COMPLETE & UNABRIDGED

It all started with a little lady with bright yellow skin.

Well, not really. As we've already seen, there were paperbacks before there were paperbacks—the nineteenth century soldiers' readers, the turn-of-the-century popular novels, the Tauchnitz-Albatross books in Europe, the Little Blue Books and other publishing experiments in the United States, and then Allen Lane's English Penguins, imported to the U.S. by Ian Ballantine.

But in 1938 another young man, Robert de Graff, came along and turned the publishing world on its ear. De Graff was not new to publishing. In 1937 he had started a company called Blue Ribbon Books, little remembered today and, to be honest, not exactly a major player even in 1937.

But Bob de Graff—by all reports a pleasant and personable individual—was familiar with the earlier experiments in paperback publishing. Surely he was aware of Allen Lane and Ian Ballantine. And he wanted to do something that was truly American and that would have a big impact on publishing.

What if he could publish major bestsellers in a small, handy format, and sell them at a price that was affordable to Everyman—and Everywoman? Most popular books were bought in bulk in that era by so-called "lending libraries." Unlike public libraries, supported by taxes or by do-gooder grants, lending libraries were commercial operations. Major department stores maintained them. Others operated from corner drugstores or even as departments within bookshops.

Customers would purchase a membership or leave a deposit—typically one dollar—and thereafter be permitted to borrow current and recent books for a few days or a week at a time, in exchange for a nominal rental fee.

If de Graff could find a way to publish books so cheaply that their purchase price was competitive with a lending library's rental fee, he thought he should be able to sell plenty of books.

De Graff set up a meeting with Richard Simon (the Simon of Simon & Schuster) and pitched his idea. Simon must have blinked, because he told de Graff that he'd had the same idea himself. Everybody knew what a paperback was. He'd been playing around with a concept that he called the Twentieth Century Library. Instead, he and his partner Max Schuster, and S&S's financial wizard, Leon Shimkin, proposed a deal whereby S&S would back de Graff's new enterprise.

The name of the new line was Pocket Books.

De Graff looked around for a suitable title to use as a trial balloon and settled on *The Good Earth*, a hugely popular novel by Pearl S. Buck, originally published in 1931. Buck was one of the most popular authors of her day, the exotic Asian settings of much of her work adding to their popularity.

After obtaining rights to the book, de Graff ordered an experimental paperback printing, legendarily comprising just 2,000 copies. The front cover featured a painting of a young woman in traditional Chinese garb, her black hair cropped short, her skin the same bright yellow as the background against which she stood. The copy on the cover read simply,

*The Good Earth*
*A Novel*
*By Pearl S. Buck*

The jacket copy included an endorsement by Will Rogers, the popular comedian, philosopher, and sometime actor of his day—a sort of New Deal era David Letterman. "Not only the greatest book about a people ever written," Rogers wrote, "but the best book of our generation."

The cover art also included a circled logo that read "Pocket Book Edition" and a banner at the bottom which contained a phrase that would become part of the language in the decade to follow: *Complete and Unabridged*.

In 1938 de Graff circulated these sample books without charge along with a questionnaire to test the potential market for such books. The response was overwhelmingly positive.

By June of 1939 Pocket Books was geared up and ready to roll. De Graff had hired a small staff. His editors were Morris E. Speare and Louise Crittendon; his marketing chief was Wallis E. Howe, better known as Pete. By the time de Graff and company had compiled their initial list of titles, Howe started calling on potential outlets for the books. His first stop was Macy's, where he allegedly hoped to sell 5,000 books and would probably have been happy to log an order for half that number. Instead, Macy's ordered 10,000. Pocket Books was successfully launched!

Pocket Books was announced in a huge newspaper ad written by Arkady Leokum of the Sherman & Marquette advertising agency. (Leokum was a handsome, pipe-smoking youngster who could easily have got work as a model himself.) It's obvious from the content of the ad that Pocket Books were originally circulated only in a small area. By modern standards the ad was heavy in text, and it's worth quoting:

"OUT TODAY—THE NEW POCKET BOOKS THAT MAY REVOLUTIONIZE NEW YORK'S READING HABITS

"Famous best sellers—complete, not digests. Unabridged and unexpurgated, in brand new pocket size editions. Beautifully printed in large, clear type on easy-to-read opaque cream paper. Sturdily bound with soil-proof, Dura-gloss cover.

"25¢ each

"Today is the most important literary coming-out party in the memory of New York's oldest book lover. Today your 25¢ piece leaps to a par with dollar bills.

"Now for less than the few cents you spend each week for your morning newspaper you can own one of the great books for which thousands of people have paid from $2 to $4.

"These new Pocket Books are designed to fit both the tempo of our times and the needs of New Yorkers. They're as handy as a pencil, as modern and convenient as a portable radio—and as good looking. They were designed specifically for busy people—people who are continually on the go, yet who want to make the most of every minute.

"Pocket Books are printed in exactly the same size, easy-to-read type as the original editions, with not so much as word or a comma left out. Thinner paper and a smaller page make them so compact they'll snuggle into your pocket or handbag without a bulge.

"Never again need you say "I wish I had time to read" because Pocket Books gives you the time. Never again need you dawdle idly in reception rooms, fret on train or bus ride, sit vacantly staring at a restaurant table. The books you have always meant to read "when you had time" will fill all the waits with enjoyment.

"How Can the Price Be So Low?

"Three factors combine to make this possible. (1) Authors, publishers, printers and paper makers have agreed to a fraction of a cent profit per volume. (2) Elimination of costly cloth and seven complicated binding operations. (3) Above all, the economies of printing quantities ten times as large as the ordinary edition.

"Despite their bargain price, Pocket Books look expensive—they even have stained edges and richly colored end sheets. You needn't hesitate to place them on the bedside tables of your weekend guests—to give them to your most finicky friends as going away presents or graduation and birthday gifts.

"Start your Pocket Book library today—ten great titles are already available. You'll find them on sale at hotel and railway newsstands, stationery shops, drug and cigar stores, book shops and department stores—wherever good books or magazines are sold.

"A Money-Back Guarantee Without Any Strings.

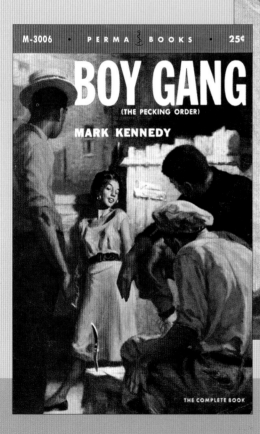

### BOY GANG
**MARK KENNEDY**
**PERMA (POCKET), 1955**

Permabooks began as an experiment by
Doubleday. Books in paperback size were
bound in laminated cardboard "hardcovers."
By 1954 Doubleday had lost interest and sold
the line to Pocket Books, where the format
was switched to normal paperbacks.

❚❚

### THE BLACKBOARD JUNGLE
**EVAN HUNTER**
**CARDINAL (POCKET), 1955**
**COVER BY CLARK HULINGS**

Evan Hunter's sensational book was probably
the most successful of all juvenile delinquent
novels. The controversial motion picture
(same year) didn't hurt sales either.

❚❚❚

### BLACK IVORY
**NORMAN COLLINS**
**POCKET, 1949**
**COVER BY BARYE PHILLIPS**

A strange distinction of the era was that
non-white women could be shown bare-
breasted but white women could not.
The blurb appealed as much to prurient
interest as to the horrors of slavery.

❚

## THE CASE OF THE BURIED CLOCK

ERLE STANLEY GARDNER
POCKET, CIRCA 1960
COVER BY ROBERT MCGINNIS

Gardner's Perry Mason novels (and his other books, including those written as "A. A. Fair") remain perennial favorites with readers and collectors. The "silver spine" McGinnis editions with their "glamour" paintings are among the most striking of all paperbacks.

## THE CASE OF THE SUBSTITUTE FACE

ERLE STANLEY GARDNER
POCKET, 1943
COVER BY BARYE PHILLIPS

Fans of the courtly (and portly) Perry Mason portrayed for so many years by Raymond Burr may be surprised at the far more vigorous, tough-talking and occasionally vulgar character created by Erle Stanley Gardner. This is a later printing of the book, by the way. Remember that the first printing in any form is always more valuable than later editions.

## CLUNY BROWN

MARGERY SHARP
POCKET, 1946

The uncredited cover painting for Margery Sharp's bright, upbeat romance was hardly sensational, but it captured the feeling of the novel. For a while, Pocket kept a running count of the number of books it had sold—by this time, total sales had exceeded 150 million.

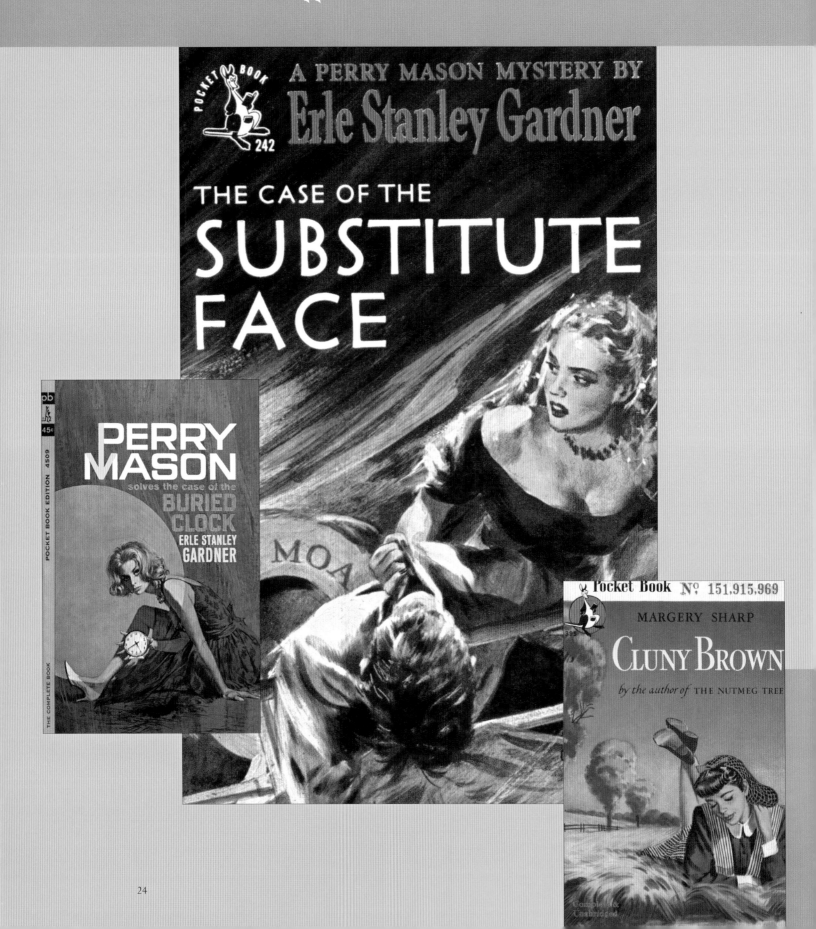

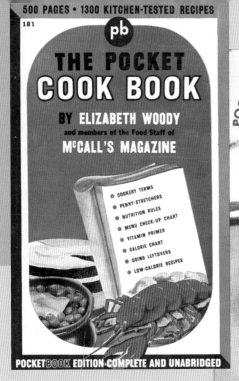

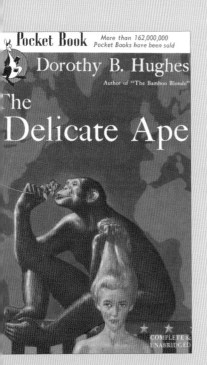

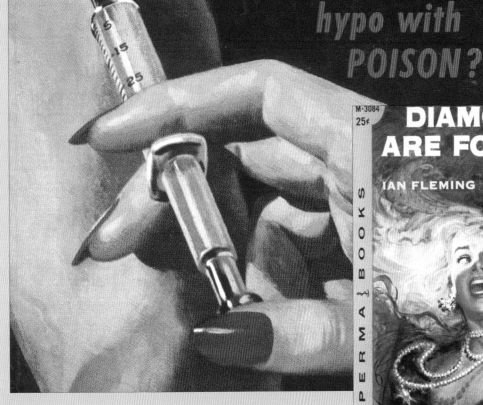

## THE POCKET COOK BOOK
**ELIZABETH WOODY**
**POCKET, 1942**

A magazine tie-in, this was meant
to be used rather than merely
read. In fact, most copies were
used until they fell apart, then
thrown away, making this a rarity
in any condition and almost
impossible to find in good shape.

## THE DELICATE APE
**DOROTHY B. HUGHES**
**POCKET, 1946**

One of the great ladies of the
mystery field for many years,
Dorothy Hughes has slipped
into undeserved obscurity. One
day she may be rediscovered
and her early editions become
sought-after items.

## CROOKED HOUSE
**AGATHA CHRISTIE**
**POCKET, 1950**
**COVER BY PAUL KRESSE**

Along with Gardner, Carr, and a
handful of other classic mystery
writers, Christie has remained
readable and collectible for many
decades. The hypodermic needle
cover also makes this a favorite
among specialists.

## DIAMONDS ARE FOREVER
**IAN FLEMING**
**PERMA (POCKET), 1957**
**COVER BY WILLIAM ROSE**

Pre-NAL James Bond editions
are a minor collecting field unto
themselves. The tough-guy image
obviously didn't work as well in
marketing Ian Fleming's superspy as did the later suave and
mildly satirical version.

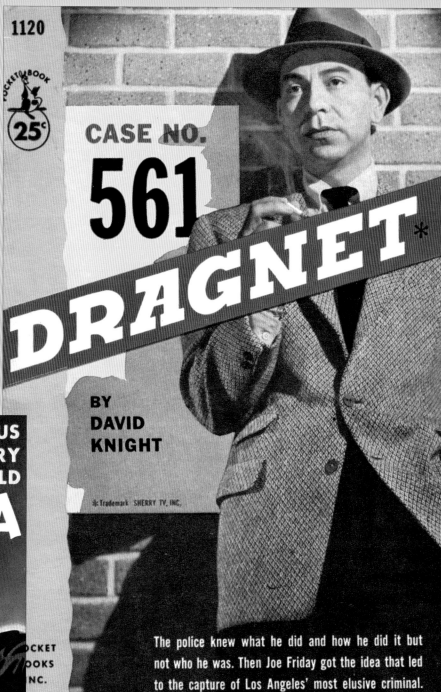

1120

POCKET BOOK 25¢

CASE NO.
**561**

**DRAGNET***

BY
DAVID
KNIGHT

* Trademark SHERRY TV, INC.

POCKET BOOKS INC.

The police knew what he did and how he did it but not who he was. Then Joe Friday got the idea that led to the capture of Los Angeles' most elusive criminal.

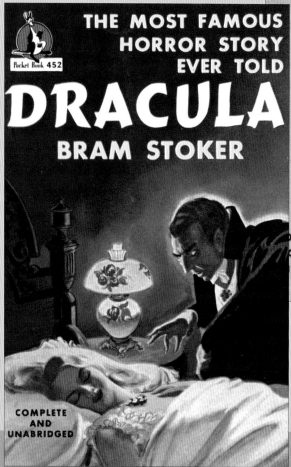

Pocket Book 452

THE MOST FAMOUS
HORROR STORY
EVER TOLD

**DRACULA**
BRAM STOKER

COMPLETE
AND
UNABRIDGED

## DRACULA
BRAM STOKER
POCKET, 1947

Unlike Mary Wollstonecraft Shelley's *Frankenstein*, famous for its adaptations but a tough nut for the modern reader to crack, *Dracula* is still a thriller that will make you go to bed with the light on!

## DRAGNET—CASE NO. 561
DAVID KNIGHT (RICHARD PRATHER)
POCKET, 1956

There *was* a mystery writer named Jack Webb but he was *not* the same man who portrayed Sergeant Joe Friday of the LAPD. This *Dragnet* novel was written by Richard Prather, author of the immensely popular Shell Scott private eye novels.

"If it's more convenient, fill in the coupon right now and send it to Pocket Books, 386 Fourth Avenue, New York, with cash, stamps, money order, or check.

"If you don't think these books are the most wonderful buy you ever saw—if you're not delighted with their "quality look"—their convenience, their ease of reading—if you're not completely satisfied in every way, send them back at our expense and we'll refund your money."

❧❧❧❧❧

That wasn't all!

The ad also featured endorsements from seven of the cultural gurus of 1939: *Nicholas Murray Butler, Hendrik Willem Van Loon, Christopher Morley, Lowell Thomas, Clifton Fadiman, Will Durant, Dale Carnegie.*

There was a coupon customers could clip and mail in to order their Pocket Books—at a uniform price of 25¢—and if they ordered four or more titles, Bob de Graff picked up the cost of postage. Otherwise, they got socked an extra nickel per book.

Let's take a look at those first ten Pocket Books:

1. *Lost Horizon* by James Hilton
2. *Wake Up and Live!* by Dorothea Brande
3. *Five Great Tragedies* by William Shakespeare
4. *Topper* by Thorne Smith
5. *The Murder of Roger Ackroyd* by Agatha Christie
6. *Enough Rope* Dorothy Parker
7. *Wuthering Heights* by Emily Bronte
8. *The Way of All Flesh* by Samuel Butler
9. *The Bridge of San Luis Rey* by Thornton Wilder
10. *Bambi* by Felix Salton

It was an interesting selection: two fantasies, one considered profound literature in its day, the other a ribald comedy; one self-help book; a collection of Shakespeare; a murder mystery; a book of light verse; a gothic; two serious novels, one classic and one modern; and a children's book.

No science fiction, no westerns, nothing resembling a bodice-ripper (not even *Topper*, although that book does contain a sexy ghost). At one time, legend had it in the paperback world that de Graff had circulated his draft list of titles before settling on the ten and received an urgent phone call from Lee Wright, a highly influential and much beloved editor of detective fiction.

"No mysteries on your list," Wright allegedly growled.

"Should there be?"

"You bet there should."

"All right. Give me a recommendation."

"Try Christie. She's as big as they come. Yes, see if you can get *The Murder of Roger Ackroyd*."

"You really think it will sell?"

"Robert, it will sell."

In a 1972 interview with paperback scholar and historian Thomas L. Bonn, de Graff set the record straight. The Christie book *had* been on the list all along. The conversation between de Graff and Wright took place *after* the first ten Pocket Books had been released. What followed was fascinating—and may have changed the entire course of modern paperback publishing.

De Graff described the performance of the first ten books to Bonn:

"Particularly with our first ten titles, we tried to find out what would be saleable. It was terribly important to find this out at an early date in the business. What would be saleable and what wouldn't. And in sufficient quantities so you could print 100,000 minimum at a time. That was our goal. To get to 100,000. Of course we increased it many times after that. So that we started out with popular fiction, *Lost Horizon*. This Shakespeare—this was 560 pages. For a quarter it was a loss leader. We lost money on it, but we wanted to find out with these *Five Great Tragedies* whether people would appreciate it. And for that reason we tried to give it a great value. Because for the money, you see, it was a terrific value. For 25 cents! It really was.

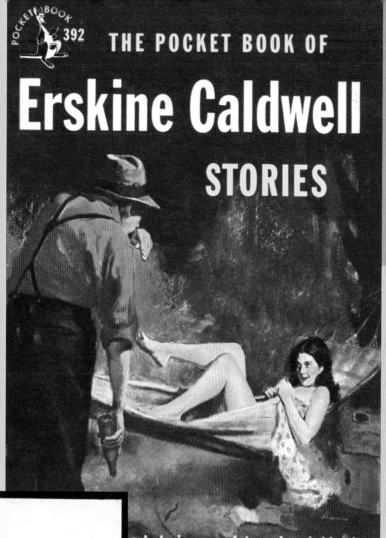

**FRANKLIN DELANO ROOSEVELT—A MEMORIAL**
EDITED BY DONALD PORTER GEDDES
POCKET, 1945
COVER BY GEORGE SALTER

Rushed into print an astonishing six days after the president of the United States died in April 1945, this was the first "instant book." Geddes, an editor at Pocket Books, was also responsible for the second "instant book," *The Atomic Age Opens*, after the bombing of Hiroshima in August, 1945.

**THE POCKET BOOK OF
ERSKINE CALDWELL STORIES**
ERSKINE CALDWELL
POCKET, 1947
COVER BY THOMAS DUNN

Caldwell was usually associated with NAL but Pocket got this collection of thirty-one short stories from him. The combination of rural setting, alcohol, and seduction was a trademark of Caldwell's books and a whole school of imitations.

**THE GIRL FROM NOWHERE**
RAE FOLEY
POCKET, 1950
COVER BY BARYE PHILLIPS

The prolific Phillips' contribution to the body-in-the-bathtub sweepstakes, the lovely blonde model also qualifies as a prime example of "strategic water level."

A magazine tie-in. In the era before *Playboy* and its far sexier imitators and competitors, *Esquire* was considered a risqué periodical. By today's standards, these jokes are barely kindergarten fare.

This was the first Pocket Book, issued in an edition of just 2,000 copies. An object of veneration by collectors, and easily distinguishable from its 1939 reissue as Pocket Number 11.

Reissued with modified artwork, revised typography, a prominent price and a number (11), Pearl S. Buck's somewhat soppy novel is also desirable in this form—but not as much so as in its unnumbered version.

# THE GOOD EARTH

A NOVEL
by PEARL S. BUCK

"Not only the greatest book about a people ever written, but the best book of our generation."
—WILL ROGERS

*Pocket*
BOOK
EDITION

COMPLETE & UNABRIDGED

THE GOOD EARTH
BY PEARL S. BUCK
Nobel Prize Winner
"Not only the greatest book about a people ever written, but the best book of our generation."
—WILL ROGERS
25¢
COMPLETE AND UNABRIDGED
*Pocket* BOOK EDITION

### HALFWAY HOUSE
ELLERY QUEEN
POCKET, 1944

Pocket experimented with its binding process on this book, producing a variant edition bound at the top instead of the edge. As a novel, this rates as typical Ellery Queen, which is to say, excellent classic-style mystery writing. As a collectible, the normal edition is an ordinary item; the variant is a treasure.

### THE GREAT IMPERSONATION
E. PHILLIPS OPPENHEIM
POCKET, 1943
COVER BY LEO MANSO

Before Ian Fleming, before John LeCarre, there was E. Phillips Oppenheim, king of the secret agent story. With no gorgeous women or high-tech gadgets, this Pocket edition evokes a more mannered, atmospheric kind of espionage novel.

### THE HIGH WINDOW
RAYMOND CHANDLER
POCKET, 1945
COVER BY E. MCKNIGHT KAUFFER

Always a favorite with hardboiled readers and collectors, Chandler's Philip Marlowe mysteries have influenced generations of writers with their brilliant metaphors and muddled plotting.

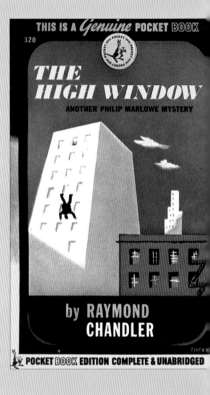

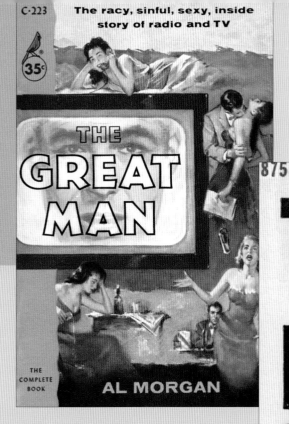

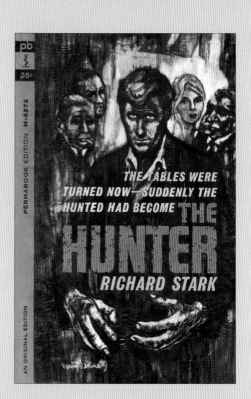

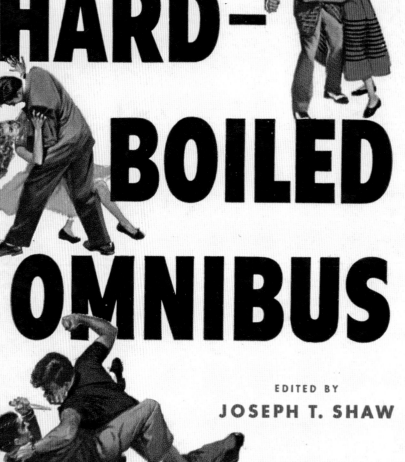

## HAVING WONDERFUL CRIME
**CRAIG RICE**
**POCKET, 1945**

The boozy, eccentric Craig Rice (Georgiana Ann Randolph) was an immensely talented and prolific author. In addition to her own several pseudonyms she ghosted celebrity mysteries for George Sanders and Gypsy Rose Lee. This book is a wonderful evocation of its era and milieu, starting with those bubbly glasses and the big city skyline.

## THE HUNTER
**RICHARD STARK**
**PERMA (POCKET), 1962**
**COVER BY HARRY BENNETT**

Richard Stark was one of Donald E. Westlake's pseudonyms, used for this series of hardboiled novels about a professional criminal named Parker. Westlake is a collected author, and his Richard Stark PBOs are especially prized.

## THE GREAT MAN
**AL MORGAN**
**CARDINAL (POCKET), 1956**
**COVER BY JAMES MEESE**

This is an early behind-the-scenes look at corruption and betrayal in the broadcast industry. Morgan adapted his novel for a brilliant motion picture released the same year—it's surprising that the paperback was not an MTI.

## THE HARD-BOILED OMNIBUS
**EDITED BY JOSEPH T. SHAW**
**POCKET, 1952**
**COVER BY MAURICE THOMAS**

Shaw had been editor of the great *Black Mask* mystery magazine in its heyday and had sponsored and guided the "hardboiled revolution" in crime fiction. This collection includes stories by many of Shaw's *Black Mask* protégés, including Hammett and Chandler. It is still a great read after half a century.

"And then there was humor: *Topper* and Thorne Smith. Then we come to a mystery. This mystery did poorly at first. It was down about seventh or eighth on the list out of the ten. We decided mysteries weren't any good. There was an editor at S&S [Simon and Schuster], for the Inner Sanctum books, named Lee Wright. She came to me and said, 'Why don't you do more mysteries?' I told her about the sales of *The Murder of Roger Ackroyd*, which was a wonderful book. She said, 'Well, you know the trouble is, you don't do them fast enough... You should do two or three of these a month, then you'll find they will go quickly; they will go much better.' I said, 'All right.' I respected her opinion, and from then on we did two-three a month, and boy, they went. The sales were terrific."

Pioneering works of Edgar Allan Poe, Wilkie Collins, Arthur Conan Doyle, and twentieth century classics by Erle Stanley Gardner, Agatha Christie, Rex Stout, and John Dickson Carr are perennials. The hardboiled school of Hammett, Chandler, MacDonald, Macdonald, Spillane, and modern mystery writers as varied in style and attitude as Elmore Leonard, James Lee Burke, Mary Higgins Clarke, Ruth Rendell, and Sue Grafton—all have built loyal audiences who come back for their new books year after year and decade after decade. Not only Pocket Books but in later years virtually every significant paperback house discovered the large and loyal readership of mysteries.

There is no question that Lee Wright had a close relationship with Pocket Books in those early days. She edited a series of mystery anthologies for the young company: *The Pocket Book of Great Detectives* (Pocket Number 103, 1941), *The Pocket Book of Mystery Stories* (Pocket Number 117, 1941), and *The Pocket Mystery Reader* (Pocket Number 172, 1942).

If you'd invested your $2.50 to order those first ten Pocket Books in 1939, and if you'd tossed the package in your attic when it arrived and not bothered to open it until today, you could probably clear something on the order of $10,000 for your investment. That sounds like a lot, but collecting is a funny institution. You could do even better if you'd bought comic books in those days before the Second World War.

De Graff told Bonn that he'd printed 2,000 copies of the "test edition" of *The Good Earth*. By the time the first ten numbered Pocket Books were ready, initial print orders were 10,000. It didn't take Pocket Books long to reach de Graff's stated goal of 100,000-copy first printings, and for some authors, even more. De Graff told Bonn that before very long the Perry Mason mysteries by Erle Stanley Gardner were up to first printings as large as 400,000 copies.

As for *The Good Earth* and its little lady on the front cover, de Graff reissued it as Pocket Book Number 11. It's easy to distinguish the unnumbered 1938 edition from the reissue. The painting has been modified, the poor lady's skin has been given a more natural tone, some additional human figures have been added to the painting, Pearl S. Buck is identified as *Nobel Prize Winner*, and—most notably—there's a funny little drawing of a kangaroo on the cover.

That's Gertrude.

Gertrude was designed by Frank Lieberman, a commercial illustrator who created cover paintings for a number of the early Pocket Books including *Topper*, *Enough Rope*, and *Bambi*. Initially Gertrude wore a pair of *pince nez* glasses similar to those worn by then-President Franklin Roosevelt. She held a book and was assiduously studying it while carrying a spare volume in her pouch or "pocket."

The Pocket Books kangaroo stayed around for a good many years, evolving through a number of redesigns before finally disappearing.

## THE KUBLA KHAN CAPER

RICHARD S. PRATHER
POCKET, 1967
COVER BY RON LESSER

This late Pocket printing of a Prather novel features a stunning painting, and note the featured sales total: forty million books! Even so, Prather regretted his move from Gold Medal.

## LOST HORIZON

JAMES HILTON
POCKET, 1939
COVER BY ISADOR N. STEINBERG

Pocket Book Number One—collectors may debate as to whether this or the unnumbered *Good Earth* was the first true Pocket Book, but either is a rare and precious collectible!

a **SHELL SCOTT**
novel by
**RICHARD S. PRATHER**

The
**Kubla Khan Caper**

Over 40,000,000
**SHELL SCOTT**
books sold!

# LOST HORIZON

## BY JAMES HILTON

COMPLETE AND UNABRIDGED

25c

*Pocket* BOOK EDITION

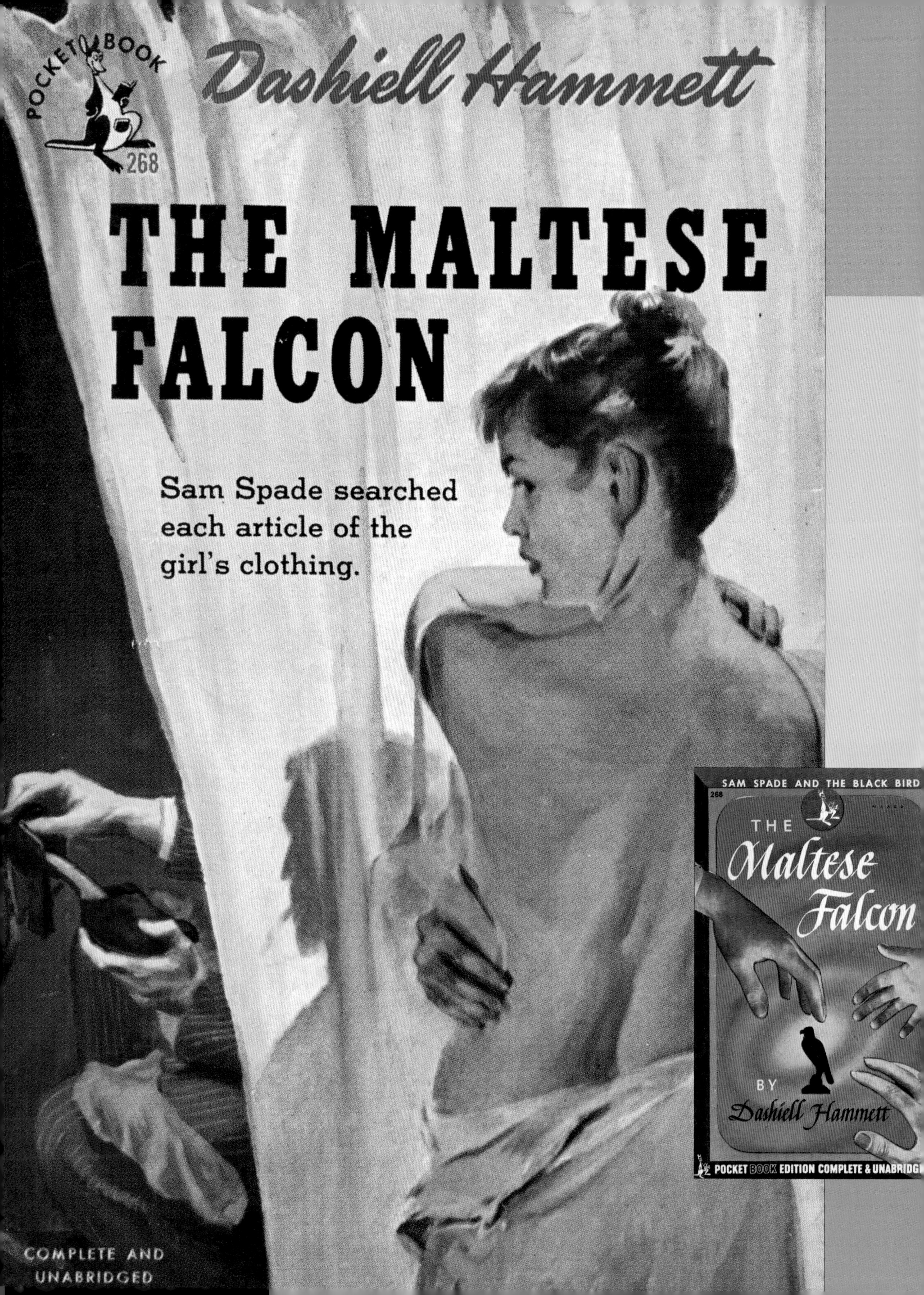
POCKET BOOK
268
Dashiell Hammett
THE MALTESE FALCON
Sam Spade searched each article of the girl's clothing.
COMPLETE AND UNABRIDGED
SAM SPADE AND THE BLACK BIRD
268
THE Maltese Falcon
BY
Dashiell Hammett
POCKET BOOK EDITION COMPLETE &

**THE MALTESE FALCON**
DASHIELL HAMMETT
POCKET, 1945
DUST JACKET BY STANLEY MELTZOFF;
BOOK COVER PAINTING BY LEO MANSO

The most important book by a highly collected author in a rare dust-jacketed paperback edition—who could ask for anything more! This is a nice but secondary item without jacket, a major prize with.

**NANA**
*By Emile Zola*

230

**The superb best seller America is taking to its heart....A touching, powerful novel about men and women you know, live with, and love!**

35¢

The Man in the Gray Flannel Suit

*a novel by* Sloan Wilson

THE
COMPLETE
BOOK

C-31
A CARDINAL EDITION
35¢

*Nelson Algren*

**THE MAN WITH THE GOLDEN ARM**

More powerful than a woman's love... more binding than a man's word... *It was DOPE!*

COMPLETE AND UNABRIDGED

POCKET BOOKS INC.

...BOOK *edition* COMPLETE AND UNABRIDGED

---

**THE MAN IN THE GRAY FLANNEL SUIT**
SLOAN WILSON
CARDINAL (POCKET), 1956

Look closely at the fellow on the cover. Is it Gregory Peck? It's hard to tell, but apparently not, which makes this edition of Sloan Wilson's bestseller *not* an MTI. It's still a striking collectible that stood out on the newsstands and bookshelves in the Eisenhower Era.

**THE MAN WITH THE GOLDEN ARM**
NELSON ALGREN
CARDINAL / POCKET, 1951

Considerable confusion exists over this book, which has been seen with a Pocket Books cover inside a Cardinal dust jacket. There was also a Fawcett Crest MTI edition in 1964, featuring cover art based on the 1955 motion picture.

**NANA**
EMILE ZOLA
POCKET, 1941

Years before the Avon *Private Life of Helen of Troy* achieved notoriety for its diaphanously-clad cover model, Pocket Books issued this daring (and rather atypical) version of Zola's classic novel.

**50¢**

# THE PROVING FLIGHT

### The thrilling story of the test flight of a luxury plane

## DAVID BEATY

**BOOKS**

**THE COMPLETE BOOK**

**A HERCULE POIROT MYSTERY**

249

# THE PATRIOTIC MURDERS

## AGATHA CHRISTIE

POCKET **BOOK** EDITION COMPLETE & UNABRIDGED

165

**pb**

# The POCKET Entertainer

Hundreds of hours of fun and mental gymnastics—over 200 pages of puzzles and braintwisters, quizzes and picture games—to play alone or at parties.

*Compiled and with an introduction by*
SHIRLEY CUNNINGHAM

POCKET **BOOK** EDITION COMPLETE AND UNABRIDGED

### THE PATRIOTIC MURDERS
AGATHA CHRISTIE
POCKET, 1943
COVER BY H. LAWRENCE HOFFMAN

Unlike Nelson Algren and others who wrote about drug addicts, Dame Agatha used hypodermic needles only to administer deadly poisons. This strikingly stylized cover by Hoffman was one of his best and is sought after by collectors.

### THE PROVING FLIGHT
DAVID BEATY
PERMA (POCKET), 1957
COVER BY ROBERT SCHULZ

A cultural reminder of the era when men wore suits and ties to travel by air. Note that the only woman on board is a nattily-uniformed stewardess. They didn't call them "flight attendants" in the 1950s.

### THE POCKET ENTERTAINER
EDITED BY SHIRLEY CUNNINGHAM
POCKET, 1942
COVER BY JAMES THURBER

With its hundreds of pages of "puzzles and braintwisters, quizzes and picture games," *The Pocket Entertainer* was clearly meant to be *used*, not just read. "Unused" copies are extremely rare and treasured by fans of the great *New Yorker* cartoonist James Thurber.

The response to de Graff's first ten books was largely favorable, although the performance of some of the titles surprised him. For one thing, Shakespeare didn't sell as well as expected. Apparently there was *not* a huge public thirst for great literature, or not one as great as de Graff had thought there would be. Readers wanted popular entertainment, in 1939 as they do today, and a publisher who sought to provide culture with a capital C was likely to wind up with a warehouse full of unsold books.

The Christie did moderately well. The famous de Graff - Wright dialog addressed that matter. And *Topper* did well, but de Graff's biggest success came with his self-help books. *Wake Up and Live!* was a grand success, and later on, when Pocket Books issued Dale Carnegie's *How to Win Friends and Influence People* (Pocket Book Number 68, 1940), they had a runaway hit. The book was the first paperback to break 1,000,000 in sales, and it went through endless printings and reprintings in later years.

De Graff was feeling his way toward a popular publishing formula that would bring books to masses of readers. It may have been coincidence that the standard price of de Graff's books was 25¢—an hour's pay for a worker earning minimum wage in those days, when the whole concept of a legal minimum wage was new.

Yet over the years, through good times and bad, through inflation, prosperity, recession, and boom, the typical price of a mass-market paperback has been close to an hour's pay for a worker earning minimum wage. Sometimes it pushes a little ahead, sometimes a little behind, but it has always been in the range of an hour's wage. By the end of the twentieth century, just over sixty years after de Graff set his price, it was still an hour's pay.

The cover designs and paintings were also relatively sedate. Compared to the Spartan appearance of Baron von Tauchnitz's paperbacks or even Alan Lane's Penguin Books with their color-coded cover bands, they were pretty lively. But they couldn't hold a candle to the sensational digest-size paperbacks of forty years earlier with their pistol-firing cops, desperadoes, spaceships, cowboys, and damsels in distress.

The very first Pocket Book (discounting the unnumbered *Good Earth*), James Hilton's *Lost Horizon*, shows a twin-engined airliner of the era winging its way over the Himalayas toward the fabled city of Shangri-La. Not bad, but not exactly knock-your-socks-off exciting, either.

Other cover designs among de Graff's original ten-book release were similarly modest looking. A bridge for *The Bridge of San Luis Rey*; a pair of gentle-looking deer, presumably Bambi and his Mom, for *Bambi*; a young man and woman looking totally bored with each other for *Wuthering Heights*; a couple of overdressed Georgian society folks gazing at each other with mild interest for *The Way of All Flesh*.

Only one of the ten books could go on sale today as anything other than a period curiosity, and that's *The Murder of Roger Ackroyd*. The book design shows poor Roger with his back to us, and a huge, but *huge*, dagger planted squarely in the middle of his back. *Complete and Unabridged. Pocket Book Edition. 25¢.*

No sign of Gertrude on the cover yet, but the book had zing, it had zip, it had eye-appeal and customer appeal, and Pocket Books was off and running and never looked back.

Some vintage Pocket Books were issued with dust jackets and a number of publishers followed the same pattern.

An important early example for Pocket Books was *The Maltese Falcon* by Dashiell Hammett. Hammett had begun publishing hard-boiled fiction in the classic *Black Mask* magazine in 1923. Six years later, in 1929, *Black Mask* ran his novel of Sam Spade and the fabulous black bird as a five-part serial, and a year later Alfred A. Knopf published the first book edition. It didn't appear as a paperback in the United States until 1945 (Pocket Book Number 268). Even then the publisher was uncertain as to how to package it. If you come across a copy of the book today you will find an attractive volume, a

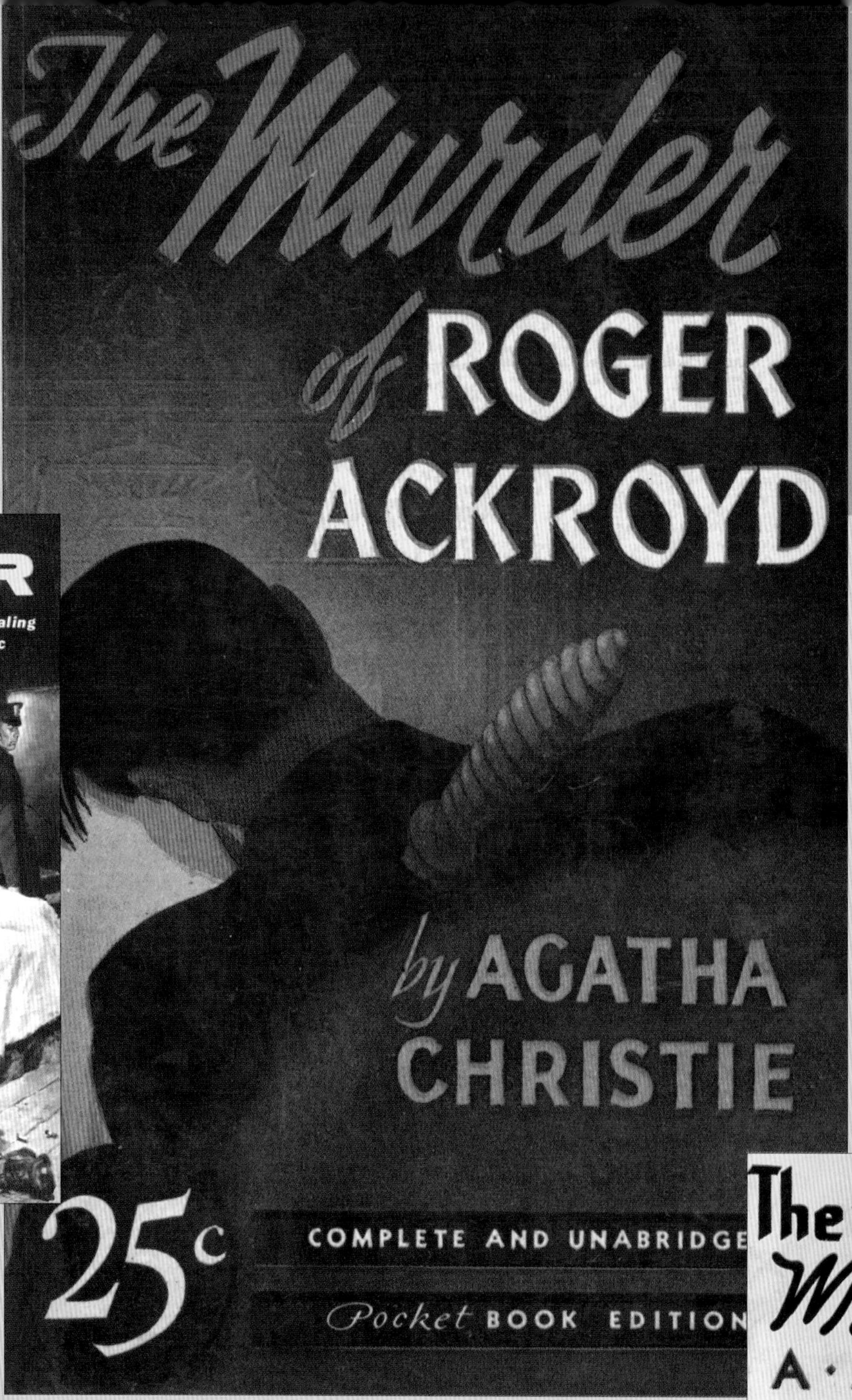

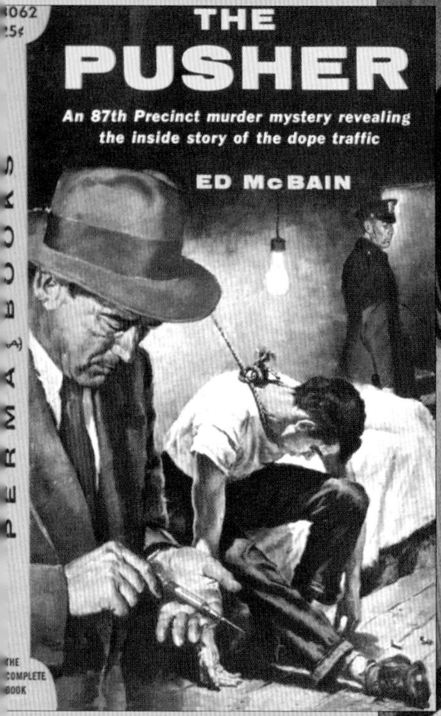

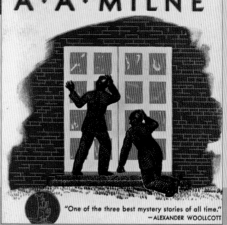

### THE PUSHER

ED MCBAIN
PERMA (POCKET), 1962
COVER BY CHARLES BINGER

Whether writing as Ed McBain, Evan Hunter, or
one of his other pseudonyms, this prolific author
has always guaranteed his fans a well-crafted,
absorbing story. This 87th Precinct PBO is part
of McBain's most popular series, and there's that
hypodermic needle in the foreground!

### THE MURDER OF ROGER ACKROYD

AGATHA CHRISTIE
POCKET, 1939
COVER BY ISADOR N. STEINBERG

One of the Pocket Books "first ten," this early
Christie is treasured by collectors. Steinberg's
cover, while mild by modern standards, was
pretty sensational in its time.

### THE RED HOUSE MYSTERY

A. A. MILNE
POCKET, 1940
COVER BY ALLEN POPE

Best known for *Winnie the Pooh* and other
children's stories, British humorist A. A.
Milne produced this classic story of deduction
in 1922. Numerous paperback editions have
appeared over the years. Milne also wrote
a number of detective short stories.

## THE ROMAN HAT MYSTERY
**ELLERY QUEEN**
**POCKET, 1940**

Cousins Manford Lepofsky and Daniel Nathan became Manfred B. Lee and Frederic Dannay, then combined their talents to create (and become) Ellery Queen. They also wrote as Barnaby Ross. *The Roman Hat Mystery* was their first novel (1929).

❏ ❏ ❏ ❏

## THE SPLINTERED MAN
**M. E. CHABER**
**PERMA (POCKET), 1957**
**COVER BY ROBERT SCHULZ**

Pulp magazine and comic book writer Kendall Foster Crossen also wrote science fiction, mysteries, and spy novels as Richard Foster and M. E. Chaber. *The Splintered Man* was a perfect distillation of Cold War paranoia: Communist brutes would take over your will with the help of that hypodermic full of mind-altering drugs!

❏ ❏ ❏

## THE SPIRIT OF THE BORDER
**ZANE GREY**
**POCKET, 1942**
**COVER BY SOL IMMERMAN AND ROBERT HOLLY ("IM-HO")**

The prolific Zane Grey was the world's most popular writer of westerns prior to the rise of Louis L'Amour. Accused of writing the same story over and over, he once replied, "Yes, and when they stop buying it I'll write another one."

❏ ❏

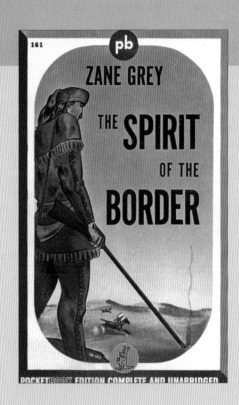

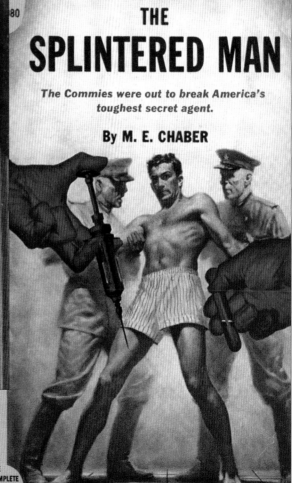

red background with three hands reaching toward a silhouetted falcon. The blurb reads simply *Sam Spade and the Black Bird*.

But if you should be fortunate enough to locate a copy with its dust jacket, you'll see a very different book. A shapely young lady (Brigid O'Shaughnessy) stands with her back to the reader, her full slip draped around her hips, her brassiere undone and apparently about to be discarded. Beyond her is a translucent cloth screen, and beyond it, fedora on head and cigarette hanging from his lips, you'll see a back-lit Sam Spade assiduously studying the young lady's red high-heeled shoe.

And the blurb? *Sam Spade Searched Each Article of the Girl's Clothing*. It was a far cry from those earliest Pockets.

Mysteries soon became a mainstay of the Pocket Books line. Year after year the company issued an eclectic mix of mainstream bestsellers, classic literature, self-help books and anthologies of poetry and prose, but mysteries were a constant. They were a favorite of travelers who would pick them up in railroad terminals and immerse themselves in a maze of corpses, clues, and deduction.

Despite forays into the hardboiled world of Dashiell Hammett and his cynical compatriots, most Pocket Books mysteries avoided violence and gore. The typical murder occurred offstage. The victim was found poisoned, shot, stabbed or hanged and the crime-solver—sometimes a police detective but more often a private eye or amateur sleuth—would set to work. With the reader peering over his (or her) shoulder, the detective would unravel the mystery by careful observation and keen deduction.

There was little bloodshed, only a few bruised knuckles or blackened eyes, and if there was such a thing as sex that messy business would be left to the blushing reader's imagination.

Early Pocket Books mysteries included *The Chinese Orange Mystery* by Ellery Queen (Number 17, 1939), *Murder Must Advertise* by Dorothy L. Sayers (Number 21, 1939), *By the Watchman's*

*Clock* by Leslie Ford (Number 33, 1939), *The Lodger* by Mrs. Belloc Lowndes (Number 43, 1940), *The Bowstring Murders* by Carter Dickson (John Dickson Carr) (Number 46, 1940), *The House Without a Key* by Earl Derr Biggers (Number 50, 1940), and *Think Fast, Mr. Moto* by John P. Marquand (Number 59, 1940).

The hugely popular Perry Mason appeared in *The Case of the Velvet Claws* by Erle Stanley Gardner (Number 73, 1940). Television addicts who know the great lawyer-sleuth solely through the many cases in which he was portrayed by the late Raymond Burr know Mason as a dignified and ponderous tower of ethics and morality. In Gardner's books Mason was a rather different character, tough and wiry, aggressive, sometimes vulgar and even violent, and not above utilizing tactics in the interests of his clients that would get him disbarred in the blink of an eye if they came to judicial attention.

Gardner must have known what he was writing about—he was a successful lawyer himself.

Westerns joined the Pocket list in 1942 with *Singing Guns* by Max Brand (Number 144). Westerns never made up a major part of Pocket's inventory, but there was a market for them and the company continued to issue them sporadically: *The Spirit of the Border* by Zane Grey (Number 161, 1942), *The Pocket Book of Western Stories* (Number 293, 1945), and *The Whoop-Up Trail* by B. M. Bower (Number 310, 1945).

Science fiction made its way onto the Pocket list in 1943 with *The Pocket Book of Science Fiction* edited by Donald A. Wollheim (Number 214). Wollheim was a former science fiction fan, a central figure in the New York Futurian Society whose members had included Elsie Balter (later Wollheim's wife), Frederik Pohl, Cyril Kornbluth, James Blish, Richard Wilson, Judith Merril, and Damon Knight. Wollheim had edited two low-budget science fiction pulp magazines, *Stirring Science Stories* and *Cosmic Stories*, and would go on to a major career as author, editor, and publisher from the 1940s through the 1980s.

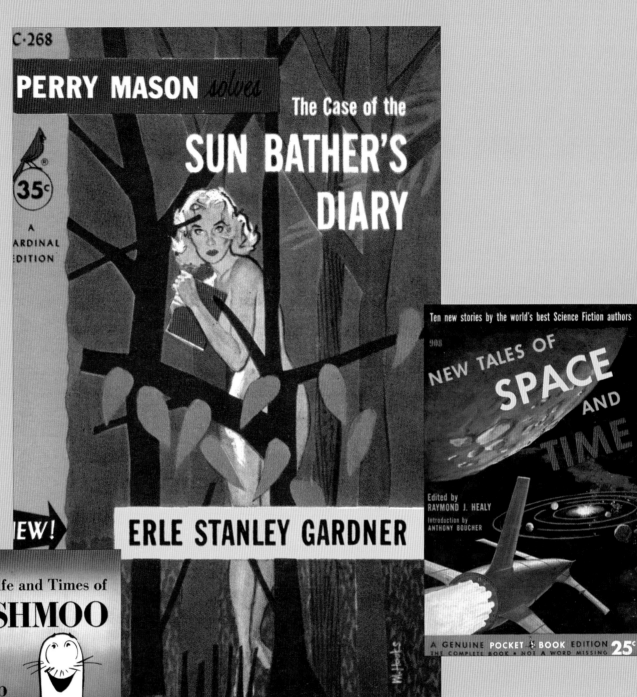

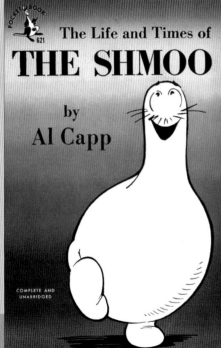

### THE LIFE AND TIMES OF THE SHMOO
AL CAPP
POCKET, 1949
COVER BY AL CAPP

Using his immensely popular "Li'l Abner" comic strip as a springboard, Capp created "Fearless Fosdick" (a parody of Chester Gould's Dick Tracy) and such national fads as Sadie Hawkins Day, Lena the Hyena, and the Shmoo.

❞❞❞

### THE CASE OF THE SUN BATHER'S DIARY
ERLE STANLEY GARDNER
CARDINAL (POCKET), 1958
COVER BY MITCHELL HOOKS

The incredibly energetic Gardner kept churning them out — not even his death in 1970 stopped him — and the public kept gobbling them up. Note the strategically placed book and botany in this evocative Mitchell Hooks painting.

❞❞

### NEW TALES OF SPACE AND TIME
EDITED BY RAYMOND J. HEALY
POCKET, 1952
COVER BY CHARLES FRANK

This "original anthology" of specially commissioned stories featured Bradbury, Asimov, Boucher, and Van Vogt — still fine reading after fifty years — plus a brilliant, almost photorealistic cover painting by the little known but highly talented Charles Frank.

❞❞

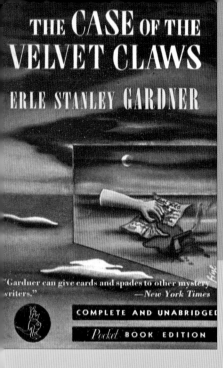

## THE CASE OF THE VELVET CLAWS
ERLE STANLEY GARDNER
POCKET, 1940
COVER BY FRYE

Veteran pulp writer (and lawyer) Gardner introduced lawyer-sleuth Perry Mason in this 1933 novel. The cover illustrator had clearly come under the influence of Salvador Dali.

## (POCKET BOOK ANNOUNCEMENT AD)

The most important advertisement in the history of publishing is copywriter Arkady Leokum's famous announcement of the first ten Pocket Books. How much credit for the rapid success of the books belongs to publisher Robert de Graff and how much to Leocum is subject to debate, but the ad must have contributed greatly to the public's awareness of the new enterprise.

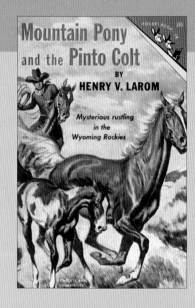

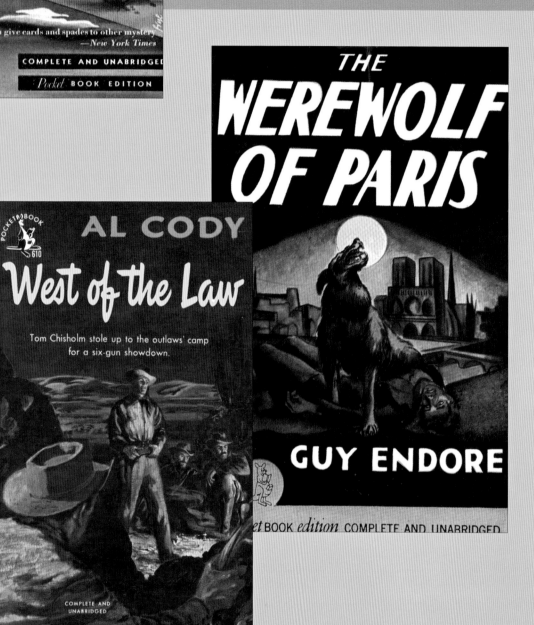

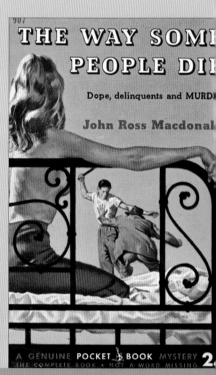

## WEST OF THE LAW
AL CODY
POCKET, 1949
COVER BY DOMINIC LUPO

By the 1940s, the Old West had disappeared and been replaced by a world of automobiles, airplanes, and big business—but the myth of the lone cowpoke, the six-gun toting outlaw, and the lovely schoolmarm arose to take its place! The spirit of Al Cody's novel was perfectly captured by Dom Lupo's atmospheric painting.

## THE WEREWOLF OF PARIS
GUY ENDORE
POCKET, 1941

The cover painting on Endore's classic novel of lycanthropy was criticized as excessively gory and sensational—note the blood pouring from the victim's mouth. Little did they know!

## MOUNTAIN PONY AND THE PINTO COLT
HENRY V. LAROM
POCKET BOOK, JR., 1951

Pocket Books, Jr., an early attempt to create a separate line of paperbacks for younger readers, didn't last very long, but over the years many paperback houses have tried this policy, and some have succeeded very well.

## THE WAY SOME PEOPLE DIE
JOHN ROSS MACDONALD
POCKET, 1952
COVER BY CLYDE ROSS

Kenneth Millar's "John Macdonald" pseudonym caused confusion with John D. MacDonald. Eventually Millar dropped "John" and wrote as "Ross Macdonald." Clyde Ross's cover painting is a superb (and unusual) example of strategically placed metalwork.

# OUT TODAY

LOST HORIZON

BY JAMES HILTON

# THE NEW POCKET BOOKS

## THAT MAY REVOLUTIONIZE NEW YORK'S READING HABITS

Famous best sellers—COMPLETE, not digests. Unabridged and unexpurgated, in brand new pocket size editions. Beautifully printed in large, clear type on easy-to-read opaque cream paper. Sturdily bound with soil-proof, Dura-gloss cover.

# 25¢ each

Today is the most important literary coming-out party in the memory of New York's oldest book lover. Today your 25¢ piece leaps to a par with dollar bills.

Now for less than the few cents you spend each week for your morning newspaper you can own one of the great books for which thousands of people have paid from $2 to $4.

These new Pocket Books are designed to fit both the tempo of our times and the needs of New Yorkers. They're as handy as a pencil, as modern and convenient as a portable radio—and as good looking. They were designed specially for busy people—people who are continually on the go, yet who want to make the most of every minute.

Pocket Books are printed in exactly the same size, easy-to-read type as the original editions, with not so much as a word or a comma left out. Thinner paper and a smaller page make them so compact they'll snuggle into your pocket or handbag without a bulge.

Never again need you say "I wish I had time to read" because Pocket Books give you the time. Never again need you dawdle idly in reception rooms, fret on train or bus ride, sit vacantly staring at a restaurant table. The books you have always meant to read "when you had time" will fill the waits with enjoyment.

**How Can the Price be so Low?**

lishers, printers and paper-makers have agreed to a fraction of a cent profit per volume. (2) Elimination of costly cloth, and seven complicated binding operations. (3) Above all, the economies of printing quantities ten times as large as the ordinary edition.

Despite their bargain price, Pocket Books look expensive—they even have stained edges and richly colored end sheets. You needn't hesitate to place them on the bedside tables of your weekend guests—to give them to your most finicky friends as going away presents or graduation and birthday gifts.

Start your Pocket Book Library today—ten great titles are already available. You'll find them on sale at hotel and railway newsstands, stationery shops, drug and cigar stores, book shops and department stores—wherever good books or magazines are sold.

**A Money-Back Guarantee Without Any Strings**

If it's more convenient, fill in the coupon right now and send it to Pocket Books, 386 Fourth Avenue, New York, with cash, stamps, money order, or check.

If you don't think these books are the most wonderful buy you ever saw—if you're not delighted with their "quality look"—their convenience, their ease of reading—if you're not completely satisfied in every way, send them back at our expense and we'll refund

Pocket BOOKS NEW YORK

But after this one very important book, Pocket showed little interest in science fiction. The company didn't return to the field until the 1950s, this time with another anthology, *New Tales of Space and Time* edited by Raymond J. Healy (Number 908, 1952). This was followed by several novels: *Space Platform* by Murray Leinster (Number 920, 1953), *Planet of the Dreamers* by John D. MacDonald (yes, the same John D. MacDonald) (Number 943, 1953), and *The War of the Worlds* by H. G. Wells (Number 947, 1953), a movie tie-in edition.

Only in the 1970s did Pocket Books, in association with its parent firm, Simon & Schuster, undertake a serious science fiction program. This was Timescape Books, edited by veteran science fiction specialist David G. Hartwell. Hartwell had previously edited for Signet, Avon, and Berkley Books, and would later go on to edit for Tor.

A scholarly man with high critical and editorial standards, Hartwell was not above publishing simple adventure stories by the likes of Lin Carter in order to generate revenue for his lines. He used the cash-flow to subsidize, in effect, the works of his more serious, "literary" authors. Within a few years Timescape was a highly regarded line. Hartwell had published numerous Hugo and Nebula award-winning books.

The science fiction community was shocked in 1984 when Pocket and S&S announced that Hartwell had been fired and the Timescape line cancelled. The books were too good; Hartwell's taste was too elevated. The bean-counters in the business office wanted to see fewer literary awards and more sales.

Timescape was to be replaced by a new science fiction line under the general editorship of a leading literary agent. A major howl went up, not just from the science fiction community but across the literary world. The new arrangement was rife with potential (in fact, inevitable) conflicts of interest. If the general editor had to decide between buying a manuscript submitted by one of his own clients and a manuscript submitted by a rival agent, how could he choose fairly? When he decided to buy a book from one of his own clients, how could he negotiate the price and contract terms when he represented both the buyer (the publisher) and the seller (the author)?

Negative reaction was widespread. The situation became untenable and the deal was cancelled. Instead, Pocket Books arranged to distribute a smaller company's science fiction paperbacks.

Let's jump back to 1945. When the U.S. president died in the spring of that year, Pocket Books rushed *Franklin Delano Roosevelt—A Memorial* into print. An anthology of essays eulogizing the late president, edited by Donald Porter Geddes, this pioneering "instant book" was issued in a dignified format. A simple black border surrounded a rectangular white field with the title and subtitle in stark black lettering.

The book was an instant classic.

On the corporate level, machinations took place almost from the creation of Pocket Books. In 1944 Marshall Field III, the Chicago-based newspaper publisher and retailer, bought both Pocket Books and Simon & Schuster. Robert de Graff and Leon Shimkin, who had created Pocket in 1938-39, remained with the company and in positions of power, although de Graff's role gradually lessened until, by the late 1940s, he was little more than a figurehead. In later years the company regained its independence only to be purchased by Gulf + Western Industries, an organization best known for its mineral drilling operations, only to be sold once again by G+W.

Pocket Books has ventured into many realms. From the viewpoint of collectors, its "silver spine" and "gold spine" periods produced many attractive volumes. Cardinal Editions, Washington Square Press, and Pocket Books, Jr. added to the company's roster of titles and authors. In 1949

Doubleday started an intriguing experimental line called Permabooks—standard format "paperbacks" bound in stiff, laminated cardboard covers. There were even a few Perma Giants in larger formats.

In 1954 Doubleday sold Perma to Pocket Books, which continued the imprint, although not the unusual binding, for several years before Perma disappeared totally into the main line of Pocket Books.

Suffering from political turmoil at the corporate level and challenged by increasing competition from powerful media conglomerates and feisty, aggressive independents, Pocket lost its dominant position in the paperback field. Mistakes on Pocket's part, especially in the realm of packaging, contributed to the company's decline.

An example of the company's experience with failed marketing was with the work of mystery writer Richard S. Prather. Prather created a hardboiled private eye named Shell Scott and in 1950 introduced him to the paperback world in *The Case of the Vanishing Beauty* (a Fawcett Gold Medal book). Scott was big, handsome, and tough. He was quirky. He raised tropical fish in his Hollywood apartment. Women loved him. He could duke it out with the toughest of opponents, drink a rival under the table, take a beating and rise in the morning to return to the battles.

His adventures tended to be zany—sometimes a variation on the hardboiled formula that bordered on parody, at other times returned to the true path of the two-fisted detective-for-hire. Most critics and collectors of hardboiled fiction rate Prather's Shell Scott equal to Mickey Spillane's Mike Hammer and John D. MacDonald's Travis McGee as champions of the genre.

Fawcett had packaged and repackaged the books with a series of splendid covers, including breathtaking paintings by Barye Phillips and Robert McGinnis. Scott was a crewcut tough guy with a winning, crooked grin. The women were gorgeous sylphs.

In the early 1960s, Pocket lured Prather away from Fawcett. Prather had done an earlier "one-off" tie-in book for Pocket: *Dragnet: Case No. 561* by "David Knight" (Number 1120, 1956). Now he would leave Fawcett and work for Pocket Books. In later years Prather would state that he had been reluctant to leave Fawcett, his association there had been a happy and lucrative one for a decade and half, but Pocket had made him the proverbial offer that he couldn't refuse.

He came to regret the move. Starting with *Dead Heat* (1963), he wrote a dozen more Shell Scott books for Pocket. Prather's new publisher decided to give the books a fresh and different look. The painted images were replaced by photographer's models. The new "Shell Scott" had fluffy white hair instead of the familiar crew cut. The idea seemed to be to bring the character and the series out of the tough-guy, macho Fifties and into the Swinging Sixties. The effort failed miserably. Eventually Pocket went back to painted covers, some of them quite attractive, but the Shell Scott series never regained its momentum.

Prather and Pocket had a falling-out over royalty statements and the last Pocket "Scott" (*The Sure Thing*), was published in 1975. Prather and Shell Scott returned with two novels from Tor Books in the 1980s, and a small-press volume from Gryphon Books in 1995.

To this day, Pocket continues to be an important force in paperback publishing. Gertrude the kangaroo is long gone. The 25¢ standard price has disappeared along with the penny postcard, the two-cent newspaper, and the nickel phone call. Pocket Books has long since ceased to be the giant it once was, but it is still a major player in its field. Pocket Books is still with us and will be for many years to come.

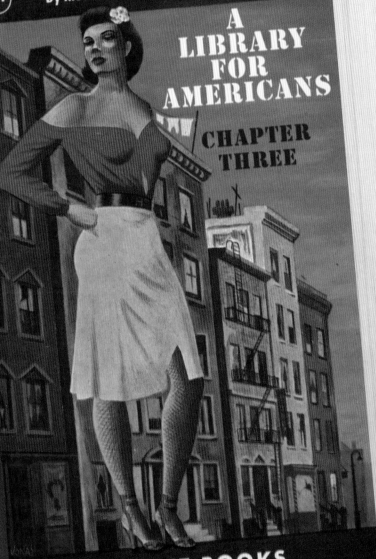

One of our great cultural archetypes is that of the growing child. His father loves him and takes pride in his achievements until the day he realizes that his son is taller, stronger, and probably smarter than he is. Or, *her* mother loves her and takes pride in her achievements until the day she realizes that her daughter is more beautiful, more accomplished, and probably smarter than she is.

Parent says (or wants to say) "Do as I tell you, this is for your own good. I know what's best for you."

Son or daughter says, "I'm grown up now, I know what's best for me, I'm going to make my own decisions. And maybe it's time for you to think about retirement."

Then there's trouble.

Think of Allen Lane as the parent. Kurt Enoch, Victor Weybright, and Ian Ballantine were the "children."

And was there ever trouble!

We've seen Ian Ballantine walk out. He would go on to a series of spectacular achievements in publishing. American Penguin would prove to be merely the launching pad from which his career took flight. But those are matters for later chapters.

What did Ballantine leave behind when he left American Penguin, taking his wife Betty and other loyal associates with him? Mainly, he left behind Kurt Enoch and Victor Weybright. These two men were also an odd couple. Enoch was conservative, punctilious, quiet and unassuming in appearance. Weybright was pudgy, sometimes flashy, characterized by some of his associates as a pretentious social climber.

Enoch and Weybright agreed on many issues, however, and they worked together well for many years. Despite their previous friction with Ian Ballantine and their decision to remain behind at American Penguin when he left, they had picked up some of his ideas about packaging and business practices.

Most notably, they knew that Ballantine's decision to use pictorial covers rather than the simple color bands of Allen Lane's British Penguins was a wise one. British Penguin might dominate its own world but American Penguin had been forced to share a larger and more varied marketplace with Pocket Books from the outset, and now faced fierce competition. American Penguin had to battle for every inch of display space and for every customer's coins.

Competition came from Avon, Dell, Popular Library, and a seemingly endless series of start-ups and newcomers to the field of paperback publishing. These companies all used pictorial covers, some of them tasteful but many garish and sensational. The kind of plain-looking books that Allen Lane preferred would have disappeared on the wire racks and wooden bookshelves of American retailers.

There was also the test of the Open Market.

A momentary aside to explain this term. Depending on the terms of contracts between publishers and authors, and on copyright laws of various nations, most books could be published in—or distributed to—only certain specified nations.

Thus, a book published in England would usually be distributed throughout what was then called the British Empire and Commonwealth of Nations. The same book might be published by a different company in the United States, and distributed in other nations. In a sense, the commercial world was neatly sliced up and parceled out among publishers.

But some nations were not included in this neat arrangement. Any publisher could distribute there. Nations not included in the exclusive rights provisions of contracts and laws, were considered the Open Market.

In some cases, the same book was published by both British Penguin and American Penguin. The British version would have a plain cover with only color-coded bands for visual appeal. The American version would feature a cover painting.

A Startling View of Life in 1984
Forbidden Love . . . . Fear . . . Betrayal

# 1984
## A Novel by GEORGE ORWELL

WAR IS PEACE

FREEDOM IS SLAVERY

...ANCE IS STRENGTH

BIG BROTH...
IS WATCH...
YOU

ANTI SEX LEAGUE

## SIGNET BOOKS
### Complete and Unabridged

S1334 SIGNET 35¢ BOOKS

Tennessee William...

Baby Doll

PRODUCED AND DIRECTED BY Elia Kazan
THE GREAT NEW PICTURE PRESENTED BY WARNER BROS.

BY THE PULITZER PRIZE-WINNING AUTHOR OF
**A Streetcar Named Desire** AND
**Cat on a Hot Tin Roof**

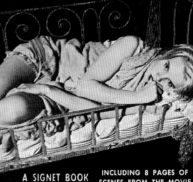

A SIGNET BOOK    INCLUDING 8 PAGES OF SCENES FROM THE MOVIE

M71    **Lincoln Barnett**    35¢
*A Clear Explanation of Einstein's Theories*

## The UNIVERSE and DR. EINSTEIN

*A Mentor Book*

1019 SIGNET BOOKS

The New Novel by the Author of
**THE NAKED AND THE DEAD**

# BARBARY SHORE
## NORMAN MAILER

NO VACANCY

---

## THE UNIVERSE AND DR. EINSTEIN
**LINCOLN BARNETT**
**MENTOR, 1954**
**COVER BY ROBERT JONAS**

The portrait of Einstein as a gentle, contemplative figure, coupled with the symbolic representation of his great theories, was intended to convince readers that they might actually understand Barnett's explanation.

❏

## 1984
**GEORGE ORWELL**
**SIGNET (NAL), 1950**
**COVER BY ALAN HARMON**

A former Communist who had fought in the Spanish Civil War of the 1930s, Orwell (Eric Blair) knew what he was writing about. This shocking satire (inspired largely by Eugene Zamyatin's earlier *We*) had immense impact in the early years of the Cold War. Alan Harmon's painting captures the mood of the novel with frightening power.

❏❏❏

## BARBARY SHORE
**NORMAN MAILER**
**SIGNET (NAL), 1953**
**COVER BY STANLEY ZUCKERBERG**

For more than half a century Norman Mailer was the *enfant terrible* of American letters; brilliant, controversial, and constantly reinventing himself. This early paperback edition of one of Mailer's lesser works capitalized on his great novel of World War II.

❏❏

## BABY DOLL
**TENNESSEE WILLIAMS**
**SIGNET (NAL), 1956**

Just in case the script wasn't enough to attract readers (Williams would certainly not have permitted a novelization), this MTI featured pages of stills from the motion picture.

📖📖

## THE CASK
**FREEMAN WILLS CROFTS**
**PENGUIN (US), 1946**

A master of the traditional British story of detection, Crofts relied on seemingly unbreakable alibis, railroad timetables, and the other paraphernalia of cold, pure logic. First published in 1920, *The Cask* is regarded as a masterpiece of its genre. The Penguin cover reflects the book's nature; the dust jacket makes it look like a steamy sex novel—and doesn't even show a publisher's logo!

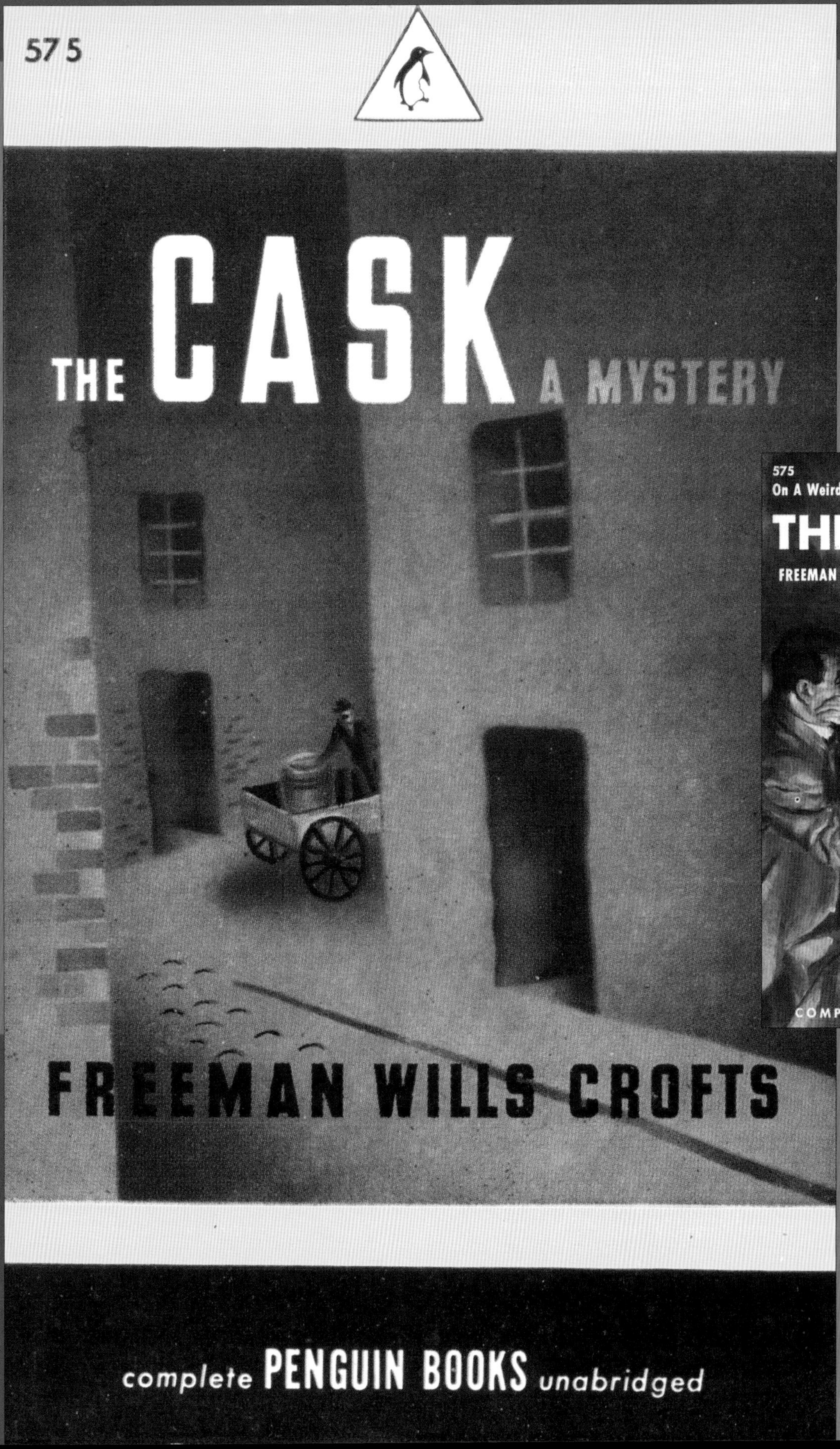

📖📖 , 📖📖📖📖

57 5

# THE **CASK** A MYSTERY

# FREEMAN WILLS CROFTS

complete **PENGUIN BOOKS** *unabridged*

575
On A Weird Trail, Three Men Stalked A Crafty Killer

## THE CASK
**FREEMAN WILLS CROFTS**

COMPLETE AND UNABRIDGED

Time after time, when both the British and American Penguin editions of the same book were offered in the Open Market, the American version with its pictorial cover would outsell the British version with its coded bands.

QED.

Even so, Eunice Frost remained loyal to Allen Lane and his ideals. There was no shaking Lane's —and Frost's—commitment to their concept of dignified publishing.

Kurt Enoch used his long experience in production, distribution, and business management to American Penguin's advantage. Victor Weybright concentrated on the selection and acquisition of properties that would sell in the American market.

American Penguin published 159 books, numbered 501 through 659. In general they reflected Penguin's longtime commitment to upscale, quality selections. The proverbial "first ten" included three murder mysteries, but all were of the traditional, genteel British type. These were *Murder by an Aristocrat*, by Mignon G. Eberhart, *Death of a Ghost*, by Margery Allingham, and *Trent's Own Case*, by E. C. Bentley and H. Warner Allen.

The others included a play by George Bernard Shaw, novels by the hugely popular Pearl S. Buck and John Steinbeck, Henry David Thoreau's philosophical diary, *Walden*, and Kenneth Walker's *The Physiology of Sex*.

This last book was a daring one for a publisher of mass market books to undertake, but the book itself was anything other than salacious. Still, it presaged a battle that would flare up again and again between the paperback publishing industry and a variety of politicians, psychologists, clergy, and self-appointed do-gooders, all of whom seemed to have trouble understanding the First Amendment to the United States Constitution.

In 1943 American Penguin dipped its toe ever so gingerly into the waters of science fiction with *Out of This World*, edited by Julius Fast (American Penguin Number 537). This anthology was barely recognizable as science fiction, in that era generally derided as "crazy Buck Rogers stuff." Most of the stories were by respectable literary figures not branded with the ugly mark of science fiction: John Collier, "Saki" (H. H. Munro), Eric Knight, Robert Arthur, John Kendrick Bangs, Stephen Vincent Benet, H. G. Wells, Oscar Wilde, Arch Oboler, Lord Dunsany, Jack London, and Julius Fast himself. Only Nelson S. Bond was a name that would have been in the everyday vocabulary of the typical science fiction fan.

Never again, in its 159 books, would American Penguin risk identification with the low-class world of spaceships and time machines. Even after the inevitable break with British Penguin it would take time for things to change —but change they did.

Not until 1950, with Edmond Hamilton's *Beyond the Moon*, would Enoch and Weybright lower themselves to publish a space opera. And when Signet (by then, the successor to American Penguin) entered the arena of science fiction, it would go for the class acts—most notably, Isaac Asimov and Robert A. Heinlein. By that time, it should be noted, Signet would have moved far from its predecessor's distinguished, if notably stodgy, traditions.

The 159 American Penguins were heavy on mystery writers, a large percentage of them British and the great majority of them firmly identified with the traditional school. One of these was J. S. Fletcher—the very prolific, very British, Joseph Smith Fletcher, by the way, not to be confused with the fictitious Jessica Fletcher later portrayed on television by Angela Lansbury.

Others were Georgette Heyer, the omnipresent John Dickson Carr, the ever-reliable Frank Gruber, Nicholas Blake, Francis Beeding, Anthony Boucher writing as H. H. Holmes, Georges Simenon, Freeman Wills Crofts, and Philip MacDonald.

1001

**NAL SiGNET BOOKS**

# J. D. SALINGER

# The Catcher in the Rye

IN PERSON
ROSEMARY CLUB SOM
3 SHOWS N

This unusual book may shock you, will make you laugh, and may break your heart— but you will never forget it

## A SIGNET BOOK
Complete and Unabridged

**THE CATCHER IN THE RYE**
J. D. SALINGER
SIGNET (NAL), 1953
COVER BY JAMES AVATI

Salinger's masterpiece of adolescent *angst* has been a classic for half a century and still resonates with young readers and with their elders who recall the pain of coming-of-age. Millions of copies have been sold, and *The Catcher* just keeps on going.

## CIMARRON
**EDNA FERBER**
**PENGUIN (US), 1946**
**COVER BY ROBERT JONAS**

An early stylized painting by
Jonas marks *Cimarron* as a serious
novel of the West, rather than a
genre "western" in the tradition
of Zane Grey, Max Brand, Louis
L'Amour, Frank Gruber, or
Clarence Mulford.

## THE CURRENTS OF SPACE
**ISAAC ASIMOV**
**SIGNET (NAL), 1953**
**COVER BY STANLEY MELTZOFF**

One of Signet's famous "blue
series" collected by science fiction
specialists, this early novel by the
remarkably prolific and successful
Asimov was also one of his best.

## DEATH IN THE FIFTH POSITION
**EDGAR BOX**
**SIGNET (NAL), 1953**

Early in his career, before
achieving fame and fortune,
novelist, historian, and essayist
Gore Vidal wrote three mystery
novels as "Edgar Box." Some
editions carry glowing blurbs
from Gore Vidal.

## THE COURTING OF SUSIE BROWN
**ERSKINE CALDWELL**
**SIGNET (NAL), 1953**
**COVER BY JAMES AVATI**

Here we have a visit to Caldwell
Country, with partially dressed
rural sirens and a libidinous male.
Note the keyhole/knothole theme;
this time it's an open window, and
we're looking *out* rather than *in*.

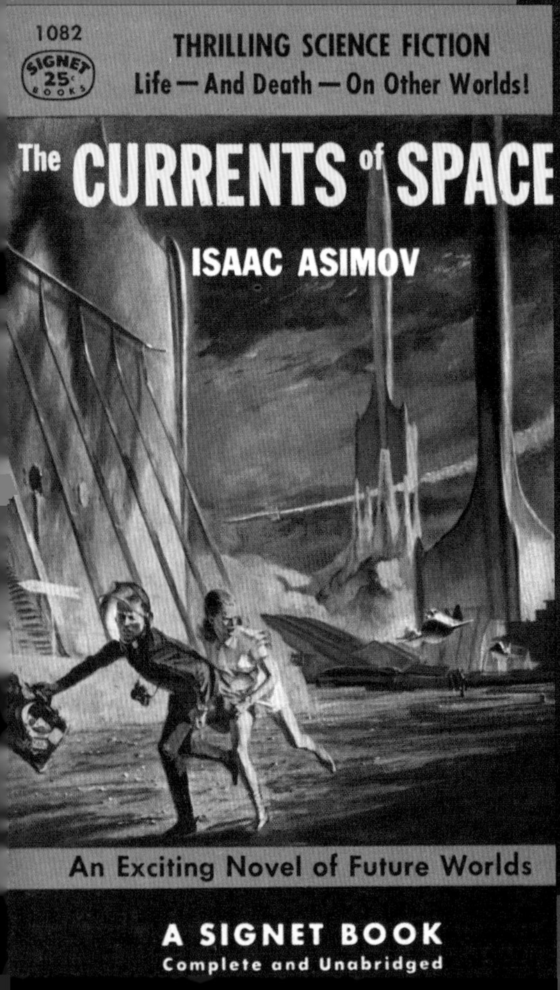

1016
**SIGNET
BOOKS**

*Erskine Caldwell*

## The Courting of
## Susie Brown

A SIGNET BOOK
*Complete and Unabridged*

605

**EDNA FERBER**
# CIMARRON

complete PENGUIN BOOKS unabridged

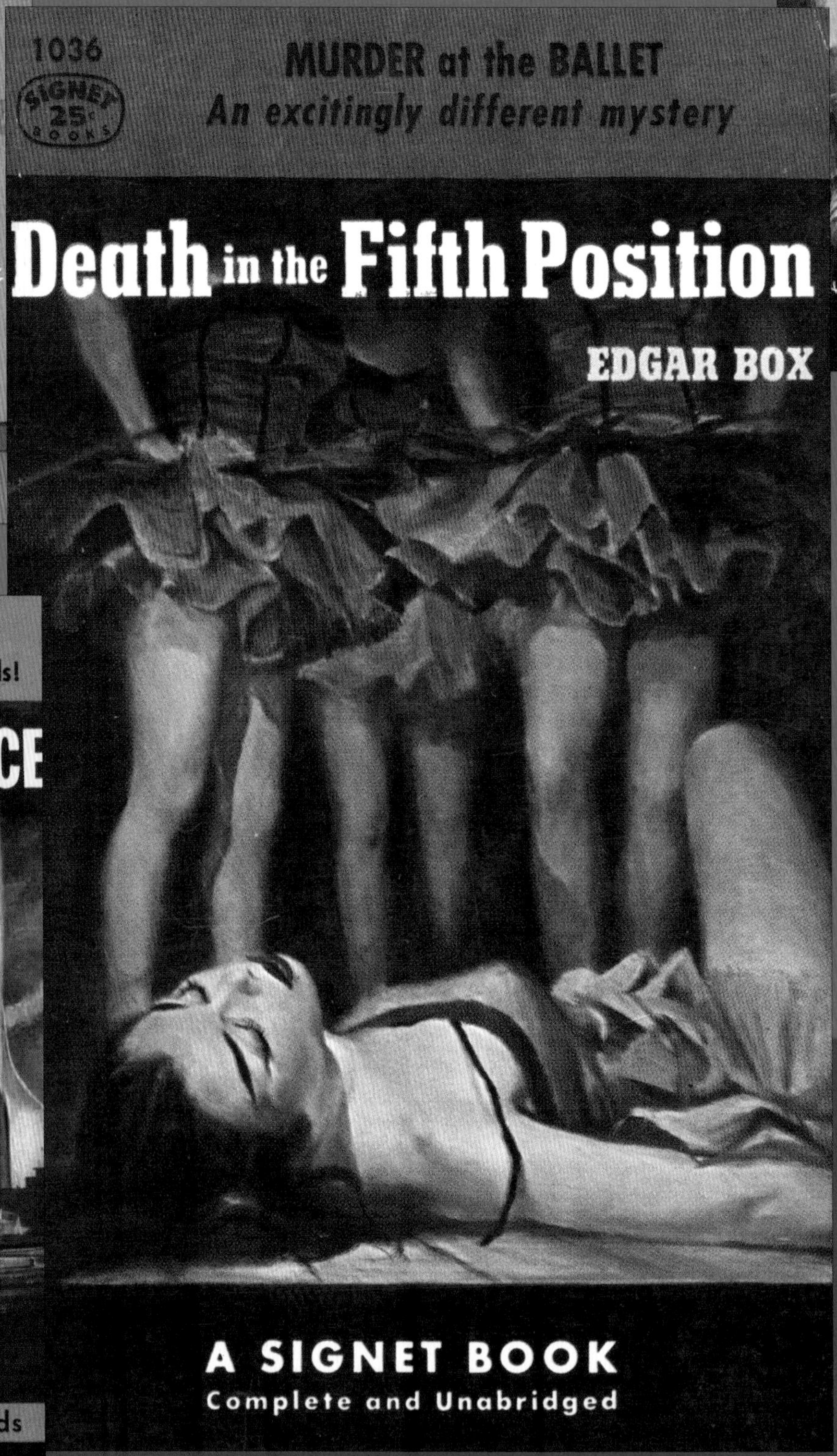

1036
**SIGNET
25¢
BOOKS**

**MURDER at the BALLET**
*An excitingly different mystery*

# Death in the Fifth Position
### EDGAR BOX

A SIGNET BOOK
**Complete and Unabridged**

1082
**SIGNET
25¢
BOOKS**

**THRILLING SCIENCE FICTION**
Life — And Death — On Other Worlds!

# The CURRENTS of SPACE
### ISAAC ASIMOV

**An Exciting Novel of Future Worlds**

A SIGNET BOOK
Complete and Unabridged

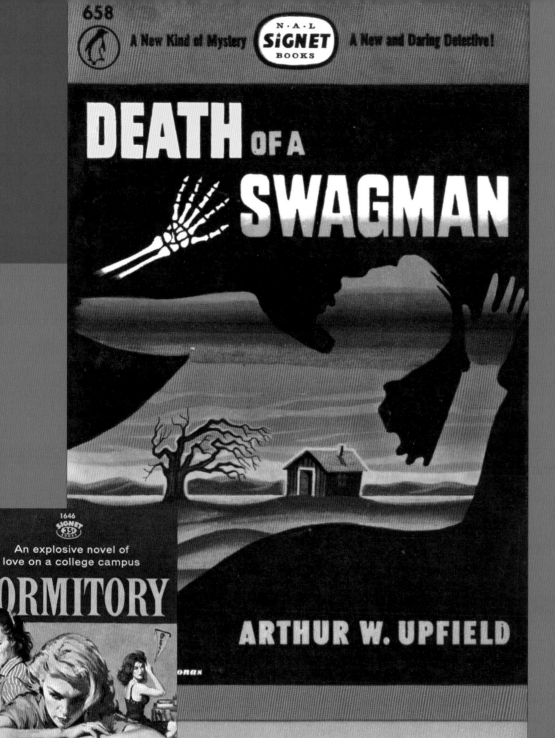

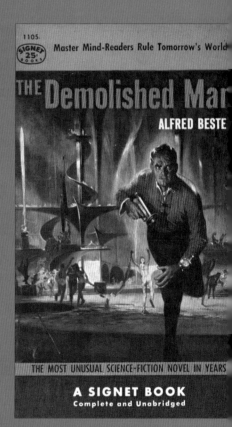

## DORMITORY WOMEN
**R. V. CASSILL**
**SIGNET (NAL), 1959**
**COVER BY ROBERT MAGUIRE**

First published as a PBO by Lion, this title was taken over when NAL bought that company's backlist. While the Lion edition is more desirable, the Signet version features a classic evocative Maguire painting.

## DEATH OF A SWAGMAN
**ARTHUR W. UPFIELD**
**PENGUIN (U.S.) / SIGNET (NAL), 1948**
**COVER BY ROBERT JONAS**

A transitional book bearing both Penguin and Signet indicia, and with a brilliant "cutout" painting by Robert Jonas, *Death of a Swagman* introduced Upfield's Australian aborigine detective, Inspector Napoleon Bonaparte, to a mass audience of American readers.

## THE DEMOLISHED MAN
**ALFRED BESTER**
**SIGNET (NAL), 1954**
**COVER BY STANLEY MELTZOFF**

Bester's brilliant *Galaxy* serial had only a small hardcover printing from a science fiction specialty publisher before this Signet "blue series" paperback brought it to a larger audience. Bester's first and finest science fiction novel, its daring stylistic advances placed the book at least a decade ahead of its time.

The Chilling Story of a Hunted Man Who Became Bait for Murder!

# FLIGHT into TERROR

## LIONEL WHITE

A SIGNET BOOK
Complete and Unabridged

T 934

TRIPLE VOLUME 75¢ SIGNET

The Sensational Bestseller of a Man and Woman Who Defied the World!

# The Fountainhead

## Ayn Rand

A SIGNET TRIPLE VOLUME
Complete and Unabridged

937
SIGNET BOOKS

Bohemian Life in a Wicked City

# Goodbye to Berli

CHRISTOPH
ISHERWOO

A SIGNET BOOK
Complete and Unabridged

## the carter brown MYSTERY SERIES

D3472
SIGNET 50¢

THE GIRL WHO WAS POSSESSED

A luscious witch practices sorcery and
sins herself into an early grave. . . .|
A SIGNET BOOK

## FLIGHT INTO TERROR
LIONEL WHITE
SIGNET (NAL), 1957
COVER BY ROBERT MAGUIRE

Journalist, magazine editor and publisher, Lionel White was a master of
caper novels. These were not of the
lighthearted variety popularized by
Donald Westlake or Lawrence Block;
White's capers are nasty and often
violent. The menacing gunman's
shadow in the Maguire painting for
*Flight into Terror* captures the mood
of the novel.

📖

## THE GIRL WHO WAS POSSESSED
CARTER BROWN
SIGNET (NAL), 1968
COVER BY ROBERT MCGINNIS

The Carter Brown mysteries of
British-born, naturalized Australian
Alan Geoffrey Yates are collectible
in their own right, along with the
lighthearted P.I. books of Robert
Leslie Bellem and Richard Prather.
The spectacular cover paintings by
Robert McGinnis raise these edi-
tions to a breathtaking level.

📖📖

## THE FOUNTAINHEAD
AYN RAND
SIGNET (NAL), 1952
COVER BY JAMES AVATI

Ayn Rand's lengthy, challenging
novels have won her loyal fans who
regard her has a great philosopher
and teacher rather than a storyteller.
The Signet Double and Triple
Volumes were a device used to
convince readers to pay premium
prices for overlength books. The
spines were designed to simulate
multi-volume sets.

📖📖

## GOODBYE TO BERLIN
CHRISTOPHER ISHERWOOD
SIGNET (NAL), 1952
COVER BY JAMES AVATI

Isherwood was the master chronicler of the Weimar Republic, the
tragic liberal-democratic society
that struggled for survival between
the end of World War I and the
rise of Hitler. Isherwood's writings
about Weimar would later become
the Broadway musical and motion
picture *Cabaret*.

📖

### I, THE JURY
MICKEY SPILLANE
SIGNET (NAL), 1948
COVER BY LU KIMMEL

The Mike Hammer novels of
Mickey Spillane rank among the
best-selling books of all time. Their
intense amalgam of suppressed
rage, paranoia, and misogyny tells
as much about their readers as it
does about the author—and the
message is not encouraging. These
books are highly collectible, especially in first editions.

### THE GRASS HARP
TRUMAN CAPOTE
SIGNET (NAL), 1953
COVER BY STANLEY ZUCKERBERG

A star of the brilliant mid-century
"Southern school" (along with
William Faulkner, Tennessee
Williams, and Erskine Caldwell),
Capote would become the gadfly
of New York, Washington, and
Hollywood high society. *The Grass
Harp* dates from his early, sensitive
period. But what the heck are all
those chickens up to?

### IF HE HOLLERS LET HIM GO
CHESTER B. HIMES
SIGNET (NAL), 1949
COVER BY JAMES AVATI

The tortured, angry Chester Himes,
ex-convict and expatriate, is best
remembered for *Cotton Comes to
Harlem* and his other Coffin Ed
Johnson and Grave Digger Jones
crime novels, but his works were
more varied and deserve wider attention than that of mystery fans. *If He
Hollers Let Him Go* is an autobio-
graphical novel, comparable to
the early works of Jim Thompson.

### THE HITCHHIKER
GEORGES SIMENON
SIGNET (NAL), 1957
COVER BY ROBERT SCHULZ

The Belgian (not French!) Georges
Simenon was one of the world's most
prolific crime novelists, turning out
a steady stream of Inspector Maigret
cases from 1932 until Simenon's
death in 1989. Critics loved or
hated him; no matter, he just kept
writing.

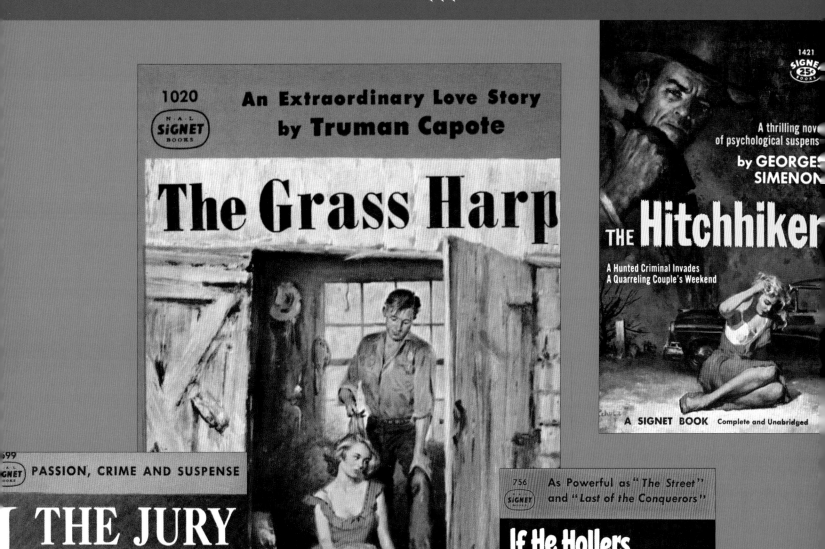

Still, American Penguin was most comfortable with high-tone literary fiction writers, and with non-fiction. When American Penguin decided to try westerns, as early as 1942, they didn't bid for the services of Max Brand or Zane Grey. They preferred the dignified likes of Walter Noble Burns (*Tombstone*, American Penguin 514; *The Saga of Billy the Kid*, 520) and Walter Van Tilburg Clark (*The Ox-Bow Incident*, 521). Try reading those bylines aloud. Let them roll off your tongue like BB's. Don't they just reek of class?

American Penguin ventured into history to resurrect *Tales of Piracy, Crime and Ghosts*, by Daniel Defoe (554, 1945).

For all the company's literary conservatism, it showed a more progressive attitude toward social issues. It was willing to face the always touchy issue of race. American Penguin brought out a paperback of Du Bose Heywood's *Porgy* (558, 1945). This novel is little remembered in its own right, but it provided the basis for George Gershwin's ground-breaking "folk opera" *Porgy and Bess*.

American Penguin was also willing to risk controversy by publishing Richard Wright's *Uncle Tom's Children* (647, 1947) and Edna Ferber's *Show Boat* (653, 1947), which was adapted into Jerome Kern and Oscar Hammerstein II's historic musical drama of the same name.

American Penguin bowed out in 1948 with still another distinguished book: *The Wild Palms*, by William Faulkner (659). The company's history had been stormy and its books distinguished. And American Penguin did not die. In 1948 it underwent a transformation to re-emerge as the New American Library of World Literature.

❧❧❧❧❧

Let's get back to that metaphor about the parent and the children. Ian Ballantine's 1947 departure might have resembled an act of adolescent rebellion—but once he had packed his sleeping bag, slammed the front door behind himself, and ventured out into the big world, Ballantine went on to major achievements in the publishing world.

What about the other "children," who remained behind?

Kurt Enoch and Victor Weybright had been brought to American Penguin by Allen Lane as a means of reasserting Lane's wobbly version of remote control. But the German-born Enoch and the American-born Weybright were on-site, observing and participating in the American paperback publishing scene with all its rough and tumble competition and its pulpish influences.

Similar competition was taking place in Britain at the same time. Although the nation's economy had been devastated by the war, new forces of enterprise and competition were coming into play. New publishers were jumping into the fray with books every bit as sensationalistic in title and packaging as the most outrageous products to appear in America.

Yet Allen Lane wished to remain above the fray, maintaining the conservative selection and sedate packaging policies of the 1930's. His drab Penguin and Pelican books faded into invisibility when displayed side-by-side with garishly covered paperbacks featuring provocative women, tough gangsters, leathery cowboys, daring spacemen and weird aliens.

*Make Mine a Virgin*, *Chicago Dames*, *Kill Her if You Can*, *Owlhoot Triggers for the Law*, *Temple of the Dead*, *The Screaming Lake*—nothing seemed too wild for the British reading public, eager to be transported from the grim realities of their postwar world.

Enoch and Weybright has seen the success of American Penguin under the influence of Ballantine's policies, and after his departure they became, surely to Lane's dismay, advocates of those policies. What had been a personal quarrel between Ballantine and his onetime mentor and sponsor, Lane, was now an irreconcilable institutional dispute between American Penguin and British Penguin.

Effective January, 1948, Enoch and Weybright bought out Allen Lane's share of American Penguin. The company was now fully independent of its parent. Under the terms of the purchase the new company, which became known as NAL, the New American Library, would continue temporarily to use the familiar names and logos. After a year-long transition period, Penguin was replaced by Signet and Pelican by Mentor.

Under the tutelage of NAL, the new Signet line even continued American Penguin's numbering. The first Signet Book was one that would have done the conservative Lane proud: *100 American Poems*, an anthology edited by Selden Rodman (Signet 660, 1948). But the second Signet was Erskine Caldwell's *Tragic Ground*, with a cover by Robert Jonas.

Caldwell had been a mainstay of American Penguin, and he continued to produce books for Signet. He was a leading advocate of what some critics called the "Southern trash" school of writing. His milieu was the rural or small-town, impoverished world of twentieth century Dixie. He was a naturalistic story-teller. His characters were lusty, vulgar, often greedy and sometimes violent. He described them realistically, often sympathetically, and frequently with a touch of ribald humor.

He had written a novel called *God's Little Acre*, published to an unenthusiastic response and a sale of some 8,000 copies, in the early 1930s. However, the book was issued as an Armed Services paperback edition and was popular with the troops.

In 1946 American Penguin had brought out a commercial paperback edition with a cover painting by Robert Jonas (Penguin 581). The book was a hit.

To get the right feel for the cover, Jonas painted it on wood rather than canvas or illustration board. The image is of a rustic fence with a large knot-hole in it. Through this hole the reader sees a rural house, a parked automobile and an old-fashioned water pump. The imagery was anything but lurid, but somehow the notion of peering through the knot-hole appealed to customers. In the following years Jonas and a school of imitators showed scenes through knot-holes, cut-outs, torn drapes, windows, doorways, brick walls, and keyholes.

As an American Penguin, and later as a Signet book, *God's Little Acre* sold an estimated 4.5 million copies.

A protegé of the Dutch painter Willem de Kooning, Jonas had worked as a factory hand, a display designer for a shoe company, and a set-painter in a nightclub. He was personally recruited for Penguin by Kurt Enoch, and while he would eventually paint a few covers for other publishers he devoted most of his career to Penguin and NAL, and it was there that he achieved his greatest success.

Caldwell also became closely identified with Penguin and Signet. In addition to the immensely successful *God's Little Acre*, his books included the equally famous and successful *Tobacco Road*, which gained stature both as a stage play and a film directed by John Ford.

Caldwell would turn out book after book, some more successful than others. Critics were confused. Was he a serious writer or a hack? A social realist or a pornographer? The reading public was not so confused. They loved his backwoods fables, and a whole school of writing and painting grew up in imitation of the Caldwell/Jonas paperbacks.

Erskine Caldwell was the first of three authors whose books brought NAL huge sales and profits.

The second was Mickey Spillane.

Born in 1918, Spillane served in the US Army Air Force in the Second World War, attended college, worked as a circus performer, and then broke into the world of fiction in the comic

D 1030
SIGNET
50¢
DOUBLE VOLUME

The Blazing Best Seller of the Year
NATIONAL BOOK AWARD WINNER

# Invisible Man
## RALPH ELLISON

A SIGNET DOUBLE VOLUME
Complete and Unabridged

754
H·A·L SIGNET BOOKS

"LOVE AS HOT AS A BLOW TORCH . . .
CRIME AS VICIOUS AS THE JUNGLE"

KISS TOMORROW GOOD-BYE
HORACE McCOY

SIGNET BOOKS
A Special Edition

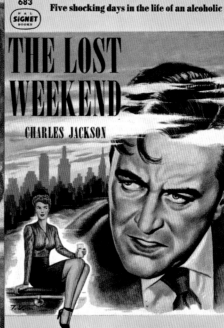

683
H·A·L SIGNET BOOKS

Five shocking days in the life of an alcoholic

THE LOST WEEKEND
CHARLES JACKSON

SIGNET BOOKS
Complete and Unabridged

### KISS TOMORROW GOOD-BYE
**HORACE MCCOY**
**SIGNET (NAL), 1949**
**COVER BY JAMES AVATI**

Former army aviator and sportswriter Horace McCoy hit it big with his first book *They Shoot Horses, Don't They?* in 1935, and wrote just six hardboiled novels (not exactly mysteries) in his career. All are well worth reading.

### INVISIBLE MAN
**RALPH ELLISON**
**SIGNET (NAL), 1953**
**COVER BY JAMES AVATI**

A Signet Double Volume (meaning double length and double price for its era, nothing like an Ace Double) *Invisible Man* is regarded as Ellison's masterpiece. One of the most important of African American writers, Ralph Ellison should not be confused with science fiction writer Harlan Ellison or JD specialist Hal Ellson.

### THE LOST WEEKEND
**CHARLES JACKSON**
**SIGNET (NAL), 1948**
**COVER BY TONY VARADY (?)**

The cover on this MTI features a portrait of actor Ray Milland, the star of the motion picture. *The Lost Weekend* was a powerful study of alcoholism in an era when drunkenness was more often regarded as funny or even chic. The painting was signed "T.V.", generally believed to be Tony Varady, but this is not a certainty.

### LIFE IN A PUTTY KNIFE FACTORY
**H. ALLEN SMITH**
**SIGNET (NAL), 1949**

Humorist H. Allen Smith was immensely popular, and Signet managed to capture the sometimes madcap, occasionally sardonic, often risqué nature of his works in this book.

### NIGHTMARE ALLEY
**WILLIAM LINDSAY GRESHAM**
**SIGNET (NAL), 1949**
**COVER BY JAMES AVATI**

A singularly ugly man himself, Gresham was fascinated by the tortured and the grotesque. He traveled with carnivals and wrote a nonfiction book as well as this shocking novel about carnival life before committing suicide. A hardcover MTI with a laminated cover featuring scenes from the Tyrone Power film exists but was apparently not issued in paperback.

### MOONRAKER
**IAN FLEMING**
**SIGNET (NAL), 1960**
**COVER BY BARYE PHILLIPS**

A brilliant combination of art, typography, and graphic design make this one of the most striking James bond novels—and there's no sign of 007 himself on the cover! Erskine Caldwell was the first Signet superstar, Mickey Spillane the second, and Ian Fleming the third.

### THE OX-BOW INCIDENT
WALTER VAN TILBURG CLARK
SIGNET (NAL), 1949
COVER BY DOMINIC LUPO (?)

When the fledgling Signet decided to try a western, their choice was a serious literary "great novel of the West." Walter Van Tilburg Clark's novel fit the bill perfectly. The cover painting was uncredited, but its style suggests the rich, atmospheric work of Dominic Lupo.

📖

### PISTOL PETE
FRANK EATON
SIGNET (NAL), 1953
COVER BY DOMINIC LUPO (?)

What did a typical frontier gunman really look like? Probably more like the grizzled character on this book cover—badly in need of a bath, a shave, and a fresh set of clothing—than the handsome cowboys so often portrayed by western movie stars. The uncredited painting may have been the creation of the talented but elusive Dominic Lupo.

📖📖📖

### ON THE ROAD
JACK KEROUAC
SIGNET (NAL), 1968
COVER BY BARYE PHILLIPS

The unusual montage by Phillips captures the episodic themes of Kerouac's most famous work. A strange, breathless wail by the alcoholic, misanthropic, mother-obsessed King of the Beats, *On the Road* became a Bible of a youthful generation.

📖📖📖

### ONLY THE DEAD KNOW BROOKLYN
THOMAS WOLFE
SIGNET (NAL), 1952
COVER BY RUDOLPH NAPPI

It's hard to imagine a collection of short stories by the rambling, verbose Thomas Wolfe, but Signet managed to issue this volume in 1952, packaging Wolfe's dense, difficult prose as if it were a juvenile delinquent book.

📖

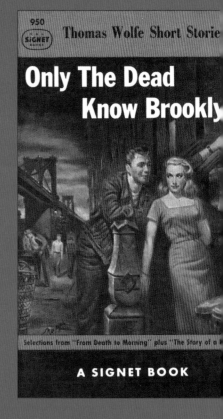

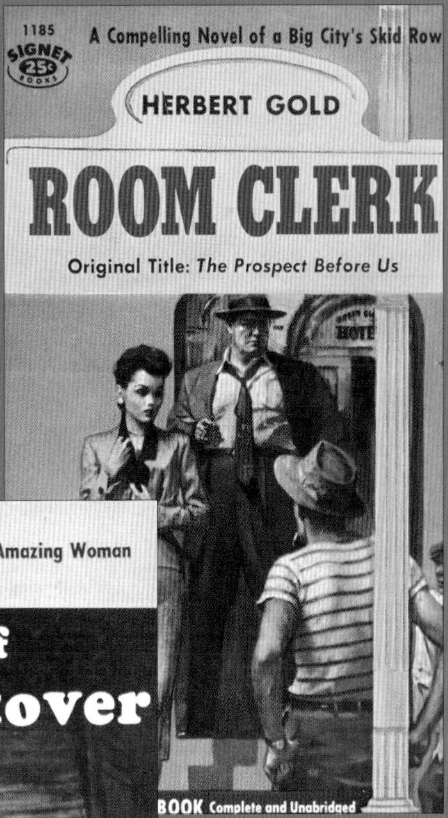

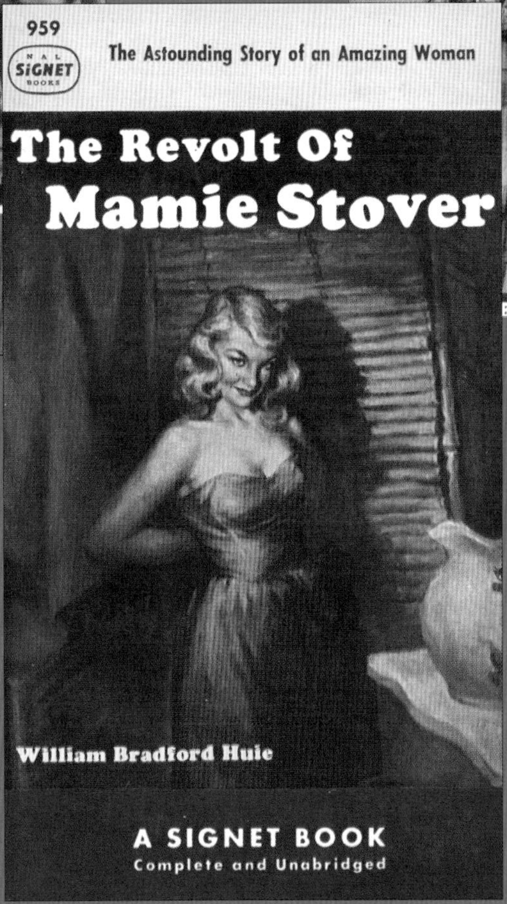

1194
SIGNET 25¢ BOOKS
A BONANZA OF SCIENCE FICTION
Intrigue and Strife in Tomorrow's U. S. A.
Revolt in 2100
ROBERT A. HEINLEIN
SIGNET BOOK
mplete and Unabridged

1185
SIGNET 25¢ BOOKS
A Compelling Novel of a Big City's Skid Row
HERBERT GOLD
ROOM CLERK
Original Title: The Prospect Before Us
BOOK Complete and Unabridged

97
A Hunt for a Beautiful and Reckless Woman
Portrait in Smoke
Bill S. Ballinger
A SIGNET BOOK
Complete and Unabridged

959
NAL SIGNET BOOKS
The Astounding Story of an Amazing Woman
The Revolt Of
Mamie Stover
William Bradford Huie
A SIGNET BOOK
Complete and Unabridged

**PORTRAIT IN SMOKE**
BILL S. BALLINGER
SIGNET (NAL), 1951
COVER BY STANLEY MELTZOFF

Bill S. Ballinger was a hardworking journalist, novelist, screenwriter, and sometime academic who produced some two dozen crime novels in addition to short stories, screenplays, and nonfiction. *Portrait in Smoke* was his third novel. Meltzoff's cover painting, with its picture-within-a-picture, was typical of the Signet "house style" of the era.

**REVOLT IN 2100**
ROBERT A. HEINLEIN
SIGNET (NAL), 1955
COVER BY STANLEY MELTZOFF

Still another of Signet's picture-within-a-picture covers, this painting is also slightly reminiscent of Signet's *1984* cover. Heinlein was one of the "big three" science fiction writers of his generation, sharing honors with Isaac Asimov and Ray Bradbury. His books remain readable, although their politics may seem naïve.

**THE REVOLT OF MAMIE STOVER**
WILLIAM BRADFORD HUIE
SIGNET (NAL), 1952

Does the model in this uncredited cover painting look familiar? She seems to have been a favorite of the artist and appears on several Signet books. Huie's novel is considered by some as a proto-feminist work.

**ROOM CLERK**
HERBERT GOLD
SIGNET (NAL), 1955
COVER BY STANLEY ZUCKERBERG

Note the type integrated into the cover design as if it were part of a street sign. Zuckerberg's superb painting with its suggestion of interracial sex, political power, and seething street violence is one of the most compelling of its genre.

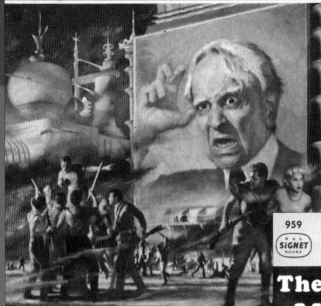

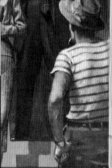

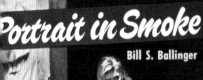

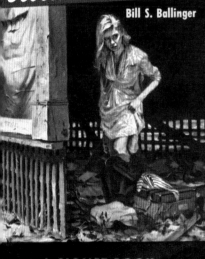

The Fabulous Story of the West's Most Daring Outlaw

THE SAGA OF
BILLY the KID

WALTER
NOBLE
BURNS

**A SIGNET BOOK**
Complete and Unabridged

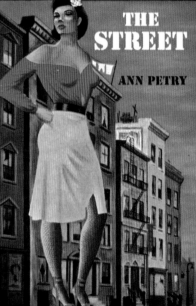

710 N·A·L SIGNET BOOKS

"The Unforgettable Story of a Beautiful Woman Beset
By the Passion, Sin, and Violence of the City"

THE
STREET

ANN PETRY

SIGNET BOOKS
A Special Edition

**THE SAGA OF BILLY THE KID**
WALTER NOBLE BURNS
SIGNET (NAL), 1953
COVER BY STANLEY MELTZOFF (?)

"Billy the Kid" (real name William Bonney, or maybe
Henry McCarty) was no western hero, and he bore
little resemblance to movie icon James Dean, who
seems to have inspired the painting. Born in New York,
Billy was, according to historian Carl Sifakis, "small,
with prominent front teeth and a short, fuzzy upper
lip, almost a harelip, which gave him a perpetual
smile. He smiled when he killed and his smile made
him look pathological, which he probably was."

**THE STREET**
ANN PETRY
SIGNET (NAL), 1949
COVER BY ROBERT JONAS

Although Ann Petry wrote at least two more novels,
both published by Signet, *The Street* was by far her most
successful book. It was reissued twice by Signet and at
least three times by Pyramid! Jonas' fine cover painting
was an early example of Signet's "urban realism" school.

**A STREETCAR NAMED DESIRE**
TENNESSEE WILLIAMS
SIGNET (NAL), 1951
COVER BY THOMAS HART BENTON

While the artist's signature is not seen, he is credited by name, as is the owner of the canvas! This edition of *Streetcar* not only contains the script of the play but eight pages of photos from the stage production.

NAL SIGNET BOOKS

# Tennessee Williams

# A Streetcar Named Desire

The complete and unabridged, illustrated text of the Pulitzer Prize play, now adapted as a great motion picture. Thomas Hart Benton's painting of a scene from the play (above) is in the collection of Irene Mayer Selznick.

# A SIGNET BOOK
### Complete and Unabridged

N·A·L
SiGNET
BOOKS

**Wine, Women and Laughter**

# TORTILLA FLAT

## JOHN STEINBECK

SiGNET
BOOKS

By the Author of "God's Little Acre"

## TOBACCO ROAD

**ERSKINE CALDWELL**

24 LARGE PRINTINGS—OVER 2,128,000 COPIES

**SIGNET BOOKS**
Complete and Unabridged

1226
SIGNET
BOOKS
25¢

More Terrifying than
THE BLACKBOARD JUNGLE

Violent
Streets

DALE
KRAMER

THE
STORY OF A
GANG'S GIRL

A SIGNET BOOK

# SIGNET BOOKS
## Complete and Unabridged

book field. He is credited with writing for the popular Captain Marvel character, but was more closely identified with the comics edited by Stan Lee: Captain America, Sub-Mariner, the Human Torch. He turned out story scripts and picked up a few extra dollars by writing short text stories for the same comics.

A colleague of Spillane's, onetime illustrator and sometime writer Don Rico, recalled that Spillane strolled into the artists' bullpen one day and announced that he was going to write a novel. Rico said that this was a common claim among comics scripters, and a goodly number of them lived up to their ambitions, including Rico himself.

Spillane's novel was *I, the Jury*. Published in hardcover in 1947, the book achieved modest success at best. It introduced Mike Hammer, Spillane's private eye / narrator. Assisted by his secretary Velma, Hammer was a throwback to the pioneering hardboiled writer Carroll John Daly's Race Williams. Hammer was violent, misogynistic, and filled with rage.

He did not care to turn over captured suspects to the courts. Rather, as the title of his first book implied, he tried and convicted the criminals purely by his own lights. Further, he usually executed them as well. As the Cold War grew increasingly intense in the late 1940s and '50s, Hammer discovered that there were Communist spies, agents, and traitors hiding under every bed and lurking around every corner. He had a quick and simple solution for how to deal with them: a dose of hot lead in the heart, the skull, or elsewhere.

The first Signet edition of *I, the Jury* (699, 1948) featured a cover painting by Lu Kimmel. The image shows Hammer, gun in hand, confronting an attractive blonde. The blonde is in the process of removing her blouse, presumably for the purpose of distracting Hammer from his punitive intention. Hammer's automatic is positioned suggestively, and it was no secret that Hammer loved to shoot women, preferably neither in the heart nor the skull.

*I, the Jury* was a sensation. Among other aspects of its popularity, the "good parts" were set in italic type. Schoolboys passed around much-read copies of the book, skipping over the rest of Spillane's crude prose in search of italicized passages.

The book sold more than 6 million copies. Spillane followed it with novel after novel, each one hugely popular. The titles were uncompromisingly tough: *My Gun Is Quick*, *Vengeance Is Mine!*, *The Big Kill*, *One Lonely Night*, *Kiss Me, Deadly*, and more. In *One Lonely Night* Spillane had varied the traditional private-eye-versus-mobsters story line by introducing a Cold War theme of private-eye-versus-Commie thugs. Later he created a second series hero, Tiger Mann, and wrote several non-series books, but these were not so popular as the Mike Hammer novels.

A Spillane trademark was the violent, even horrific, climaxes of his novels. The hysterical rage in these scenes was usually directed at women. Consider these closing passages:

"The hate was all there in my face now and she must have known what I was thinking. She gave me a full extra second to see her smile for the last time, but I didn't waste it on the face of evil.

"I saw the kid grab the edge of the table and reach up for the thing he had wanted for so long, and in that extra second of time she gave me his fingers closed around the butt safety and trigger at the same instant and the tongue of flame that blasted from the muzzle seemed to lick out across the room with a horrible vengeance that ripped all the evil from her face, turning it into a ghastly wet red mask that was really no face at all."

*The Big Kill*, 1951

"She laughed and I heard the insanity in it. The gun pressed into my belt as she kneeled forward, bringing the revulsion with her. "You're going to die now…but first you can do it. Deadly…deadly…kiss me."

"The smile never left her mouth and before it was on me I thumbed the lighter and in the moment of time before the scream blossoms into the wild cry of terror she was a mass of flame tumbling on the floor with the blue flames of alcohol turning the white of her hair into black char and her body convulsing under the agony of it. The flames were teeth that ate, ripping and tearing, into scars of other flames and her voice the shrill sound of death on the loose.

"I looked, looked away. The door was closed and maybe I had enough to make it."

*Kiss Me, Deadly*, 1952

One Spillane oddity was *The Veiled Woman*. This "complete novel" (actually a novelette) was a rare foray by Spillane into the realm of science fiction, appearing in *Fantastic* magazine in 1952. At least it was published under Spillane's byline, but in later years Howard Browne, the editor of the magazine, claimed that he had written it. If you come across a copy of the magazine with Spillane's name blazoned on the cover, beware!

Throughout the 1950's Spillane was one of the world's most popular authors. Even after 50 years his books cycle in an out of print, episodes of the old Mike Hammer TV series turn up in reruns, old Mike Hammer movies are revived on the small screen (and occasionally, the big one), and Spillane is himself a cult figure to a loyal band of admirers.

What was his appeal? It's hard to say. He remains a controversial figure in the detective fiction field and in the world of mass culture to this day. One thing is certain. Whether by design or by instinct he managed strike a chord that resonated for generations of readers.

Today his books seem almost quaint. The writing is crude, the mindset borders on the pathological. To some critics the books were never anything other than crude and pathological. Maybe Spillane was crazy. If so, he was crazy like a fox.

---

**THE YOUNG LIONS**
IRWIN SHAW
SIGNET (NAL), 1950
COVER BY BARYE PHILLIPS

Irwin Shaw was one of the fine novelists to emerge from World War II, standing alongside Norman Mailer, James Jones, and Kurt Vonnegut. Phillips contributed one of his many fine covers, complete with the Signet trademark "picture-in-a-picture."

**YOUNG MAN WITH A HORN**
DOROTHY BAKER
SIGNET (NAL), 1953
COVER BY STANLEY ZUCKERBERG

This Signet edition is a reprint of a book that had previously been issued by Penguin (U.S.) in 1945 and had also appeared as an Armed Services Edition. The later Signet is therefore of little value as a collectible, but its Zuckerberg cover painting is outstanding.

**YOUNG LONIGAN**
JAMES T. FARRELL
PENGUIN (U.S.), 1947
COVER BY ROBERT JONAS

Farrell was one of the originators of the gritty novel of modern urban realism. His books were sometimes condemned for dealing too much in the sordid and corrupt. Jonas's cover was an early, semi-abstract approach to the tenements-and-gangs school so common on later Signet books.

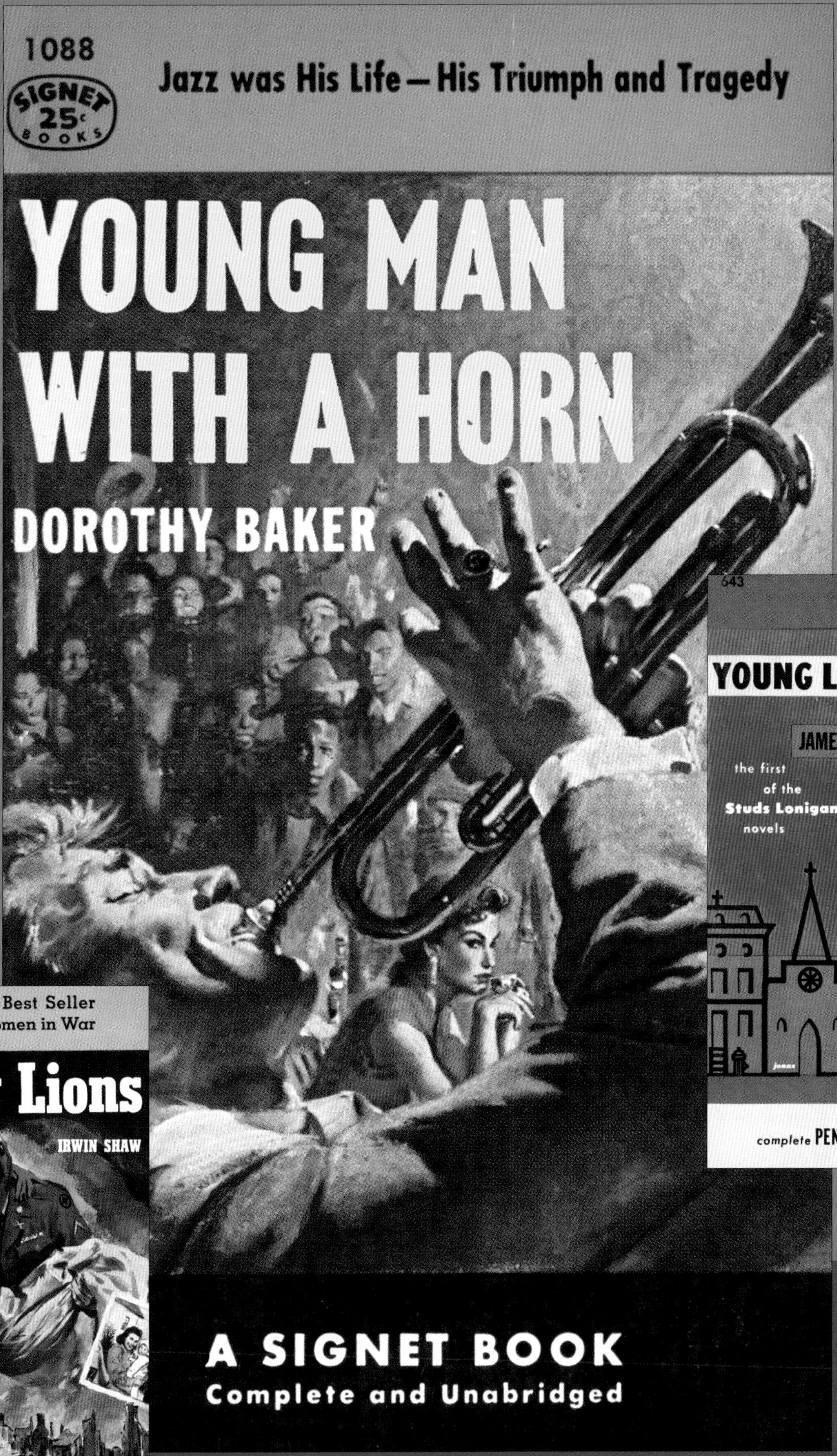

1088
SIGNET 25¢ BOOKS
Jazz was His Life — His Triumph and Tragedy
YOUNG MAN WITH A HORN
DOROTHY BAKER
A SIGNET BOOK
Complete and Unabridged

643
YOUNG LONIGAN
JAMES T. FARRELL
the first of the Studs Lonigan novels
complete PENGUIN BOOKS unabridged

SIGNET 50¢ DOUBLE VOLUME
The Powerful Best Seller of Men and Women in War
THE Young Lions
IRWIN SHAW
A SIGNET DOUBLE VOLUME
Complete and Unabridged

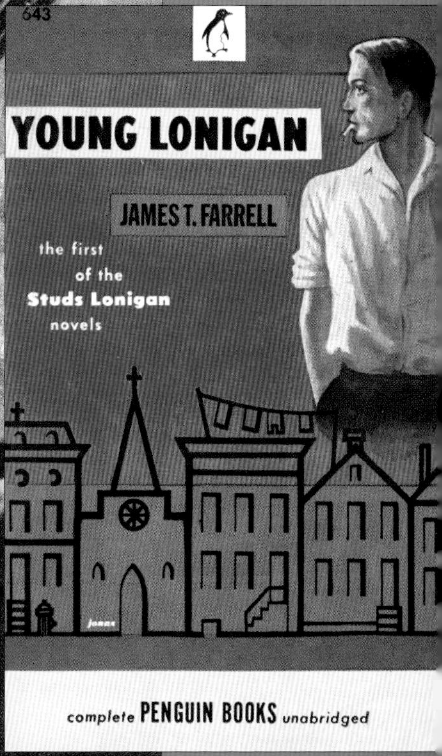

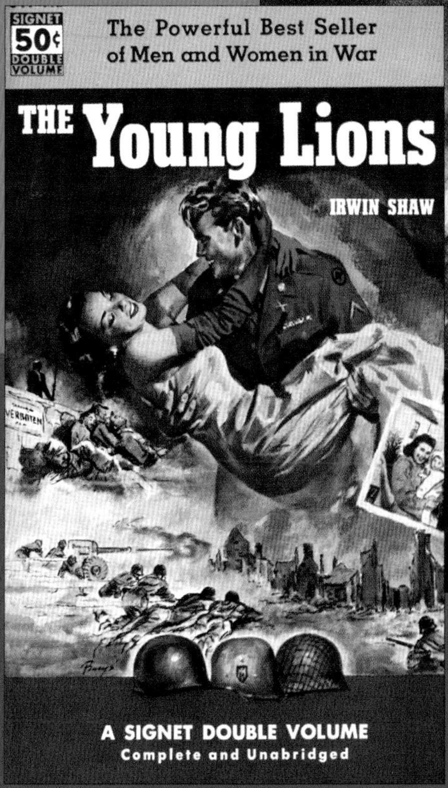

¶¶¶¶¶

The third of Signet's Big Three authors was Ian Fleming.

Born in 1908, Fleming was the perfect author to update the spy story tradition of E. Phillips Oppenheim, Talbot Mundy, and John Buchan. He had been in Stalin's Soviet Union in the 1920s and '30s, working as a correspondent for the Reuters New Agency and the *Times* of London. He had become an officer in the Royal Navy and spent six years in the intelligence service.

By the time his first novel, *Casino Royale*, was published in 1954, the Cold War was well under way and exposés of espionage rings were popping up in daily newspapers, radio newscasts, theatrical newsreels and on that newfangled thing called television. *Casino Royale* introduced the superspy James Bond, agent 007. The "double O" meant, *licensed to kill*.

The Bond adventures featured a mixture of Cold War intrigue, wild super-villains who might have been fully as comfortable in comic books or the dying pulp magazines of the era as in Ian Fleming's novels, gorgeous women, and high-tech gadgets and plot devices to delight the boy in every man who read them.

At first, paperback publishers weren't quite sure how to handle James Bond. *Casino Royale* was retitled *You Asked for It* by Popular Library in 1955. The second Bond novel, *Moonraker*, was a borderline science fiction adventure. Permabooks retitled it as *Too Hot to Handle* in 1957.

Once NAL got its hands on Bond, things started to change. Signet issued *From Russia with Love* (S1563, 1958) with a striking cover by Barye Phillips, a highly talented artist more often associated with Fawcett paperbacks. This was followed by *Dr. No*, *Live and Let Die*, *Goldfinger*, *On Her Majesty's Secret Service*... a dozen Bond novels produced in one productive decade, the last of them published in 1965, the year after Fleming's death.

The adventure-packed, at times self-parodistic books caught the spirit of the early 1960s, just as Spillane's angry, venomous Mike Hammer novels had caught the feeling of paranoia and seething rage of the early 1950s. Fleming's sales spiked when it was revealed that the young President John F. Kennedy was a fan of James Bond.

On a more serious note, one of the Cold War era's most important books was a huge seller for Signet and is still read more than half a century after its first appearance. This was *1984*, by George Orwell (Signet S798, 1950). The cover painting by Alan Harmon, all the more frightening for its low-keyed approach, remains in the memories of countless readers. George Orwell (Eric Blair) had been a Communist as a young man. He traveled to Spain during that country's civil war in the 1930's, became disillusioned with Communism, and wrote a terrifying satire of the system.

Other important authors continued to appear on Signet's list. A sampling of Signet's authors in the 1950s and '60s reads like a Who's Who of American (and to a lesser degree, World) Literature: Truman Capote, William Faulkner, Sherwood Anderson, Carson McCullers, E. M. Forster, John Dos Passos, W. Somerset Maugham, John O'Hara, Richard Wright, Howard Fast, Virginia Woolf, Dylan Thomas, Herman Wouk, Irwin Shaw, Tennessee Williams, Norman Mailer, Chester Himes, Eugene O'Neill, James Baldwin and J. D. Salinger appeared side-by-side with beatnik hero Jack Kerouac and popular writers like Spillane and Fleming. Gore Vidal graced Signet's list, both in his own persona and under his mystery-writer pseudonym, Edgar Box.

Signet tried a few westerns by L. P. Holmes, Charles Siringo, Nelson Nye, Homer Croy, William Colt MacDonald, and Evan Evans (Max Brand). But they never discovered "their" Zane Grey or Louis L'Amour, and the line enjoyed only limited success. Signet's science fiction program received more emphasis. This time there was no pussy-footing as there had been with American Penguin's Julius Fast experiment. Signet's science fiction was clearly identifiable, and the authors were among the best that science fiction had to offer: Alfred Bester, James Blish, Arthur C. Clarke, A. E. van Vogt, Heinlein, and Asimov.

Among collectible Signets of the era are the many mysteries by "Carter Brown" (Alan Geoffrey Yates). Born in England in 1923, Yates emigrated to Australia after the Second World War. He began writing his mysteries in 1953, with *Venus Unarmed*; his Signet career didn't begin until 1958, with *The Body*.

Yates was amazingly prolific. His "Carter Brown" novels featured an array of recurring private eye heroes, the most notable of whom was Mavis Seidlitz, a dazzlingly beautiful if not excessively bright operative. They were generally rather short, lightweight, and filled with wisecracks and zany humor that caused readers to compare them to Richard Prather's Shell Scott capers.

But it was inspired packaging that in all likelihood brought Yates his success at Signet. A number of artists painted covers for the books, starting with Barye Phillips, but eventually "Carter Brown" and the cover paintings of the brilliant Robert McGinnis became synonymous.

Born in 1926, McGinnis worked in the art department of Walt Disney Studios after completing art school. Like Yates, McGinnis was astonishingly prolific. His total output of paintings—mostly book covers but also movie posters—is estimated in the thousands. He began painting paperback covers in 1958, and over the years worked for most of the major houses: Avon, Bantam, Berkley, Dell, Fawcett and Popular Library, in addition to NAL.

His greatest strength—and certainly much of the appeal of his "Carter Brown" covers—was beautiful women. Typically, McGinnis women are tall, slim, and graceful. McGinnis had a way of making them beautiful, sensuous, and sexually charged, yet utterly without a trace of vulgarity.

◣◣◣◣◣

But all good things come to an end. In 1966 NAL was purchased by the Times Mirror company, a media conglomerate whose crown jewel was the Los Angeles *Times* newspaper. Kurt Enoch became a Vice President of Times Mirror and President of its Book Division. He stayed on for a number of years, mostly devoting himself to the business aspects of publishing rather than the editorial or creative.

He moved slowly into retirement, and died in 1982 at the age of 77.

Enoch's partner, Victor Weybright, left NAL to found a new publishing firm, Weybright and Talley, in partnership with his stepson, Truman "Mac" Talley.

NAL is still in business, still a class operation for the most part, yet with frequent forays into populist publishing. Ironically, through the exigencies of globalization, it is now part of an international conglomerate. Signet and several other NAL lines are part of Penguin USA.

The children have returned to the nest.

FIGHTING
FORCES
SERIES

# "BOOKS ARE WEAPONS"

CHAPTER FOUR

THE
INFANTRY
JOURNAL

By Lt. Col. Randolph Leigh

Anytime you go to a paperback collectors' show or swap-meet, there's a fair chance that you'll see a few Armed Services Editions. They're odd little books. Most of them are about the size of a standard paperback, but the format is short and wide instead of tall and narrow.

You'll find them on occasion in used book stores, antique shops, or flea markets. A lot of people have no idea what they are worth—or even what they are—and they are offered at an astonishing range of prices. If you're lucky you can pick up a great bargain. If you're unwary, you may pay far more than a book is worth.

A battered Armed Services Edition (ASE) of a run-of-the-mill book may be worth only a couple of dollars. A fine copy of a heavily collected ASE can be worth many hundreds. *Caveat emptor!*

There aren't many of them around these days; that may seem a little bit odd. Nobody knows exactly how many of these little paperbacks were printed. Even the exact number of titles is disputed, but we know there were well over 1,300 titles (counting some reissues), and a total in the vicinity of 125,000,000 total copies. That's 125 *million*—roughly the total population of the United States during World War II.

But the books were expendable. They were shipped by case lots to Americans in uniform serving all around the world. They were immensely popular, not especially durable, and were often read to shreds and then discarded.

They were distributed free to American soldiers, sailors, and marines. It was illegal to sell them, and they were expressly forbidden to the civilian market. There was a reason for that.

The ones that survive in the hands of dealers and collectors are thus the ones that servicemen and women happened to have in their pockets, packs, or footlockers when they were mustered out. The books wound up in living rooms or attics, were passed down to heirs, were donated to thrift shops or disposed of in garage sales.

Technically they were always government property, but nobody paid much attention to that in the 1940s, and certainly no federal marshal is going to clap you in handcuffs today for

proudly showing off a copy of *The Case of the Half-Wakened Wife* by Erle Stanley Gardner (ASE 1039).

Nobody knows exactly how many of these little books survive. But it's more than half a century since the last one was produced, and there surely aren't many.

We know that Johnny Reb and Billy Yank read nineteenth century paperbacks around the campfires. Teddy Roosevelt's Rough Riders probably had dime novels stuffed into their packs as they charged up San Juan Hill.

Anybody who's ever served in the military will tell you that boredom is a major problem. You spend long hours in barracks or in rear area "repple depples" (replacement depots) waiting for something to happen. When it does, all hell breaks loose. But until then you can't spend *all* your time polishing your boots or cleaning your rifle.

By World War I, Uncle Sam had got into the act and purchased huge quantities of books for free distribution to his doughboys and swabbies. After the war, leftover government stocks were dumped on the civilian market at bargain-basement prices. Publishers protested angrily, but there wasn't much they could do about it—then.

The Second World War broke out in Europe in 1939. By 1940 the United States was doing everything it could, short of actually declaring war itself, to assist Great Britain and its allies in resisting Hitler's aggression. A peacetime draft was instituted in the U.S.—a first—and there was massive growth in the armed forces. From a low in the 1930s of a few hundred thousand servicemen, the military grew to 10,000,000 once the nation formally entered the war.

All those young men and women found themselves in basic training camps or Officer Candidate Schools, overseas preparing to invade North Africa and then Europe to drive the Nazis back, island hopping across the Pacific, on makeshift airfields or fighting Japanese forces all the way from the Aleutian Islands to Okinawa.

**751**

# THE
# Big Sleep

### A MYSTERY BY

### *Raymond Chandler*

Overseas edition for the Armed Forces. Distributed by the Special Services Division, A.S.F., for the Army, and by the Bureau of Naval Personnel for the Navy. U. S. Government property. *Not for sale.* Published by Editions for the Armed Services, Inc., a non-profit organization established by the Council on Books in Wartime.

**1043**

# The
# Diamond as Big
# as the Ritz

### and other stories

### by **F. SCOTT FITZGERALD**

Overseas edition for the Armed Forces. Distributed by the Special Services Division, A.S.F., for the Army, and by the Bureau of Naval Personnel for the Navy. U. S. Government property. *Not for sale.* Published by Editions for the Armed Services, Inc., a non-profit organization established by the Council on Books in Wartime.

## SELECTED SHORT STORIES

## THE BIG SLEEP
**RAYMOND CHANDLER**
**ARMED SERVICES EDITION**

Chandler's first novel was originally published by Knopf in 1939. Note the "Black Widow Thriller" indicia on the reproduction of hard cover jacket.

📖📖

## THE DIAMOND AS BIG AS THE RITZ AND OTHER STORIES
**F. SCOTT FITZGERALD**
**ARMED SERVICES EDITION**

This rare paperback original Armed Services Edition ("PBO/ASE") collects Fitzgerald's short fiction. While best known for his "jazz age" stories and novels, Fitzgerald also experimented with fantasies, such as the title story of this collection, and even borderline science fiction.

📖📖📖📖

## A ROSE FOR EMILY AND OTHER STORIES
**WILLIAM FAULKNER**
**ARMED SERVICES EDITION**

The hardcover edition shown on this ASE is only a mock-up. There was no such book in hardcover, making this PBO by the great Mississippi writer a rare treasure.

📖📖📖📖📖

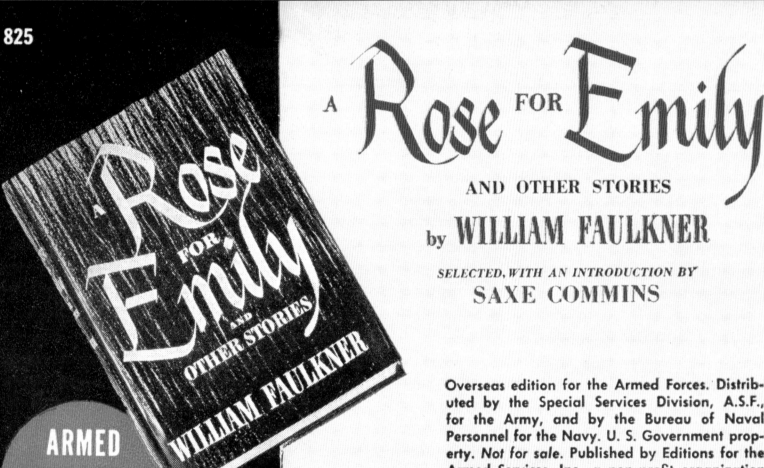

825

A Rose FOR Emily
AND OTHER STORIES
by WILLIAM FAULKNER
SELECTED, WITH AN INTRODUCTION BY
SAXE COMMINS

ARMED SERVICES EDITION

Overseas edition for the Armed Forces. Distributed by the Special Services Division, A.S.F., for the Army, and by the Bureau of Naval Personnel for the Navy. U. S. Government property. *Not for sale.* Published by Editions for the Armed Services, Inc., a non-profit organization established by the Council on Books in Wartime.

## SHORT STORIES

They needed food, arms, fuel, and medical supplies. And they wanted books!

At first the existing commercial publishers tried to fill the demand for books, but they were simply unable to keep up. An industry-wide association, the Council on Books in Wartime, was formed early in 1942. Some seventy publishers became members. The council's motto was "Books are Weapons in the War of Ideas."

The council cast about for new ways to meet the need for books. The organization was heavily weighted with Simon & Schuster and Pocket Books executives. Other publishers including Doubleday, Doran and Company, and G. P. Putnam's Sons were also represented. The council worked closely with the heads of the military services' own libraries: Ray Troutman of the Army and Isabel DuBois of the Navy.

Another military man, Stan Thompson, suggested that the military print its own books, or at least that a special production facility be created to print books for the military. While Thompson's initial scheme didn't work out, his idea took root.

It took until September, 1943, nearly two years after the United States' entry into the war, before the first Armed Services Edition rolled off the press. The books were "gang-printed" two at a time, then sliced horizontally and bound at the edge. This produced books approximately the size of standard paperbacks but with a peculiar two-column layout. Some of the books were slightly larger; it was just a matter of which printing presses were available.

Books were chosen by a panel of volunteer editors, but the greatest influence came from Philip Van Doren Stern. Another great literary name, that!

Stern had worked for Pocket Books and had compiled several anthologies for that company. When the United States entered the war, he left Pocket Books and signed up for government service, working for the Office of War Information. The OWI was responsible for getting accurate war news and morale-building material to the public. (A less friendly interpretation would be to call it Uncle Sam's own little propaganda factory. Take your pick.)

An obvious question was, Which books should Armed Services Editions publish? This of course is a profound question for *all* publishers. In the field of commercial paperback publishing there was a struggle from the outset. Those like Allen Lane had a kind of missionary attitude toward publishing, feeling that it was their duty to bring great literature to the reading public, thereby elevating their intellectual and moral level. Other publishers decided that they were in the business of providing entertainment rather than enlightenment to readers.

This was nothing new. The same struggle existed between "pulp" and "literary" publishers at the beginning of the twentieth century. It had existed in the 1830s, when the first wave of popular paperbacks came into being.

Until now, however, the forces of the marketplace had held sway over the preferences of the publishers. Those whose books met the needs (or the wishes) of readers and buyers survived and prospered. Those whose books did not either changed their ways or failed.

But Armed Services Editions would be given away. Free books! No need to sell them! No "bottom line."

Philip Van Doren Stern, Mrs. Stephen Vincent Benet, Louis Untermeyer, and other editors at the Council on Books in Wartime produced an amazingly eclectic list of books. Turning out thirty to forty titles a month, there seemed to be room for every taste from the most sophisticated to the most rudimentary.

There was remarkably little interference from the political arena. An exception was George Dondero, a Republican congressman from Michigan. According to Kenneth Davis, Congressman Dondero found an objectionable paragraph in *Native's Return* by Louis Adamic (ASE B-54). Dondero was a right-wing extremist who built a career on finding Communists everywhere. He was particularly sensitive to what he considered dangerous Communist influences in literature and the arts. As a result of Dondero's complaint, later ASEs were vetted for political content.

As late as 1956, Dondero was still serving in Congress and attacked President Dwight Eisenhower (also a Republican, and anything but a Communist sympathizer) for visiting the Museum of Modern Art in New York and endorsing the artistic freedom of painters. Dondero's criticism of Eisenhower was typical of the convoluted logic of censors: "Frankly, I do not understand some of the statements made by the President regarding the Museum of Modern Art. Modern art is a term that is nauseating to me. We are in complete accord in our thinking regarding this subject and its connection with Communism. No one is attempting to stifle self expression, but we are attempting to protect and preserve legitimate art as we have always known it in the United States."

While the Dondero/Adamic incident seems almost laughable today, it was a serious matter in 1944, and comparable events continued to occur in later years. During the Cold War there was controversy over the inclusion of politically questionable books in libraries sponsored by American embassies in foreign countries. Senator Joseph McCarthy of Wisconsin dispatched a team of aides to visit these libraries in European capitals and root out what were considered unAmerican books. Forty years later there was an uproar over the inclusion of photographs made by Robert Maplethorpe in an exhibit sponsored by the National Endowment for the Arts.

In fact, ordinary citizens and their elected representatives have a strong case to make when they feel that their tax dollars are being used to promote images and ideas that they themselves find repugnant. In response to this, artists vehemently defend their own right of free expression. It seems that this dispute is inevitable as long as there is such a thing as "official culture."

The very first ASE book was *The Education of H*y*m*a*n K*a*p*l*a*n*, the humorous account of an immigrant's struggles to become a true American. The author was "Leonard Q. Ross" (Leo Rosten). The range of books in ASE's "first ten" was extremely broad: one humor book, one non-fiction book about the war, three classic novels, two modern novels, one thriller, one general nonfiction book, and an anthology of dog stories!

The books were snapped up at military bases wherever they appeared. Stories found their way back to civilian newspapers and magazines of how much GI Joe and his counterparts in other branches loved them. The *New York Post* quoted an Air Force officer on the subject: "I was gratified when I saw a GI lying in the shade of a bomber reading *Huckleberry Finn*. Somehow I knew that this particular GI's mind wasn't dwelling on the mud and mire this war had placed him in, but rather he was floating down the Mississippi on a raft with Tom and Huck.... I saw men in chow-lines reading worn copies of *Moby Dick*, *The Robe*, and dozens of other good books."

Soldiers and sailors who read the books often wrote to their authors. The all-time champion may have been Betty Smith, author of *A Tree Grows in Brooklyn* (ASE K-28), a gentle, sentimental tale of immigrant family life at the beginning of the twentieth century. Apparently, all those young men, thousands of miles from home, were touched by this literary visit to safer, happier days in a more secure world.

It was estimated that these millions of books cost the government only about six cents apiece. The government paid a royalty of one cent per copy, divided equally between the original publisher and the author. In some cases, the authors waived their royalties.

The basic design of Armed Services Editions was uniform for most titles. It was pretty straightforward: the original hardcover edition of the book was shown, tilted at an angle. Beside it was a simple circular logo reading *Armed Services Edition*.

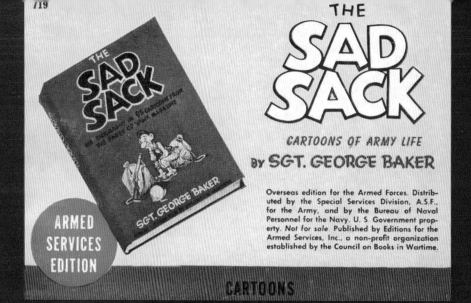

719

# THE SAD SACK
CARTOONS OF ARMY LIFE
By SGT. GEORGE BAKER

Overseas edition for the Armed Forces. Distributed by the Special Services Division, A.S.F., for the Army, and by the Bureau of Naval Personnel for the Navy. U. S. Government property. *Not for sale.* Published by Editions for the Armed Services, Inc., a non-profit organization established by the Council on Books in Wartime.

CARTOONS

887

# THE VIRGINIAN
A HORSEMAN OF THE PLAINS
BY
OWEN WISTER

Overseas edition for the Armed Forces. Distributed by the Special Services Division, A.S.F., for the Army, and by the Bureau of Naval Personnel for the Navy. U. S. Government property. No... Armed... establis...

ARMED SERVICES EDITION

THIS IS THE COMPLETE BOOK

S-26

# SELECTED SHORT STORIES OF ALGERNON BLACKWOOD
STORIES OF MYSTERY AND IMAGINATION

Overseas edition for the Armed Forces. Distributed by the Special Services Division, A.S.F., for the Army, and by the Bureau of Naval Personnel for the Navy. U. S. Government property. *Not for sale.* Published by Editions for the Armed Services, Inc., a non-profit organization established by the Council on Books in Wartime.

SELECTED SHORT STORIES

## THE SAD SACK
**GEORGE BAKER**
**ARMED SERVICES EDITION**

*Yank* was a semi-slick, heavily graphics-oriented magazine published as a morale-builder for servicemen and women. George Baker's cartoons about the Sad Sack, a G.I. forever getting into hilarious scrapes, were immensely popular with young soldiers. They could laugh at the poor Sad Sack and feel a little better about themselves.

## THE VIRGINIAN
**OWEN WISTER**
**ARMED SERVICES EDITION**

Wister's famous novel of "a horseman of the plains" had become an early "talkie" in 1929, with Gary Cooper uttering the immortal line, "Smile when you say that." Apparently the ASE was the book's first paperback edition, followed by a Pocket Cardinal version in the postwar years.

## SELECTED SHORT STORIES OF ALGERNON BLACKWOOD
**ARMED SERVICES EDITION**

This collection of Blackwood's "stories of mystery and imagination" was a PBO and while the individual stories were separately available, this was their only appearance in this form. The Armed Services Edition is sought by horror and fantasy fans as well as ASE aficionados.

### 48 MILLION TONS TO EISENHOWER

**LT. COL. RANDOLPH LEIGH,**
**INFANTRY JOURNAL BOOKS**

Under the guidance of Colonel Walter Greene, the *Infantry Journal* was one of several semi-official newspapers and magazines published for a military readership. Greene and Ian Ballantine worked out a deal whereby American Penguin became a partner in Infantry Journal Books.

### THE LAST TIME I SAW PARIS

**ELLIOT PAUL**
**ARMED SERVICES EDITION**

This is a nostalgic look at prewar France and a bright reminder of the days before the Nazi conquest.

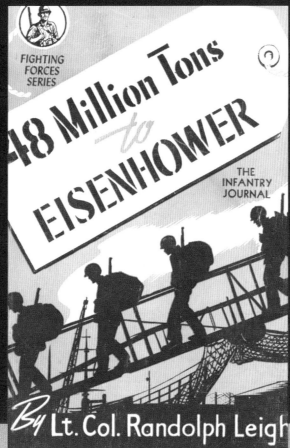

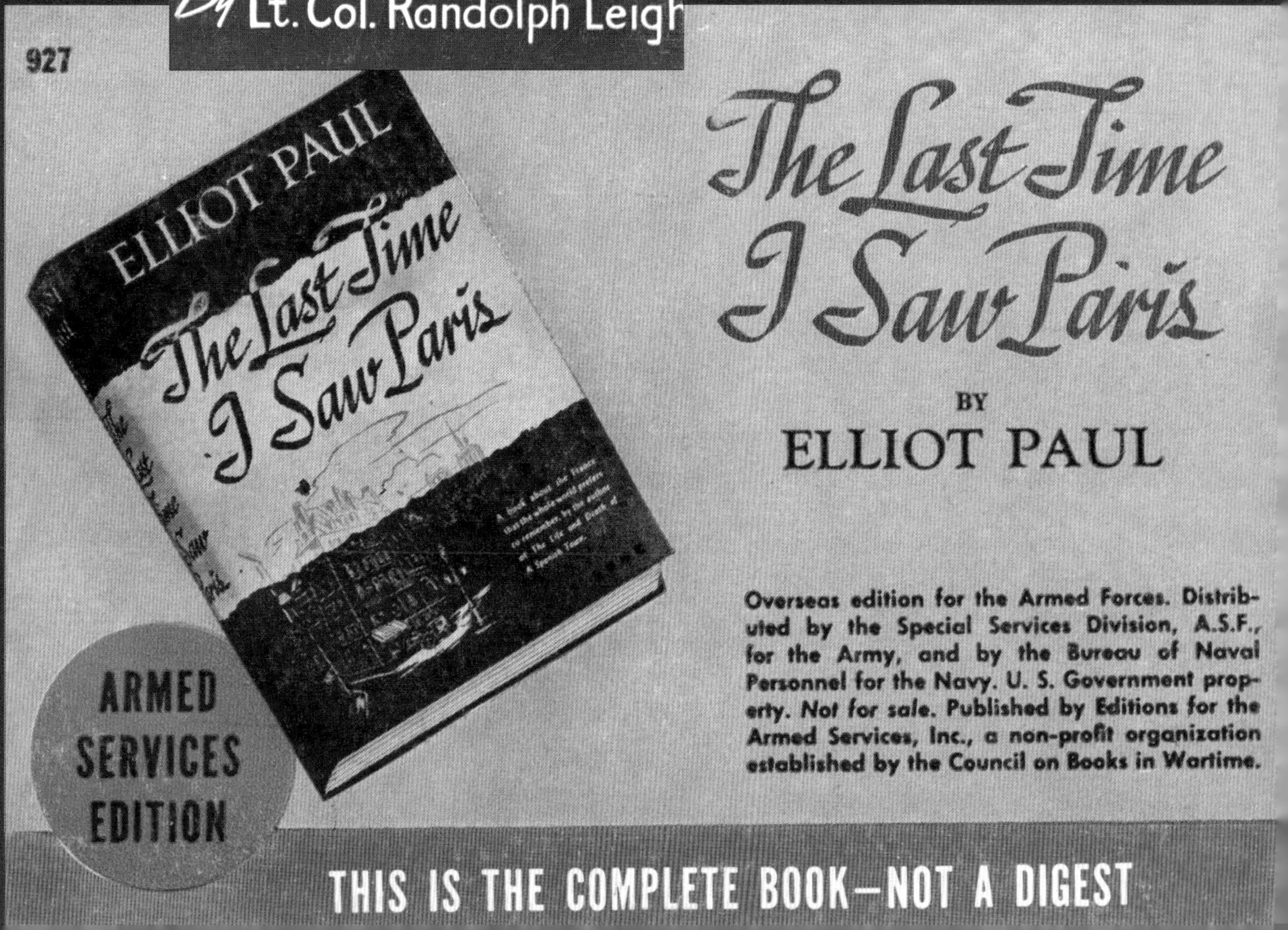

FIGHTING FORCES SERIES
48 Million Tons to EISENHOWER
THE INFANTRY JOURNAL
By Lt. Col. Randolph Leigh

927
ELLIOT PAUL
The Last Time I Saw Paris
The Last Time I Saw Paris
BY
ELLIOT PAUL
Overseas edition for the Armed Forces. Distributed by the Special Services Division, A.S.F., for the Army, and by the Bureau of Naval Personnel for the Navy. U. S. Government property. Not for sale. Published by Editions for the Armed Services, Inc., a non-profit organization established by the Council on Books in Wartime.
ARMED SERVICES EDITION
THIS IS THE COMPLETE BOOK—NOT A DIGEST

**BOOMERANG!**
WILLIAM C. CHAMBLISS
INFANTRY JOURNAL BOOKS / BANTAM, 1945

This book contains two novelettes, "Boomerang!" and "Baby Fights Back." It was issued in both Infantry Journal and Armed Services Edition formats. Remaining stock was issued as a Bantam book by simply placing a new Bantam dust jacket over the Infantry Journal version.

❚❚ without dj, ❚❚❚❚ with dj

J101

# Boomerang
### Two Novelettes
#### by
## WILLIAM C. CHAMBLISS

THE INFANTRY JOURNAL

SHE WAS A DECOY IN A TROPICAL BRAWL...

BOOMERANG!

WILLIAM C. CHAMBLISS

# G.I. Sketch BOOK

S 225

G. I. SKETCH BOOK

INFANTRY JOURNAL · PENGUIN BOOKS

FIGHTING FORCES PENGUIN SPECIAL

## Guadalcanal Diary

### RICHARD TREGASKIS

*An hour-by-hour, eyewitness account of the invasion of the Solomons by the U. S. Marines*

NEW YORK        WASHINGTON

## G.I. SKETCH BOOK
**INFANTRY JOURNAL / PENGUIN (US)**

This unusual book consists of drawings by American service personnel serving around the world. It includes many color plates, some of them paradoxically beautiful.

📖📖📖

## GUADALCANAL DIARY
**RICHARD TREGASKIS**
**INFANTRY JOURNAL / PENGUIN**

Tregaskis was one of the outstanding battlefield correspondents of World War II. Guadalcanal, a small island in the western Pacific Ocean, was the scene of a terrible, costly struggle between U.S. Marines and Japanese army troops.

📖📖

What looked like a front-cover blurb was actually more a "publisher's indicia," uniform from one book to another. This read:

*Overseas edition for the Armed Forces distributed by the Special Services Division, A.S.F., for the Army, and by the Bureau of Naval Personnel for the Navy. U.S. Government property.* **Not for Sale** *Published by Editions for the Armed Services, Inc., a non-profit organization established by the Council on Books in Wartime.*

Across the bottom of the cover, in a band of contrasting color, each book carried a very brief description of its contents: *This is the complete book—not a digest,* or *Selected Short Stories,* or *Cartoons,* and so on.

While most Armed Services Editions were reprints of books previously published in standard commercial editions, a few ASEs were "originals." These weren't actually books *written* for ASE but were compilations of previously published material. They were PBOs (paperback originals) from the viewpoint of collectors because they had not previously existed in that form, but all their contents *had* previously appeared elsewhere.

These "ASE/PBOs" are especially sought after by collectors and are valued more highly than most other ASEs. Even so, they vary widely in subject matter and collectibility. Two such ASE/PBOs were *Collected Short Stories of Sherwood Anderson* (Q-9) and *Collected Short Stories of Dorothy Parker* (R-4). Norman Corwin's *Selected Radio Plays* (R-7) is also in demand.

But even more important are ASEs by authors whose works are collected in their own right. For instance, Edgar Rice Burroughs' *Tarzan of the Apes* (M-16) and *The Return of Tarzan* (O-22), and H. P. Lovecraft's *The Dunwich Horror and Other Weird Tales* (730) are all hotly pursued and can be extremely pricey. Similarly, *The Adventures of Superman* by George Lowther (656) is seldom seen and highly prized.

Why is this?

Edgar Rice Burroughs (1875-1950) was an immensely popular author in his lifetime. He was a prolific science fiction writer, and of course he is best known as the creator of Tarzan. Pulp magazine editors competed for rights to his stories, and enthusiastic readers eagerly awaited the next volume in the sagas of Tarzan of the Apes, John Carter of Mars, and other Burroughs heroes. Book collectors built libraries of his novels. Following Burroughs' death most of his books lapsed from print and he was largely forgotten except for Tarzan comic books and screen adaptations, but in the 1960s interest in Burroughs and his works revived, and he has become more heavily collected than ever.

For this reason, a paperback collector seeking a run of ASEs will find himself in competition with a Burroughs collector who could hardly care less about *The Best from Yank* (ASE 934) or *Green Dolphin Street* by Elizabeth Goudge (ASE S-39) but who will willingly pay through the nose for *Tarzan of the Apes* or *The Return of Tarzan.*

*The Dunwich Horror and Other Weird Tales* is especially noteworthy. Howard Phillips Lovecraft (1890-1937) was an eccentric, reclusive *afficionado* and writer of atmospheric horror stories. He envisioned himself as a twentieth-century Edgar Allan Poe, affected old-fashioned orthography and mannerisms in his correspondence, and placed his stories with low-paying pulp magazines when he wasn't giving them away outright to fanzines.

Only after Lovecraft's death did his admirers August Derleth and Donald Wandrei create a publishing firm, Arkham House, for the specific purpose of rescuing Lovecraft's works from oblivion. The Armed Services Edition of Lovecraft's stories contains no material that a collector won't find elsewhere, but it is the only edition of this particular selection of stories *in this form.*

Lovecraft has remained consistently popular with a loyal core group of readers and collectors. In recent years major biographies of Lovecraft have appeared, one by L. Sprague de Camp and another by S. T. Joshi. Horror master Stephen King shows strongly the influence of Lovecraft, and literary doyenne Joyce Carol Oates has championed Lovecraft.

Some of his early commercial paperbacks are among the most desirable of paperback collectibles. And in the case of his Armed Services Edition, as with the Burroughs books, general paperback collectors must compete with Lovecraft specialists for the book.

*The Adventures of Superman* is still another case of a "double collectible." Comics collectors seek the book as an important associational item; paperback collectors seek it in its own right.

World War II ended in 1945, and Philip Van Doren Stern returned to Pocket Books, but Armed Services Editions continued under the supervision of Stan Thompson. The nation's forces were still scattered around the world, for the most part serving as armies of occupation in conquered Germany and Japan.

ASEs continued to appear until September, 1947, four years almost to the day after the ASE version of *The Education of H*y*m*a*n K*a*p*l*a*n* shipped. The final ASE was *Home Country* (1322). Its author, Ernie Pyle, had spent the war years as a combat journalist and was killed by enemy fire.

Leftover stock of ASEs remained in warehouses and were still in circulation in the 1950s. Frank M. Robinson, who would go on to an outstanding literary career in his own right, had served in the U.S. Navy during World War II and was recalled to duty during the Korean Conflict.

Assigned to the attack cargo ship *USS Alshain* as an electronics technician, Robinson pulled an additional duty as ship's librarian. He recalls that every time the *Alshain* made port, there would be another fresh carton of Armed Services Editions waiting on the dock.

There was no ordering of particular titles, Robinson recalls. You took whatever was in the carton — always a mix of serious literature and popular entertainment reading. There was a definite division of literary taste. Ship's officers, generally well-educated, preferred intellectual reading fare. Petty officers and ordinary seamen "went for anything adventurous."

What were the most popular of all the books in the ship's library? "*Tarzan of the Apes* and *The Return of Tarzan*," says Robinson. "And anything with adventure in it. Mysteries were very popular. And the sailors really loved books by Nordhoff and Hall." The most famous book by the last named was of course *Mutiny on the Bounty*.

Robinson also recalls visiting a bookstore in Norfolk, Virginia, when the *Alshain* returned to the United States. "There was a new author and he was immensely popular. They cleared a whole table and just covered it with his books. He was Mickey Spillane." As for the Spillane book, "I bought it for me, though it may have ended up in the ship's library."

But Spillane had arrived on the scene too late to be included in the Armed Services Editions program. Robinson had to buy a copy of Spillane's latest, out of his seaman's pay.

The United States has participated in several wars since the 1950s, and soldiers continue to seek diversion by reading, but commercial publishers have managed to meet their needs. There has never been another effort like the Armed Services Editions, and there probably never will be again.

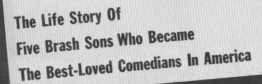

Government policy during the Second World War was anything but consistent. On the one hand, paper supplies were rationed and publishers were limited in their ability to obtain newsprint or book paper. A great many periodicals cut their pagination or frequency of publication or suspended publication altogether pending the end of the war. When the war ended some of them resumed publication; others simply ceased to exist.

And yet, the government encouraged book publication. Many volumes published in the early 1940s contained notices like this one:

"Books in Wartime

"Books are weapons in the war of ideas.

"President Roosevelt

"This book is manufactured in compliance with the War Production Board's ruling for conserving paper.

"It is printed on lighter weight paper, which reduces bulk substantially…and has smaller margins and more words to each page. The text is complete and unabridged.

"Thinner and smaller books will not only save paper, plate metal, and manpower but will make more books available to the reading public.

"The reader's understanding of this wartime problem will enable the publisher to cooperate more fully with our Government."

❚ ❚ ❚ ❚ ❚

The great paperback boom that had begun with Bob de Graff's Pocket Books in 1939 might have been squelched by wartime restrictions, or so it would seem. But somehow publishers managed to find paper. In fact, an astonishing number of new publishers entered the field, including three of the classic "majors"—Avon, Dell, and Popular Library.

One of the three new majors, Avon, actually succeeded in launching in 1941. The war had begun in Asia in the early 1930s and in Europe in 1939 with Hitler's invasion of Poland. The United States did not formally enter the war until December 8, 1941—the day after aircraft of the Japanese Imperial Navy attacked Pearl Harbor, Hawaii. But the nation had been edging closer to war for some time through the so-called Atlantic Charter and the Lend-Lease Program, which forged alliances with Great Britain and the Soviet Union.

Both Dell and Popular Library were launched in 1942.

Avon was a surprising innovation. While both Penguin and Pocket Books had been created by bookmen who simply wanted to publish books, and had to find a means of distributing their product, Avon was created to order by a distributor in need of a product.

Pocket Books had been distributed by the giant American News Company. ANC was the nation's largest distributor of periodicals, operating its own chain of retail stands under the name Union News Company. But after the first couple of years, Pocket Books became dissatisfied with its distribution by ANC/UNC and moved on to a complex chain of independent distributors ("IDs"). This left ANC without the mass-market paperback books that it had been distributing like magazines and that had proved a lucrative addition to its business.

Executives at ANC decided to create and fund a paperback book company of their own. ANC would thus be assured of a steady source of paperback books.

They hired two executives with backgrounds in both book and pulp magazine publishing: Joseph Meyers and Edna B. Williams. Meyers and Williams had no illusions about bringing great literature to the hungry minds of the masses. They were creating product for ANC to sell.

The design of the earliest Avon Books was eclectic to say the least. The very first "Avon Pocket-Size Book" was *Elmer Gantry* by Sinclair Lewis. The illustration is a dull and crudely executed painting of a man, presumably the title character, with a similarly dressed man half-hidden behind him and three vignetted human heads seemingly floating above them. The background is a featureless orange-yellow field.

### SEVEN FOOTPRINTS TO SATAN
A. MERRITT
AVON, 1945

Abraham Merritt was a longtime editor at Hearst's *American Weekly* and part-time pulp fantasy writer. The unknown artist who created this cover and others for early Avon editions achieved a lurid combination of eroticism, sadism, and imagination that drew loud criticism but made books jump off the revolver racks. They are collected mainly for these paintings.

〟〟〟

### THE AGONY COLUMN
EARL DERR BIGGERS
AVON, 1951

Originally published in 1916, this early novel was given a modern look for its Avon edition. Biggers was a journalist and playwright who had achieved huge success with his first novel, *Seven Keys to Baldpate*, but would achieve his greatest fame with Charlie Chan, the Chinese-Hawaiian-American detective.

〟〟

### ALL SHOT UP
CHESTER HIMES
AVON, 1960
COVER BY GEORGE ZEAL

A troubled man, Himes had trouble getting his books published as well. Often he was forced to cut or revise them, or his publishers cut them against his will. In recent years, Himes (1909-1984) has been the subject of increasing interest and respect. His paperback originals, including *All Shot Up*, are increasingly in demand.

〟〟〟〟

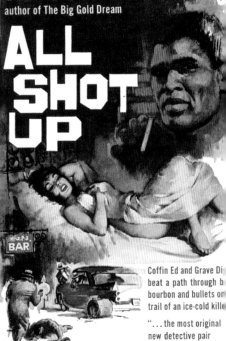

84

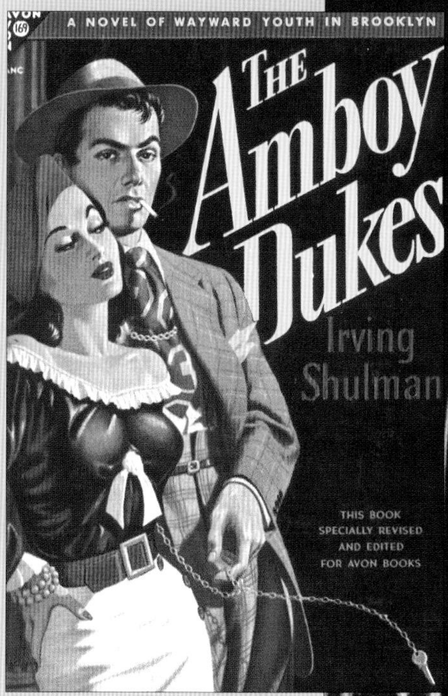

Through space and time
to worlds of tomorrow!

AVON 548
25¢

AWAY and BEYOND

A. E. Van Vogt

COMPLETE AND UNABRIDGED

A NOVEL OF WAYWARD YOUTH IN BROOKLYN

THE Amboy Dukes

Irving Shulman

THIS BOOK
SPECIALLY REVISED
AND EDITED
FOR AVON BOOKS

**THE AMBOY DUKES**
IRVING SHULMAN
AVON, 1949
COVER BY ANN CANTOR

One of the first and best "JD" novels, *The Amboy Dukes*
was "specially revised and edited", presumably to avoid
legal problems. Ann Cantor's cover painting is a classic,
with its zoot-suited, keychain-swinging wise guy and
his beret-wearing, tight-skirted moll.

👍👍👍👍

**AWAY AND BEYOND**
A. E. VAN VOGT
AVON, 1953

There could be no doubt about this collection by
science fiction star A. E. Van Vogt, one of whose stories
would later inspire the *Alien* motion pictures. You do
have to wonder about those spacemen's hands—or
maybe they're wearing flesh-colored gloves!

👍👍

## BIG LEAGUE BASEBALL
**ANTHOLOGY**
**AVON, 1950**

Those were the top-rank sports writers of their generation, and most of their names are still spoken with hushed respect by serious baseball historians. There has always been a market for nonfiction sports books, and the vintage photos in this one add to its desirability.

## THE BIG SLEEP
**RAYMOND CHANDLER**
**AVON, 1943**
**COVER BY PAUL STAHR**

Early Chandlers in either mass or trade paperback format are in huge demand and almost nonexistent supply. The lurid corpse-and-orchids theme of Stahr's painting may be in questionable taste, but the book is a prime collectible.

### A BULLET FOR BILLY THE KID
NELSON NYE
AVON, 1952
COVER BY JAMES BAMA

Neither the battered gunslinger nor his two-fisted opponent bears the slightest resemblance to Billy the Kid—nor was he even mentioned in the original title of the book, *Pistols for Hire*—but Avon's retitling and Bama's colorful, exciting painting sold copies.

### CORPSE IN THE WAXWORKS
JOHN DICKSON CARR
AVON, 1943

Both under his own name and that of his alternate persona, Carter Dickson, this detective writer has been a staple of paperback publishers for more than sixty years. The uncredited artist who painted this cover managed to make Carr's rather static, wordy novel look like an action-packed thriller.

### THE DAUGHTER OF FU MANCHU
SAX ROHMER
AVON, 1949
COVER BY ANN CANTOR

A stunning portrait by artist Ann Cantor marks this early paperback of one of (Arthur Sarsfield Ward) Rohmer's lurid Oriental mysteries. Rohmer claimed that the sinister genius was based on a mysterious Mr. King who ruled the London docks in Rohmer's boyhood.

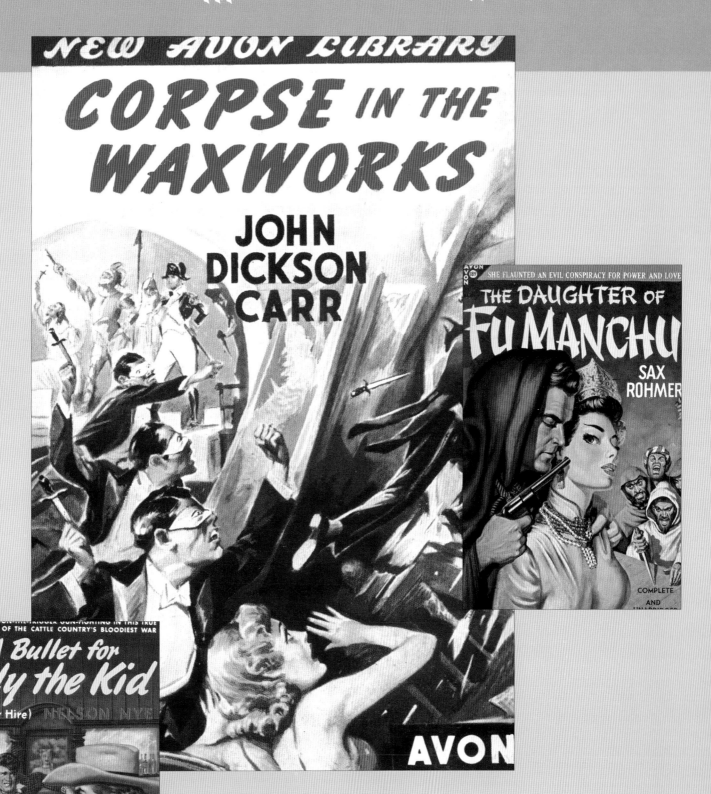

## THE DEVIL THUMBS A RIDE

ROBERT C. DU SOE
AVON, 1949
COVER BY ANN CANTOR

This odd novel by (possibly pseudonymous) Robert Du Soe, apparently his only book, was a forerunner of the popular "road" novels of later decades. Partly because of its low-budget film version starring Lawrence Tierney, it has become a minor cult item.

## ELMER GANTRY

SINCLAIR LEWIS
AVON, 1941

The very first Avon Book, this otherwise undistinguished edition of Lewis's famous novel is a major collectible.

## EUROPA

ROBERT BRIFFAULT
AVON, 1950

Nudity, sadism, bondage—and those high society toffs in their evening clothes and fancy gowns—you have to wonder how Avon got away with it. Apparently Avon did, too, and issued an alternate version with a much toned-down cover. You can guess which one the collectors look for.

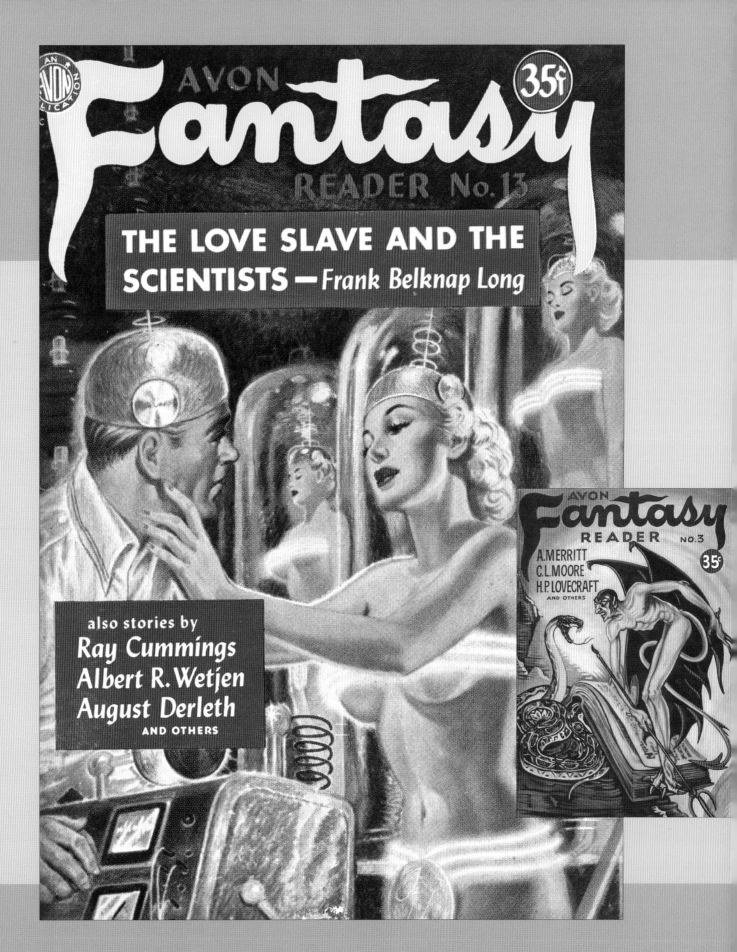

AVON FANTASY
Fantasy
READER No. 13

35¢

THE LOVE SLAVE AND THE
SCIENTISTS — Frank Belknap Long

also stories by
Ray Cummings
Albert R. Wetjen
August Derleth
AND OTHERS

AVON
Fantasy
READER No. 3
A. MERRITT
C. L. MOORE
H. P. LOVECRAFT
AND OTHERS
35¢

**AVON FANTASY READER NUMBER 13 AND NUMBER 3**
EDITED BY DONALD A. WOLLHEIM, 1947

Were these anthology series or magazines? They are
collected as both. Eighteen editions of the *Avon Fantasy
Reader* were published between 1947 and 1952, plus
three of the *Avon Science Fiction Reader* and a bewildering
array of other Avon series, most of them issued in digest
size but a few in mass paperback format.

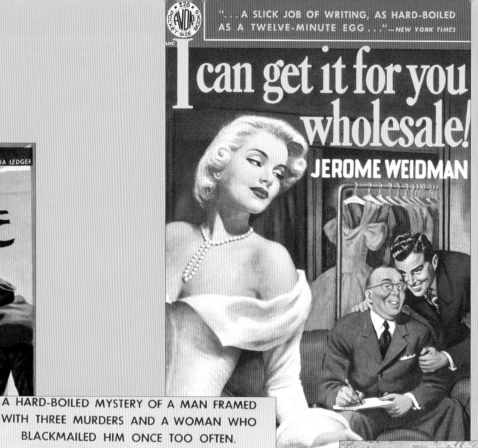

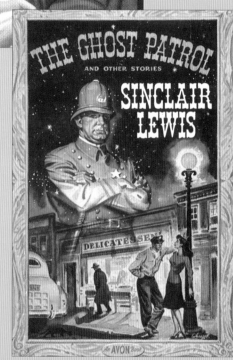

## FAST ONE
**PAUL CAIN**
AVON BOOKS, 1948

George Carrol Sims (1902-1966) wrote just one hardboiled novel and a volume of short stories under the byline Paul Cain, and a number of screenplays as Peter Ruric. His prose was so terse that readers are sometimes uncertain as to what's going on, but that that doesn't prevent his books from being collected. Note that there was a 1952 Avon reissue of *Fast One*.

## FRIDAY FOR DEATH
**LAWRENCE LARIAR**
AVON, 1951

Almost totally forgotten today, Lawrence Lariar was in his prime a popular hardboiled writer under his own name and a variety of pseudonyms. Those few readers who remember him do so fondly, and he may well be a candidate for rediscovery and renaissance. With its brilliant chrome yellow background and unusual typography, *Friday for Death* is a bargain collectible.

## I CAN GET IT FOR YOU WHOLESALE
**JEROME WEIDMAN**
AVON, 1950
COVER BY ANN CANTOR (?)

Weidman's exposé novel of the garment industry was a bestseller and shortly became a successful motion picture starring Susan Hayward and George Sanders; an MTI was published in 1951. The painting on the 1950 edition, probably by Ann Cantor, is superb. It looks like something painted by Norman Rockwell's evil twin!

## THE GHOST PATROL AND OTHER STORIES
**SINCLAIR LEWIS**
AVON, 1946
COVER BY SCHRAGGE (?)

For a while, Avon tried for a classy look by placing its cover paintings in elaborate golden frames. This edition is desirable for its lovely, evocative portrait of the ghostly turn-of-the-century officer presiding over a modern street scene. The line had come a long way from its first Lewis book, the 1941 *Elmer Gantry*.

What does it mean? Who would be attracted by such a cover?

The selection of titles was fairly incoherent. Avon's first ten releases ranged from an illustrated edition of *The Rubaiyat of Omar Khayyam* to *Mosquitos* by William Faulkner. But also included in the first ten were no fewer than six murder mysteries including books by Agatha Christie and John Dickson Carr (again, writing as Carter Dickson). The group also included *The Haunted Hotel*, a collection of ghost stories.

Where Penguin and Pocket Books had tried for a middlebrow or higher literary level, Avon was solidly populist from the outset.

The first Avon Books went on sale on November 21, 1941—just sixteen days before Japanese bombs fell on Pearl Harbor.

The first forty Avon Books were unnumbered, but Avon eventually assigned numbers to them "after the fact," to the great comfort and assistance of collectors. Avon Number 41 was *The Narrow Corner* by W. Somerset Maugham, and it did not appear until 1944, indicating a low rate of production. Maybe those wartime restrictions were taking their bite after all, although other factors may have been involved.

Remembering that Avon Books were originally intended to fill the vacuum left in ANC/UNC's racks by the desertion of Pocket Books, the early Avons imitated certain features of Pocket Books. Paper edges were stained red, as were the edges of Pocket Books. And the cover line *Avon Pocket-Size Books* was suspiciously suggestive of *Pocket Books*. The latter publisher sued Avon, and Avon was forced to drop the phrase "Pocket-Size." They also discontinued the red edge stains. Avon also adopted a miniature portrait of William Shakespeare as its symbol.

Drawing upon Meyers' and Williams' pulp magazine experience, veteran pulp illustrators were brought in to paint covers for Avon. Images that had been familiar to pulp aficionados now appeared regularly on paperback covers. A group of macabre icons—grinning skulls, danc-

ing or menacing skeletons, bony pointing fingers, flying bats silhouetted against the moon, and of course the ever-present Grim Reaper with his hooded robe and scythe—meant murder mysteries. There was seldom a ghostly or supernatural element in these books, despite their covers.

In fact, many of them were old-style, genteel whodunits written by the likes of John Rhode, Earl Derr Biggers, Dorothy L. Sayers, or Margery Allingham.

Other Avon mysteries harked back to the tradition of the gangster pulps, both in content and in design. One such early Avon was *Little Caesar* by W. R. Burnett (Number 66). Avon got double duty out of this cover by using it on a comic book as well.

By contrast there was *Over My Dead Body* by Rex Stout (Number 62). The cover features a corpse as well as a well-endowed young woman falling out of her dress. One of Stout's perennially popular Nero Wolfe novels, *Over My Dead Body*, is neither sexy nor gory, but the conventions of packaging were served.

One reason for Avon's slow production of books may well have been its diversion of resources—both literary and material—into a bewildering array of separately numbered series, most but not all of them digest sized, that might be considered either books or magazines. These included the *Avon Detective Mysteries, Avon Fantasy Novels, Avon Fantasy Reader, Avon Love Book Monthly, Avon Modern Short Story Monthly, Avon Monthly Novel, Avon Murder Mystery Monthly, Avon Romance Novel Monthly, Avon Science Fiction Reader, Avon Science Fiction and Fantasy Reader, Avon Western Novel Monthly*, and *Avon Western Reader*.

Many of these series were edited or inspired by Donald A. Wollheim, a former pulp magazine editor and anthologist who joined Avon in 1947 and would remain with the company until 1952 when he left to make publishing history with the fledgling Ace Books.

### THE GORGEOUS GHOUL MURDER CASE
DWIGHT V. BABCOCK
AVON, 1943, 1951

The uncredited painting makes this 1951 edition
look like *The Invisible Man Returns*, but in fact it is
a delightful comedy-mystery featuring Babcock's
amateur sleuth Hannah Van Doren. Babcock had
written standard hardboiled fiction for *Black Mask*
magazine but changed his tone for the madcap
adventures of Homicide Hannah in three wonderful
novels. The 1943 Avon paperback is very scarce and
of course is more desirable than this 1951 reissue.

◖◖◖.◖◖

### THE GIRL WITH THE HUNGRY EYES
EDITED BY DONALD A. WOLLHEIM
AVON, 1949

In later years editor Wollheim revealed that
he had lobbied Avon for authority to start a
new science fiction magazine and had got as
far as buying stories for the first issue when
the project was cancelled. Instead, the stories
were used in this superb PBO anthology. The
cover painting is sometimes attributed to Ann
Cantor, and the style is certainly hers, but the
signature is "RS." Go figure.

◖◖

### GOD WEARS A BOW TIE
LYLE STUART
AVON, 1950

Before starting his career as a muckraking
publisher, Lyle Stuart was a Broadway journalist
on the Damon Runyon/Earl Wilson/Walter
Winchell/Ed Sullivan model. His tell-all book
was really less sensational than its clever cover
suggested.

◖◖◖

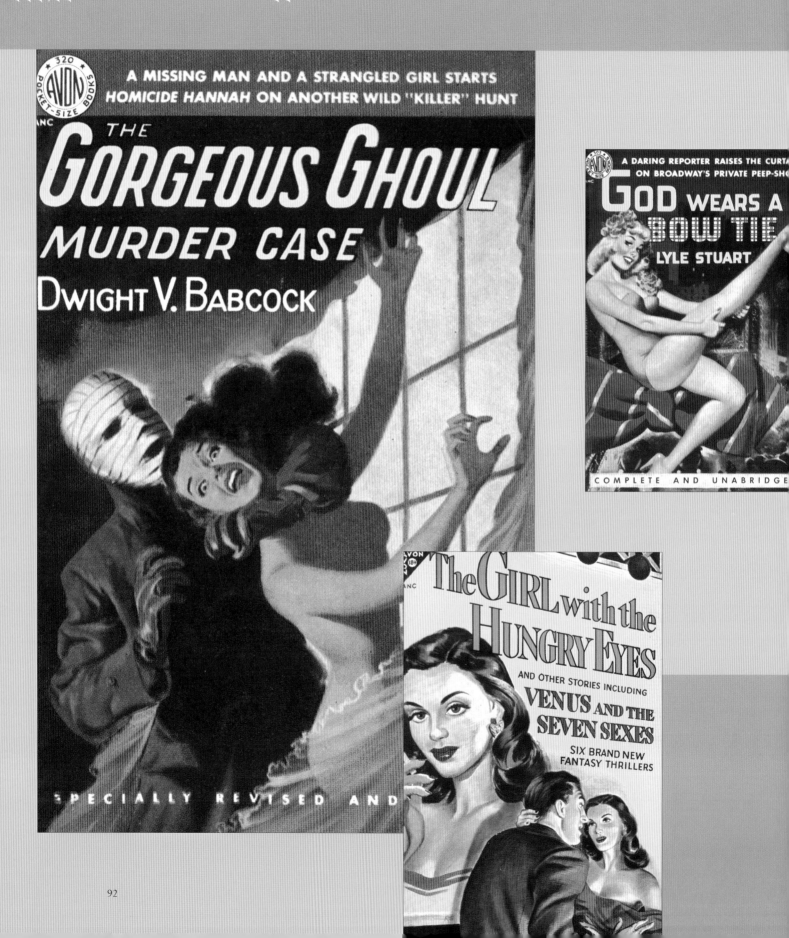

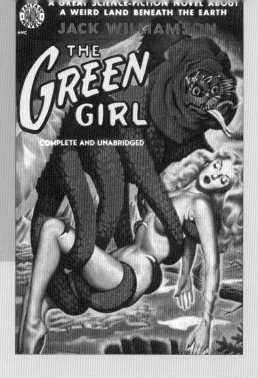

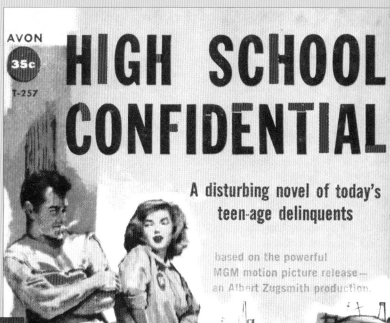

### THE GREEN GIRL
JACK WILLIAMSON
AVON FANTASY NOVEL 2, 1950

Jack Williamson is the undisputed record-holder for longevity as a science fiction writer. His career spans the classic pulp era, the fan-owned specialty publishers, and the paperback revolution. *The Green Girl* is pure-quill early Williamson, lurid cover and all. There were only two volumes in this series; Avon Fantasy Novel 1 was *Princess of the Atom* by Ray Cummings.

### HOME TO HARLEM
CLAUDE MCKAY
AVON, 1951
COVER BY ANN CANTOR (?)

Claude McKay (1899-1948) was a brilliant and much-traveled, Jamaican-born member of the Harlem Renaissance. *Home to Harlem* was a bestseller in 1928 and is a serious novel of contemporary African American life. Highly collectible on its own merits, it features the brilliant if controversial cover painting, probably by Ann Cantor.

### HIGH SCHOOL CONFIDENTIAL
MORTON COOPER
AVON, 1958

Beloved of fans of Jerry Lee Lewis, juvenile delinquents, marijuana, and movies so bad that they're good, the Jack Arnold film of 1958 inspired this collectible MTI/PBO.

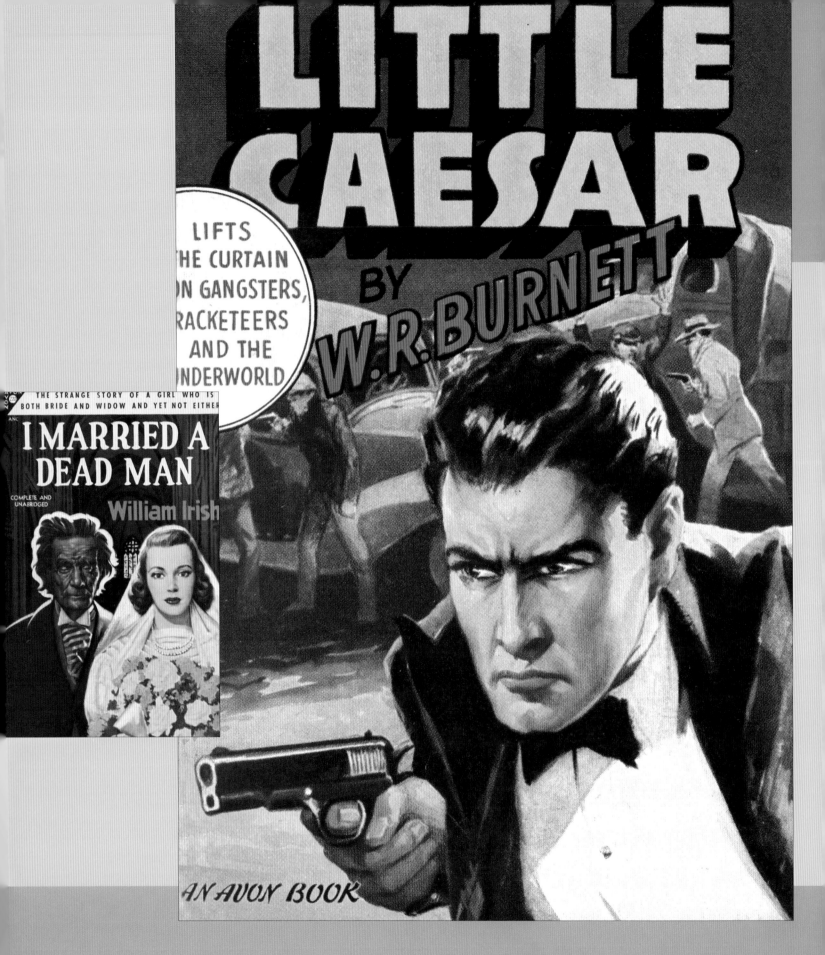

### I MARRIED A DEAD MAN
**WILLIAM IRISH**
**AVON, 1950**

William Irish was a pseudonym of Cornell
Woolrich (as was George Hopley); Woolrich
is collectible under all three names. The
uncredited painting for this reissue of the 1948
hardcover is certainly a leading candidate for
most gruesome book cover of all time.

🕮🕮🕮

### LITTLE CAESAR
**W. R. BURNETT**
**AVON, 1945**
**COVER BY PAUL STAHR**

The most famous of Burnett's many gangster
novels, *Little Caesar* brought Edward G. Robinson
to fame as a cinema tough-guy. Avon got double
duty out of Paul Stahr's painting, using it as a
comic book cover as well.

🕮

### THE LURKING FEAR AND OTHER STORIES
**H. P. LOVECRAFT**
**AVON, 1947**
**COVER BY A. R. TILBURNE**

Howard Phillips Lovecraft (1890-1937) was
seldom well served by cover illustrators, but
first editions of books by this eccentric anti-
quarian and horror writer are highly desirable
nonetheless. Avon editor Donald A. Wollheim
had befriended Lovecraft and published him in
semi-professional magazines in the 1930s.

🕮🕮🕮🕮

### MISS JILL FROM SHANGHAI
EMILY HAHN
AVON, 1950
COVER BY DALE RANDALL

This is not an MTI for the 1948 film *The Lady from Shanghai*, although Randall's portrait of the blonde heroine might have suggested the blonde version of Rita Hayworth who starred in that film with Orson Welles. The film was based on another novel by Sherwood King.

### LOVE'S LOVELY COUNTERFEIT
JAMES M. CAIN
AVON MURDER MYSTERY MONTHLY, 1947
COVER BY DON MILSAP

This digest-size series was filled with brilliant, collectible (and expensive) novels and collections by many of the top names in crime fiction: Chandler, Stout, Simenon, Sayers, Woolrich, Allingham, and others. It is both seldom seen and highly collectible!

### MURDER AT MIDNIGHT
R. A. J. WALLING
AVON, 1942

Walling was one of the most traditional of all English mystery writers, much admired in his own time but sadly outdated. Mystery writer, collector, and critic Bill Pronzini said that, "Walling wrote some of the dullest mysteries ever committed to paper." Still, *Murder at Midnight* has an interesting cover painting if nothing else.

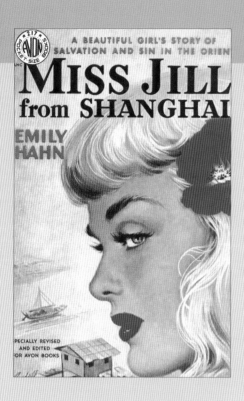

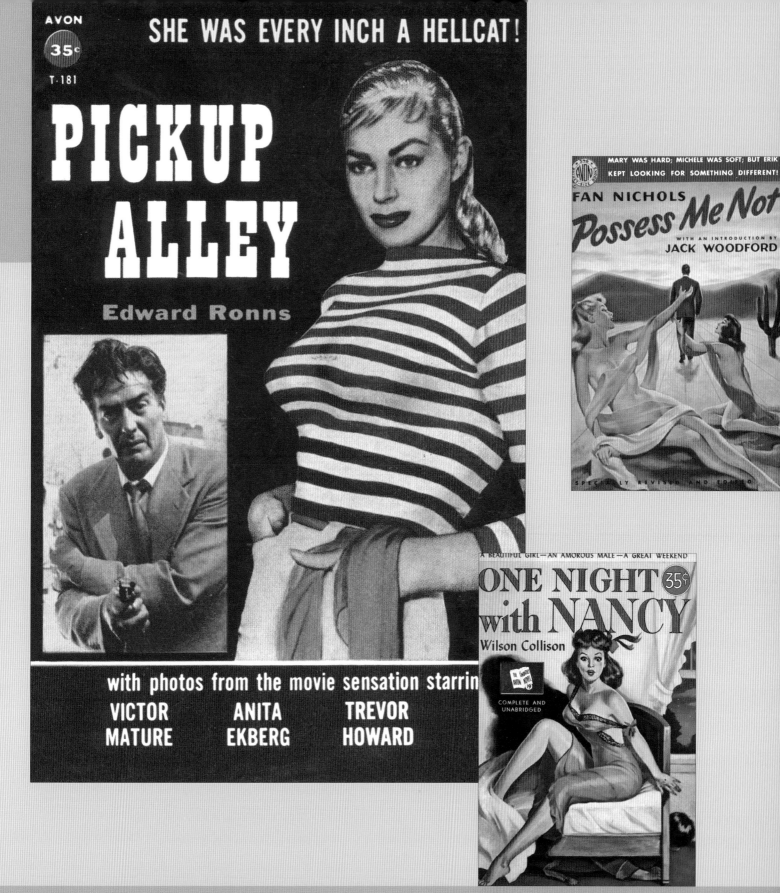

SHE WAS EVERY INCH A HELLCAT!

AVON
35¢
T-181

PICKUP ALLEY

Edward Ronns

with photos from the movie sensation starrin

VICTOR MATURE    ANITA EKBERG    TREVOR HOWARD

MARY WAS HARD; MICHELE WAS SOFT; BUT ERIK KEPT LOOKING FOR SOMETHING DIFFERENT!

FAN NICHOLS
Possess Me Not
WITH AN INTRODUCTION BY JACK WOODFORD

A BEAUTIFUL GIRL—AN AMOROUS MALE—A GREAT WEEKEND

ONE NIGHT with NANCY    35¢

Wilson Collison

COMPLETE AND UNABRIDGED

### PICKUP ALLEY
EDWARD RONNS
AVON, 1957

This screenplay novelization, PBO/MTI features 1950s screen siren Anita Ekberg and tough-guy actor Victor Mature. "Ronns" was also Edward Aarons (1916-1975), whose name gave him the distinction of always appearing first in reference works and alphabetized book collections.

### POSSESS ME NOT
FAN NICHOLS
AVON, 1951

Fan Nichols was one of the many writers of her era who combined traditional romance, soft-core pornography, and sometimes remarkable psychosexual insights in her novels. The endorsement by Jack Woodford, an earlier practitioner of the craft, couldn't have hurt, but the chief interest in this book comes from its astonishing cover painting. Dali meets Vargas? GGA on an abstract landscape?

### ONE NIGHT WITH NANCY
WILSON COLLISON
AVON MONTHLY NOVEL, 1951

This digest-size series included both mysteries and borderline, soft-core porn. Very, very soft-core. It is sought after by collectors of GGA ("good girl art").

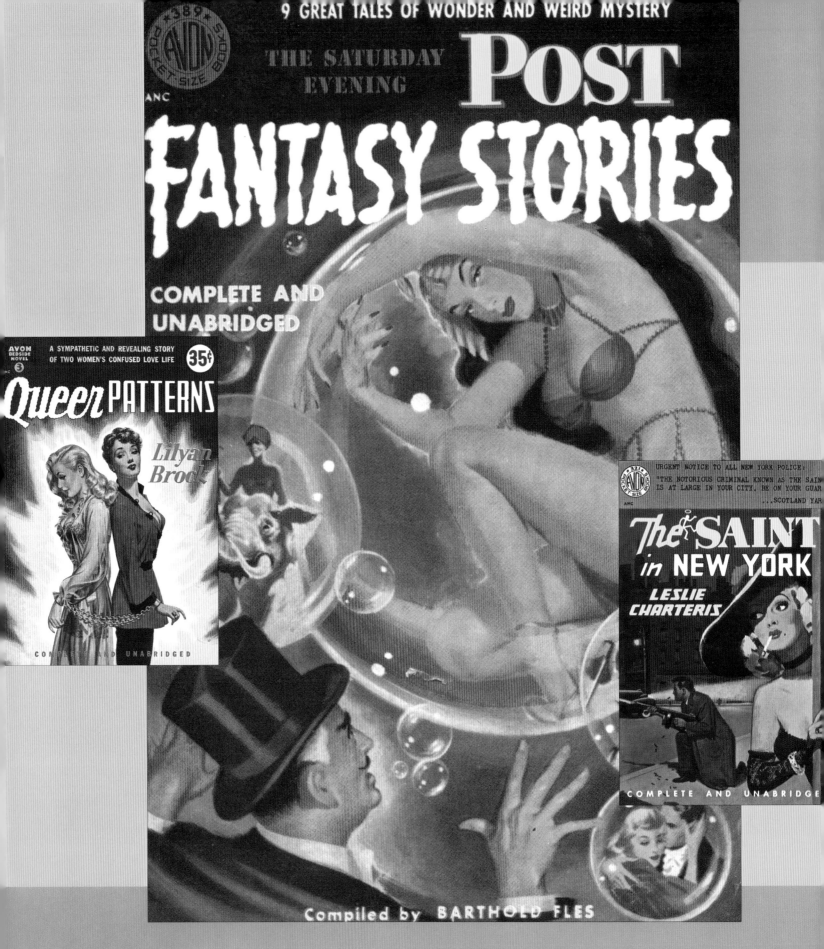

9 GREAT TALES OF WONDER AND WEIRD MYSTERY

THE SATURDAY EVENING **POST**
FANTASY STORIES

COMPLETE AND UNABRIDGED

A SYMPATHETIC AND REVEALING STORY
OF TWO WOMEN'S CONFUSED LOVE LIFE

35¢

*Queer* PATTERNS

*Lilyan Brock*

COMPLETE AND UNABRIDGED

URGENT NOTICE TO ALL NEW YORK POLICE:
"THE NOTORIOUS CRIMINAL KNOWN AS THE SAINT
IS AT LARGE IN YOUR CITY. BE ON YOUR GUAR
...SCOTLAND YAR

*The* SAINT
*in* NEW YORK

LESLIE
CHARTERIS

COMPLETE AND UNABRIDGE

Compiled by BARTHOLD FLES

### QUEER PATTERNS
LILYAN BROCK
AVON BEDSIDE NOVEL, 1951, ETON (AVON), 1952

The striking Lesbian cover on still another Avon digest-size series makes this a highly collectible book. The reissue by Eton Books, an Avon companion line, is less desirable.

### THE SATURDAY EVENING POST FANTASY STORIES
EDITED BY BARTHOLD FLES
AVON, 1951

*The Saturday Evening Post* was so popular in the 1950s that Avon didn't bother to mention any of the contributors to this book, even though they included such luminaries as Gerald Kersh, Will F. Jenkins, and Admiral Daniel Gallery. The cover was also magical.

### THE SAINT IN NEW YORK
LESLIE CHARTERIS
AVON, 1951

Leslie Charles Bowyer Yin, born in Singapore, educated in England and naturalized American, lived a life as peripatetic and amusing as that of his most famous creation, Simon Templar, the Saint. A gentleman rogue, chased by police on both sides of the Atlantic Ocean, subject of successful motion picture and television series, the Saint is collected in all his many manifestations.

## SINFUL WOMAN
**JAMES M. CAIN**
**AVON, 1948**
**COVER BY PHILLIPS AND TROEGER**

This rare PBO by James M. Cain looks like a sex novel and in a sense it is, but Cain was a serious novelist who blended hardboiled crime with emotional and psychological depth. Some bibliographers don't seem to realize that this is a PBO, despite the publisher's loud pronouncement of that fact.

📖📖📖📖

## THE TRAGEDY OF X
**ELLERY QUEEN**
**AVON, 1952**

The Ellery Queen name is still with us in the form of a leading mystery magazine, despite the death of both cousins who created the joint pseudonym. The Queen novels evolved from stuffy "classic" style to a more modern, realistic approach over the years. Collectors abound.

📖📖

## AVON SCIENCE FICTION READER NUMBER 1
**EDITED BY DONALD A. WOLLHEIM**
**AVON, 1951**

This short-lived (three issues) companion to the *Avon Fantasy Reader* reprinted numerous pulp stories by fine authors. With its combination of GGA and bondage, the cover painting has almost nothing to do with the contents.

📖📖

Wollheim's chief interest was science fiction, and under his tutelage Avon produced many striking science fiction novels and "readers." But Wollheim also had an interest in Westerns, and Avon successfully published these as well.

Avon was not above self-praise, as indicated by this notice that appeared on *The Avon Ghost Reader* (Number 90, 1946). By now Avon Pocket-Size Books were called the New Avon Library. On the back cover of the *Ghost Reader*, headed by a portrait of the Bard of Avon himself, the text reads:

"GOOD BOOKS—GREAT AUTHORS

"Mysteries - Crime & Detective Stories

"Anthologies - Novels - Classics

"LOOK FOR THE *Shakespeare-Head* Imprint!

"AVON BOOKS are always excellent reading —but more than that—they are good books. Every volume is printed on a sturdy, opaque paper in a clear, modern, and easy to read type-face. Bound in heavy weight covers, they have a delightful flexibility in handling and stand up well under reading and rereading. The covers are specially processed to make them resistant to dirt, damp, and rough usage and can easily be washed clean. And finally, the books are color-fully stained on all three sides with fast book dyes, serving to keep the pages free of dust.

"AVON BOOKS are grand books in every way—and every AVON volume carries its distinctive hallmark: the SHAKESPEARE-HEAD. Look for this imprint on the back cover of every volume."

Joseph Meyers died in 1957. Edna Williams' name had already disappeared from the Avon masthead, and in 1959 the company was sold to Hearst, who put Avon under his magazine operation. The company had produced many intriguing and collectible books in its nearly two decades of operation, but had never been a truly major player, and under Hearst's control it was almost lost within a huge multimedia empire that ranged from newspapers and magazines to motion pictures and newsreels.

In 1963 Peter Mayer (no relation to Joseph Meyers) joined Avon and began revamping and upgrading the company. In later years Mayer would move on, eventually joining Penguin Books. In the years that followed, Avon rose in prestige and impact on the publishing field and remains to this day a major player.

WHOSE BODY?
by Dorothy L. Sayers
A Lord Peter Wimsey Mystery

COMPLETE AND UNABRIDGED

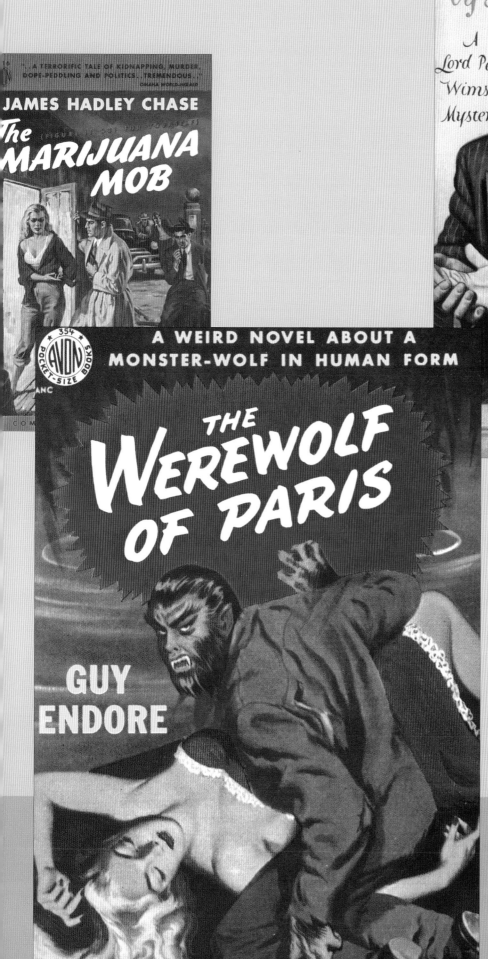

"...A TERRORIFIC TALE OF KIDNAPPING, MURDER, DOPE-PEDDLING AND POLITICS...TREMENDOUS..."
OMAHA WORLD-HERALD

JAMES HADLEY CHASE
The MARIJUANA MOB

354 AVON
POCKET-SIZE BOOKS

A WEIRD NOVEL ABOUT A MONSTER-WOLF IN HUMAN FORM

THE WEREWOLF OF PARIS

GUY ENDORE

SPECIALLY REVISED AND EDITED

WHOSE BODY?
DOROTHY L. SAYERS
AVON, 1948

Sayers' (1893-1957) Lord Peter Wimsey may have been the original and ultimate aristocrat amateur sleuth, the model for uncounted tiresome imitations. Sayers' wicked wit and high intelligence raised Lord Peter above the crowd and has made her a cult figure (and collected writer) for decades.

¶¶¶¶¶

Popular Library (originally called Popular Books) hit the newsstands in 1942. Like Avon it was encouraged by American News Company and distributed via ANC/UNC, but it had greater independence than had Avon. Popular was the creation of Ned Pines, a longtime periodicals publisher whose earlier properties (most of which continued in parallel with Popular Library) included comic books, pulp magazines, and even astrology guides.

Pines had operated under a number of corporate titles including Standard Publications and Thrilling Publications, and Pines Publications. for his new book line he experimented with several logos. By 1956 he settled on a visual pun —a stylized pine tree.

One of Pines' favorite words was *thrilling*, and his pulp magazines included *Thrilling Wonder Stories*, *Thrilling Western*, and *Thrilling Adventures*. He also liked the word *startling*, and for some years published *Startling Stories*. His comic books included *Startling Comics* and *Thrilling Comics*.

For many of his editorial enterprises he employed Leo Margulies as editor. When he started Popular Library, he added Charles Heckleman, a Western novelist, as editor.

Popular Library books had a look that was more slick and professional than the early Avons. Pines selected green as a theme color, and most of his early paperback books—known among collectors as "Pops"—had green end papers and green edges.

He also brought a number of pulp magazine cover painters over to Popular Library, most notable among them being Rudolph Belarski and Earle K. Bergey. Belarski specialized in spectacular costume scenes, square-jawed men reminiscent of the Norman Saunders pulp school and voluptuous women of a rather Junoesque build.

Bergey had come to prominence as a cover artist for Pines' science fiction pulps, where he was known as the "King of the Triple Bs." This appellation referred to a common configuration of a BEM (Bug-Eyed Monster), a Bum (heroic, ray-gun wielding spaceman), and a Babe (generally semi-nude or wearing such odd outfits as a cellophane spacesuit over a set of riveted brass undies).

Two of the most famous and sought-after Pops featured Bergey covers. One was *Gentlemen Prefer Blondes* by Anita Loos (Number 221, 1950). Bergey's painting shows a bosomy blonde in plunging, lace-edged black lingerie, surrounded by the floating heads (shades of Avon's *Elmer Gantry*) of an assortment of leering males. There's a top banner on the book, "She Knew Her Way Around Men", and another at the bottom, "The Intimate Story of a Professional Lady." It was a most striking and effective cover.

Even more famous was Bergey's cover painting for *The Private Life of Helen of Troy* by John Erskine (Number 147, 1948). Ask any paperback collector about "the nipple cover" and you'll get a knowing nod. Only the most prurient-minded could consider Bergey's painting of Helen as pornographic, but his anatomically correct portrayal of Helen's charms, covered but hardly concealed by a diaphanous gown, left nothing to the imagination.

Ned Pines' pulp magazines covered a broad spectrum from jungle tales to horror stories, but his books were at least initially far more sharply focused. The very first Pop—unnumbered, but by courtesy considered Number 1—was a crime novel, *Saint Overboard* by Leslie Charteris. Next came *Murder in the Dark* by Mignon G. Eberhart, *Crime of Violence* by Rufus King, *Murder in the Madhouse* by Jonathan Latimer, *Miss Pinkerton* by Mary Robert Rinehart, *Three Bright Pebbles* by Leslie Ford, *Death Demands an Audience* by Helen Reilly, *Death for Dear Clara* by Q. Patrick (Patrick Quentin), *The Eel Pie Murders* by David Frome, and *To Wake the Dead* by John Dickson Carr.

## 7 KEYS TO BALDPATE
EARL DERR BIGGERS
POPULAR LIBRARY, 1948
COVER BY H. LAWRENCE HOFFMAN (?)

Earl Derr Biggers (1884-1933) had achieved his greatest popularity decades earlier and in fact had been dead fifteen years when this handsome edition of his first novel (1913) was issued. The spectacular cover and the continuing popularity of Biggers' detective Charlie Chan gave the old book new life.

## ALL OVER BUT THE SHOOTING
RICHARD POWELL
POPULAR LIBRARY, 1946
COVER BY FIEDLER

Born 1908, Richard Powell was the author of ten novels published in the 1940s and 1950s. Except for the Arab and Andy Blake novels, they tended to be hardboiled and even *noir*-ish, but the Blakes, who resembled Hammett's Nick and Nora Charles, took part in a series of lighthearted, reader-friendly adventurers.

## THE BIG EYE
MAX EHRLICH
POPULAR LIBRARY, 1950
COVER BY EARLE K. BERGEY

Max Ehrlich (1909-1983) wrote ten science fiction novels, several other books, and a number of screenplays. *The Big Eye* was his first extravaganza, reminiscent of Philip Wylie and Edwin Balmer's *When Worlds Collide* (1933), a theme revived in the 1990s by the actual impact of huge meteors on Jupiter. "Big Eye" covers are a highly specialized department of paperback collecting.

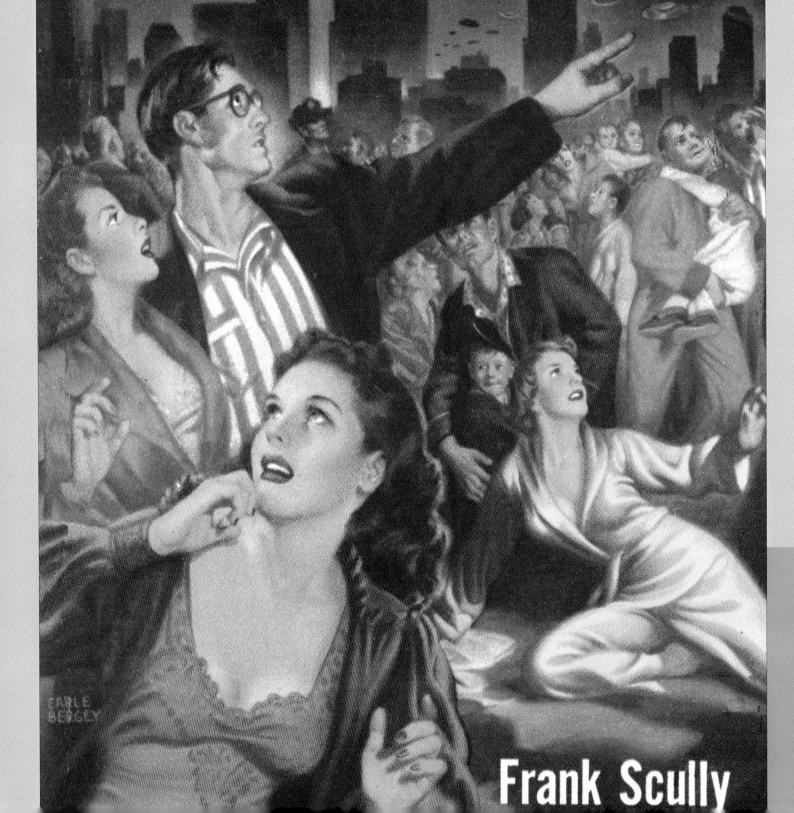

POPULAR LIBRARY

The Book Everyone Is Talking About

326

# BEHIND THE FLYING SAUCERS

Frank Scully

## BEHIND THE FLYING SAUCERS

FRANK SCULLY
POPULAR LIBRARY, 1951
COVER BY EARLE K. BERGEY

For a while the competition among paperback houses to capture the UFO market was fierce. Probably the most successful of all UFO books was Donald Keyhoe's *The Flying Saucers are Real* (Fawcett Gold Medal, 1950) but "Pop" wasn't far behind. Half a century later, UFO books are still a staple!

A TEXAS RANGERS NOVEL

# BUCKAROO

## EUGENE CUNNINGHAM

PULAR LIBRAR

A MICHAEL SHAYNE MYSTERY

POPULAR LIBRARY 192

# Bodies ARE WHERE YOU FIND THEM

BRETT HALLIDAY

LAUGHS AND FUN FOR EVERYONE

POPULAR LIBRARY

# POPULAR BOOK OF
# Cartoons

Featuring
SYDNEY HOFF · LAWRENCE LARIAR
JEFFERSON MACHAMER · LOUIS PRISCILLA
JACK MARKOW · W. P. TRENT · DOROTHY McKAY
BARNEY TOBEY · AL ROSS · COURTNEY DUNKEL

---

## BODIES ARE WHERE YOU FIND THEM

BRETT HALLIDAY
POPULAR LIBRARY, 1949
COVER BY RUDOLPH BELARSKI

Davis Dresser (1904-1977) used several pseudonyms, the best known being Brett Halliday. His Mike Shayne series ran to dozens of titles starting in 1940, became a popular radio series, and was filmed with Lloyd Nolan as Shayne. While the classic Shayne paperbacks were Dells with stunning McGinnis covers, the Belarski version is also a fine collectible.

## BUCKAROO

EUGENE CUNNINGHAM
POPULAR LIBRARY, 1946
COVER BY H. LAWRENCE HOFFMAN

Westerns were more popular in the 1940s and 1950s (in part thanks to their endorsement by President Eisenhower) but have declined in popularity in recent decades. There are a few western specialist collectors, but mostly they are sought by hobbyists trying to complete a run by publisher.

## POPULAR BOOK OF CARTOONS

ANTHOLOGY
COVER BY SYD HOFF AND OTHERS

Cartoon books have always had a market; everybody needs a laugh now and then.

## BORDER TOWN GIRL

There Was No Turning Back For Her

John D. MacDonald

25c

750

COMPLETE AND UNABRIDGED

A TREASURY FOR PUZZLE FANS

POPULAR LIBRARY

150

## CROSSWORD PUZZLES BOOK TWO

MORE PUZZLES BY AMERICA'S ACE PUZZLE-MAKERS

POPULAR LIBRARY

220

Intimate Tales of Broadway's Guys and Gals

## The DAMON RUNYON STORY

BY ED WEINER

Introduction by WALTER WINCHELL

POPULAR LIBRARY

331

She Defied Their Moral Code

## Campus Town

HART STILWELL

**CROSSWORD PUZZLES BOOK 2**
POPULAR LIBRARY, 1950
Most puzzle books are pretty uninteresting visually, but they are hard to find and assiduously pursued by "publisher completists."

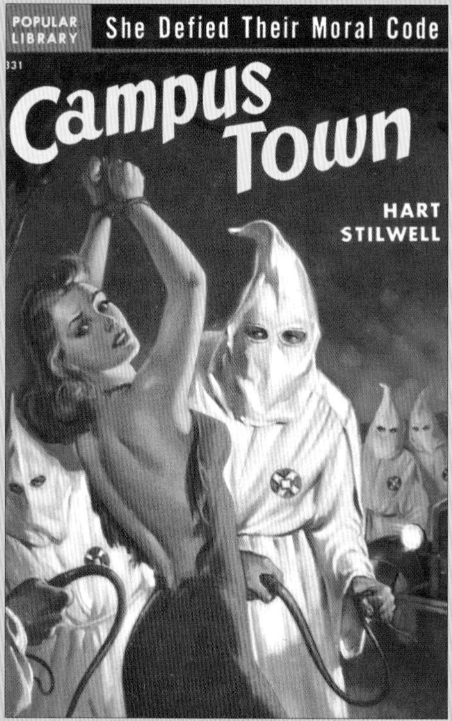

📖📖📖

**BORDER TOWN GIRL**
JOHN D. MACDONALD
POPULAR LIBRARY, 1956
John D. MacDonald made a home for himself with Fawcett Gold Medal Books, but he did stray occasionally. His books for other pulishers, like this PBO, are vigorously pursued by MacDonald collectors.

📖📖📖

**THE DAMON RUNYON STORY**
ED WEINER
POPULAR LIBRARY, 1950
COVER PAINTING PROBABLY BY BELARSKI
This biography of the famous journalist, courtroom reporter, Broadway columnist, sometime sports writer, and short story writer (best known for *Guys and Dolls*) features an unusual cover treatment: a combination of GGA painting, newspaper columns, and a photograph of Runyon. Runyon's pal Walter Winchell, then a popular columnist and radio personality himself, boosted the book.

📖📖

**CAMPUS TOWN**
HART STILWELL
POPULAR LIBRARY, 1951
COVER BY EARLE K. BERGEY
Segregation was the rule—in much of the country, the law—in the early 1950s. Publishers, distributors, and retailers risked severe retaliation for selling books like *Campus Town* or *KKK* by Paul E. Walsh (Avon PBO).

📖📖📖📖

## DON'T EVER LOVE ME
OCTAVUS ROY COHEN
POPULAR LIBRARY, 1951
COVER BY RUDOLPH BELARSKI

Octavus Roy Cohen (1890-1959) was a journalist, playwright, lawyer, and prolific author of
short stories and novels. One of his sleuths,
Florian Slappey, "the Black Beau Brummell
of Birmingham," was a pioneering portrayal
of an African American as the lead character
in a detective series. *Don't Ever Love Me*, with
its astonishing GGA Belarski cover, features
another of Cohen's detectives, Max Gold.

## THE DREAM PEDDLERS
FLOYD MILLER
POPULAR LIBRARY, 1956

Little is known about the mysterious Mr. Miller,
save for his year of birth, 1912. His only books
seem to have been *The Dream Peddlers* (PBO) and
the earlier *Savage Streets*, also published by
Popular Library.

## EPITAPH FOR AN ENEMY
GEORGE BARR
POPULAR GIANT, 1960
COVER BY STANLEY ZUCKERBERG (?)

George Barr, author of this war novel,
should not be confused with the artist
George Barr, whose lush, brilliant fantasy
and science fiction covers have appeared
on Ace, DAW, and other books.

## EXCUSE MY DUST
BELLAMY PARTRIDGE
POPULAR LIBRARY, 1951

In the bewildering world of the 1950s,
jarred by the shriek of jet planes,
atomic bombs, television sets, and the
earliest computers, readers turned
toward the "simpler, better world" of
earlier decades. Of course, it's always
like that — today, aging Baby Boomers
yearn for the "simpler, better world"
of the 1950s!

## FOCUS
ARTHUR MILLER
POPULAR LIBRARY, 1950
COVER BY RUDOLPH BELARSKI

This thriller was indeed an early work by Arthur Miller, the famous playwright. Maybe it's not a world-class novel for the ages, but it makes a great curiosity and a nice collectible.

📖📖

## THE FORTUNES OF CAPTAIN BLOOD
RAFAEL SABATINI
POPULAR LIBRARY, 1950
COVER BY RUDOLPH BELARSKI

Good old Rafael Sabatini, king of the swash-bucklers—the Spanish Main, cutlass-wielding pirates, gorgeous wenches in low-cut blouses, the wind in your sails and rum in your cup! This nice MTI edition features a fine Belarski cover.

📖📖

## GENTIAN HILL
ELIZABETH GOUDGE
POPULAR LIBRARY , CIRCA 1972
COVER BY ROBERT MCGINNIS

This is a distinctly upscale historical by a respected novelist. Goudge was able to portray historical characters with all the color and detail of costume and lifestyle beloved by myriad readers of her sweeping sagas.

📖

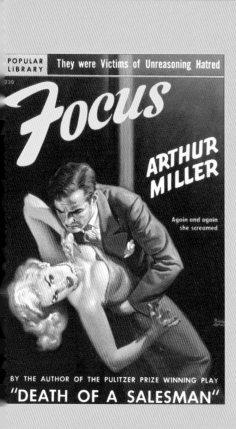

## THE DOLL'S TRUNK MURDER

HELEN REILLY
POPULAR LIBRARY, 1949
COVER BY RUDOLPH BELARSKI

Bondage, sexual titillation, a not-so-subtle hint of sadism—not at all the kind of thing that Helen Reilly (1891-1962) went in for with her well-characterized and ingeniously plotted police procedurals. Belarski's painting is a classic study both of what worked for the pulp-oriented paperback houses, and what drew such strong criticism from many quarters.

❚❚❚❚

## GENTLEMEN PREFER BLONDES

ANITA LOOS
POPULAR LIBRARY, 1950
COVER BY EARLE K. BERGEY

The famous novel by Anita Loos was brought to life onstage by actress Carol Channing as the temptress Lorelei Lee and on the screen by Marilyn Monroe—with Jane Russell as her sidekick, no less! Can you sing "Diamonds Are a Girl's Best Friend?" This book, highly collectible for Bergey's brilliant painting if for no other reason, is a masterpiece!

❚❚❚❚

## THE GREAT MAIL ROBBERY

CLARENCE BUDINGTON KELLAND
POPULAR LIBRARY, 1952
COVER BY RUDOLPH BELARSKI

This versatile and prolific author was most famous for creating New England shopkeeper Scattergood Baines, but Kelland (1881-1964) wrote historical romances and dozens of mystery novels, including this series about postal inspector Will Scarlett.

❚

## THE PRIVATE LIFE OF HELEN OF TROY

JOHN ERSKINE
POPULAR LIBRARY, 1948
COVER BY EARLE K. BERGEY OR RUDOLPH BELARSKI

Although some historians attribute the famous cover painting on this book to Belarski, a majority of paperback experts believe it was the work of Earle K. Bergey. In any case, this is probably one of the least read but most collected books in the history of paperback publishing.

❚❚❚❚

We could go on, but you get the point—at least, if you recognize those titles and by-lines. Popular Library didn't call itself a mystery specialty house, and in due time it would branch out with westerns, science fiction, sex-oriented books, and a full spectrum of topics. But initially, Pop published mysteries, mysteries, and more mysteries.

Even when Popular Library took a flier on a "celebrity novel", that was a mystery: *Mother Finds a Body* by Gypsy Rose Lee (Number 37). Allegedly ghosted by Craig Rice, this book remains a subject of debate.

Never pretentious and never very adventurous, Popular Library lived up to its name, pumping out hundreds and hundreds of books, always maintaining its base among mystery readers with additional lines of westerns, science fiction, historical novels, and such occasional oddities as crossword puzzle books, volumes of advice for readers who thought they could get rich betting on horse races, and "cute baby" books.

Late in Popular Library's history the company returned to its roots and ran a series of books based on pulp magazines. Two such collectible groups are the "Captain Future" space adventure novels, from the 1940s magazine of the same name, and the Jules de Grandin horror/detective books gleaned from the pages of *Weird Tales* magazine.

By this time Leo Margulies had returned to his roots and became publisher of a series of magazines including *Mike Shayne's Mystery Magazine*, *The Saint*, *Shell Scott Mystery Magazine*, and *Fantastic Universe*.

Popular Library finally disappeared in the usual tangle of corporate buy-outs and mergers. By the time Popular ceased to exist, it had published a great many good, readable books. Its packages were often colorful and attractive, highly prized by paperback collectors.

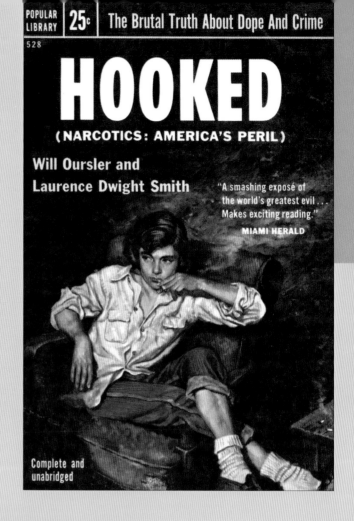

## HOOKED

WILL OURSLER AND LAURENCE DWIGHT SMITH
POPULAR LIBRARY, 1953
COVER BY RAFAEL DESOTO

A "scare" book aimed at susceptible teenagers and their
worried parents, the depraved young lady in DeSoto's
fine painting looks like anybody's little sister. The worst
thing likely to happen is a burned table top. The title is
still popular with collectors of drug books, JD covers,
or maybe borderline sleaze.

◗◗◗

## HOPALONG CASSIDY TAKES CARDS

CLARENCE E. MULFORD
POPULAR LIBRARY, 1948

According to Clarence Mulford's biographer, Francis
M. Nevins, Mulford was a career civil servant who
lived in Brooklyn and learned his western lore from
Owen Wister's *The Virginian* and other books. Finally
he created Hopalong Cassidy and never looked back!

◗

## I'LL GET MINE

THURSTON SCOTT
POPULAR LIBRARY, 1952
COVER PAINTING BY A. LESLIE ROSS (?)

What a blurb! "She loved men, money, and
marijuana." "Thurston Scott" was the joint
pseudonym of George Thurston Leite and
Jody Scott; this was apparently their only book.
Attribution of the fine cover painting is uncertain,
but it was probably the work of A. Leslie Ross,
a Popular Library and Thrilling pulp regular.

◗◗◗

## I DIVE FOR TREASURE

HARRY E. RIESEBERG
POPULAR LIBRARY, 1954
COVER BY JOHN FLOHERTY, JR.

There's no escaping that cliché: heroic diver fights
for life against murderous devilfish. It's as old as
Jules Verne, but in fact octopods are rather gentle
and extremely shy, far more likely to hide from
divers than to face them. Still, books about deep
sea diving always have an audience.

◗

## LADY CHATTERLEY'S DAUGHTER

EDITED BY LAWRENCE LARIAR
POPULAR LIBRARY, 1963
COVER BY CASEY JONES

Lawrence Lariar (1908-1981) was the author
of ten mystery novels. He also had a sense of
humor, was fond of cartoons, and compiled
this collection for Popular Library. The title
reflects the 1960s controversy surrounding
D. H. Lawrence's famous novel.

◗◗

## THE LAST PRINCESS
CHARLES O. LOCKE
POPULAR LIBRARY, 1954

Lost races and ancient empires have always been popular. Think Rider Haggard, Talbot Mundy, Edgar Rice Burroughs. Charles O. Locke's entry in the exotic romance sweepstakes did well enough to warrant a 1959 reissue by Popular, but his only other book (or at least his only other paperback) was a western.

## THE LEATHER PUSHERS
H. C. WITWER
POPULAR LIBRARY, 1950
COVER BY EARLE K. BERGEY

Witwer may indeed have been one of the world's great humorists, as the cover blurb asserts, but he seems to be totally forgotten today. This attempt at a hardboiled boxing novel was apparently his only book. It is collected by boxing specialists and Bergey fans who agree that the cover painting is certainly a knockout!

## THE MARX BROTHERS
KYLE CRICHTON
POPULAR LIBRARY, 1952
COVER BY EARLE K. BERGEY (?)

Fine semi-caricature portraits of the five famous brothers are the chief collecting point of this joint biography. Can you name them? Clockwise, starting with Groucho (with cigar): Chico, Gummo, Zeppo, Harpo.

## THE MORTAL STORM
PHYLLIS BOTTOME
POPULAR LIBRARY, 1946
COVER BY "IM-HO" (SOL IMMERMAN, H. L. HOFFMAN, ROBERT HOLLY)

Phyllis Forbes-Dennis (1884-1963) wrote several novels and a number of short stories; *The Mortal Storm* was her most successful. It dealt with the impact of Hitler's rise on an ordinary middle-class German family and was also a successful film.

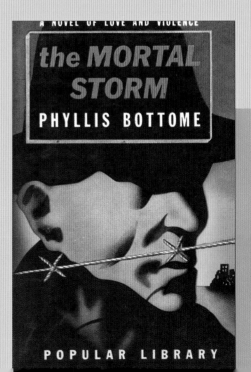

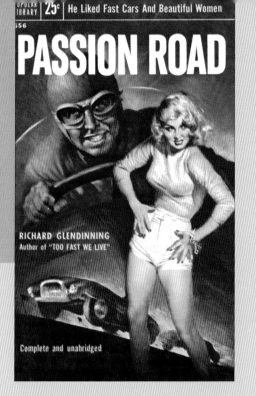

**PASSION ROAD**

POPULAR LIBRARY 25¢ · 56 · He Liked Fast Cars And Beautiful Women

RICHARD GLENDINNING
Author of "TOO FAST WE LIVE"

Complete and unabridged

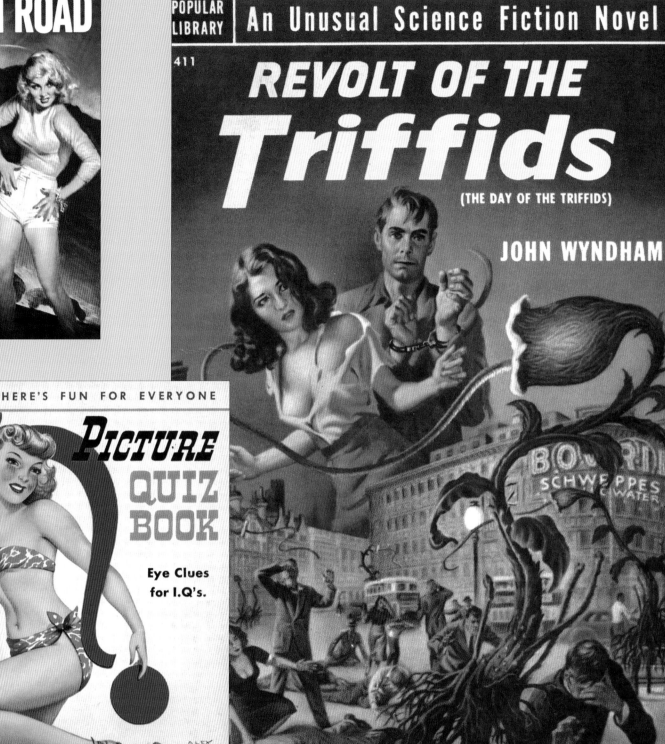

POPULAR LIBRARY · 411 · An Unusual Science Fiction Novel

**REVOLT OF THE Triffids**

(THE DAY OF THE TRIFFIDS)

JOHN WYNDHAM

SCHWEPPES WATER

COMPLETE AND UNABRIDGED

POPULAR LIBRARY · 223 · HERE'S FUN FOR EVERYONE

**PICTURE QUIZ BOOK**

Eye Clues for I.Q.'s.

ALEX SCHOMBURG

*Featuring –*
an entertaining roundup of quiz games
illustrated by eye-pleasing photos!

---

### PASSION ROAD
RICHARD GLENDINNING
POPULAR LIBRARY, 1955

Richard Glendenning was a semi-regular producer of PBOs for Popular Library and Fawcett Gold Medal. Not many collectors specialize in race car novels, but you can never tell—and the uncredited cover is quite striking.

### PICTURE QUIZ BOOK
JOHN PAUL ADAMS
POPULAR LIBRARY, 1950
COVER BY ALEX SCHOMBURG

It's hard to find quiz and puzzle books in good condition—this one is a beauty; extremely rare and very valuable. Alex Schomburg was a talented calligrapher and painter of pulp magazine covers; he also worked for comic books. The innocent pin-up on this book is unusually sunny for Schomburg.

### REVOLT OF THE TRIFFIDS
JOHN WYNDHAM
POPULAR LIBRARY, 1952
COVER BY EARLE K. BERGEY

John Wyndham Parkes Lucas Beynon Harris (1903-1969) wrote science fiction novels and short stories for almost fifty years. His most successful novels were *Day of the Triffids* (*Revolt of the Triffids* in this edition) and *The Midwich Cuckoos*. The striking cover was one of the last works of longtime pulp science fiction painter Bergey, who died in 1952.

## THE SECRET OF FATHER BROWN AND OTHER STORIES
GILBERT K. CHESTERTON
POPULAR LIBRARY, 1948
COVER BY "IM-HO" (?)

London-born G. K. Chesterton (1874-1936) was an astonishingly prolific novelist, poet, illustrator, editor, and radio personality. His finest novel, in the opinion of some critics, was *The Man Who Was Thursday*, but his most enduring works are the Father Brown stories, about a gentle priest who seems to solve crimes by divine inspiration and to bring the culprits to justice by moral suasion. This is an attractive edition of a collectible book.

## SAINT OVERBOARD
LESLIE CHARTERIS
POPULAR BOOKS, 1943
COVER BY H. LAWRENCE HOFFMAN

This is the very first "Pop" - originally called Popular Books before the name Popular Library was adopted. Hoffman's "porthole" cover is reminiscent of the Penguin/Signet cut-out covers. It's highly collectible; a must for "Pop" enthusiasts. Lotsa luck!

## SHE'LL BE DEAD BY MORNING
DANA CHAMBERS
POPULAR LIBRARY, 1950
COVER BY RUDOLPH BELARSKI (?)

Writing as Dana Chambers, Albert Leffingwell (1895-1966) created several popular detectives, the best known of them being Jim Steele, featured in this novel. Chambers seems to be totally forgotten today—who knows when he'll be rediscovered.

POPULAR LIBRARY
STORIES OF MYSTERY AND SUSPENSE

# SIX TIMES DEATH
## WILLIAM IRISH

"WELL WORTHY OF THE ATTENTION OF ALL LOVE[RS]
[O]F GOOD SHORT STORIES."
*NEW YORK TIM[ES]*

POPULAR LIBRARY
217
SHE WAS SEDUCTIVE AND DANGEROUS

# TALES OF Chinatown
## SAX ROHMER

Ten stories of macabre mystery by the creator of the famous Dr. Fu Manchu

POPULAR LIBRARY
She Broke Every Rule To Get Her Man

# Soldiers' Daughters Never Cry
## AUDREY ERSKINE LINDOP

Special abridged edition

POPULAR LIBRARY  25¢  A Lusty Saga Of A Half-Breed Romeo
548

# STAY AWAY, JOE
## Dan Cushman
A Book-of-the-Month Club Selection

Complete and unabridged

---

## SIX TIMES DEATH
WILLIAM IRISH
POPULAR LIBRARY, 1948
COVER BY FIEDLER (?)

Whether writing as Cornell Woolrich, George Hopley, or William Irish, this brilliant, troubled man is always worth reading. This collection of his short stories is truly splendid.

## SOLDIERS' DAUGHTERS NEVER CRY
AUDREY ERSKINE LINDOP
POPULAR LIBRARY, 1951
COVER BY RUDOLPH BELARSKI

Credited with three novels, all published in the 1950s, Audrey Erskine Lindop has become something of a mystery woman. Belarski provides a lovely, appealing portrait of the model on this cover, as well as two nude sketches.

## TALES OF CHINATOWN
SAX ROHMER
POPULAR LIBRARY, 1950
COVER BY RUDOLPH BELARSKI

Rohmer's insidious Dr. Fu Manchu had his ups and downs in popularity, but he was never far from the reading public's mind. Here's a collection of Rohmer's shorter works, all of them wonderfully trashy and absorbing, packaged in a splendid cover painting. Oh, that green, claw-tipped hand! This is one of Belarski's most pulpishly grand.

## STAY AWAY, JOE
DAN CUSHMAN
POPULAR LIBRARY, 1953
COVER BY RAFAEL DESOTO

Dan Cushman favored exotic settings for his novels, although this one takes place closer to home. The jug of moonshine, the rustic cabin, the lusty siren-slut and the suggestion of interracial romance are all suggestive of the Erskine Caldwell "trash" school of writing, but in fact, this is a fine and sensitive novel about life on an Indian reservation.

### THE TOUGH ONES
EDITED BY WHIT AND HALLIE BURNETT
POPULAR LIBRARY, 1959

This looks like a minor JD anthology and is not much sought after, but the Norman Mailer story makes the book a potential sleeper.

### TO WAKE THE DEAD
JOHN DICKSON CARR
POPULAR LIBRARY, 1943
COVER BY H. LAWRENCE HOFFMAN

John Dickson Carr's popular detective Gideon Fell was allegedly based on his friend G. K. Chesterton. Bulky and bibulous, Fell was featured in no fewer than twenty-three books by the industrious and immensely popular Carr (1906-1977). A slim, dapper man, Carr favored detectives who were often bulky and seldom fastidious.

### VALCOUR MEETS MURDER
RUFUS KING
POPULAR LIBRARY, 1944
COVER BY H. LAWRENCE HOFFMAN

Rufus King (1893-1966) wrote dozens of novels (most of them mysteries but a few dog stories) in addition to several plays. His series detective, Inspector Valcour, was quite popular, and King's books are informed with intelligence, ingenuity, humor, and human warmth. The "Pop" logo resembling the famous Crime Club gunman, and slogan *mysteries of proven merit* add to the appeal of this book.

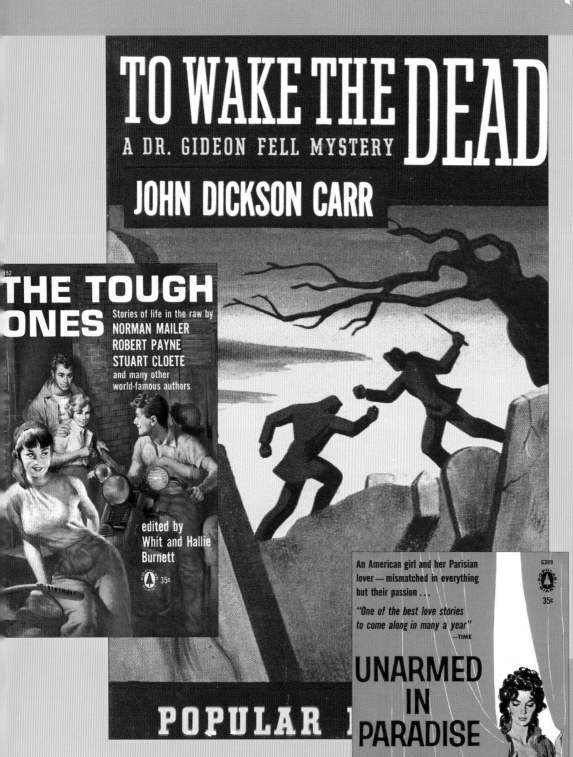

### UNARMED IN PARADISE
ELLEN MARSH
POPULAR GIANT, 1960
COVER BY MITCHELL HOOKS

*Time* magazine praised this novel —apparently Ellen Marsh's only one—but both the book and the author have slipped into obscurity. It is noteworthy for the excellent Mitchell Hooks painting (and strategically placed pajamas).

**POPULAR LIBRARY** | **25c** | A Girl On The Town — Looking For Trouble

570

# THE VIOLENT WEDDING

**Robert Lowry**
Author of
"THE WOLF THAT FED US"

"A fast-moving,
brutally frank novel."
Hollywood CITIZEN NEWS

Complete and Unabridged

---

**POPULAR LIBRARY** | **25c** | She Played A Man's Game With A Woman's Weapons

660

# YOU ASKED FOR IT
(CASINO ROYALE)

**IAN FLEMING**

"Intensely Exciting"
HARPER'S MAGAZINE

---

# THE WHEEL SPINS
## ETHEL LINA WHITE

Alfred Hitchcock's famous
movie thriller THE
LADY VANISHES
was based on
this novel.

te and unabridged

MYSTERIES OF
PROVEN MERIT

**POPULAR LIBRARY**

---

### THE VIOLENT WEDDING

ROBERT LOWRY
POPULAR LIBRARY, 1954

Robert Lowry was a regular "Pop" author for
a number of years but seems to have slipped
off the radar screen in recent decades. His
books were of the tough, gritty, urban-realism
school with overtones of dangerous interracial
relationships.

### THE WHEEL SPINS

ETHEL LINA WHITE
POPULAR LIBRARY, 1944
COVER BY H. LAWRENCE HOFFMAN

Despite a relatively late start as a novelist, Ethel
Lina White (1887-1944) became one of the
Grande Dames of the mystery story. Her first
book appeared in 1931, her last in the year of
her death. *The Wheel Spins* was filmed by Alfred
Hitchcock as *The Lady Vanishes* (1938) and again
by Hammer Films (1979). The 1944 paperback
was an MTI, and another MTI was issued in
1979, retitled as *The Lady Vanishes*.

### YOU ASKED FOR IT

IAN FLEMING
POPULAR LIBRARY, 1955

This book is a retitling of Ian Fleming's *Casino
Royale*, avidly sought by James Bond collectors
who keep hoping (usually in vain) that they'll
stumble across a copy in a thrift store or paperback exchange and pick it up for a buck or so.

¶ ¶ ¶ ¶ ¶

Unlike the relatively humble beginnings of Avon and Popular Library, Dell Books started from a position of strength—and a sizable financial war chest. Created by George T. Delacorte in 1921, the Dell Publishing Company was a successful publisher of magazines and comic books. The Dell magazine line offered a wide range of publications including sports magazines, movie "fan" magazines, *Modern Romance*, *Inside Detective*, and *Danger Trail*. Dell also held the comic book license for Disney characters and over a period of years published a variety of hugely successful comics featuring Donald and Daisy, Mickey and Minnie, Bucky Bug, and assorted other funny animals.

Dell was closely affiliated with the Western Publishing and Lithographing Company in Wisconsin. Western had made an earlier attempt at publishing paperbacks as early as 1939—the so-called "L.A. Bantams." This was an early line that sold for a dime, mostly from vending machines as if they were candy bars. There were only twenty-eight "L.A. Bantams," and they included a Tarzan novel, a Shadow novel, and mysteries by Agatha Christie, Mignon G. Eberhart, Ellery Queen, and Rex Stout. These books, in fact any L.A. Bantams, are considered the Holy Grail of paperback collectors.

The "L.A. Bantams" were not connected in any way to the better-known Bantam Books, although by an irony of the publishing world, a peculiar, indirect relationship would eventually occur.

To return to the origins of Dell Books, important editors working for Delacorte included Frank Taylor and Knox Burger. In the books themselves Delacorte was listed as president of the company, while a brilliant, hard-driving executive named Helen Meyer (no relation to Peter Mayer or Joseph Meyers) was named vice-president. She would eventually become president of Dell, a remarkable achievement in what was considered a male-dominated field.

Like Popular Library, Dell Books were initiated with a line consisting entirely of mysteries. The first Dell Book was a "bibliomystery", *Murder in the Library* by Philip Ketchum. The cover painting by William Strohmer was semi-abstract: a huge book featuring the title and byline, a bullet hole in the cover, parts of a corpse emerging from between the pages, and a puddle of blood. Prominent on the cover is a stylized keyhole with an eye peering through it. The keyhole became a familiar trademark on early Dell Books—with an eye for mysteries (or any mapback), a steamship for adventure novels, a steer's skull for westerns, a heart for romances, and a quill pen for historicals.

With the fifth Dell book, *Four Frightened Women* by George Harmon Coxe, Delacorte and Meyer initiated another feature that gave the books character in their own day and that have become beloved of collectors. This was the addition of a map to the back of the book in lieu of a sales-oriented blurb.

The map might show anything from a sector of the Pacific Ocean (*Queen of the Flat-Tops* by Stanley Johnston), a diagram of an apartment building (*Death in Five Boxes* by John Dickson Carr writing as Carter Dixon), the surface of the moon (*First Men in the Moon* by H. G. Wells), Hopalong Cassidy's ranch (*Bar-20 Days* by Clarence E. Mulford), the Caribbean Sea (*Men Under the Sea* by Frank Meier), or the city of San Francisco (*Dead Yellow Women* by Dashiell Hammett).

The mapbacks were popular in their day and it's hard to understand why Dell dropped them. Presumably it was felt that the space was more profitably used as a billboard for a sales pitch

### DEATH IN THE LIBRARY
PHILIP KETCHUM
DELL BOOKS, 1943
COVER BY WILLIAM STROHMER

Philip Ketchum was the pseudonym of Miriam Leslie (1902-1969), who wrote half a dozen novels as Ketchum and just one under her own name. *Death in the Library* was one of the few volumes issued by the ill-fated Red Arrow Books in 1939; it got another chance as the very first Dell Book and is of course a keystone for any Dell collector.

### FEAR AND TREMBLING
EDITED BY ALFRED HITCHCOCK
DELL BOOKS, 1948
COVER BY GERALD GREGG

Hitchcock actually farmed out the work of compiling "his" anthologies, most often to Robert Arthur (Feder) although this book was edited by Don Ward. In any case, it was Hitch's name that sold these always very readable but seldom outstanding books. Note the keyhole and mapback: both features add to the collectibility of this book.

### A BUNDLE FOR THE CORONER
BRETT HALLIDAY
DELL MYSTERY NOVELS, 1955
COVER BY ROBERT STANLEY

Is it a magazine or is it a digest-size book? The presence of stories by William Campbell Gault and Bruno Fischer suggests the former, but it's close enough for inclusion in some paperback book collections. Take your pick!

## ALDER GULCH
**ERNEST HAYCOX**
**DELL BOOKS, 1950**
**COVER BY BOB MYERS**

Like so many fictioneers, Ernest Haycox
(1899-1950) worked first as a journalist and
then graduated to the pulps. He continued on,
writing for the slicks as well (*Saturday Evening
Post, Colliers, Ladies Home Journal*) as well as
selling several of his stories to Hollywood.

## THE BIG FIST
**CLYDE B. RAGSDALE**
**DELL BOOKS, 1953**
**COVER BY CARL BOBERTZ**

This obscure novel by the obscure Clyde B.
Ragsdale (apparently his only book) features
a pretty nasty painting. A previous edition
had been published by Harlequin in 1952
and is more desirable than the Dell.

## APRIL EVIL
**JOHN D. MACDONALD**
**DELL FIRST EDITION, 1956**
**COVER BY ROBERT MAGUIRE**

MacDonald's non-Gold Medal and non-Travis
Magee PBOs are generally tougher to find than
the Fawcetts and always worth the trouble. The
fine Maguire cover adds to the desirability of
*April Evil.*

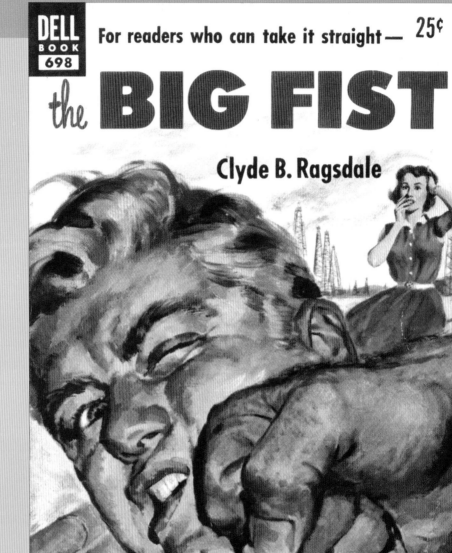

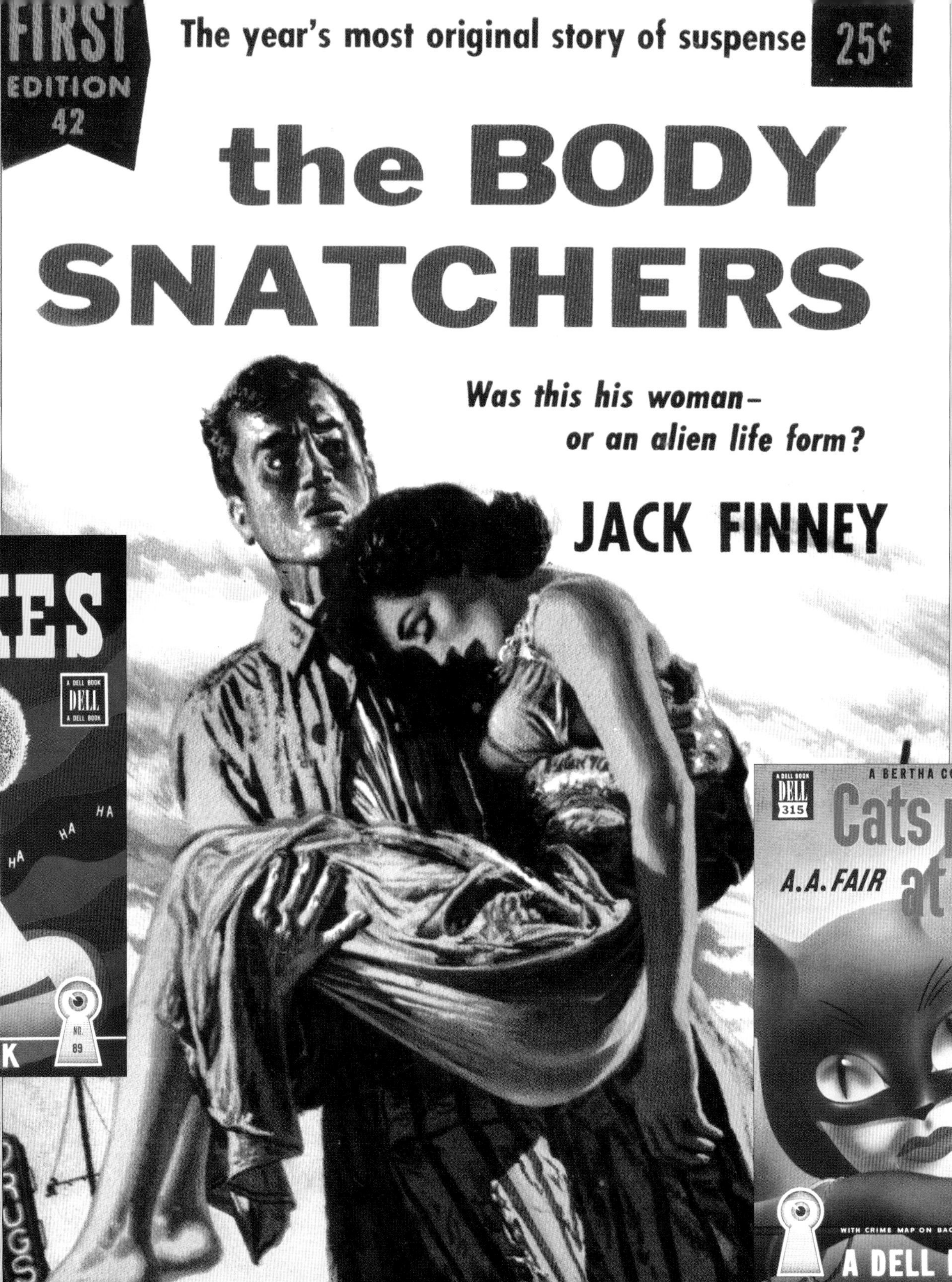

# the BODY SNATCHERS

Was this his woman—
or an alien life form?

## JACK FINNEY

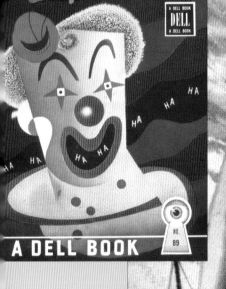

DELL BOOK OF JOKES

DELL

A DELL BOOK

NO. 89

A DELL BOOK

DELL
315

A BERTHA COOL MYSTERY

Cats prowl
at night

A.A. FAIR

WITH CRIME MAP ON BACK COVER

A DELL MYSTERY

NOT A REPRINT

---

**DELL BOOK OF JOKES**
EDITED BY CAVANAGH AND WEIR
DELL BOOKS, 1945
COVER BY GERALD GREGG

Along with puzzle and game books, this is exactly the kind of paperback that readers left on trains or buses or simply browsed through and then tossed in the garbage, which makes finding them all the more difficult for collectors. The striking cover on this PBO makes it all the more desirable.

♟ ♟ ♟ ♟

**THE BODY SNATCHERS**
JACK FINNEY
DELL BOOKS, 1955
COVER BY JACK MCDERMOTT

This PBO became a classic film as *Invasion of the Body Snatchers* (1956) and was remade at least twice. It is not to be confused with the Karloff-Lugosi film, *The Body Snatchers*, which is a different story altogether.

♟ ♟ ♟

**CATS PROWL AT NIGHT**
A. A. FAIR
DELL BOOKS, 1945
COVER BY GERALD GREGG

Of course A. A. Fair was Erle Stanley Gardner, in this mystery writing about his portly female shamus, Bertha Cool. A book by a collected author, a truly spectacular cover painting, and a Dell mapback at that make this title a collector's dream.

♟ ♟ ♟

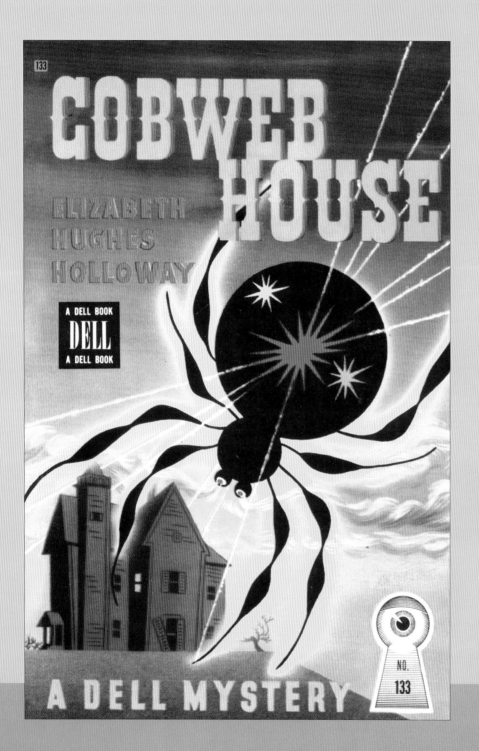

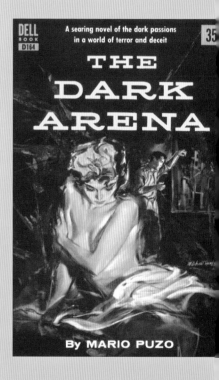

### COBWEB HOUSE
ELIZABETH HUGHES HOLLOWAY
DELL BOOKS, 1946
COVER BY GERALD GREGG

If you have never heard of the
author or the book, join the party!
But the brilliant cover would be
a valuable addition to anyone's
collection.

### CAVE GIRL
EDGAR RICE BURROUGHS
DELL BOOKS, 1949
COVER BY JOHN DES VIGNES

That's Nadara the cave girl herself
dancing in John Des Vignes' painting. Burroughs is highly collected,
and his minor books, like this
one, are all the more difficult
to come by.

### THE DARK ARENA
MARIO PUZO
DELL BOOKS, 1956
COVER BY MITCHELL HOOKS

That's the same Mario Puzo, a
good, solid, journeyman writer,
who finally hit it big with *The
Godfather*. This earlier book is
certainly worthwhile.

This Donald Lam-Bertha Cool mystery by Erle Stanley Gardner became a favorite collectible—or rather, two. The original painting and cover blurb were considered too risqué so Dell had Stanley zip up the skirt and button the blouse and chose a different line to quote. They are most collectible as a pair.

❡❡❡

25¢
DELL BOOK 1542

"You've got to get out of here! Sergeant Sellers is on his way up."

A. A. FAIR
FOOLS DIE on FRIDAY

A Donald Lam and Bertha Cool Mystery

COMPLETE AND UNABRIDGED

5¢
DELL BOOK 42

"Get your clothes on — just enough to cover yourself, and get out of here."

A. A. FAIR
FOOLS DIE on FRIDAY

A Donald Lam and Bertha Cool Mystery

AND UNABRIDGED

## GREENMASK
JEFFERSON FARJEON
DELL BOOKS, 1946
COVER BY GERALD GREGG

Jefferson Farjeon (1883-1955) was a typical
early Dell choice—an English old-timer of
impeccable credentials. Almost unreadable
today, *Greenmask* is collectible as a Dell mapback
with a fine, stylized cover painting by Gregg.

## THE HEADLESS LADY
CLAYTON RAWSON
DELL BOOKS, 1947

In addition to writing mysteries of his own,
Clayton Rawson (1906-1971) was a busy book
and magazine editor and a professional magi-
cian, performing as the Great Merlini. He wrote
his alter ego into many of his stories, including
this collectible mapback.

## THE HALF-CASTE
DAN CUSHMAN
DELL, 1960
COVER BY ROBERT MCGINNIS

This PBO is one of Cushman's trademark
"exotics," always readable but actually more
sought-after for the fine McGinnis painting.

124

rather than the map, but they are avidly collected and fondly remembered. In an interview in the year 2000, Art Spiegelman, Pulitzer Prize winner and creator of the powerful *Maus* books, commented on his encounter with the mapbacks as a young man:

"I found myself collecting old paperbacks in the early 1970s when they weren't so 'commodified.' I felt like I was rescuing trash. And while I found myself, ultimately, reading some of them, I was primarily drawn to the graphic qualities of the covers, and most particularly to those Dell mapback books…cause they had a very strong and efficient sense of graphic design communicating in a very small surface area. I found them influencing my approach to jacket design, when I found myself making forays into that field. Specifically, I designed a series of book jackets for the German editions of Boris Vian's novels.

"They're not rendered in the same style, but the idea of finding a small, powerful image to give it a vaguely pulp look did grow from my affection for those Dell mapbacks. Most specifically, when I did my *Maus* books, it's no accident that there are maps on the back."

If anything, Dell Books were user-friendly. Many of them contained a page-long summary of "Persons this Mystery is about", offering descriptions such as this:

"*Evelyn Zarinka*, a pretty, smartly dressed young lady whose brown hair is carefully coifed and whose white, even teeth are complemented by full, red lips and a small, strong chin.

"*Captain Duncan MacLain*, erect and handsome, is a truly amazing gentleman. Despite the fact that he is totally and hopelessly blind, he is a most accurate and self-confident detective. With his dog Schnucke and his partner Spud Savage, he is a threat to crime in all quarters."

There was also a page devoted to "Things this Mystery is about."

A jigsaw PUZZLE…
Two white MICE in a birdcage…
A Mills HAND GRENADE…
A few MARIHUANA cigarettes…
A slim, shiny DAGGER…
A disused TUNNEL…
A Seeing Eye DOG…

In a sense, the Dell Books resembled magazines. They didn't offer just the main text in an attractive package. There were features galore that identified them not merely as books but as *Dell Books*.

Knox Burger, a Dell editor, supervised the development of the Dell First Editions, a series of PBOs (paperback originals) whose popularity added luster to the Dell Books line, important exposure to the authors, and great books to the readers. Eventually Burger would leave Dell for Fawcett, where he was instrumental in developing the hugely successful (and hugely important) Gold Medal originals.

The Dell First editions were not the first PBOs, of course, but they were the first consistent series of originals in the modern era. The series began with *Down* by Walt Grove (1953), followed by Fredic Brown's *Madball*. Brown was a prolific writer of mysteries and science fiction and remains a highly collected author. Another important Dell First Edition was *Area of Suspicion* by John D. MacDonald (1954). MacDonald came to be closely associated with Fawcett Gold Medal, but in fact he placed almost a dozen PBOs with Dell, including the anthology *The Lethal Sex* (1959). MacDonald seemed to inspire cover artists to outdo themselves, and several of his Dell First Edition covers —especially those by Robert McGinnis—are miniature gems. MacDonald's books from other publishers than Fawcett are necessary to MacDonald collectors and often among the most difficult to obtain.

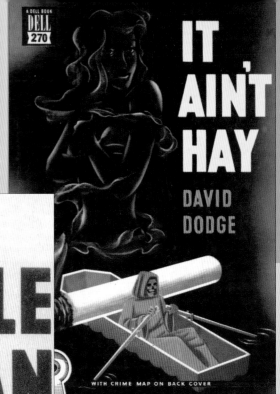

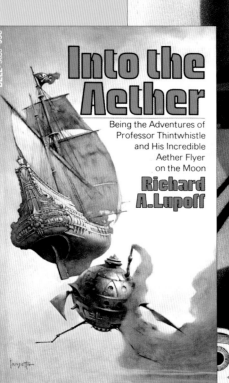

### INTO THE AETHER
RICHARD A. LUPOFF
DELL BOOKS, 1974
COVER BY FRANK FRAZETTA

This PBO is collectible primarily for the sake of its spectacular cover painting. Frazetta was known chiefly for his muscular male and well-endowed female semi-nudes, but he juxtaposes a Spanish galleon with a wacky "spaceship" worthy of the late Rube Goldberg.

### THE INVISIBLE MAN
H. G. WELLS
DELL BOOKS, 1949
COVER BY GERALD GREGG

Fifty years after Wells wrote his great science fiction novels, they were still readable—and after another fifty years they are *still* readable. This is Gregg at his wittiest and a mapback to boot.

### IT AIN'T HAY
DAVID DODGE
DELL BOOKS, 1949
COVER BY GERALD GREGG

Californian David Dodge was an accountant, a mystery writer, and the author of travel books. His most famous novel was *To Catch a Thief* (yes, think Grace Kelly and Cary Grant). An early drug book (the title refers to cannabis) and dearly sought by collectors, the price of a copy of this book ain't hay either!

### LAURA
VERA CASPARY
DELL BOOKS, 1961
COVER BY FORTÉ

Although Vera Caspary (1904-1987) had a long and productive career as novelist and playwright, she never surpassed her 1943 novel, *Laura*, which became a brilliant film with Gene Tierney in the title role.

## I WAS A NAZI FLIER
**GOTTFRIED LESKE**
**DELL, 1943**
**COVER BY GERALD GREGG**

This is "A Dell War Book" indeed. The skull, swastika, and Nazi regalia make this book collectible.

## MADBALL
**FREDRIC BROWN**
**DELL FIRST EDITIONS, 1953**
**COVER BY GRIFFITH FOXLEY**

This Fredric Brown PBO is highly sought, both because Brown is himself a collected author and because the carnival-setting cover painting is still another collecting specialty.

## THE LONG LOUD SILENCE
**WILSON TUCKER**
**DELL BOOKS, 1954**
**COVER BY RICHARD POWERS**

Wilson Tucker and his lifelong friend Robert Bloch were Midwestern science fiction fans in the 1930s, then advanced to careers as both mystery-suspense and science fiction writers. Powers' cover is less abstract than most of his work.

## MESSALINA
**JACK OLECK**
**DELL BOOKS, 1960**
**COVER BY JAMES BAMA**

This reissue of a 1960 Dell title is most notable for its lush, colorful cover painting. And then there are those who go in for whips.

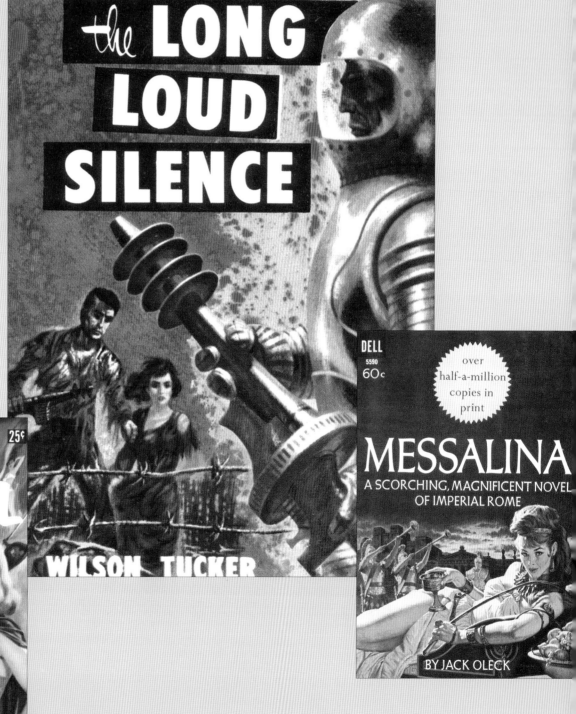

127

## NOTHING MORE THAN MURDER

JIM THOMPSON
DELL, 1953
COVER BY GEORGE GEYGAN

Most of the books of Jim Thompson (1906-1977) were PBOs, and are very heavily collected. *Nothing More than Murder* was a 1949 hardcover, but this first paperback edition is also an important collectible.

📖📖📖

## THE PHANTOM OF THE OPERA

GASTON LEROUX
DELL BOOKS, 1943
COVER BY GERALD GREGG

Leroux's melodrama was already a relic by the time this Dell edition appeared, but Gregg's manic depiction of the phantom is irresistible.

📖📖📖

## THE RAT BEGAN TO GNAW THE ROPE

C. W. GRAFTON
DELL BOOKS, 1947
COVER BY GERALD GREGG

Remarkably modern looking for 1947, this mapback was the first of Cornelius William Grafton's three mystery novels. His daughter, Sue Grafton, went on to great fame in the same field.

📖📖

## QUEEN OF THE FLAT-TOPS

STANLEY JOHNSTON
DELL BOOKS, 1944
COVER BY GEORGE A. FREDERICSON

One of Dell's war books, *Queen of the Flattops* included a photo section.

📖📖

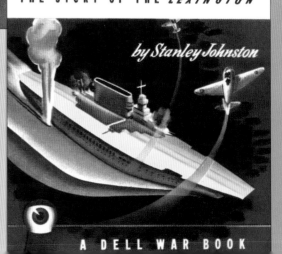

# Scarecrow

EATON K. GOLDTHWAITE

**A DELL MYSTERY**

WITH CRIME MAP ON BACK COVER

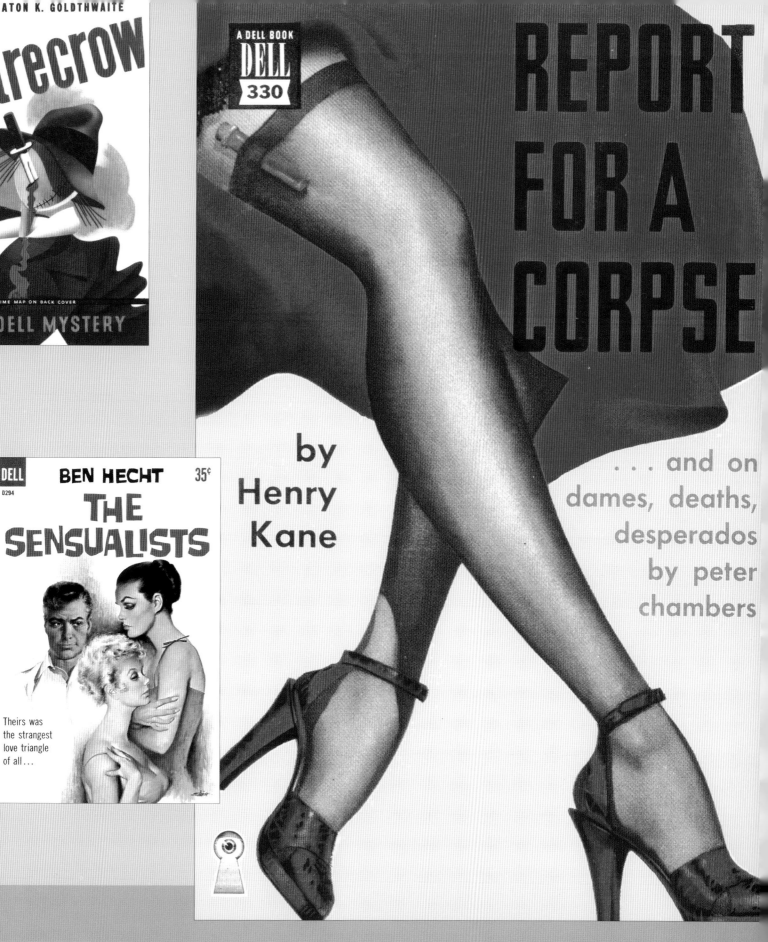

A DELL BOOK

**DELL**
**330**

# REPORT FOR A CORPSE

by
Henry
Kane

. . . and on
dames, deaths,
desperados
by peter
chambers

BEN HECHT 35¢

**DELL**
D294

# THE SENSUALISTS

Theirs was
the strangest
love triangle
of all . . .

## SCARECROW
EATON K. GOLDTHWAITE
DELL BOOKS, 1947
COVER BY GERALD GREGG

Another popular author of his day
who has been largely forgotten,
Goldthwaite featured his series
detective, Lt. Joe Dickerson, in
this mapback.

## THE SENSUALISTS
BEN HECHT
DELL BOOKS, 1959
COVER BY FREEMAN ELIOTT

Journalist, playwright, novelist
and general literary gadfly, Hecht
was famous (or infamous) in his
own day and largely forgotten
today. Eliott's cover is outstanding.

## REPORT FOR A CORPSE
HENRY KANE
DELL BOOKS, 1949

Spectacular leg art with drug-
book overtones make this volume
of Kane's stories collectible. The
Peter Chambers mentioned on
the cover is Kane's PI.

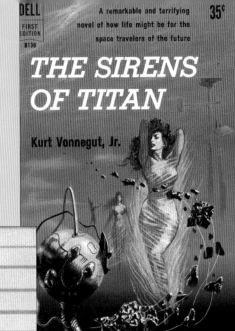

DELL
FIRST
EDITION
B138

35¢

# THE SIRENS OF TITAN

Kurt Vonnegut, Jr.

A DELL BOOK

DELL
236

FAITH BALDWIN

*Skyscraper*

A DELL ROMANCE

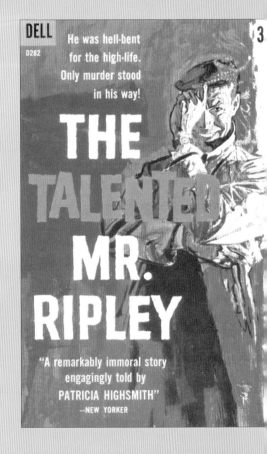

DELL
D282

3

He was hell-bent
for the high-life.
Only murder stood
in his way!

# THE TALENTED MR. RIPLEY

"A remarkably immoral story
engagingly told by
PATRICIA HIGHSMITH"
—NEW YORKER

### SKYSCRAPER
FAITH BALDWIN
DELL, 1948
COVER BY EARL SHERWAN

Romance writer Faith Baldwin jerked many a tear
in the 1940s and 1950s. *Skyscraper* is notable for its
fine Art Deco design.

### THE SIRENS OF TITAN
KURT VONNEGUT, JR.
DELL FIRST EDITION, 1959
COVER BY RICHARD POWERS

A grand prize for Vonnegut fans, this PBO didn't
draw the attention that it deserved—at first.
Collectors have been kicking themselves ever
since and paying through the nose for copies.

### THE TALENTED MR. RIPLEY
PATRICIA HIGHSMITH
DELL, 1959
COVER BY WILLIAM TEODECKI

The talented Ms. Highsmith had a long and distinguished career as a writer of psychologically subtle
and complex fiction, typified by *Strangers on a Train*
as well as her Ripley books. The sexual ambigui-
ties of many of her novels were given full vent in
at least one pseudonymous book, *The Price of Salt*.

### TARGET: MIKE SHAYNE
**BRETT HALLIDAY**
**DELL BOOKS, 1960**
**COVER BY ROBERT MCGINNIS**

### DICK TRACY AND THE WOO WOO SISTERS
**CHESTER GOULD**
**DELL BOOKS, 1947**
**COVER BY CHESTER GOULD**

### THE GLASS MASK
**LENORE GLEN OFFORD**
**DELL BOOKS, 1947**
**COVER BY GERALD GREGG**

There are two reasons to scout up a copy of this book: the story— Halliday could always tell a good hardboiled P.I. yarn with just a hint of tongue-in-cheek, and the lovely painting by Robert McGinnis, the most collected of paperback cover artists.

This PBO, along with its companion volume (*Blondie and Dagwood in Footlight Folly*, by Chic Young) were early examples of the novelization of cartoon characters. A spectacular book, it is almost never seen.

An early member of the "malice domestic" school (in fact, one of its founders) Lenore Glen Offord specialized in the lives of women, surrounded by the minutiae of domesticity and invaded by menace. This book is an especially attractive early Dell and a mapback.

Similarly, Jim Thompson's Dell First, *The Nothing Man* (1954), is sought after, although Thompson is generally associated with Lion Books, one of the "major minor" publishers in paperback history.

Other important Dell First Editions include Jack Finney's *The Body Snatchers* (1955) and *The House of Numbers* (1957); *This is Little Lulu* (1956), a compilation of the popular cartoons by "Marge" (Margery Henderson Buell), 1956; *Dangerous Dames*, an anthology of stories allegedly selected by the fictitious Mike Shayne; and *The King and Four Queens*, a movie tie-in (MTI) by Theodore Sturgeon. While most often regarded as a science fiction writer (and heavily collected by science fiction fans), Sturgeon also had a strong interest in Westerns, and this unusual MTI is highly prized.

Perhaps the most important of all Dell First Editions was *The Sirens of Titan* by Kurt Vonnegut (1959, cover by Richard Powers). Vonnegut's first novel, *Player Piano*, had been published in hardcover in 1952 and retitled *Utopia 14* by Bantam Books for its 1954 paperback. *Sirens* was a PBO and is still another treasure for collectors.

For many years PBOs were held in low esteem, seldom reviewed and stigmatized as "a second-rate form of publication, perfect for second-rate books by second-rate authors." Yet many distinctly first-rate authors, of whom Vonnegut and MacDonald were only two, were willing to publish in this form. Why?

The answer lies in traditional publishing contracts. Dating to the 1930s, before the era of modern paperback publishing, these contracts normally included provisions for reissues as "cheap editions" at reduced royalty rates and royalty sharing on subsidiary rights such as book club sales. Once paperback houses entered the picture, hardcover publishers treated paperback reprints as cheap editions or subsidiary sales and simply cut themselves in for half the money received.

Paperback royalties were paid at a lower rate than hardcover royalties, typically four to six percent of cover price versus ten percent or more. And of course paperback cover prices were drastically lower than hardcovers. In an era when paperbacks sold for 25¢ or 35¢, hardcover editions of the same books might sell for $2.00 to $3.00, with "cheap editions" selling for $1.00.

Let's do the math. A six percent royalty on a 25¢ paperback is just 1.5¢. A ten percent royalty on a $2 book was 20¢. Yet the print runs of paperbacks could be huge; a paperback bestseller could move several *million* copies. Even a very modest paperback, in an era when competition was limited and shelf life almost indefinite, would sell between 75,000 and 100,000 copies.

At 1.5¢ per copy, 100,000 sales would produce royalties of $1,500.00. This is small potatoes by present-day standards, of course, but half a century ago that was pretty good money. You could buy a low-end Ford or Chevrolet fresh off the dealer's floor for that amount. As cover prices rose, and as an author would (he or she hoped) move into higher sales ranges, the money improved dramatically. At 35¢ instead of 25¢, at a sales level of 500,000, and at a royalty rate of six percent, an author would earn $10,500.00. You could buy a very nice house in a good neighborhood for that sum half a century ago.

# TUGBOAT ANNIE

*Norman Reilly Raine*

WITH MAP ON BACK COVER

A DELL BOOK

## WHAT A BODY
ALAN GREEN
DELL BOOKS, 1947
COVER BY GILBERT DARLING

Possibly the most famous *back* cover in publishing history on this PBO by a husband-and-wife writing team. It is so Politically Incorrect it'll take your breath away.

## VANISH IN AN INSTANT
MARGARET MILLAR
DELL BOOKS, 1953
COVER BY GRIFFITH FOXLEY

Margaret Millar was one of the most sophisticated of mystery novelists. The fine cover painting by Griffith Foxley adds to the interest of this book.

## WAKE FOR A LADY
H. W. RODEN
DELL BOOKS, 1949
COVER BY WILLIAM GEORGE JACOBSON

Henry Wisdom Roden (1895-1963) was nothing if not consistent. A career executive in the food industry, he wrote four mystery novels, each one featuring detective Sid Ames, each one published in hardcover by Morrow, and each one issued in paperback by Dell.

Why is it more interesting to spend an evening with this book than with a beautiful woman?

### A DELL BOOK
### A COMPARISON TEST CHART
BOOK ➡      WOMAN ➡

| BOOK | | | WOMAN |
|---|---|---|---|
| 49% | | TEXTURE | 100% |
| 100% | | AVAILABILITY | 2-100% (depending on competition) |
| 60,000 | | NUMBER OF WORDS | 11 |
| 97% | | LAUGHTER PRODUCTION | 3% average |
| 0 | | MISERABILITY (capacity to make you feel terrible) | 73% |
| 80% | | INSOMNIABILITY (ability to keep you up all night, one way or another) | 79% |
| 100% | | OVERCOATABILITY (ease of placing in overcoat pocket) | 11% |
| 25¢ | | COST | $45 for dinner (wine and cabs not included) |

DELL BOOK 730

A Superlative Mystery
(See back cover)

25¢

# VANISH in an INSTANT

## MARGARET MILLAR

A DELL BOOK DELL 345

## Wake FOR A Lady

H.W. Roden

10¢
DELL BOOK 20
TOM W. BLACKBURN
A Texan fights for a huge ranch,
a trail herd, and a pretty girl.

# Broken Arrow Range

COMPLETE

In the look she gave him Carl saw the promise of a night of love... but he didn't see murder.

## e case of the DANCING SANDWICHES

FREDRIC BROWN

COMPLETE AND UNABRIDGED

10¢
DELL BOOK 11
WILLIAM IRISH
A cheap and evil girl sets a hopped-up killer against a city.

# MARIHUANA

COMPLETE AND UNABRIDGED

10¢
DELL BOOK 36
Robert Heinlein

# UNIVERSE

Their world was a giant spaceship, its purpose and destination lost in centuries of drifting among the stars.

COMPLETE AND UNABRIDGED

**BROKEN ARROW RANGE**
TOM W. BLACKBURN
DELL TEN-CENT BOOKS, 1951
COVER BY ROBERT STANLEY

**THE CASE OF THE DANCING SANDWICHES**
FREDRIC BROWN
DELL TEN-CENT BOOKS, 1951
COVER BY ROBERT STANLEY

**MARIHUANA**
WILLIAM IRISH (CORNELL WOOLRICH)
DELL TEN-CENT BOOKS, 1951
COVER BY BILL FLEMING

**UNIVERSE**
ROBERT A. HEINLEIN
DELL TEN-CENT BOOKS, 1951
COVER BY ROBERT STANLEY

Dell's experiment with slim volumes that sold for ten cents apiece (hence, "Dell Dimers") lasted for thirty-six books, all highly collectible. Not all were PBOs, but these four were, and three of them (except for the Blackburn) are by highly collected authors.

**CHART of PACIFIC AREA of THE BATTLE of THE CORAL SEA in "QUEEN of THE FLAT-TOPS"**

TRUK ISLAND···JAPANESE NAVAL BASE WHERE STRIKING FORCE WAS ASSEMBLED WHICH SAILED SOUTHWARD TOWARD THE CORAL SEA···

ROUTE OF NO.1 JAP STRIKING FORCE

*Pacific Ocean*

To Hawaii

Equator

BISMARCK ARCHIPELAGO

NEW IRELAND
NEW BRITAIN
RABAUL
GASMATA

TULAGI HARBOR···WHERE, ON MAY 4, 14 OUT OF 15 JAP WARSHIPS & TRANSPORTS WERE SUNK···BURNED OR BEACHED

BOUGAINVILLE IS.
CHOISEUL IS.
SOLOMON IS. (BR.)
YSABEL IS.
MALAITA IS.
FLORIDA IS.
TULAGI

JAP CARRIER RYUKAKU & CRUISER SUNK MAY 7···

PORT MORESBY

ROUTE FOLLOWED BY PLANES FROM AMERICAN CARRIERS

MISIMA I.
DE BOYNE
ROSSEL
JOMARD PASSAGE

JAP HELD AREAS IN BLACK

GUADALCANAL I.

JAP CARRIER SHOKAKO DAMAGED

CARRIER
CARRIER
CARRIER

SAN CRISTOBAL (BAURO I.)

ROUTE OF NO.2 JAP STRIKING FORCE

THE ATTACK
THE FIRE
SANK

*Coral Sea*

ON MAY 8, WHILE HER PLANES WERE AWAY CONTACTING FORCE, THE LEXINGTON W ATTACKED BY JAPANESE TORPEDO & BOMBER PLANES··· RECEIVING DAMAGE THAT RESULTED IN EVENTUAL SINK-ING BY U.S. DESTROYER·····

**HOUSE IN GREAT RUSSELL STREET SCENE OF MURDER IN "DEATH IN FIVE BOXES"**

Bath
Wardrobe
Bedroom
Steps to Flat
Stairs to 3rd Fl.

Felix Haye's Flat

Anglo-Egyptian Importing Co.

Chas. Dellings' Sons

Mason + Wilkins

**CRIME MAPS OF SIX TOUGH DETECTIVE CASES BY DASHIELL HAMMETT**

A DELL BOOK

GREENWICH
FILBERT
UNION
GREEN
VALLEJO
BROADWAY
PACIFIC
JACKSON
WASHINGTON
CLAY
SACRAMENTO
CALIFORNIA
PINE
BUSH
SUTTER
POST
GEARY
O'FARRELL
ELLIS
EDDY
TURK
GOLDEN GATE AVE.

CHINATOWN
NOB HILL

TACOMA
YAKIMA

RAPHAEL
RICHMOND
BERKELEY
OAKLAND
SAN FRANCISCO BAY
SAN MATEO
BELMONT
PALO ALTO
SAN JOSE
PORTLAND
SAN MATEO CO.
PACIFIC OCEAN
HALF MOON BAY

SANTA ROSA
SAN RAFAEL
SAN FRANCISCO
OAKLAND
SANTA CRUZ

SULU SEA
SULU
BORNEO
TAWITAWI PROV.
SULU ARCHIPELAGO
CELEBES SEA

**GUIDE**

**DEAD YELLOW WOMEN**
1. SHAN MANSION
2. PIGATTI'S PLACE WAVERLY PL. (JAIR QUON) SPOFFORD ALLEY (CHANG LI CHING)
3. "BIG FAT" THOMSON'S PLACE
4. GLENWAY APTS.
5. HALL OF JUSTICE

**THE GOLDEN HORSESHOE**
1. POST OFFICE
2. JOHN RYAN'S ROOM
3. MRS. ASHCRAFT'S HOME.
4. TIJUANA

**HOUSE DICK**
1. MONTGOMERY HOTEL
2. PIGATTI'S PLACE

**WHO KILLED BOB TEAL**
1. BOB TEAL IS SHOT
2. WHITACRE'S APT.
3. QUIRK'S APT.
4. OGBURN'S APT.

**THE GREEN ELEPHANT**
1. SPOKANE
2. SEATTLE

**THE HAIRY ONE**
1. SULU ARCHIPELAGO

**HOPALONG CASSIDY'S ADVENTURES IN "BAR-20 DAYS"**

TEXAS

TO EL PASO

BIG BEND COUNTRY

CLOUDBURST
MARSHAL OF RAWHIDE
WINCHESTER
APACHE FIGHT
COYOTE PASS
PERRY'S BEND
COAST TOWN
SAN MIGUEL CANYON
TOWN OF GRANT

RIO GRANDE RIVER

MEXICO

A DELL BOOK

**THE SURFACE OF THE MOON SCENE OF ADVENTURE IN "THE FIRST MEN IN THE MOON"**

A DELL BOOK

CLAVIUS
MAGINUS
TYCHO
MAUROLYCUS
STOEFLER
PICCOLOMINI
MARE NUBIUM
MARE HUMORUM
STRAIGHT WALL
MARE NECTARIS
PTOLEMAEUS
HERSCHEL
LALANDE
COPERNICUS
MARE UNDITATIS
MARE TRANQUILLITATIS
PINIUS
MARE CRISIUM
MARE SERENITATIS
OCEANUS PROCELLARUM
POSIDONIUS
ARCHIMEDES
MARE IMBRIUM
SINUS IRIDUM
VALLEY OF THE ALPS
MARE FRIGORIS

**ROUTE OF FLEETWING EXPEDITION SEARCHING FOR THE TREASURE OF THE ORINOCO IN "MEN UNDER THE SEA"**

A DELL BOOK

NORTH AMERICA
NEW YORK
START OF EXPEDITION
NORFOLK
HATTERAS
ATLANTIC OCEAN
CHARLESTON
SAVANNAH
JACKSONVILLE
GULF OF MEXICO
NASSAU
BAHAMA IS.
MONA PASSAGE WEST INDIES
JAMAICA
PUERTO RICO
CARIBBEAN SEA
CENTRAL AMERICA
LOCATION OF THE ORINOCO
PUERTO CABELLO
VENEZUELA
PACIFIC OCEAN
SOUTH AMERICA

As paperback editor Donald Wollheim used to say, "Authors may be crazy, but they're not stupid." They didn't want to split their paperback royalties with hardcover houses that typically produced prestigious but small editions and that paid them little money. This principle applies to most journeyman authors, not to the elite few who scored breakout bestseller sales. However, the more successful an author became, the more money he had riding on the sales of a mass-market paperback edition—and on the terms of his contract.

In addition to the successful PBO line, Dell tried another intriguing experiment in 1951. These were the Dell Ten-Cent Books, affectionately known as Dell Dimers. There were just thirty-six of these, starting with *Trumpets West* by Luke Short. Any Dell Dimer is a collectible, but the most sought-after are *Marihuana* (a PBO by Cornell Woolrich writing as William Irish), *The Case of the Dancing Sandwiches* (a PBO by Fredric Brown), and, the last in the Dime series, *Universe* (a PBO by Robert A. Heinlein).

Dell moved into the big time with a series of bestsellers—*Bonjour Tristesse* by Francoise Sagan, *Peyton Place* by Grace Metalious, *Anatomy of a Murder* by "Robert Traver" (James Voelker), and *Return to Peyton Place* by Grace Metalious.

Dell was "mainstreaming" now. It had begun as a marginal publisher, operating in the shadow of Pocket Books and Signet, but had become a power in its own right. Gone were the mapbacks, the keyholes, the little summaries of people and things that the book was about.

*Dell Mapbacks* were popular with readers in their day and have grown in popularity with collectors. This selection ranges in scale from a single building to a hemisphere of the moon. While the maps were not credited, paperback scholar Piet Schreuders researched the question and determined that most if not all of them were the work of Ruth Belew, one of the great unsung heroes (or heroines) of publishing history!

In the 1970s Dell became a major player in the science fiction field. Building on earlier one-offs like *The Sirens of Titan* by Vonnegut, and *The Cosmic Rape* by Sturgeon, Dell established a program under the tutelage of a series of talented editors. Unfortunately, the company was becoming increasingly bureaucratized, and one editor after another either resigned in frustration or fought the system until he got himself fired. Talented men who came and went included Larry T. Shaw (who had edited a brilliant science fiction series for Lancer Books), Fred Feldman (who would go on to Fawcett), and David Harris (who would later create the highly collected Millennium hardcover line for Walker).

Finally James Frenkel arrived on the scene. He developed a line of hardcovers and paperbacks for Dell and Delacorte under the rubric Quantum Books. On a more modest level he instituted a series of Dell Doubles, although without the front-and-back gimmickry of the beloved Ace Doubles. Frenkel promoted important younger writers like John Varley, Orson Scott Card, and Joan Vinge.

Dell was going through a series of mergers and takeovers, eventually becoming part of a publishing empire with Bantam Books and Doubleday, the entire company in turn owned by the German Bertelsmanns company. The science fiction line was cancelled, reinstated, and canceled again. Authors whose manuscripts were already in Dell's hands found themselves stranded. Dell refused either to publish the books or to return the rights to the authors. Some bought their books back from Dell. Others simply waited out their contracts, at which time the rights reverted to the authors who were then free to sell them elsewhere.

The modern Dell Books are typically well chosen, slick, and attractively packaged. But somehow they just don't have the charm of the *old* Dells with their keyholes, maps, and summaries.

# Brave
# New
# World

## Chapter Six

BANTAM BOOKS
COMPLETE AND UNABRIDGED

Allen Lane, Kurt Enoch, and Ian Ballantine made a fascinating team. As long as they pulled together they could perform prodigies but all too often they found themselves tugging in different directions. These were three men of the highest intelligence, fine taste, sound instincts, and dedication to their craft. But all were strongwilled, and when they differed (which they often did) the fur would fly. They're all deceased now so there's no consulting them about their disagreements, but the battles must have been monumental.

I did know Ian Ballantine. In the 1960s I was editing for a hardcover publisher in New York and negotiated reprint rights and joint projects with Ian. He was a brilliant bookman and he knew exactly what he wanted. He could be as hard as iron, and as inflexible, when it came to getting his way. By 1970 our paths had diverged, but we renewed our acquaintanceship some years later. In his earlier days, Ian had seemingly taken pride in being a curmudgeon of the publishing world. In his later years he outgrew this persona, or perhaps he simply abandoned it and transformed himself into a jolly old elf.

Historians tell us that most world leaders thought World War II would be a brief war that would cease before the end of 1942. But each side proved more resilient and determined than the other had expected, and the war dragged on through 1945 before coming to an end with the conquest of Germany and the collapse of the Nazi regime, the nuclear destruction of Hiroshima and Nagasaki, and the surrender of Japan.

British paper restrictions were even more stringent than those in the United States, and submarine warfare made any attempts to ship civilian goods risky at best. Thus, as the war continued, Allen Lane's Penguin Books became unable to supply American Penguin with books. The brash young Ian Ballantine grew from importer and salesman to publisher in his own right, with Lane's blessing (perhaps reluctantly granted).

As Ballantine flexed his muscles, adopting a more and more independent attitude, Lane became increasingly unhappy. He dispatched Kurt Enoch to work at Ballantine's elbow and bring American Penguin back under control.

Thus the trio was formed.

Allen Lane was a proper, conservative British gentleman, the scion of a traditional publishing family. Despite his Jewish heritage, Enoch tended toward a Teutonic punctilio. Ballantine, with his roots in American radicalism and his aggressive energy, was the embodiment of New World boisterousness and excitement. The Continental sophisticate, Enoch, tended to support Lane when disagreements arose. This is not surprising: he had been sent to America, in effect, as Lane's spokesman and proconsul. Ian Ballantine bridled at Lane and Enoch's attempts to bring him to heel. The arrangement couldn't last, and it didn't.

By 1945 Ian Ballantine stomped out of American Penguin. He took key staffers with him: Walter Pitkin, a talented editor, and Sidney Kramer, who was doubly qualified as lawyer and accountant. Other Penguin employees followed. Ballantine took other things with him that were actually more important than the staffers. After all, publishing is one of those "magnet" industries that seems eternally besieged by eager and talented young men and women, happy to work long hours in dingy surroundings for inadequate pay. They could do better pushing papers in a bank or insurance office, but, to paraphrase the old joke — "What, and leave the book business?"

When Ian Ballantine left American Penguin, he took that company's agreements with *Infantry Journal* and the Military Services Publishing Company. Even more important, he took the distribution deal with Curtis.

He set up shop as an independent and managed to get several books out, the most notable being a reprint of *The Informer* by Liam O'Flaherty. But

## ASYLUM
**WILLIAM SEABROOK**
**BANTAM, 1947**
**COVER BY CHARLES ANDRES**

A travel writer and student of voodoo, Seabrook told the story of his struggle with alcohol in this remarkable early memoir.

📖📖

## BABBITT
**SINCLAIR LEWIS**
**BANTAM, 1946**
**DUST JACKET BY B. BARTON, BOOK COVER BY CIRLIN**

Lewis's satire on American boosterism had an appropriate but decidedly unexciting cover design, so Bantam decided to pump up sales with a more colorful and suggestive treatment.

📖📖📖📖 with jacket, 📖 without jacket

## BAT MASTERSON
**RICHARD O'CONNOR**
**BANTAM BOOKS, 1958**

Yes, that's good ol' Gene Barry as the title character in this TVTI (television tie-in) from the late-1950s series.

📖

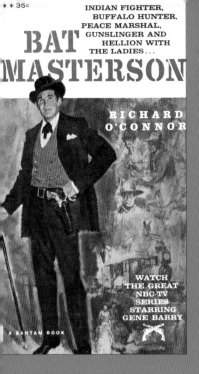

## BELVEDERE
GWEN DAVENPORT
BANTAM BOOKS, 1949
COVER BY CASEY JONES

Those aren't quite Clifton Webb, Maureen O'Hara, and Robert Young, the actors who starred in the films about the nation's favorite babysitter in the late 1940s, but they're close enough.

## BLUES FOR THE PRINCE
BART SPICER
BANTAM BOOKS, 1951

The arts often overlap, and novels about the world of music, especially so-called "jazz novels," are a subgenre unto themselves.

## THE BURNING HILLS
LOUIS L'AMOUR
BANTAM, 1956

Veteran pulp writer Louis L'Amour turned out hardboiled crime stories, air war adventures, and whatever it took to earn a living prior to finding his true *metier* as a western writer. He became a mainstay for Bantam and inherited the title of king of the western from Zane Grey. Note that L'Amour, who is heavily collected, also wrote several novels as Jim Mayo and as Tex Burns. If you're lucky, you may get a bargain on one of those.

the new enterprise, Ballantine and Company, was undercapitalized. Lacking a bankroll, Ballantine had trouble acquiring properties. He was also forced to juggle creditors, holding off payroll and royalty payments while he waited for receipts to arrive. This couldn't go on for long, and he went looking for backers.

He found them. Bennett Cerf of Random House offered no money but a sympathetic ear and a strong recommendation to John O'Connor, President of Grosset & Dunlap, who wound up taking a major interest in the new company. Curtis took a similar large chunk. Ballantine wound up with a smaller share, and Walter Pitkin and Sidney Kramer each took a still smaller share.

Ballantine now had a company, a war chest, and a staff. The new company was named Bantam Books. The board of directors included Cerf, O'Connor, Cass Canfield (of Harper & Brothers), Charles Scribner, and Meredith Wood (of the Book of the Month Club). Curtis Circulating Company insisted on reserving *four* positions on the board for themselves. (For this information, and for much more, I am indebted to Kenneth C. Davis.)

The first ten Bantam Books reveal a schizophrenic tendency which not only marked Bantam but the entire paperback industry. The very first Bantam Book was *Life on the Mississippi* by Mark Twain. Twain was himself a contradictory and controversial figure in American letters. In his own time he was a rebel and a populist. In later years his works (with certain notable exceptions) were accepted as part of the American canon, and Twain became an icon.

Mark Twain (Samuel Langhorne Clemens) had died in 1910. Dead authors are always safer than living ones, and the longer they've been dead, the better for publishers. They're not going to write or say or do anything embarrassing, and the longer they've been dead, the fewer people who actually knew them still remain.

*Life on the Mississippi* wasn't a dangerous book, like Twain's famous *Huckleberry Finn* or his largely suppressed *Christian Science*. It was a solid, respectable book, and Bantam published it in a solid, respectable package.

The cover harked back to the disagreement between Ballantine's American Penguin and Allen Lane's British Penguin. There was a picture on the cover, but it was minimal. An old-fashioned Mississippi River steamer drawn by H. Lawrence Hoffman in black-and-white made its way across a solid greenish background. (The steamer was shown three times, in fact.) The author's name and the title of the book appeared in a simple box in the middle of the cover. A Bantam rooster logo appeared in vignette, and across the bottom of the image the words *Bantam Books Complete and Unabridged* were printed.

I remember it well. I bought a brand-new copy off the racks. The year was 1945, and I was just ten years old, but I could see that something significant was going on.

I wish I'd saved the book, too.

The back cover of *Life on the Mississippi* was also notable. Paperback publishers varied their practices here. Some used the back cover for a sales pitch for the book—the equivalent of flap copy on the dust jacket of hardcovers. Others used the back covers for other purposes, most notably the famous (and highly collectible) Dell mapbacks. Others, like Avon, used the back cover to promote their entire line.

Bantam followed this last policy. The back cover of *Life on the Mississippi* featured another version of the crowing Bantam rooster. Then there was a wonderful little homily designed to convince the reader that Bantam Books ranked right up there with holiness, Godliness, and Mom's apple pie:

"Four Bantam Books are published each month. Like this book, all are chosen to give you maximum reading enjoyment.

"Bantam Books include novels, mysteries and anthologies, besides works of humor and information. You can recognize Bantam Books by the tasteful pictures on the covers, by their famous authors, and by the tough bantam rooster on the front of all the books. Look for the four new Bantam Books this month, next month, and every month.

"Only 25¢ each.

"The Bantam Book you are now holding in your hand contains the complete text of the original edition, shown on the right. **Not one word has been changed or omitted**. This low-priced Bantam edition is made possible by the large sale and effective promotion of the original edition published by Harper & Brothers."

❧ ❧ ❧ ❧ ❧

And right there, in thumbnail size, is a reproduction of the hardcover version of *Life on the Mississippi*, pictorial dust jacket and all.

Was the reference to "tasteful pictures on the covers" a dig at Lane and Enoch, and their resistance to Ballantine's putting pictures on the covers of his American Penguin books? Was the reproduction of the pictorial dust jacket from the Harper edition more of the same?

Other early Bantams reproduce the self-serving sermon with the last line revised, of course, to reflect the hardcover publisher of the book. Bantam's connections with Random House, Harpers, Scribners, and G&D gave the new company convenient access to those publishers' books. This was especially important when you consider Pocket Books' cozy relationship with Simon & Schuster.

By this time there were six major paperback houses in the U.S. Avon, Dell, and Popular Library were determinedly populist in nature, pulpish in ancestry, and "down-market" in their choice of titles and marketing practices. This is not to suggest that they were trashy publishers or that they produced no books of serious intent and real literary merit. But their fiction consisted *primarily* of mysteries, westerns, and innuendo-laden romance titles.

Pocket, American Penguin, and now Bantam were in competition for the "high-end" segment of the paperback field. Having a close relationship with an important hardcover house was a boost for de Graff and Pocket. Having connections with several such houses gave upstart Bantam a huge boost. At the same time, living in part on nourishment received through a three thousand mile umbilical cord was a serious handicap for American Penguin.

Ian Ballantine and editor Pitkin made obeisance to Quality Literature with a capital Q with *Life on the Mississippi* but they totally reversed their field with Bantam Book Number 2, *The Gift Horse* by Frank Gruber.

Born in 1904, Gruber was a veteran writer with credentials as a journalist, pulp author and novelist by 1945. He had also started what would prove a long and successful career as a screenwriter, scoring heavily with the 1944 *noir* drama *Mask of Dimitrios*, adapted from Graham Greene's *A Coffin for Dimitrios*.

Gruber had written for *Black Mask*, *Dime Detective*, Ned Pines' *Thrilling Detective*, *Short Stories*, *Ranch Romances*, *Operator #5* and *Ace Sports*. In short, Gruber could write whatever the market demanded: mysteries, westerns, sports stories—anything except science fiction. He despised science fiction and contended that all the people he called "pseudoscience fiction writers" were weirdos. And ugly, to boot. He even complained that they hated him!

Eventually Gruber would write more than fifty novels, the majority mysteries and the rest westerns, as well as a biography of Zane Grey, an autobiography, and literally hundreds of motion picture and television screenplays.

MURDER WEARS AN UGLY MAS

361

THE **DEAD RINGER**

Fredric Brown

1093 A BANTAM BOOK Every Book Complete

AN UNFORGETTABLE PICTURE OF PEOPLE INHABITING THE BIZARRE AND EROTIC UNDERSIDE OF HOLLYWOOD

THE **DAY** OF THE **LOCUST**

**NATHANAEL WEST**

71 A BANTAM BOOK Every Book Complete

GRAHAM GREENE

THE **CONFIDENTIAL AGENT**

"BREATHLESS EXCITEMENT . . . ORIGINAL AND POWERFUL." New York TIMES

COMPLETE & UNABRIDGED

Complete & Unabridged

---

**THE CONFIDENTIAL AGENT**
GRAHAM GREENE
BANTAM BOOKS, 1951

Not as well known as Greene's *The Third Man* or *Our Man in Havana*, this spy novel nonetheless sports a fine cover by Mitchell Hooks.

**THE DAY OF THE LOCUST**
NATHANAEL WEST
BANTAM BOOKS, 1951

Do you think the artist had any idea what this book is about? It looks like a disaster novel, with hordes of killer bugs about to eat people alive. It's actually a tell-all novel about nasty infighting in the motion picture industry.

**THE DEAD RINGER**
FREDRIC BROWN
BANTAM BOOKS, 1949
COVER BY ROBERT STANLEY

Here is a three-ring collectible: Fred Brown, a carnival setting, and that lovely gorilla peering through the window!

### DEATH IN THE BLACKOUT
**ANTHONY GILBERT**
**BANTAM BOOKS, 1946**

A fine cover was done for this novel, with its striking yellow-and-black color scheme and skeleton motif; it's too bad the artist wasn't credited. Anthony Gilbert was the pseudonym of British writer Lucy Beatrice Malleson (1899-1973), whose deceptively inept lawyer-detective Arthur G. Crook was a likely ancestor of John Mortimer's famous Rumpole. This book was first published as *The Case of the Tea-Cosy's Aunt*.

### DRAWN AND QUARTERED
**CHARLES ADDAMS**
**BANTAM BOOKS, 1946**
**COVER BY CHARLES ADDAMS**

A grand master of macabre humor, Charles Addams created an immortal "family" of ghoulishly hilarious characters. This is a highly collectible early cartoon book with a gorilla on the cover!

### THE DRAGON MURDER CASE
**S. S. VAN DINE**
**BANTAM BOOKS, 1949**
**COVER BY A. FREUDEMANN**

Writing as S. S. Van Dine, Willard Huntington Wright (1888-1939), a sometime art critic, alcoholic, heroin addict, and kept man, was also the world's favorite mystery writer. Almost forgotten today, his books offer a window into the fantasy world of the millionaire-genius, insufferable snob, and amateur-sleuth.

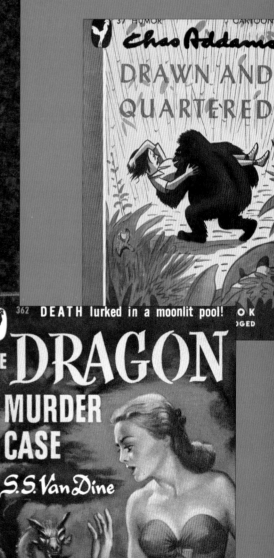

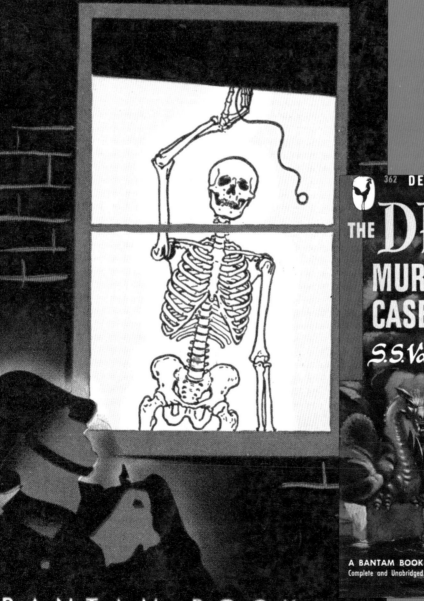

*The Gift Horse* was one of Gruber's mysteries. It featured the team of hardboiled, wisecracking Johnny Fletcher and muscle-man Sam Cragg. The cover was an impressionistic design that was hardly great art (not even great commercial art) but would still have given Allen Lane the collywobbles.

Next came a western, *Nevada*, by Zane Grey. Then a mystery, *Evidence of Things Seen*, by Elizabeth Daly. Daly was another veteran, born in 1878, and was reputedly Agatha Christie's favorite American mystery writer. Her detective, Henry Gamadge, was a cultured New Yorker who lived in a brownstone house with his wife, his son, and his cat. Gamadge was a great bibliophile.

Independently wealthy, Gamadge nonetheless offered his services as an authenticator of rare volumes and manuscripts. He had numerous hobbies and a fulltime assistant. Anthony Boucher has been quoted as saying that Gamadge was "a man so well-bred as to make Lord Peter Wimsey seem a trifle coarse."

*Evidence of Things Seen* had been published in hardcover in 1943, when the United States was deeply embroiled in warfare, and Gamadge was in the army. He managed nonetheless to get away long enough to visit his wife at a vacation cottage in the mountains and to solve the seemingly supernatural murder of their landlord. Henry Gamadge thus achieved the unusual distinction of actually wanting to solve the murder of his landlord, but let's leave that alone.

Bantam's first four-book release thus comprised a literary novel, a hardboiled mystery, a western, and a traditional "genteel" detective story. Bantam's second four-book release was also mixed, although it turned slightly more in the direction of upscale literature.

The lead title (or at least, the first of the four) was *Scaramouche*, that grand swashbuckler by the master of foppish finery and fancy fencing, Rafael Sabatini. Next came *Murder by Marriage*, by Robert George Dean, a mystery featuring Dean's series hero Tony Hunter.

Then Bantam turned upscale with *The Grapes of Wrath*, by John Steinbeck, and *The Great Gatsby*, by F. Scott Fitzgerald. Aside from being a masterpiece and one of the finest novels of the twentieth century, the Bantam *Gatsby* was notable as the first Bantam issued with a dust jacket. It was not, of course, the first paperback to sport a jacket, but that extra bit of colorful laminated paper makes it a prize for paperback collectors.

A number of publishers experimented with dust jackets for paperbacks in the early years of the industry, including the British "2-4-1" books that preceded the Ace Doubles by several years. Book jackets had evolved in the nineteenth and twentieth centuries, starting out as plain opaque or translucent paper covers intended to protect unbound sheets until they were bound or to protect expensive leather or cloth bindings. Hence, the term "dust jacket."

It didn't take publishers long to start printing a bit of promotional copy on their jackets, and from there it was a natural development to add colorful illustrations, elaborate typography, and extensive text designed to sell the book.

Typically, the hard binding would have only the title, author's by-line, and publisher's identification stamped on the spine. The jacket could be sensational and, from the viewpoint of collectors, came to have great importance. Today collectors often cover the jackets themselves with clear protectors.

When it came to paperback books, the pattern was similar. The book itself might sport a quiet, dignified design in subdued colors with an unprepossessing illustration, if any. The jacket, by contrast, would be printed in glaring colors, feature an exciting illustration, and carry provocative text that was often misleading if not exactly false. An interesting example is Bantam Number 22, *Babbitt*, by Sinclair Lewis (1946). The book cover ("wraps") features a painting by Cirlin of George Babbitt. Our perspective is from behind Mr. Babbitt, who is clad in a conservative

## EVIDENCE OF THINGS SEEN
**ELIZABETH DALY**
**BANTAM, 1945**

A typical back cover of a very early Bantam Book. Note the reproduction of the hardcover edition and the promotional copy for Bantam's publishing program rather than Elizabeth Daly's very cozy, British-style mystery novel. Daly (1878-1967) was reputedly Agatha Christie's favorite American author.

## FOR WHOM THE BELL TOLLS
**ERNEST HEMINGWAY**
**BANTAM BOOKS, 1951**
**COVER BY MAYAN**

That's not quite Gregory Peck as the American adventurer and Ingrid Bergman as the unlikely blonde, blue-eyed Spanish Republican guerrilla fighter from the 1943 film of Hemingway's novel, but they're close enough.

Four Bantam Books are published each month. Like this book, all are chosen to give you maximum reading enjoyment.

Bantam Books include novels, mysteries and anthologies, besides works of humor and information. You can recognize Bantam Books by the tasteful pictures on the covers, by their famous authors, and by the tough bantam rooster on the front of all the books. Look for the four new Bantam Books this month, next month, and every month.

ONLY **25¢** EACH

The Bantam Book you are now holding in your hand contains the complete text of the original edition, shown on the right. **Not one word has been changed or omitted.** This low-priced Bantam edition is made possible by the large sale and effective promotion of the original edition, published by Farrar & Rinehart, Inc.

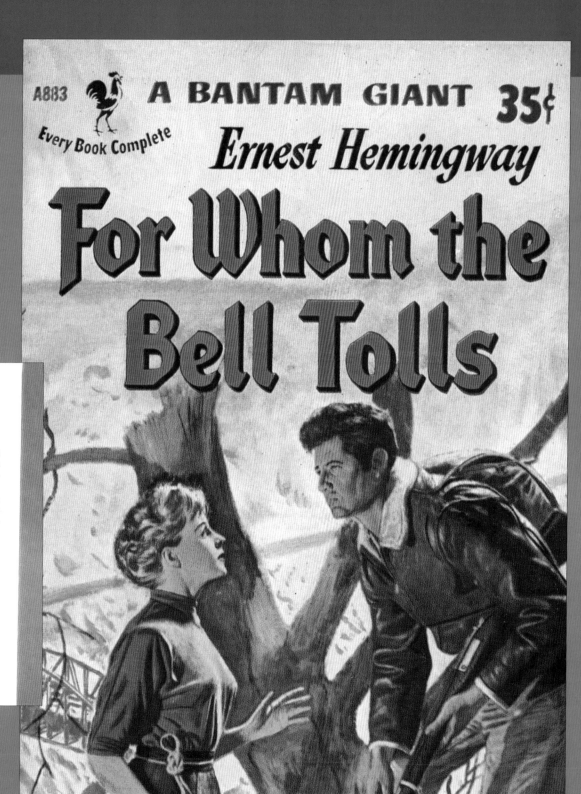

A8&3  **A BANTAM GIANT**  35¢
Every Book Complete
*Ernest Hemingway*
**For Whom the Bell Tolls**

715

SAMMY BAUGH, DON HUTSON,
FRANK LEAHY, AND 34 OTHERS

# My Greatest Day in FOOTBALL

Foreword by
**LOU LITTLE**

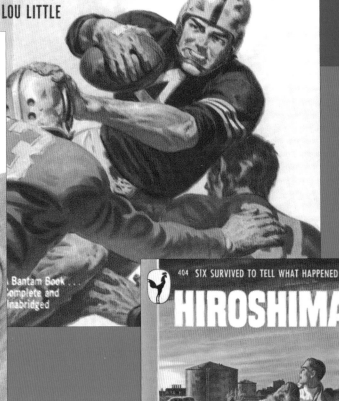

A Bantam Book...
Complete and
Unabridged

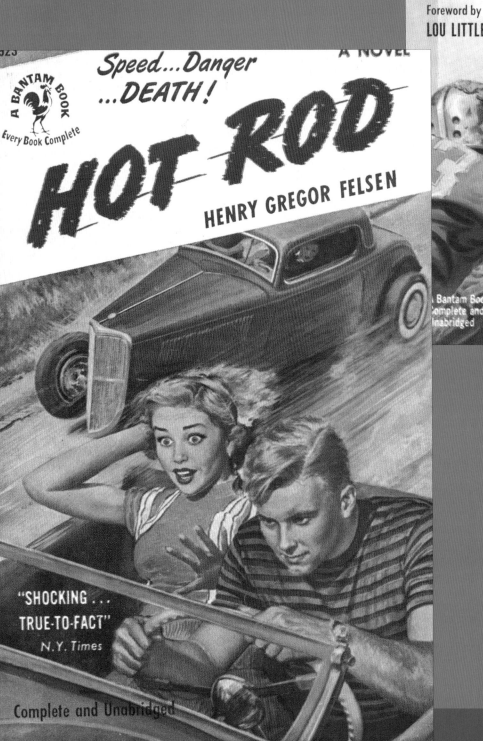

Speed...Danger
...DEATH!

*A NOVEL*

A BANTAM BOOK
Every Book Complete

# HOT ROD

HENRY GREGOR FELSEN

"SHOCKING...
TRUE-TO-FACT"
N.Y. Times

Complete and Unabridged

404    SIX SURVIVED TO TELL WHAT HAPPENED

# HIROSHIMA

John
Hersey

A BANTAM BOOK
Complete and Unabridged

## HOT ROD
**HENRY GREGOR FELSON**
**BANTAM BOOKS, 1951**

It's hard to believe that, at the time, the nastiest thing we could imagine teen-agers doing was drag racing. The uncredited painting captures the emotions of the boy and girl to perfection.

📖

## MY GREATEST DAY IN FOOTBALL
**EDITED BY MURRAY GOODMAN AND LEONARD LEWIN**
**BANTAM BOOKS, 1949**
**COVER BY NORMAN SAUNDERS**

Ah, those were the days when football stars played on both sides of the ball and face-masks were for Halloween! This is a collectible and remarkably readable collection of first-person accounts of gridiron heroics.

📖📖

## HIROSHIMA
**JOHN HERSEY**
**BANTAM BOOKS, 1948**
**COVER BY GEOFFREY BIGGS**

Bantam's gamble on this early description of the horrors of nuclear warfare paid off, even though the painting didn't look much like the scene of the bombing.

📖📖📖

## THE HUCKSTERS

**FREDERIC WAKEMAN**
**BANTAM BOOKS, 1948**
**COVER BY BERNARD D'ANDREA**

Certainly no equal of the Clark Gable/Deborah Kerr 1947 film, this edition qualifies as one of the few specifically "non-MTIs" ever issued.

## LIFE ON THE MISSISSIPPI

**MARK TWAIN**
**BANTAM BOOKS, 1947**
**COVER BY H. LAWRENCE HOFFMAN**

This is one of the key books in the history of paperback publishing. Sometimes undervalued as it is neither a very important literary work nor a particularly striking image, the very first Bantam should nevertheless have a place in any serious collector's heart, if not on his shelf.

## HOW TO SURVIVE AN ATOMIC BOMB

**RICHARD GERSTELL**
**BANTAM BOOKS, 1950**

The best way to survive an atomic bomb is not to have it go off. The second best is to be far away when it does. Far, far away.

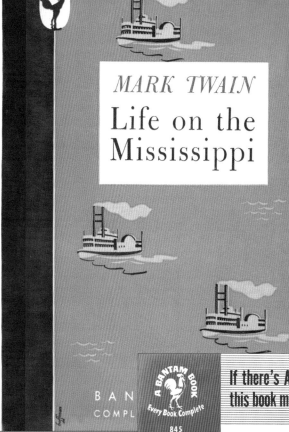

## LONG, LONG AGO

**ALEXANDER WOOLLCOTT**
**BANTAM BOOKS, 1946**
**COVER BY W. COTTON (?)**

How many of the celebrities surrounding the avoirdupois-gifted Woolcott can you identify?

📖📖

## LOUISVILLE SATURDAY

**MARGARET LONG**
**BANTAM BOOKS, 1951**
**COVER BY ROBERT SKEMP**

Military service was part of almost every young man's life in the Cold War days of the 1950s, and novels based on their experiences were common. This one, written by a woman and from the female viewpoint, was very unusual.

📖

## MAN ALONE

**WILLIAM DOYLE WITH SCOTT O'DELL**
**BANTAM BOOKS, 1954**

Prison memoirs are a subgenre world unto themselves, whether written by Adolf Hitler, Fidel Castro, George Sylvester Viereck, Jack Woodford, or Charles Colson. Novels of prison life are another matter. The signature on this unusual painting is hard to make out (paperback covers rarely feature nude males). Is it Binger? Bingham? Or maybe Barye Phillips?

📖📖

**NOW YOU CAN READ THEM!**

704

**MEMOIRS OF**
*Sherlock Holmes*

**ELEVEN FAMOUS CASES**

**SIR ARTHUR CONAN DOYLE**

**THE GREAT DETECTIVE MEETS MORIARTY, KING OF CRIME!**

A BANTAM Book Complete and Unabridged

406   THIS TOMBOY COULD UPSET ANYBODY!

*Mickey*
(CLEMENTINE)

Lois Butler stars in "MICKEY" an Eagle Lion Cinecolor Production

PEGGY GOODIN

WHAT EVERY YOUNG GIRL SHOULD KNOW

A Bantam Book... Complete and Unabridged

**MEMOIRS OF SHERLOCK HOLMES**
ARTHUR CONAN DOYLE
BANTAM BOOKS, 1949

No publisher ever lost money on a Sherlock Holmes book, and there's hardly a paperback house that didn't try at least one. Bantam's early effort was adequate but far from striking.

**MICKEY**
PEGGY GOODIN
BANTAM BOOKS, 1948
COVER BY CASEY JONES?

This bit of MTI fluff has a sweet appeal to it, although the story of a tomboy who "learns how to be a girl" might not match the spirit of the times half a century later.

044 Muscle-Man! Dizzy Dame! Trunk Murder!

THE MIGHTY BLOCKHEAD

FRANK GRUBER

COMPLETE AND UNABRIDGED

**THE MIGHTY BLOCKHEAD**
FRANK GRUBER
SUPERIOR REPRINT, 1945, BANTAM DUST JACKET, 1946

This is one of those paperbacks where the dust jacket
is far more valuable than the book itself.

M655 A JOHNNY FLETCHER MYSTERY

THE MIGHTY BLOCKHEAD

BY

FRANK GRUBER

COMPLETE and UNABRIDGED

25c A SUPERIOR REPRINT

blue pinstripe suit. He's looking up at the familiar Bantam rectangle with title and author. There's that good old Bantam rooster logo, book number, and the message, *A Novel*, plus the customary *A Bantam Book Complete and Unabridged*.

But the jacket—wow! Old George is strolling down the street in front of his real estate office. He's wearing a conservative suit and Mrs. Babbitt is clutching him by the elbow, looking extremely peeved. George is making eyes at a shapely young lady in a red dress and she's returning his glance with more than polite interest. He's holding a cigar cocked at a suggestive angle that we can only call, to put it delicately, phallic. The lady in the red dress has one braceletted hand extended toward him.

The blurb blazoned across the top of the cover: *What did this man want?* What did he want, indeed!

Pocket Books had tried the technique with *The Maltese Falcon* and others, and collectors today value these jacketed editions highly. One leading authority has estimated that the presence of a good condition jacket can raise the value of a paperback as much as 100 times that of the identical book without its jacket.

Dust jackets were used on paperbacks for more reason than to spice up otherwise quietly packaged books. The ever-creative Ian Ballantine would sometimes buy up the remaining stock of a defunct publisher for what he liked to call "distress prices"—just pennies on the dollar. The bankrupt publisher would take even those few pennies rather than be stuck with a warehouse full of utterly worthless books.

Ballantine would then print up Bantam jackets to go on the books and market them at full cover price. One such example was *The Mighty Blockhead*, another Johnny Fletcher and Sam Cragg mystery by Frank Gruber. Originally published in hardcover in 1942, the book had been reprinted by Ballantine's old pals at the Military Services Publishing Company in 1945. The book was part of MSPC's Superior Reprints

line. The Superior paperback sports a striking drawing in red, yellow, and black and powerful lettering. But the war was just about wrapped up, MSPC had nowhere to go, and Ian Ballantine was happy to take away their overstock—or at least selected titles.

Thus, Superior M655 was transformed into Bantam 144 (1946) with a screaming yellow dust jacket and a painting of two toughs (are they Fletcher and Cragg?) batting around a third mean-looking bozo. Both an automatic and a pair of handcuffs figure in the action, and the top banner reads *Muscle-Man! Dizzy Dame! Trunk Murder!*

In dust jacket format the book is worth many, many times its value without the jacket.

With the war over the paperback industry faced a new reality. Until then there had been more demand for books than there were books to read—and sell. Millions of paperbacks had been printed as Armed Services Editions and distributed free to servicemen and women around the world. Millions more had been purchased by civilians at home, carefully packed with homebaked cookies and lovingly knitted socks, and shipped off to soldiers and sailors.

But peacetime competition was increasing. Instead of keeping books on display until they sold, retailers were faced with a shortage of display space. New product kept arriving from the majors and from an endless parade of new, smaller publishers looking either for a niche where they could fit comfortably and profitably, or hoping to hit the big time and compete with the Pockets and the Bantams of the world.

Bantam continued its eclectic policy, mixing westerns, mysteries, swashbucklers, mainstream novels, the occasional classic, and—every so often—a title so quirky that it defied categorization. Seen from the perspective of half a century, the era of the late 1940s seems like a golden age of publishing. Books were selected with a freedom that would later disappear under the onslaught of conglomerization and the rule of bean-counters.

### MY FLAG IS DOWN
**JAMES MARESCA**
**BANTAM BOOKS, 1949**
**COVER BY CASEY JONES**

While racy for 1949, this "diary" seems far more innocent today, and is a true window into the past.

### MY MAN GODFREY
**ERIC HATCH**
**BANTAM BOOKS, 1947**

If this were an MTI related to the 1936 film, that would be William Powell carrying Carole Lombard up the stairs.

### THE NARROW CORNER
**W. SOMERSET MAUGHAM**
**BANTAM BOOKS, 1951**

Even the great Mr. Maugham tried his hand at the tropical island romance theme.

126

# Quality

SHE "PASSED" FOR WHITE
BUT SHE FOUND LOVE
AND HAPPINESS AMONG
HER NEGRO FRIENDS

CID
RICKETTS
SUMNER

A BANTAM BOOK
COMPLETE AND UNABRIDGED

---

THE NOVEL OF A LOVE SOCIETY FORBIDS

# THE PRICE OF SALT

CLAIRE MORGAN

"[handles] explosive material...
with sincerity and good taste." New York Times

---

1156

BANTAM BOOKS

25¢

A NOVEL OF A SOUTHERN
ARMY POST IN PEACETIME

## CARSON McCULLERS

# REFLECTIONS
in a GOLDEN EYE

"One of the most compelling, one of the most uncanny
stories ever written in America." —LOUIS UNTERMEYER

---

## QUALITY
**CID RICKETTS SUMNER**
**BANTAM BOOKS, 1947**
**COVER BY BERNARD D'ANDREA**

"Crossing the color line" was far
more difficult and could be far
more dangerous in the 1940s than
younger generations may realize.

## THE PRICE OF SALT
**CLAIRE MORGAN**
**BANTAM BOOKS, 1953**

Patricia Highsmith wrote this
lesbian novel under a pseudonym.

## REFLECTIONS IN A GOLDEN EYE
**CARSON McCULLERS**
**BANTAM BOOKS, 1953**

This cover offers a strangely
effective, Dali-esque painting
for McCullers' moody novel
of Army life and sexual identity
in the early 1950s.

Ian Ballantine was, in a sense, a precursor of those number-crunching MBAs. He had a reputation for being able to look at a book and predict its sales before the print-run was determined. Whether he did this by calculation or instinct, it led to great success, avoiding the waste of overspending on a project of limited potential and maximizing the benefits of a likely bestseller.

He was also a bookman to the core, and if he believed in a book, if he truly loved it and felt that it deserved to live, he would support it.

Thus, in its early, Ballantine years, Bantam published a number of possibly surprising titles.

Two of them dealt with the new threat of nuclear disaster. One of these was John Hersey's hugely successful *Hiroshima* (Bantam 404, 1948). Hersey had been born in China in 1914 and spent several years there reporting for *Life* magazine during World War II. When the war ended in August 1945, after atomic bombs were dropped on Hiroshima and Nagasaki, Hersey visited what was left of Hiroshima.

When he returned to the United States he wrote a lengthy report which appeared in *The New Yorker*. A hardcover edition of the book which evolved from this piece of journalism was only modestly successful, but Ian Ballantine saw its potential. He obtained paperback rights and made the book a success. In edition after edition it sold for decades, racking up total sales in the millions of copies.

The first Bantam version was rather surprisingly packaged. In Geoffrey Biggs' painting a man and woman are seen trudging away from a partially destroyed city. Both are wearing American-style clothing and the woman's hair seems to be honey-blonde. The sky is orange; a brilliant light glows on the horizon—it might be the rising or setting sun for all we can tell. Judged solely by its cover, the book might have been a soaper in the fashion of *Peyton Place*.

Nor was the blurb particularly enlightening: *Six survived to tell what happened.*

But one way or another the public understood what the book was about, and they bought it. It's interesting to note, however, that later Bantam editions of the book featured new cover art and different blurbs that made it clear what *Hiroshima* was all about.

Two years after publishing *Hiroshima*, Bantam issued *How to Survive an Atomic Bomb* (Bantam 845) by Richard Gerstell, "Consultant, Civil Defense Office." This may be the most peculiar book Bantam ever issued. Its patriotic-looking red-white-and-blue cover informs the reader that *If there's ATOMIC WARFARE this book may save your life!* It was a *Complete easy-to-read guide for every home, office and factory*.

The artwork was a black-and-white sketch of an all-American family, 1950 style: Dad in his suit and tie, Mom in her below-the-knees dress, Junior and Sis holding hands as they all gaze at something. We can't see what. Based on the drawing it might have been a new Kelvinator refrigerator, an exciting DuMont television set, or a shiny Hudson Hornet sedan. But it was none of the above: it was only a nuclear explosion.

Of course there were other notable Bantam books of the era. One was *Asylum*, by William Seabrook (Bantam 106, 1947). Seabrook was a talented anthropologist and ethnographer. His most famous book on the peoples and history of Haiti, *The Magic Island*, remains a riveting classic to this day.

He became a serious alcoholic and, after agonizing years of treatment and struggle, made his way back to sobriety. When he wrote the story of his years with alcohol, Bantam issued the book in a powerful package, the main image a haunting portrait by Charles Andrés.

Alexander Woollcott's memoir of the famous Algonquin Round-table, *Long, Long Ago* (Bantam 39, 1946) would be collectible if only for its brilliant cartoonish cover painting by Cotton. But of course Woollcott was an illustrious wit and a brilliant raconteur, and the words inside the cover are equally worthy.

Bantam went for the big names like Ernest Hemingway, issuing *For Whom the Bell Tolls* (Bantam A883, 1951), and the tried-and-true like Arthur Conan Doyle (*Memoirs of Sherlock Holmes*, Bantam 704, 1949). They hopped on trends, as with *The Hucksters* by Frederic Wakeman, (Bantam 405, 1948), and on headlines as with *Hot Rod* by Henry Gregor Felson (Bantam 923, 1951). The latter book carried the blurb, *Speed... Danger... DEATH!*—great formula for selling books.

In an era when publishers were competing ever more fiercely, the common practice was to spice up the package in order to capture the attention of the customer. Bantam's practices were far from the most egregious in this regard, but they were not above adding a dash of hot pepper to an otherwise bland stew. A good example was *The Dragon Murder Case* by S. S. Van Dine (Bantam 362, 1949).

"Van Dine" was the *nom de plume* of Willard Huntington Wright, a self-styled aesthete, a successful art critic, and a sometime alcoholic and heroin addict. He had achieved immense success with his Philo Vance mysteries, announcing at one point that it was impossible to write more than six novels in such a series without ruining the enterprise.

*The Dragon Murder Case*, originally published in 1933, was Van Dine's seventh Philo Vance novel out of a total of thirteen, and the fifth to be published by Bantam. Van Dine was the author of a famous set of rules for writing detective stories which he prefaced by stating that, "The detective story is a kind of intellectual game. It is more—it is a sporting event." One of his rules reads, "There must be no love interest. The business in hand is to bring a criminal to the bar of justice, not to bring a lovelorn couple to the hymeneal altar."

In fact, Van Dine's novels are shining examples of the type. Characters are paper-thin (although Philo Vance himself comes across as an obnoxious, arrogant snob), there is absolutely no sex or "love interest," there is remarkably little violence, and in fact there is hardly any action at all.

The crime is discovered, the police are baffled, the millionaire-playboy-amateur-sleuth Philo Vance is called in, and he then spends the next several hundred pages questioning witnesses, analyzing clues and eliminating suspects until the mystery is solved.

For some reason this kind of detective story was immensely popular, and Van Dine himself was one of the world's most successful authors.

To get back to *The Dragon Murder Case*, the Freudeman cover shows a shapely young lady in a one-piece maroon swimsuit. Her costume would be conservative, almost dowdy, by today's standards, but in 1949 it was pretty daring. There really is a dragon in the painting but it's one of those fancy fountains and it spouts water, not flames. The blurb reads, *DEATH lurked in a moonlit pool!*

Another detective whom Bantam offered a tryout was Rex Stout's Nero Wolfe. Bantam's first Stout book was *The Silent Speaker* (Bantam 308, 1948). In the early years of the paperback era Stout titles were all over the place, and nowadays collectors who specialize by author find him one of the most attractive and rewarding of all authors to pursue.

Rex Stout (1886-1975) did not start his writing career with Nero Wolfe. In fact, he had a substantial publishing record dating back several decades before he offered the world his most famous creation, starting (as so many did) in the pulps. He tried his hand at swashbucklers, novels of manners, love stories, even a hollow-earth-lost-race adventure ("Under the Andes," *All-Story Weekly*, 1914). This last was not a very good book (to put it mildly)—which must have been a great relief to Edgar Rice Burroughs who was just starting his own hollow earth series at the same time.

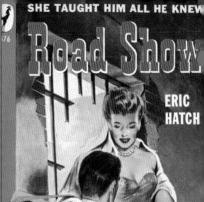

SHE TAUGHT HIM ALL HE KNEW

**Road Show**

ERIC HATCH

A DIFFERENT KIND OF MYSTERY THRILL!

**Shot in the Dark**

751

23 astounding
stories that are
out of this world

A BANTAM BOOK

356

*She dialed..* D-E-A-T-H

**SORRY,
WRONG NUMBER**

ALLAN ULLMAN &
LUCILLE FLETCHER

BARBARA STANWYCK and
BURT LANCASTER star in
the Hal Wallis production
"SORRY, WRONG NUMBER"
released by
Paramount Pictures

A BANTAM BOOK · COMPLETE & UNABRIDGED

## SHOT IN THE DARK
**EDITED BY JUDITH MERRIL**
**BANTAM BOOKS, 1950**
**COVER BY H. E. BISCHOFF**

Designed to fool readers
into thinking it was a book
of detective stories, Merril's
early PBO anthology remains
one of the finest science fiction
collections ever published.

## SORRY, WRONG NUMBER
**ALLAN ULLMAN AND LUCILLE FLETCHER**
**BANTAM BOOKS, 1948**
**COVER BY GILBERT DARLING**

Here is a nice MTI with Barbara
Stanwyck doing her best to look
terrified.

## ROAD SHOW
**ERIC HATCH**
**BANTAM BOOKS, 1949**
**COVER BY FRITZ WILLIS**

The novel of carnival life and jail-
breaking is written by the author
of *My Man Godfrey*.

## STEP RIGHT UP!
**DAN MANNIX**
**BANTAM BOOKS, 1952**
**COVER BY HARRY SCHAARE**

The author used the more formal Daniel P. Mannix on most of his books. The book is another prize for the carnival-theme collector.

📖

## TAMERLANE
**HAROLD LAMB**
**BANTAM, 1955**

This one in Lamb's series of biographies of great conquerors of history is remarkably readable.

📖

## STRANGERS ON A TRAIN
**PATRICIA HIGHSMITH**
**BANTAM BOOKS, 1951**
**COVER BY STANLEY ZUCKERBERG**

Highsmith's classic novel of a murder swap, this Bantam paperback was released the same year as Hitchcock's classic adaptation but is not an MTI.

📖📖

## TOMBOY
HAL ELLSON
BANTAM BOOKS, 1951, 1957, 1965
COVERS BY ROBERT MAGUIRE, MITCHELL HOOKS, JAMES BAMA
Three versions of this JD novel by the king of gang
fiction show changing styles of hair and clothing—
social history before your very eyes!

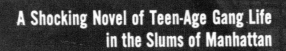

## TRAIL BOSS
PETER DAWSON
BANTAM BOOKS, 1946
The striking and very un-pulplike cover on this early
Bantam western is still effective and modern in effect.

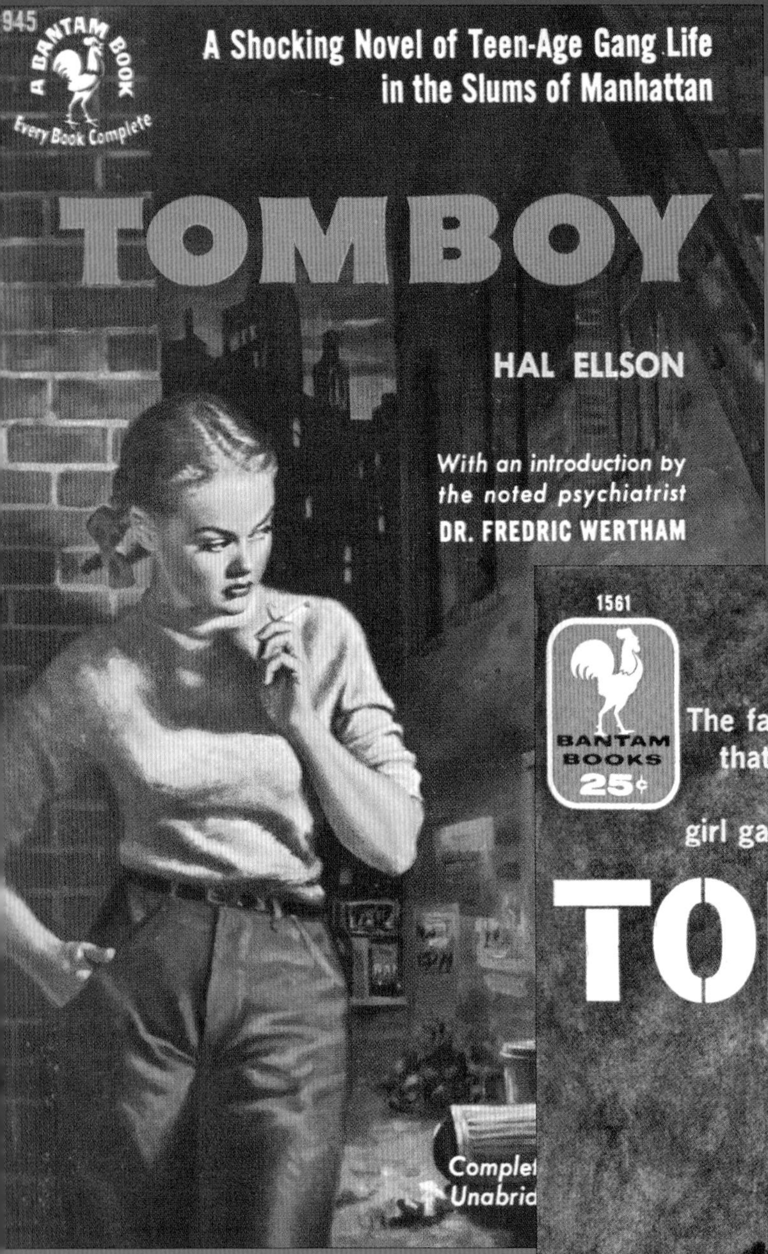

945
A BANTAM BOOK
Every Book Complete

A Shocking Novel of Teen-Age Gang Life
in the Slums of Manhattan

# TOMBOY

### HAL ELLSON

*With an introduction by
the noted psychiatrist*
**DR. FREDRIC WERTHAM**

Comple
Unabri

F3067 ★ 50¢

Tomboy
by Hal Ellson
The famous novel of
juvenile delinquency
OVER 1,000,000 COPIES IN PRINT

1561

BANTAM
BOOKS
25¢

### HAL ELLSON
AUTHOR OF DUKE

The famous novel of juvenile delinquency
that made millions gasp—the utterly
revealing story of a teen-age
girl gang-leader in the slums of New York

# TOMBOY

6TH BIG BANTAM PRINTING

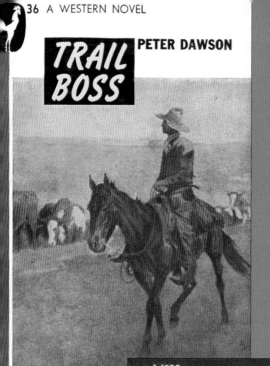

PETER DAWSON

TRAIL BOSS

A BANTAM
COMPLETE AN

A 1262

A BANTAM
GIANT

35¢

925

NERO WOLFE does the impossible!

REX STOUT

Trouble in Triplicate

**3** of the toughest cases ever cracked
by America's favorite detective

COMPLET

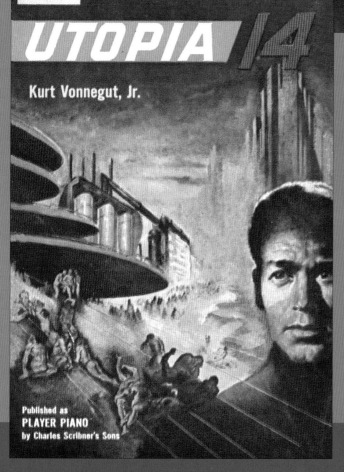

MAN'S REVOLT AGAINST
A GLITTERING, MECHANIZED
TOMORROW

UTOPIA 14

Kurt Vonnegut, Jr.

Published as
PLAYER PIANO
by Charles Scribner's Sons

83

Up Front

Bill Mauldin

A BANTAM BOOK
COMPLETE AND UNABRIDGED

## UTOPIA 14
**KURT VONNEGUT, JR.**
**BANTAM BOOKS, 1953**

This retitling of Vonnegut's first novel, *Player Piano*, looks a lot more like a standard science fiction adventure in a dystopian future than the bitterly funny social satire that it really is. It exists both as Bantam 1262 and A1262; priority unknown.

## TROUBLE IN TRIPLICATE
**REX STOUT**
**BANTAM BOOKS, 1951**
**COVER BY HARRY SCHAARE**

Early on, Stout was published by many paperback houses. Eventually he found a home at Bantam Books, and a quarter century after the author's death he is still in print from Bantam and still widely beloved.

## UP FRONT
**BILL MAULDIN**
**BANTAM BOOKS, 1947**
**COVER BY BILL MAULDIN**

The great cartoonist's pictorial memoir of World War II was his way of coping with the horrors of combat, and brought that reality home to millions who never saw the inside of a foxhole. Those are Mauldin's two G.I. Everymen, Willie and Joe, on the cover.

It was not until 1934 that Stout introduced his detective team of Nero Wolfe and Archie Goodwin in *Fer-de-Lance*. They were a great hit, and Stout would eventually write some seventy of their cases, both in novels and in shorter versions.

This remarkable and admirable man also took time to write several other books, to participate in the creation of the progressive publisher Vanguard Press, to perform war work as a civilian (he was too old to don a uniform), and to take up the cudgels against J. Edgar Hoover's FBI during the McCarthy era. That last took great courage.

The appeal of Wolfe and Goodwin has fascinated critics and scholars for almost seventy years. Wolfe's brownstone house on West 35th Street in Manhattan is as familiar and as beloved to millions of fans as Sherlock Holmes' lodgings at 221b Baker Street in London. Stout himself has been the subject of a full-scale biography and Nero Wolfe of another. Stout's famous creations have appeared on the radio, in motion pictures, and on television.

One theory as to their popularity is that the stories straddle the chasm between old-style genteel detection and modern hardboiled crime-fighting. Wolfe is cast very much in the mold of the eccentric, brilliant detective—a tradition created by Edgar Allan Poe, perfected by Arthur Conan Doyle, and imitated by hundreds of authors over the past century or more. Wolfe is grotesquely fat, spends four hours a day with the orchids in his "plant rooms," eats gargantuan portions of gourmet delicacies, and quaffs beer endlessly. He is a self-described genius and a petulant tyrant.

In some ways, he resembles Ian Ballantine.

Archie Goodwin, Wolfe's legman and amanuensis, is a slang-talking, sharp-dressing, womanizing wise-guy. Yes, he *does* carry a concealed firearm, and he uses his fists when he likes and his revolver when he must.

Whether it was this surprising amalgam of contradictory traditions, the ingenuity of the cases, or some other factor that made the books a success, they have retained their popularity to this day. In recent years Bantam has undertaken to republish the Wolfe canon, and a number of other Rex Stout books, issuing and reissuing the titles in rotation; one would hope, in perpetuity.

Another publisher, Carroll & Graf, has mined ancient pulp files for Stout stories and issued a set of his scarce, early works in paperback.

Bantam Books was a success, but the offices of the company were the scene of almost constant turmoil. Ian Ballantine was a serious bookman and a brilliant publisher but he was headstrong and often inflexible, even abrasive, in his dealings with colleagues.

Bantam was supposed to be "his" company, but in fact he owned only nine percent of its stock. Even if Sidney Kramer and Walter Pitkin threw in with him, their voting bloc amounted to just fifteen percent. The other eighty-five percent was divided equally between Grosset & Dunlap and Curtis, Bantam's distributor. The board of directors was loaded with other talented but strongwilled veteran publishers: Cerf, Scribner, Canfield. Curtis pushed Ballantine to concentrate on sure money-makers. Cerf, Scribner, Canfield, and Grossett's O'Connor all had their ideas of what Bantam should be doing and how it should be doing it.

By 1952, Ian Ballantine had had all he could take. He left Bantam, repeating his act of seven years before when he had left American Penguin to create Ballantine and Company. This time he and his wife, Betty, created Ballantine Books, which of course is another chapter.

Bantam surely felt the shock of Ballantine's departure, but it had its back-list, its talented staff, its powerful backers, and its prestigious directors. It took Bantam a while to right itself, but once it did it went right on crowing.

Half a century later it is the paperback bellwether of Bantam-Doubleday-Dell. It has its own hardcover line and is well financed. Its books are beautifully designed, carefully manufactured, effectively marketed, and very well distributed. It might be realistic for Bantam to change its symbol from the familiar feisty, crowing rooster to the six-hundred pound gorilla of the paperback world.

**THE WILD BUNCH**
**ERNEST HAYCOX**
**BANTAM BOOKS, 1949**
**COVER BY NORMAN SAUNDERS**

The *actual* Wild Bunch was portrayed decades later in
the film *Butch Cassidy and the Sundance Kid*. This earlier fictitious outlaw gang makes for good reading but bears little resemblance to reality.

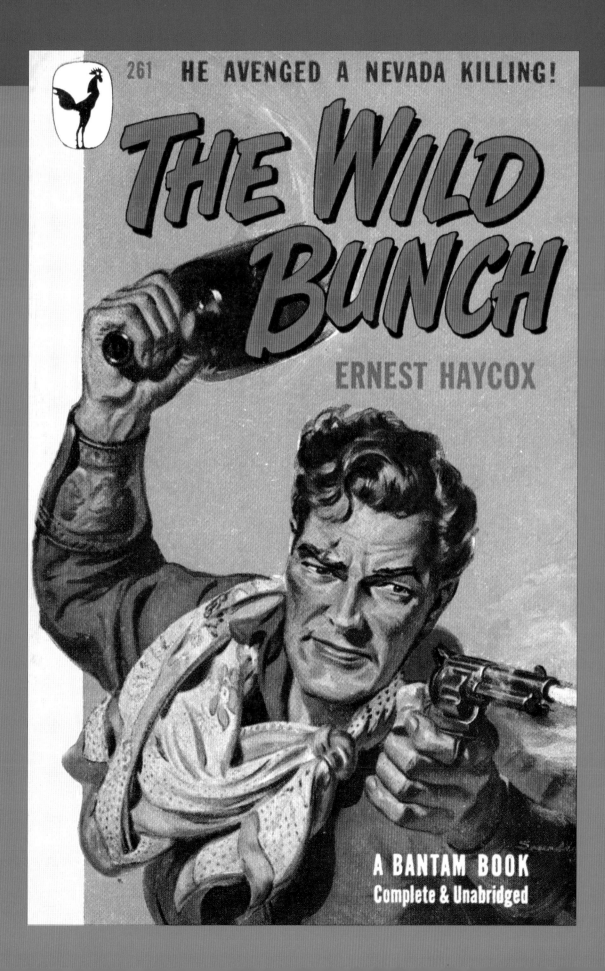

261    HE AVENGED A NEVADA KILLING!

# THE WILD BUNCH

## ERNEST HAYCOX

**A BANTAM BOOK**
Complete & Unabridged

639

GOLD
MEDAL
BOOK

25c

Chapter Seven

# A MEDAL FOR
# CAPTAIN BILLY

## GORDON D. SHIRREFFS
### Author of RIO BRAVO

The story of Fawcett Publications is a classic. The company started as a family business, the creation of Wilford Fawcett, a Minnesota farm boy who found himself, probably to his great surprise, bogged down in the trench warfare of World War I. A young officer, Fawcett started a humor magazine called *Captain Billy's Whiz-Bang*. It was named for an artillery shell known to the troops for coming in with a *whiz* followed by its explosion —*bang*.

In the years after the war, Fawcett was joined by his brother, Roger, and eventually by four younger Fawcetts. The little humor magazine was spiced up with pin-up photos that were tame by today's standards but considered risque in the 1920s. Numerous successful magazines joined *Captain Billy's Whiz-Bang*: *Mechanix Illustrated*, *True*, *Motion Picture*, *Woman's Day*, and others. Fawcett added a pulp line, led by *Triple-X*, originally a "variety pulp" ("Air-War-West"), later a specialized Western. Fawcett was also one of the leading comic book publishers, with a line of superheroes including Captain Marvel, Spy Smasher, Bulletman, Commando Yank, and Ibis the Invincible. These in turn led to a series of four Fawcett Dime Action Books, more like Big Little Books than the Dell Dimers.

By the late 1940s Fawcett had set up a distribution system that reached newsstands and other outlets throughout the country. They had become the distributor of the New American Library paperbacks and had great success with these.

As NAL's distributor, Fawcett had access to the numbers of NAL's print runs, copies distributed, and sell-through and return numbers. These were very impressive. In fact, Fawcett decided that they would like to publish their own mass paperback line. But there was a problem: Fawcett's contract with NAL prevented Fawcett from competing with NAL.

But Fawcett could slide around this prohibition if they published originals rather than reprints, and thus was born the Fawcett Gold Medal line. Important editors were longtime Fawcett employee Ralph Daigh, William Lengle, and later, coming from Dell, Knox Burger. The reason for Burger's defection is shrouded in mystery, but the domineering influence of Helen Meyer was most likely a factor.

Fawcett started with a couple of trial balloons. The very first was a non-fiction anthology, *The Best from True*. The second was *Marriage and Sex*, a non-fiction anthology from *Today's Woman*.

Gold Medal numbering began at 101 with a PBO titled *We Are the Public Enemies* by Alan Hynd (actually the third Fawcett Gold Medal book). Fawcett Gold Medal Books established a personality immediately.

We've already seen the almost schizophrenic division in American paperback publishing. On the one hand there were the publishers who sought to bring great reading to the masses: the English Allen Lane, his American surrogate Ian Ballantine, Victor Weybright, and Robert de Graff. On the other hand there were the populist, pulp-oriented executives and editors at Avon, Popular Library, Dell (and Aaron Wynn and company, whom we will meet shortly, with Ace Books).

Fawcett came down emphatically on the populist side. The packages on Gold Medal Books were sensational, and most of them could have come directly from pulp magazines. In fact, the very term "pulp paperback" has come into common use as a reference to the notion that some lines of paperbacks were at least a spiritual and esthetic continuation of the dying pulp magazines.

The Gold Medal covers were bright and action-filled. Leading painters were Stanley Meltzoff, Barye Phillips, Walter Baumhofer, Robert Maguire, Mitchell Hooks, Robert Abbett, Stanley Zuckerberg, Robert McGinnis, and Richard Powers. Each cover featured a stylized gold medal, Fawcett's answer to Pocket's Gertrude the Kangaroo, Avon's Shakespeare head, and Dell's famous keyholes.

The cover paintings were highly representational; the images were familiar: Snarling tough guys in fedoras, blazing gats in hand; beautiful women in tight costumes and low-cut blouses; unshaven cowboys on sweating cayuses. They could have come directly from pulp magazines. The books were immensely successful. A set of early Gold Medals, perhaps the first hundred, would represent a spectrum of genre illustration worthy of art gallery exhibition.

Powers was the exception. In later years he would become the trademark artist for Ballantine science fiction and for other publishers' science fiction lines. In Powers' paintings the traditional, almost photorealistic scenes of spaceships, planetscapes, and aliens were replaced by ragged-looking, semi-abstract images. Some fans hated these images, others applauded them, but no one was neutral and no one failed to notice them.

The selection of books was just what you'd expect of Fawcett's canny, talented, populist-oriented, pulp-based editorial staff. Top choices for Fawcett were mysteries, and there was no mincing words about the mystery story as intellectual exercise or of sweet little old ladies turned amateur sleuth. Fawcett featured Edward Ronns/Edward Aarons, Theodore Pratt, Bruno Fischer, Cornell Woolrich, Octavus Roy Cohen, Wade Miller, A. S. Fleischmann, Gil Brewer, Day Keene, and Howard Hunt (who would achieve notoriety as an operative deeply involved in the Watergate scandal that led to the downfall of Richard Nixon).

But the Big Two of Gold Medal Books were John D. MacDonald and Richard S. Prather.

A native Pennsylvanian who would eventually settle and write in the Sarasota, Florida area, John Dann MacDonald was a paradox and yet a perfect fit for the fledgling Gold Medal line. MacDonald was highly educated, with an M.B.A degree from Harvard University, and an intelligence officer in the United States Army throughout World War II, rising to the rank of lieutenant colonel.

He had his choice of careers. He could have remained in the military and would almost certainly have wound up with stars on his shoulders; he could have gone into business and become a huge success; or he could have returned to academia and become a distinguished professor.

None of these appealed to him. Instead, he chose to become a pulp fiction writer. Late in his career he spoke of the rejection slips he'd received when he was starting out: "I papered a whole office with them." That would surely have been a unique bit of wallpaper. And did those slips survive? "Oh no. I've painted it over since then. They were depressing."

But MacDonald persisted and eventually sold to a wide variety of magazines ranging from *Weird Tales* and *FBI Detective Cases* to *Planet Stories* and *Galaxy Science Fiction*. He even wrote a few westerns, and he cracked the pages of the legendary *Black Mask*. This was after the magazine's glory days under the editorship of the legendary Joseph Shaw, but ironically Shaw was MacDonald's literary agent at one time.

CREST BOOK
191

**1st PRIZE**
Best Mystery Novel
of the Year!
MWA AWARD

25

# A DRAM
# OF POISON

## CHARLOTTE ARMSTRONG

S1047
GOLD
MEDAL
BOOK

35¢

# ANGEL'S FLIGHT

**LOU
CAMERON**

erybody—
ging novel
nty years!"
THORNHILL

CREST BOOK
299

35¢

EST
OK

# Venus
# in Sparta

LOUIS AUCHINCLOSS

ve, marriage and infidelity
dern Manhattan…"Penetrating
and utterly absorbing."
— Boston Herald

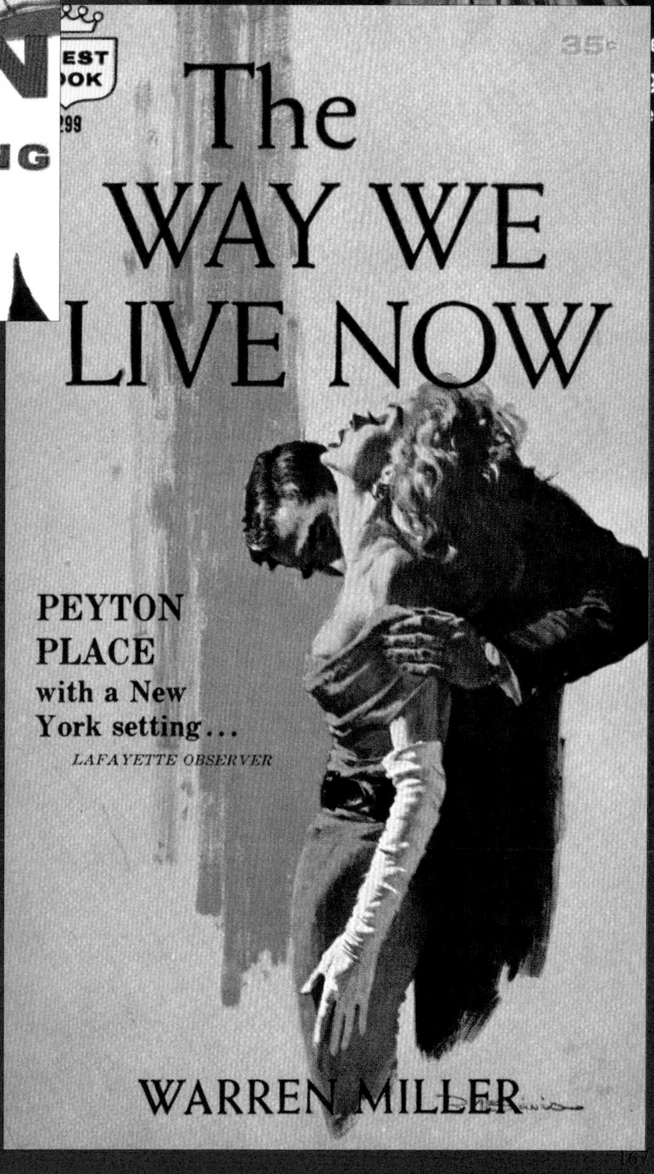

35¢

# The
# WAY WE
# LIVE NOW

PEYTON
PLACE
with a New
York setting…
*LAFAYETTE OBSERVER*

## WARREN MILLER

## ASSIGNMENT: MARA TIRANA

**EDWARD AARONS**
FAWCETT GOLD MEDAL, 1960
COVER BY ROBERT MCGINNIS

Edward Aarons (1916-1975) turned out thirty of his Sam Durrell "Assignment" novels, and that was only one aspect of this hard-working crafts-man's production! This almost-science fiction PBO features a McGinnis semi-nude painting, splendid as ever.

📖📖

## BAD DAY AT BLACK ROCK

**MICHAEL NIALL**
FAWCETT GOLD MEDAL, 1954
COVER BY BARYE PHILLIPS

Count Spencer Tracy's arms in this MTI/PBO. Have you ever seen the movie?

📖📖

## THE BEATS

**EDITED BY SEYMOUR KRIM**
FAWCETT GOLD MEDAL, 1960

This is a truly fine and quite important PBO anthology of writers whose works and reputa-tions are still relevant. Look at those names: Kerouac, Mailer, Ginsberg, Ferlinghetti. This one's a keeper!

📖📖📖

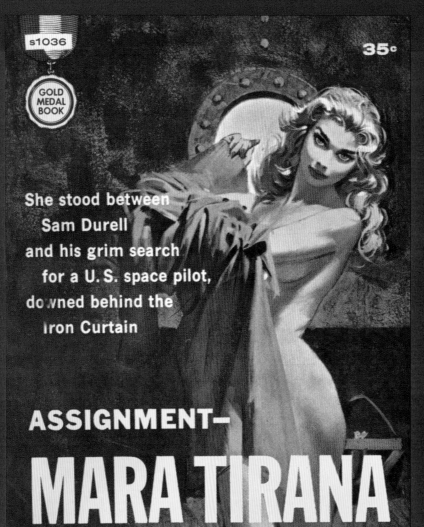

s1036

GOLD MEDAL BOOK

35¢

She stood between Sam Durell and his grim search for a U.S. space pilot, downed behind the Iron Curtain

ASSIGNMENT—
MARA TIRANA
EDWARD S. AARONS

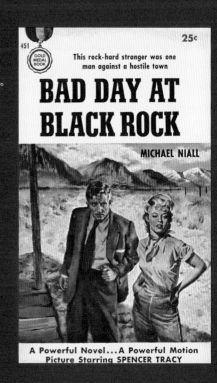

451 GOLD MEDAL BOOK

25¢

This rock-hard stranger was one man against a hostile town

BAD DAY AT BLACK ROCK
MICHAEL NIALL

A Powerful Novel...A Powerful Motion Picture Starring SPENCER TRACY

Here are the most vital and controversial writers on the American scene

THE BEATS

Raw, penetrating stories, poems and social criticism by JACK KEROUAC
NORMAN MAILER
ALLEN GINSBERG
LAWRENCE FERLINGHETTI
and many others

Edited by Seymour Krim

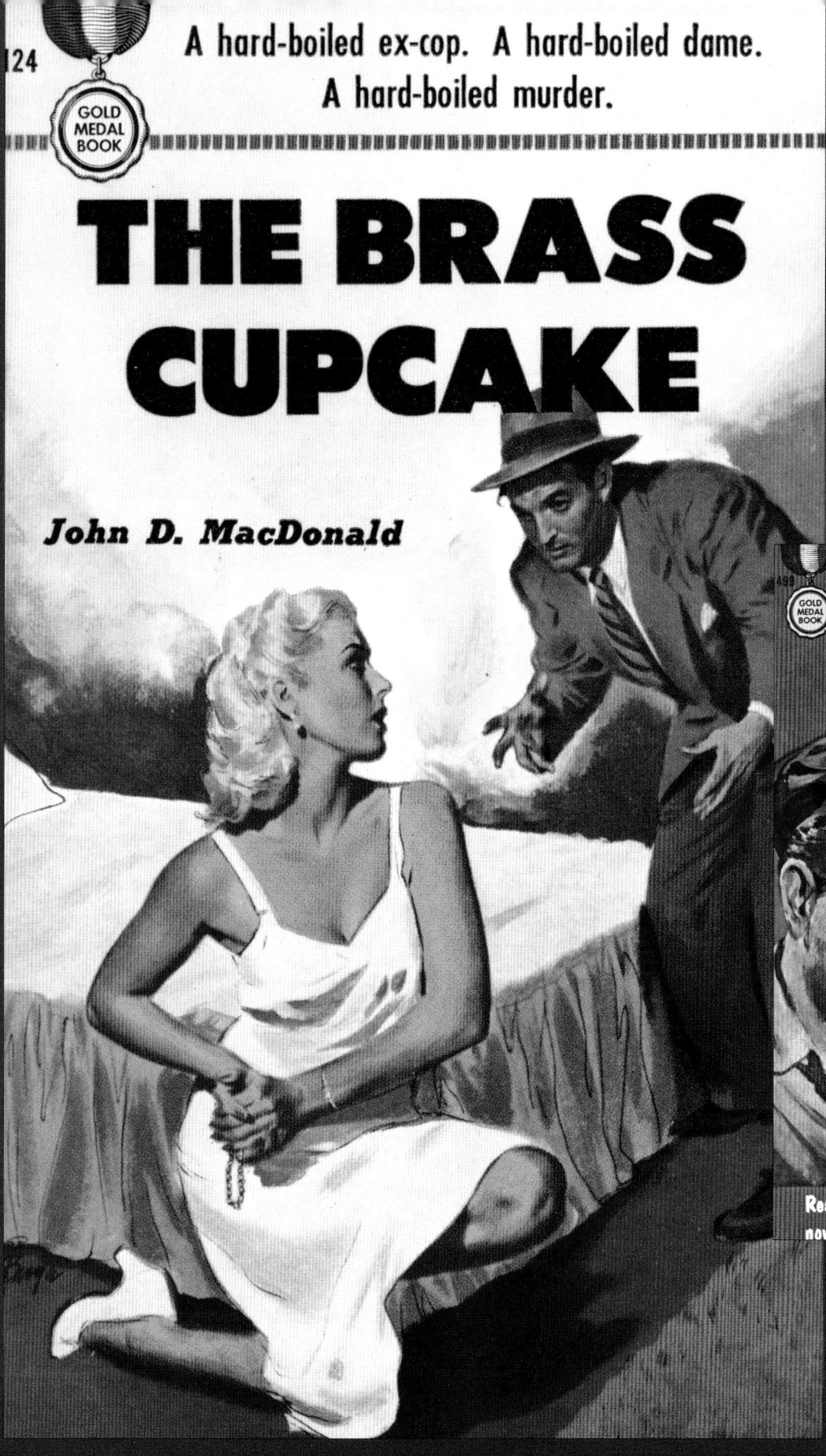

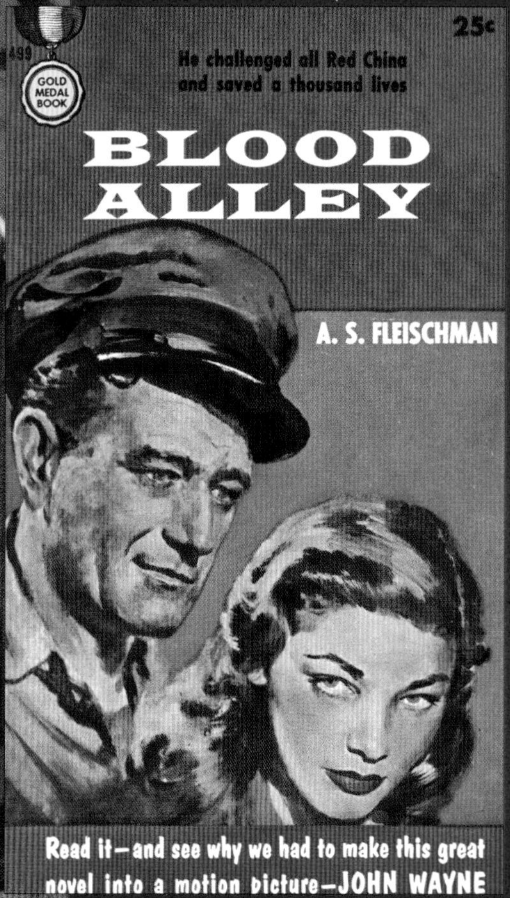

A hard-boiled ex-cop. A hard-boiled dame.
A hard-boiled murder.

124

GOLD MEDAL BOOK

# THE BRASS CUPCAKE

John D. MacDonald

25¢

499

GOLD MEDAL BOOK

He challenged all Red China
and saved a thousand lives

# BLOOD ALLEY

A. S. FLEISCHMAN

Read it—and see why we had to make this great
novel into a motion picture—JOHN WAYNE

## THE BRASS CUPCAKE
**JOHN D. MACDONALD**
**FAWCETT GOLD MEDAL, 1950**
**COVER BY BARYE PHILLIPS**

Who would have known that John D. MacDonald, a pulp
writer who tackled everything from westerns to science
fiction and detective yarns, would become one of the
world's most popular (and most collected) authors when
this hardboiled PBO appeared?

## BLOOD ALLEY
**A. S. FLEISCHMAN**
**FAWCETT GOLD MEDAL, 1955**
**COVER BY BARYE PHILLIPS**

Here's a PBO/MTI to make the hearts of John Wayne
or Lauren Bacall fans throb!

Perhaps it was MacDonald's training at Harvard that influenced him to work out royalty numbers and to decide that it was more advantageous to write paperback originals than it was to sell hardcover rights to his novels. He was a methodical and prolific writer with a distinctly populist appeal, yet he won literary prizes in both the United States and Europe and was awarded the degree of Doctor of Human Letters by several universities.

He placed his first novel, *The Brass Cupcake* (1950), with Gold Medal, and stayed with them for ten books. Eventually he sold novels elsewhere but always returned to Fawcett, even in later years when he did sell hardcover rights and Fawcett had gone into the reprint business. MacDonald went on to a long and productive career, including almost seventy PBOs. His last novel, *Barrier Island*, was published in 1986, the year of his death. Since then his works continue to be repackaged, reissued, and enthusiastically read and collected.

MacDonald's huge output of PBOs continued until 1958 when Simon & Schuster issued *The Executioners* (successfully filmed as *Cape Fear* in 1962 and again in 1991). Even then, Fawcett obtained reprint rights and issued a paperback edition in 1962.

Most of MacDonald's books were hardboiled mysteries, executed with a sure hand and razor-sharp insight into human emotions. They often bordered on the *conte cruel*, a time-honored story form in which the author creates a sympathetic character only put him (or her) through a series of harrowing experiences while the readers sit on the edge of their chairs, biting their fingernails in vicarious anxiety. MacDonald's heroes, sometimes private eyes, sometimes innocent citizens in peril, suffered their fair share of beatings and shootings. They consumed their share of alcohol and encountered more than their share of beautiful women (sometimes willing and sometimes not).

In 1962 Gold Medal published *The Girl, the Gold Watch, and Everything*, a PBO in which MacDonald returned to science fiction. His early pulp production had included two science fiction novels, *Wine of the Dreamers* (also published as *Planet of the Dreamers*) and *Ballroom of the Skies*. These were first published in *Startling Stories* and then as hardcover books in the early 1950s. They eventually became Fawcett paperback reprints.

But *The Girl, the Gold Watch, and Everything* was MacDonald's only PBO science fiction novel, although MacDonald referred to it as "a fantasy, wish-fulfillment sort of thing… I think it's more, I think, of the Thorne Smith genre than anything else."

In 1964 Gold Medal published MacDonald's *The Deep Blue Good-bye*, and with this novel he struck pure gold. The book introduced Travis McGee, a self-styled "salvage consultant"; in effect an unlicensed private eye. McGee lived on a boat, the *Busted Flush*, berthed in Bahia Mar, Florida, an imaginary town remarkably resembling Sarasota. Like MacDonald, McGee was a war veteran, although as the years passed it became unclear as to which war McGee had served in (World War II, the Korean War, or Vietnam).

McGee's best friend was the bear-like Meyer, a professional economist based on MacDonald himself. McGee claimed to have taken early retirement and to take his retirement in pieces. Whenever he was in danger of running out of funds he would accept a salvage operation, claim a portion of the recovered amount as his fee, and then retire again.

To a degree, McGee was a throwback to the "eccentric sleuth" as created by Edgar Allan Poe in C. August Dupin and perfected by Arthur Conan Doyle in Sherlock Holmes. The eccentric sleuth was used by Willard Huntington Wright (S. S. Van Dine) in his Philo Vance stories, by John Dickson Carr in his Gideon Fell novels, by Agatha Christie in her Hercule Poirot series, and by Rex Stout in his Nero Wolfe books. In fact there were scores of eccentric sleuths in the pages of detective fiction throughout the nineteenth and twentieth centuries.

But they usually appeared in genteel, intellectual fiction. Hardboiled heroes — Carroll John Daly's Race Williams, Dashiell Hammett's Sam Spade, Raymond Chandler's Philip Marlowe — were usually much more straightforward men, their lives stripped of quirks and peculiarities.

Travis McGee had quirks galore. There were his odd choice of profession and his peculiar attitude toward retirement. He lived on a boat. He drove an electric-blue Rolls Royce which he had converted (perhaps a better word would be "perverted") into a pickup truck. He had a favorite brand of gin. He referred to himself as a knight in rusty armor. MacDonald said that he always knew where a Travis McGee adventure was going to start and end, but he did not plan the path between starting and ending points. In writing that, he simply followed the trail of characters and events.

Some critics prefer MacDonald's one-off novels and consider the McGee books as little more than yard goods, but the readers loved them. MacDonald responded to the demand for more McGee, following *The Deep Blue Good-bye* with *Nightmare in Pink*, *A Purple Place for Dying*, *The Quick Red Fox*, *A Deadly Shade of Gold*, *Bright Orange for a Shroud*, *Darker than Amber*, and *One Fearful Yellow Eye* — eight Travis McGee novels, all Gold Medal PBOs, between 1964 and 1966. Eventually there would be a total of twenty-one McGee novels — the last of them, *A Lonely Silver Rain*, published in 1985.

MacDonald was unique: a brilliant, prolific, compelling, always conscientious, always readable writer. He was one of the last and greatest gifts of the pulp magazine tradition to the world of books.

The other great pillar of Gold Medal was Richard S. Prather. As MacDonald defected, for a time, to Dell, Prather defected to Pocket Books. Unlike MacDonald, who returned to Fawcett's open arms, Prather was to become embroiled in a protracted lawsuit with his new publisher. He would retire from the world of books and become an avocado farmer in California for eleven years before returning to the newsstands as a Tor author in 1986.

Richard Scott Prather, a native Californian, was born in 1921. He served in the Merchant Marines in World War Two. His first book, *Case of the Vanishing Beauty* (1950), was a Gold Medal PBO and it introduced Prather's Southern California private eye, Shell Scott.

It's not easy to pin down the Scott character. At times the Scott character seemed to be a serious private eye, cast in the classic mold of Sam Spade. He was muscular and tough, with prematurely white hair that he wore in short, military style. He lived alone in a Hollywood apartment, was a hard drinker and an enthusiastic woman chaser. He had the common private eye's ability to engage in the most ferocious bout of fisticuffs, drag himself home a battered wreck of a man, get a good night's sleep, and awake ready to take on the world all over again.

But he raised tropical fish. And he had a huge and hideous nude painting on the wall of his home.

His capers were sometimes so silly that reading a Shell Scott novel was like reading an adventure of Robert Leslie Bellem's *Dan Turner, Hollywood Detective*. Yet at other times the puzzles, the suspense, and the action seemed quite serious.

Somehow Prather made it work, and book after book in the Shell Scott series hit the million-plus mark for Fawcett.

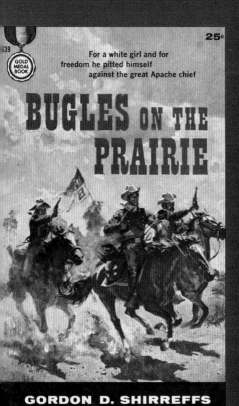

For a white girl and for freedom he pitted himself against the great Apache chief

25¢

GOLD MEDAL BOOK

# BUGLES ON THE PRAIRIE

## GORDON D. SHIRREFFS
### Author of RIO BRAVO

Meet Shell Scott, Fast with Gun or Gal
Fast with the Answer for Murder, Too...

127

GOLD MEDAL BOOK

# CASE OF THE VANISHING BEAUTY

Richard S.

She was lush
as the countrysid
as fertile—
and as hard to ta

GOLD MEDAL BOOK

611

# DESIRE IN THE DUST

## HARRY WHITTINGTON

25¢ Capt. Billy's OCT.

# Whiz Bang

A CORKING GOOD TIME!

---

## BUGLES ON THE PRAIRIE
**GORDON D. SHIRREFFS**
**FAWCETT GOLD MEDAL, 1957**
**COVER BY FRANK MCCARTHY**

Gordon Shirreffs returned from World War II, intending to write a history of the Civil War. Once into his studies he decided that he could express himself better in fiction, and turned out a series of solidly researched, complexly plotted, and extremely well-written westerns.

## CASE OF THE VANISHING BEAUTY
**RICHARD S. PRATHER**
**FAWCETT GOLD MEDAL, 1950**
**COVER BY DOWNES**

Prather introduced Shell Scott in this PBO, his first published novel. 1950 was a banner year for Gold Medal with Prather's and MacDonald's debuts, Torres' sensational *Women's Barracks*, Woolrich's *Savage Bride*, and Keyhoe's UFO book, all PBOs. This is a record unmatched by new publishers before or since.

## DESIRE IN THE DUST
**HARRY WHITTINGTON**
**FAWCETT GOLD MEDAL, 1956**
**COVER BY BARYE PHILLIPS**

Incredibly prolific and highly collected, Whittington wrote something like one hundred novels. About half his books are crime fiction, another third are westerns, and the remainder are a scattering of spy stories, "rurals," historicals, and novelizations. In his spare time he wrote motion picture and television scripts.

## CAPT. BILLY'S WHIZ BANG
**MAGAZINE, CIRCA 1920**

The ancestor of the Fawcett publishing empire was this little gags'n'gals magazine published by Wilford "Captain Billy" Fawcett. The *Whiz Bang* led to a string of pulp, confession, and slick magazines (*True*), comic books, and finally the great Gold Medal series of PBOs.

## DEVIL'S LEGACY

JOSEPH CHADWICK
FAWCETT GOLD MEDAL, 1952
COVER BY A. LESLIE ROSS

While Gold Medal was best known for its hardboiled mysteries, they maintained a sprinkling of westerns and other genres among the gangsters, gun molls, and private eyes.

◗

## DRUM BEAT—BERLIN

STEPHEN MARLOWE
FAWCETT GOLD MEDAL, 1964
COVER BY STANLEY ZUCKERBERG

Stephen Marlowe's earliest PBOs were published by Ace and Graphic, but he hit his stride with a series of tough, intelligent novels for Gold Medal. His Chester Drum series is of special interest; Zuckerberg's atmospheric painting for *Drum Beat —Berlin* evokes that city's Cold War tension.

◗◗◗

## THE FLYING SAUCERS ARE REAL

DONALD KEYHOE
FAWCETT GOLD MEDAL, 1950
COVER BY FRANK TINSLEY

Veteran fictioneer Donald E. Keyhoe emphasized his military record and pointedly ignored his career turning out pulp yarns of square-jawed heroes and sinister menaces when he wrote this classic UFO exposé. It was a huge best-seller when first issued and a key item in any ufological library.

◗◗

## FIND THIS WOMAN

RICHARD S. PRATHER
FAWCETT GOLD MEDAL, CIRCA 1972
COVER BY ROBERT MCGINNIS

Originally published in 1951, this Shell Scott PBO was part of a repackaged series featuring spectacular McGinnis covers. This is a must for the McGinnis collector, although Prather's first editions, many with fine Phillips covers, are also excellent.

◗◗◗

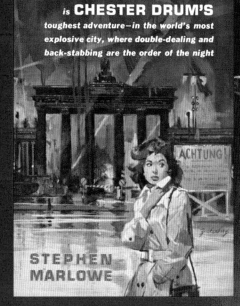

173

## THE GIRL IN THE RED VELVET SWING
**CHARLES SAMUELS**
FAWCETT GOLD MEDAL, 1953

Among Fawcett's innovations was a series of true crime books, all with titles beginning with *The Girl*… Charles Samuels' treatment describes the murder of architect Stanford White by millionaire playboy Harry K. Thaw over the love of showgirl Evelyn Nesbit. A wonderfully trashy film version was released in 1955.

## THE GIRL FROM MIDNIGHT
**WADE MILLER**
FAWCETT GOLD MEDAL, 1962
COVER BY ROBERT ABBETT

Collaborators Robert Wade and Bill Miller created an array of joint pseudonyms, the best known of which were Wade Miller and Whit Masterson. Most of their novels were grim and very much on the hardboiled side, although on occasion they would produce a remarkably lighthearted yarn, or conversely, turn to exploitation.

## THE GOLDFISH MURDERS
**WILL MITCHELL**
FAWCETT GOLD MEDAL, 1950

This book is one of the great mysteries of paperback history. It is not a great novel, but who was Will Mitchell? Who painted the cover? Gold Medal completists of course seek this book in competition with people who collect books with goldfish on the cover.

## HOUSE OF FLESH
**BRUNO FISCHER**
FAWCETT GOLD MEDAL, 1950

Born in Germany, Fischer emigrated to the United States as a small child. Under the name Russell Gray he was a prolific contributor to the "shudder pulps," magazines that specialized in gruesome horror stories. The cover painting for *House of Flesh* is among the most striking of early Gold Medals—if only the artist had signed his work!

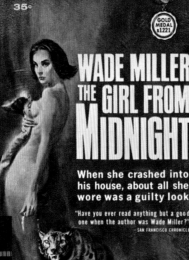

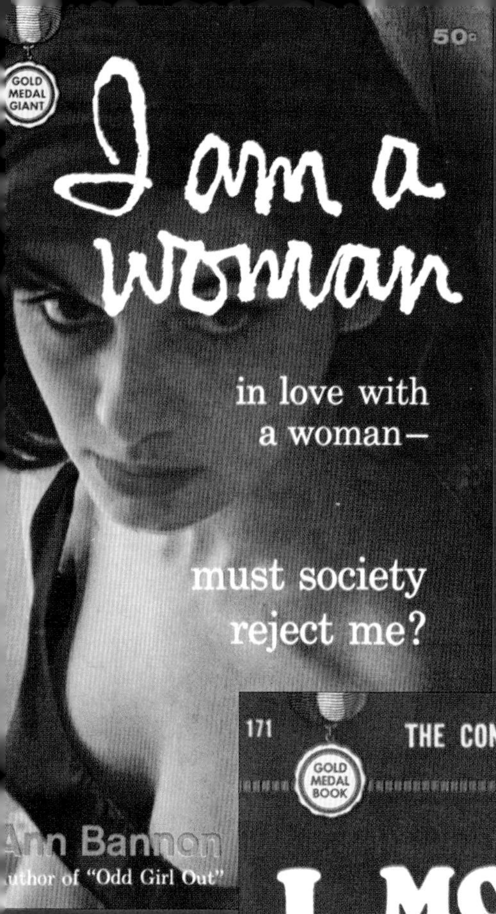

50¢

*I am a woman*

GOLD MEDAL GIANT

in love with
a woman—

must society
reject me?

Ann Bannon
author of "Odd Girl Out"

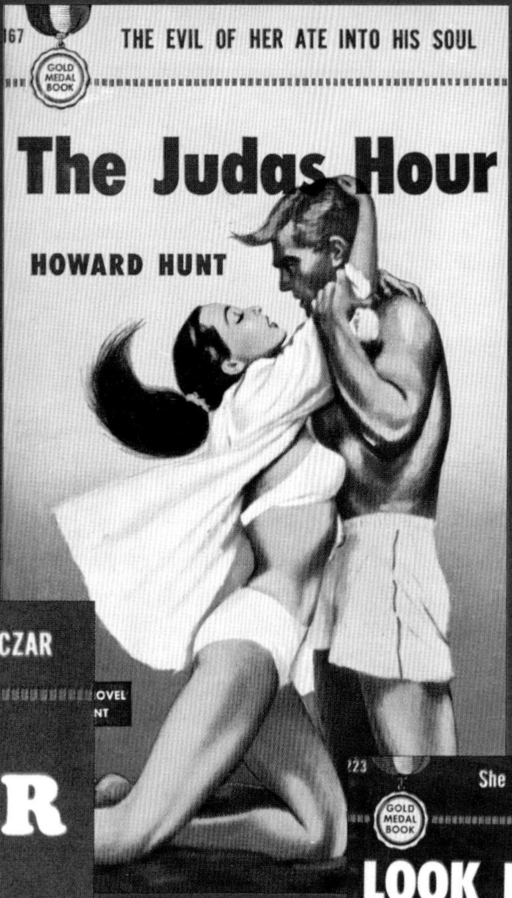

167

GOLD MEDAL BOOK

THE EVIL OF HER ATE INTO HIS SOUL

# The Judas Hour

HOWARD HUNT

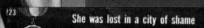

171

GOLD MEDAL BOOK

THE CONFESSION OF A CRIME CZAR

# I, MOBSTER

Anonymous

An original book—not a reprint

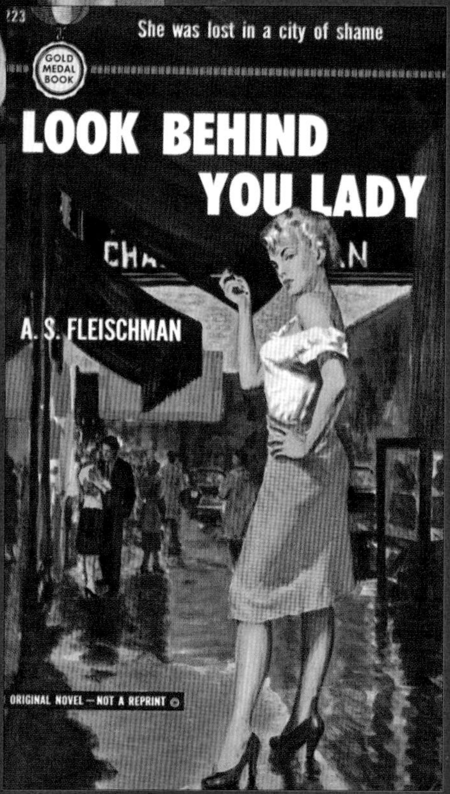

223

GOLD MEDAL BOOK

She was lost in a city of shame

# LOOK BEHIND YOU LADY

A. S. FLEISCHMAN

ORIGINAL NOVEL—NOT A REPRINT

## I AM A WOMAN
**ANN BANNON**
**FAWCETT GOLD MEDAL, 1959**

One of the most famous paperback covers (a photograph) for this Lesbian novel. Fawcett published quite a few of these books, and Fawcett executive Ralph Daigh was summoned onto the Congressional carpet to answer for it.

## I, MOBSTER
**ANONYMOUS**
**FAWCETT GOLD MEDAL, 1951**

The cover artist, as anonymous as the author, may or may not have been working from publicity stills of film stars Maureen O'Hara and Victor Mature when he painted this one

## THE JUDAS HOUR
**HOWARD HUNT**
**FAWCETT GOLD MEDAL, 1951**

Everette Howard Hunt, born 1918, wrote as Howard Hunt, John Baxter, Gordon Davis, Robert Dietrich, and David St. John. He turned up as a Nixon operative during the Watergate affair and his books were rediscovered for all the wrong reasons.

## LOOK BEHIND YOU LADY
**A. S. FLEISCHMAN**
**FAWCETT GOLD MEDAL, 1952**
**COVER BY SOL LEVINE**

Albert Sidney Fleischman was one of the many journeyman (and journeywoman) writers who produced PBOs for Ace, Fawcett, and other publishers. Never famous and perhaps not brilliant, these writers knew their craft and produced readable, intelligent books in impressive numbers.

**FREDRIC BROWN**
# MADBALL

s1132

35¢

GOLD MEDAL BOOK

Step right up, gents—
They're all alive inside.
Here's the sizzling classic
of carny life by the
celebrated author of
*The Fabulous Clipjoint,*
*The Screaming Mimi,* etc.

GOLD MEDAL k1276

40¢

# WALTER TEVIS

He made the lonely journey, leaving
behind a broken world and a promise
to rescue his fellow-beings from the
devastation their wars had wrought

# THE MAN WHO FELL TO EARTH

---

## MADBALL
**FREDRIC BROWN**
**FAWCETT GOLD MEDAL, 1961**
**COVER BY MITCHELL HOOKS**

This reissue of Brown's 1953 novel is collected
for Mitchell Hooks' provocative cover painting,
one of that talented artist's finest.

## THE MAN WHO FELL TO EARTH
**WALTER TEVIS**
**FAWCETT GOLD MEDAL, 1963**
**COVER BY LEO AND DIANE DILLON**

Walter Tevis (1928-1984) was equally at home
in the world of mainstream fiction (*The Hustler,*
*The Queen's Gambit*) and that of science fiction.
He once told an interviewer that this novel of a
strange, sensitive being stranded on a primitive
world was based on his own experience as a
child, when his family moved from bustling
San Francisco to a small town in Kentucky.

## MARRIAGE AND SEX
**FAWCETT PUBLICATIONS, 1949**

Fawcett tested the waters with two non-fiction
anthologies, one from *Today's Woman* magazine,
the other from *True,* before launching Gold
Medal Books. Not strictly Gold Medals, these
are important associational items.

## THE MOON IN THE GUTTER
DAVID GOODIS
FAWCETT GOLD MEDAL, 1953
COVER BY VICTOR OLSON

David Goodis (1917-1967) wrote magazine fiction for markets ranging from *Horror Stories* and *Western Tales* to *The Saturday Evening Post* as well as screenplays, radio scripts, and almost twenty novels. His skill and depth of commitment were great, as was, unfortunately, his unremitting pessimism. One look at Victor Olson's painting for this PBO tells you what you need to know.

## MOTHER NIGHT
KURT VONNEGUT, JR.
FAWCETT GOLD MEDAL, 1962
COVER BY LEO AND DIANE DILLON

Vonnegut accomplished that rare feat, writing genre fiction throughout his career yet gaining acceptance with mainstream critics and readers. His few PBOs (of which *Mother Night* is one) are in demand of almost fanatical intensity.

## WE NEVER CALLED HIM HENRY
HARRY BENNETT
FAWCETT GOLD MEDAL, 1951

An oddity for the company that made its fortune on private eyes, sexy babes, and the occasional lone cowhand, this is a pretty straightforward biography of one of the founders of the American automobile industry.

35¢

GOLD MEDAL s1191

KURT VONNEGUT, JR.

author of
CANARY IN A CAT HOUSE & THE SIRENS OF TITAN

*An American traitor's astonishing confession—mournful, macabre, diabolically funny—written with unnatural candor in a foreign death cell*

MOTHER NIGHT

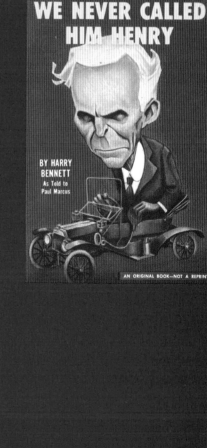

Ford—Giant and Genius
Pigmy and Puppet

GOLD MEDAL BOOK

WE NEVER CALLED HIM HENRY

BY HARRY BENNETT
As Told to
Paul Marcus

AN ORIGINAL BOOK—NOT A REPRINT

They met on the street of vagrant love,
the stevedore and the girl from uptown

GOLD MEDAL BOOK

THE MOON IN THE GUTTER

DAVID GOODIS
thor of STREET OF THE LOST

Prather turned out five Shell Scott PBOs in rapid succession for Gold Medal: *Case of the Vanishing Beauty* (1950), *Bodies in Bedlam* (1951), *Everybody Had a Gun* (1951), *Find this Woman* (1951), and *Way of a Wanton* (1952). Also in 1952 he did three one-offs: *Lie Down, Killer* (Lion), *Dagger of Flesh* (Falcon), and *The Peddler* (Lion), returning to Gold Medal with *Darling, It's Death* (1952).

The pace at which writers like Prather and MacDonald turned out their early novels is truly astonishing. They didn't just produce books in rapid-fire manner. The books themselves were populated with vivid characters, often complex plots, and always powerful writing.

Prather turned out some sixteen Shell Scott books for Gold Medal before defecting to Pocket Books in 1963. Fawcett had two more Shell Scott novels in inventory and published them in 1964; then Prather and Pocket Books spent a dozen years in a troubled relationship.

Collectors and bibliographers have to be careful with Prather books. Several of them appeared in more than one version, sometimes with Shell Scott as the protagonist, sometimes with a surrogate. Another oddity was the Gold Medal PBO *Double in Trouble* (1959), written in collaboration with Stephen Marlowe. In this novel Prather's Shell Scott works rather uncomfortably with Marlowe's series private eye, Chester Drum.

If Fawcett had published only the works of John D. MacDonald and Richard S. Prather in the 1950s, they would still have had an immensely popular and successful line. But of course they had many other authors.

Their army of tough-guy private eyes and gorgeous women was unmatched. Their line of western fiction was also strong, and the Westerns were gorgeously packaged. Their leading western authors included Les Savage, Jr. (*The Wild Horse*, 1950), Clifton Adams (*The Desperado*), Will F. Jenkins (*Dallas*, MTI), William Heuman (*Guns at Broken Bow*), Walt Grove (*Hell-Bent for Danger*), Logan Stewart (*War Bonnet Pass*), and Leslie Ernenwein (*Gunfighter's Return*)—all published in 1950!

But even there, Fawcett was not ready to draw the line. They published a series of PBOs by Sax Rohmer (Arthur S. Ward). An Englishman who moved to the United States in his later years, Rohmer had been an immensely popular and successful author of sensational fiction.

Born in 1883, Rohmer had worked as a journalist and in this capacity came to know the seamy underbelly of Edwardian London. He wrote songs for music-hall entertainers and then began a long career writing fiction for both slick-paper and pulp magazines. His first book, *The Mystery of Dr. Fu-Manchu*, was published in 1913. Fu Manchu (Rohmer dropped the hyphen after a few years) was the ultimate embodiment of the Yellow Peril. He was a suave, idealistic genius, convinced that only a universal dictatorship headed by himself could bring about a new Golden Age for the world. To achieve his aims he would use any means necessary, including blackmail, hypnosis, assassination, poison, and seduction. To accomplish the last he enlisted his breathtakingly lovely daughter, Fah Lo Suee. Dr. Fu Manchu's arch-rival was the Englishman, Sir Dennis Nayland Smith, assisted by the loyal but bumbling Dr. Petrie.

Does all of this sound vaguely familiar? It should—Rohmer had simply appropriated the imagery that Conan Doyle had established in the triad of Sherlock Holmes, Dr. Watson, and the malevolent genius Dr. Moriarty. But Rohmer placed his focus on the "Moriarty" figure—Dr. Fu Manchu—and downplayed his "Holmes" and "Watson" (Nayland Smith and Dr. Petrie).

Rohmer wrote dozens of other books, many of them with elements of fantasy and evoking the exoticism of the ancient civilizations of Egypt and China as well as the fog-shrouded mystery of London's Limehouse.

By 1950 Rohmer's formula was old and getting pretty creaky, so Rohmer made still another change to it. He dropped Fu Manchu and Nayland Smith—Dr. Petrie had disappeared from the series some years before—and shone his spotlight on a female Yellow Peril named Sumuru. She was as lovely and seductive as Fah Lo Suee—in fact, she might have been Fah Lo Suee under another name—and as brilliant and dangerous as Dr. Fu Manchu.

Gold Medal titled the book *Nude in Mink*. Whose idea was that? It's hardly a Rohmeresque title (the British edition was called *Sins of Sumuru*) but it evoked a suggestion of sexuality mixed with luxury and decadence, and it sold. Rohmer wrote five Sumuru novels, all Gold Medal PBOs and all luridly wonderful in a creaky, old-fashioned way. The covers were evocative, a fine example being *Return of Sumuru* (1954). It features a gorgeous painting of Sumuru herself, by the under-appreciated James Meese, and a blurb that says it all: *Every woman was her disciple and every man her slave.*

After five Sumuru novels, Rohmer brought his greatest villain out of retirement for two curtain calls: *Re-Enter Fu Manchu* (Gold Medal PBO, 1957) and *Emperor Fu-Manchu* (Gold Medal PBO, 1959). Rohmer died while his final novel was in press, seventy-six years old and turning out his wonderful, lurid thrillers to the end.

Rohmer did not create the Yellow Peril in literature, but he was the greatest exponent of this genre. In fact, Dr. Fu Manchu was so popular that a great many imitations were created by other authors. Any number of these appeared in pulp magazines, and at least two 1930s-era pulps were devoted entirely to Fu Manchu imitations. A former military man and prolific pulp writer named Donald Keyhoe was responsible for the adventures of one such clone, Dr. Yen Sin.

In 1950, thanks to a wonderful synchronicity, Keyhoe once again crossed paths with Sax Rohmer. The UFO craze was still in its infancy when Keyhoe wrote a Gold Medal PBO called *The Flying Saucers are Real*. The cover painting by Frank Tinsley shows three spacecraft, actually more oblong than disk-shaped, zooming above the earth and shooting out rays.

Flying saucer books were pouring from publishers' presses, and several of them made successful paperbacks. One highly collected example was Frank Scully's *Behind the Flying Saucers*, published by Popular Library in 1951 with a fine cover by science fiction veteran Earle Bergey.

But Keyhoe—and Gold Medal—got there first, and the book was a huge success. A patchwork of solid research, wild speculation, and pulp hokum, the book convinced armies of readers that hostile aliens were swooping overhead and maybe sneaking around our planet disguised as humans.

It was the era of Cold War paranoia, when Senator Joe McCarthy or some other politician or journalist was ready to warn us that there was a spy in every closet and a Communist lurking under every bed. Science fiction books like Jack Finney's *The Body Snatchers* (Dell, 1955), later filmed and reissued as *Invasion of the Body Snatchers*, would simultaneously play into this fear and replace the menace from the teeming hordes or the Evil Empire with invading monsters from outer space.

Fawcett's Gold Medal Books were an attractive market for writers, not only because those writers collected their whole royalty checks and didn't have to split them with hardcover publishers but also because Fawcett paid royalties based on print runs rather than actual sales.

In the early days of paperback publishing, almost all copies were sold. There was little competition for rack space and books simply remained on display until somebody bought them. But as

### RETURN OF SUMURU
**SAX ROHMER**
FAWCETT GOLD MEDAL, 1954
COVER BY JAMES MEESE

Rohmer's brilliant, gorgeous, seductive supervillainess was as hokey as all get-out, but was she ever fun! And who could resist Meese's GGA cover? Rohmer is collected, too.

### THE PERSIAN CAT
**JOHN FLAGG**
FAWCETT GOLD MEDAL, 1950
COVER BY DOWNES

John Gearon wrote at least one book under his own name and eight more as John Flagg, all eight Gold Medal PBOs. The model in Downes' splendid painting seems to have borrowed her pose from a famous Rita Hayworth pin-up photo.

### ROGUE MOON
**ALGIS BUDRYS**
FAWCETT GOLD MEDAL, 1960
COVER BY RICHARD POWERS

Arguably the best novel of Budrys' relatively sparse output, *Rogue Moon* struck the science fiction readership like a meteorite when it appeared as a PBO and has been a favorite, almost a cult novel, ever since.

### RIPE FRUIT
**JOHN MCPARTLAND**
FAWCETT GOLD MEDAL, 1958
COVER BY ERNEST CHIRIAKA

Another novel of the world of big business, big money, and beautiful women. A beautiful nude smiles seductively while smoking a cigarette. How 1950s can you get?

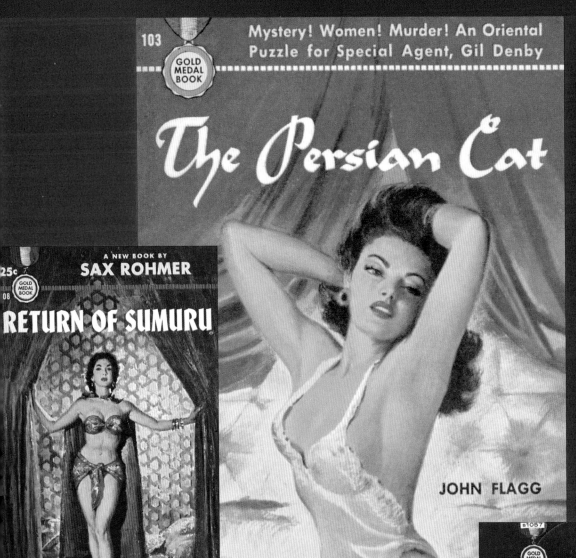

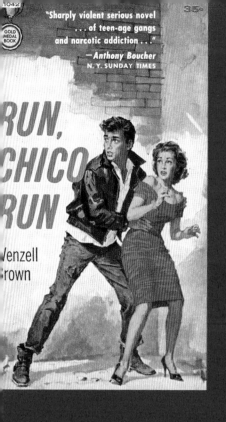

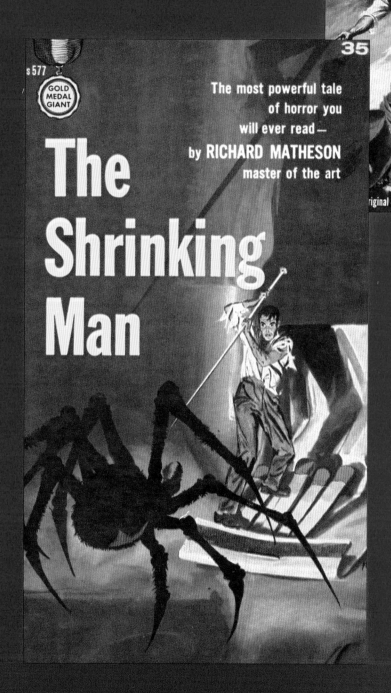

### RUN, CHICO RUN
WENZELL BROWN
FAWCETT GOLD MEDAL, 1960

The boy on the cover of this reissue of Brown's 1953 PBO is a splendid example of JD chic, 1950s style. Note his pompadour, leather jacket, torn jeans, biker boots. How is his girlfriend ever going to keep up in her tight skirt and stiletto heels? This is one of the mysteries of the universe!

### SAVAGE BRIDE
CORNELL WOOLRICH
FAWCETT GOLD MEDAL, 1950
COVER BY BARYE PHILLIPS

This is one of Woolrich's lesser efforts with little suspense and too much suggestion of fantasy without sufficient payoff. Still, it is an important book by a heavily collected author.

### THE SHRINKING MAN
RICHARD MATHESON
FAWCETT GOLD MEDAL, 1956
COVER BY MITCHELL HOOKS

This PBO by the highly talented and avidly collected Richard Matheson is one of the most desirable Gold Medals. When the novel was filmed as *The Incredible Shrinking Man,* Fawcett issued an MTI, also prized by tie-in collectors but otherwise relatively unimportant.

### SEMINOLE
THEODORE PRATT
FAWCETT GOLD MEDAL, 1964
COVER BY JOHN FLOHERTY, JR.

Floherty's startling painting exemplifies the rule of the era: women may be shown bare-breasted unless they are Caucasian; then they must be covered, however flimsily. How did this practice come about? Why? Leave it for the sociologists. Pratt was a good, solid writer, always worth reading.

**455** 25¢

GOLD MEDAL BOOK

UNCLE GOOD'S GIRLS hit the glory trail when the preacher comes to CABIN ROAD

# The Sin Shouter of Cabin Road

**JOHN FAULKNER**

**201**

GOLD MEDAL BOOK

Ride the plains with Johnny Colt who feared no man...and all women

# STAMPEDE

### YUKON MILES

AN ORIGINAL NOVEL—NOT A REPRINT

**222**

GOLD MEDAL BOOK

A story once told in whispers now frankly, honestly written

# SPRING FIRE

### Vin Packer

INAL NOVEL—NOT A REPRINT ©

## THE SIN SHOUTER OF CABIN ROAD

JOHN FAULKNER
FAWCETT GOLD MEDAL, 1945
COVER BY BARYE PHILLIPS

What goes around comes around. If Erskine Caldwell put his own spin on William Faulkner's South, then the great Mississippian's brother, John Faulkner, put his own counterspin back on it with a series of backwoods novels. Obviously not as famous as William, John Faulkner was not without talent, and his books make an interesting byway for the paperback collector.

## STAMPEDE

YUKON MILES
FAWCETT GOLD MEDAL, 1951
COVER BY A. LESLIE ROSS

This cover features one of the classic blurbs of all time: *Johnny Colt...feared no man...and all women.* It is strictly for the western collector.

## SPRING FIRE

VIN PACKER
FAWCETT GOLD MEDAL, 1952
COVER BY BARYE PHILLIPS

With Ann Bannon, Tereska Torres, and Vin Packer (Marijane Meaker) all producing PBOs for them, Gold Medal didn't corner the Lesbian market, but they did much to bring it into the mainstream. These books are highly collected today.

## THE WRECKING CREW
**DONALD HAMILTON**
FAWCETT GOLD MEDAL, 1960

Yes, that's Hamilton's tough adventure hero Matt Helm in the trenchcoat. Featured in a series of Hollywood potboilers with Dean Martin as a bibulous lightweight, Helm was actually a tougher and more serious cross between a secret agent and a hardboiled private eye. There were a slew of them at the time, and Hamilton's was really one of the best.

📖📖

## WOMEN'S BARRACKS
**TERESKA TORRES**
FAWCETT GOLD MEDAL, 1950
COVER BY BARYE PHILLIPS

This is the allegedly scandalous novel that got the Gathings Committee in such an uproar and is now highly collectible. This is the original version of the Phillips cover—it makes an interesting pairing with the tamed-down 1954 reissue.

📖📖 , 📖📖

## THE TORMENTED
**THEODORE PRATT**
FAWCETT GOLD MEDAL, 1950
COVER BY BARYE PHILLIPS

Here is one of the versatile and talented Phillips' earliest Gold Medal covers, for the versatile and talented Pratt's first Gold Medal PBO. While Pratt seems to be in a state of literary eclipse, his books remain both collectible and readable and he is definitely on the "A list" as a candidate for rediscovery.

📖📖

## THIS WOMAN
**ALBERT IDELL**
FAWCETT RED SEAL, 1952
COVER BY BARYE PHILLIPS

*This Woman* was apparently Idell's only book, but it was certainly successful for Fawcett, first as a Red Seal release and then reissued twice as a Gold Medal Book. Red Seal was a short-lived Fawcett line, apparently designed to break the 25¢ price barrier.

📖

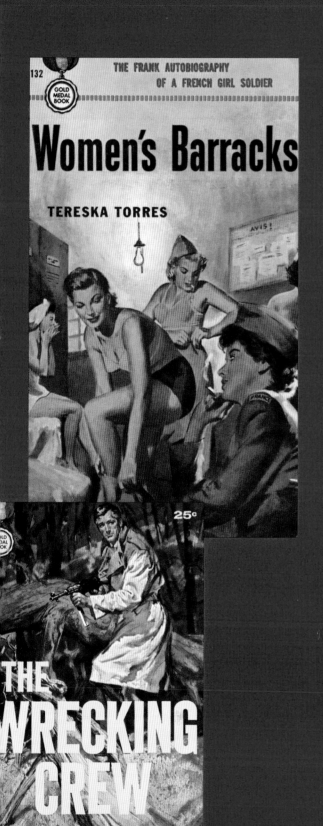

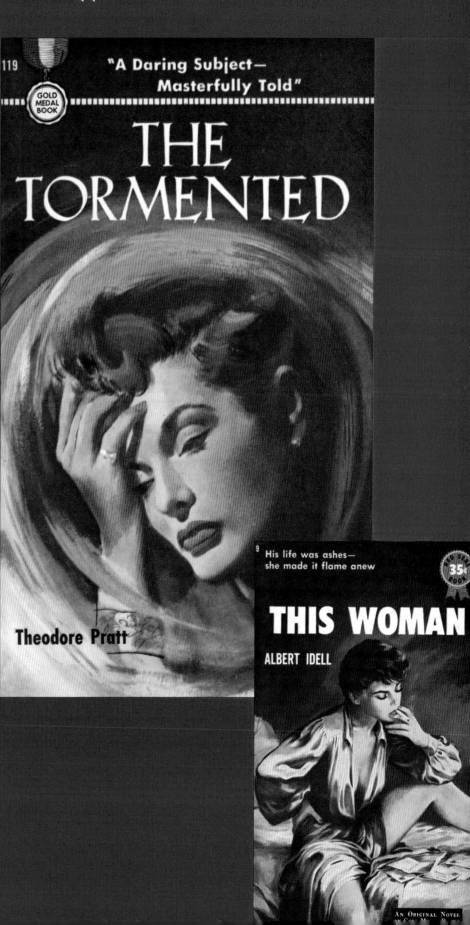

ever more companies entered the fray and ever more titles jostled for display space, it became customary for retailers to return unsold copies to their publishers.

In time it was discovered that the cost of packing, shipping, unpacking, counting, and re-shelving returned books was greater than the cost of simply printing more copies, if and when they were needed. "Whole book returns" were largely discontinued in the mass paperback field; retailers or distributors tore off the front covers of books and returned these for credit.

Gradually "sell-through" rates slid from well over ninety percent to, typically, substantially under fifty percent. The waste was terrible, costs of books rose to make up for losses on unsold (and destroyed) copies, and everybody lost — the reader, the publisher, and the author.

Eventually Fawcett switched to paying on the basis of sell-through rather than that of print run.

Gold Medal also had great success with books that either hinted at Lesbianism or dealt directly with the subject. An early effort was *Women's Barracks* (Gold Medal PBO 132, 1950) by Tereska Torres. Barye Phillips' cover painting shows a typical scene, familiar in 1950 to millions of World War Two and Cold War veterans. It's set in a military barracks or locker room, a squad of soldiers in varying stages of uniformed dress and undress slouch around smoking cigarettes and apparently planning to leave the post and head into town.

But the soldiers in this case are all female. The blurb reads, *The frank autobiography of a French girl soldier*. And the female soldier in the foreground, fully clothed, is eyeing one of her comrades, mostly unclothed, with an interest that is obviously not military. Her barracks buddy is apparently gazing back (we can't see her shaded eyes), returning that interest.

The book was controversial to say the least. It ran through printing after printing and was even cited in a hearing by the United States Senate on dangerous trends in publishing. Fawcett repackaged *Women's Barracks* with a tamer cover painting, still by the talented Phillips but without the wink-wink-nudge-nudge sexual innuendo of the first edition.

*Women's Barracks* spawned a whole school of books about women's prisons, girls' schools, female juvenile delinquents, and girl gangs. Such books — as well as books dealing with male homosexuality — had of course been around from time immemorial. But until then they had been published clandestinely, sold under the counter, passed from hand to hand with a whispered word and a covert nod. At best they were packaged and treated as "sleaze"; at worst, as outright pornography.

With *Women's Barracks* Lesbianism had gone mainstream — virtually overnight.

Were these books bought primarily by women, or by men? Hold the question — we have some testimony on the subject.

One of the most successful Lesbian books of the 1950s was *I Am a Woman* by the pseudonymous Ann Bannon (Gold Medal PBO d833, 1959). The illustration is an extreme close-up of a stunning dark-haired model. The camera angle is high and we see her face and low-cut black blouse. The title is scrawled across the cover and "reads" directly into the blurb, to create a question for the reader:

*I Am a Woman*

> *in love with a woman —*

>> *must society reject me?*

Forty years later, in the foreword to a book devoted to the artwork on such books, Bannon herself gave her theory:

"As for outerwear, many of the covers exhibit young women in torn blouses, unbuttoned blouses, sheer blouses, and the occasional peignoir — standard issue, of course, for all self-respecting Lesbians of the 1950s and 1960s.

"What was the goal? Again, it was the calculated and clever representation of female gender displayed as an incentive to the boys to buy the book."

But, Bannon points out, Lesbians did buy the books, and the question as to the proportion of male to female readers, while intriguing, remains unanswered. Bannon does point out, however, that a sizable proportion of these Lesbian novels were written by male authors, sometimes quite prominent and successful male authors. The list includes mystery writers Donald E. Westlake and Lawrence Block, science fiction master Robert Silverberg, literary novelist Patricia Highsmith, fantasy and science fiction author Marion Zimmer Bradley, hardboiled novelist (and sometime humorist) Fletcher Flora, novelist R. V. Cassill, and the versatile and prolific Michael Avallone.

Doubtless many other writers, better known in other realms of literature, wrote sex fiction. Some did so under their own names; others, under pseudonyms.

¶¶¶¶¶

In 1955 Fawcett's distribution contract with NAL expired, and Fawcett was freed from the shackles of its no-compete clause. Fawcett could now enter the bidding wars for books previously published in hardcover by other houses. Fawcett continued Gold Medal Books as a PBO house, adding two new lines, Crest and Premier.

Fawcett had already added Fawcett Red Seal, prior to the expiration of the NAL contract, and had used this line for longer and more expensive books. In content and design, however, they weren't much different from the Gold Medal PBOs.

Crest and Premier were a different story. New editors were brought in from other publishers or promoted from within the ranks. Most notable among these was Leona Nevler, whose chief claim to fame had been picking the manuscript of *Peyton Place* out of the slushpile at another publisher where she was a part-time employee. Premier Books was a non-fiction line from the outset.

For the most part the Crest Books were really just another Fawcett line, including a great many Gold Medal titles remarketed under the new logo. However, they could now include reprints of hardcovers as well as originals, and some notable books did appear under this heading: *A Walk on the Wild Side* by Nelson Algren (1956) and *Psycho* by Robert Bloch (MTI, 1961).

But Fawcett was now inclined to shed its modest, populist roots and compete for Big Books. The company bid for (and won) reprint rights to a bestseller called *By Love Possessed* by James Gould Cozzens. Fawcett Crest got *Lolita* by Vladimir Nabokov, and *The Ugly American* by Eugene L. Burdick and William J. Lederer.

In 1961 Fawcett paid a record-breaking price for paperback rights to William L. Shirer's huge history of Nazi Germany, *The Rise and Fall of the Third Reich*.

The brash upstart that had started with Wilford Fawcett's little gags-and-gals sheet had burgeoned with slicks and pulps and comic books, had made PBOs a major element of mass culture, had become just one more publisher among many. The once family-owned business was sold and became part of the Columbia Broadcasting System.

By the early 1980s CBS was steadily losing money on Fawcett and opted to get out of the publishing business. Fawcett was essentially shut down cold, its assets (that is, its backlist of titles and its name) were sold to Random House. Eventually Fawcett was folded into Ballantine Books, and for all practical purposes ceased to be a player in the world of books.

What went wrong? One theory is that Fawcett simply got too big for its britches and finally got its come-uppance. Those are a couple of old-fashioned expressions, but then Fawcett was a grand, old-fashioned company. Another way to put it is that Fawcett lost its identity. Then it lost its life.

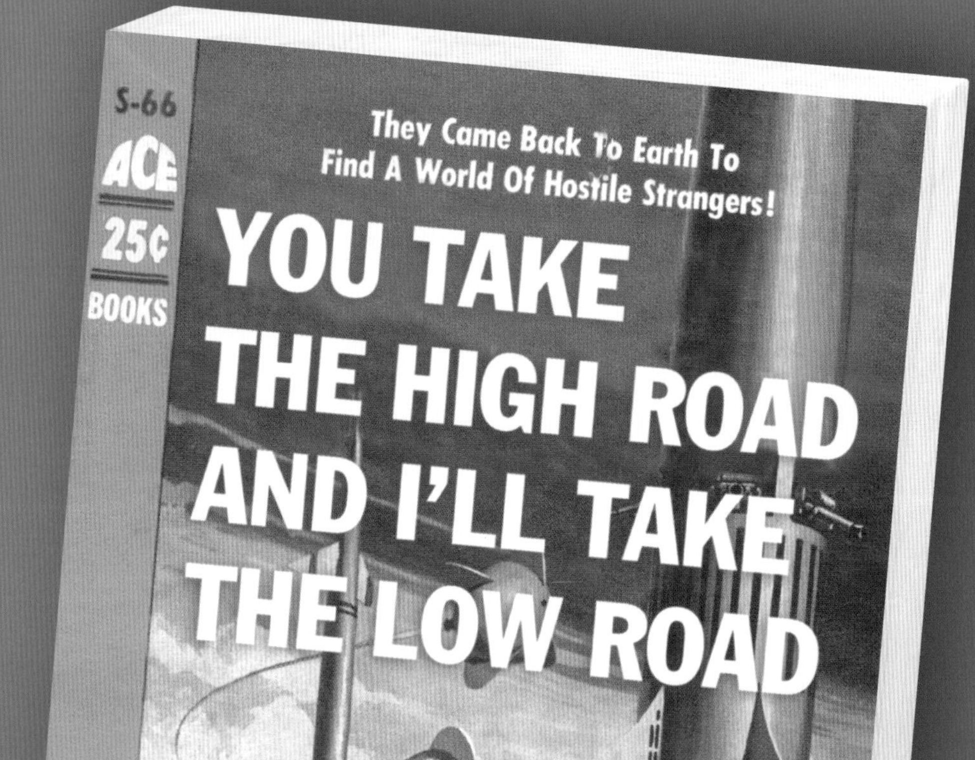

S-66

ACE

25¢

BOOKS

They Came Back To Earth To
Find A World Of Hostile Strangers!

# YOU TAKE THE HIGH ROAD AND I'LL TAKE THE LOW ROAD

CHAPTER
EIGHT

This is the story of two men, Ian Ballantine and Donald A. Wollheim. Ballantine was one of the true pioneers of paperback publishing in America. He was instrumental in bringing Penguin Books to the U.S. and became one of the founders and owners of Bantam Books. Wollheim had worked as a pulp magazine editor and author, had compiled two of the earliest and most significant anthologies in the history of science fiction, and had been employed as editor of Avon Books.

In 1952 each struck out on his own, creating two major and long-lived independent paperback houses. Each would introduce innovations into paperback publishing which are felt to this day, and each achieved great success. But before we go into details about those events of half a century ago, it is worth taking a look at each of these men. In many ways they were markedly different. They clashed repeatedly and held each other in cordial disdain, and yet they seemed to be drawn together again and again by a mischievous and ironic fate.

Ballantine was the more polished of the two. He was well educated, well dressed, well mannered, and immaculately groomed. But there was a surprising streak in Ian Ballantine, which emerged at times to astonish those around him. He claimed the radical leader Emma Goldman as a somewhat distant aunt, and those who knew him would find that, just when they had him figured out, he would defy their expectations.

If the young Ian Ballantine was unquestionably a brilliant and energetic bookman, he could also be difficult, headstrong, and even abrasive. Having left American Penguin to become cofounder and part owner of Bantam Books, he managed in short order to alienate his partners at Bantam. By February of 1952, he was ousted from his position with that company, but Ian Ballantine was not one to take such treatment lying down.

He promptly began a series of visits to the publishing moguls he had not irreparably offended.

By May of that year, he was ready to announce the formation of Ballantine Books, and before the year was out Ballantine would publish its first title, *Executive Suite* by Cameron Hawley.

*Executive Suite* was a novel of ambition and intrigue in the world of wealthy and powerful corporations. The cover illustration, painted by Harry Bennett, could have been taken for a movie poster or the official portrait of a corporate executive. It featured a dignified, gray-haired, immaculately tailored, middle-aged businessman.

While the novel itself was barely noteworthy, Ballantine's publishing strategy drew attention, not only to *Executive Suite* but to the new company and its entire line of books. Prior to this event, mass-market paperback books had been almost exclusively reprints of previously published hardcovers. This, in fact, had been the basic marketing strategy of Penguin, Pocket Books, Bantam, and Avon, along with assorted smaller houses: bring to the public low-priced, conveniently formatted editions of successful books, whether classics, newly published "important" volumes, or popular entertainment such as westerns or murder mysteries.

Fawcett Gold Medal had moved to the opposite extreme, producing original paperbacks from the outset. Even the earliest Gold Medals, collections of feature articles from Fawcett magazines, had appeared without prior hardcover publication. Once Gold Medal moved into the realm of fiction, sales boomed. Nor was Fawcett the first company to publish "PBOs" (paperback originals); their achievement was to make the PBO a staple and to achieve huge sales of a line consisting entirely (or nearly entirely) of PBOs.

But *Executive Suite* was published *simultaneously* by a prestigious, long-established hardcover house, Houghton-Mifflin, and by the brash upstart Ballantine Books. There had been a few earlier experiments at simultaneous publication

### BIG BUNNY
JOE GOLDBERG
BALLANTINE, CIRCA 1966
COVER BY LEROY NEIMAN

Starting with the creation of *Playboy* in the early 1950s, Hugh M. Hefner managed to turn himself into the personification of The Good Life—or at least, his personal version of it. This PBO actually merited a cover by Leroy Neiman!

❧❧

### SGT. BILKO JOKE BOOK
BALLANTINE, 1959

Writer Nat Hiken's superb comedy series with Phil Silvers as the conniving Sergeant Bilko and a brilliant supporting cast hit the nation's television screens in an era when military service was part of virtually every young man's life. The PBO/TVTI is highly collectible.

❧❧

### AFTER DOOMSDAY
POUL ANDERSON
BALLANTINE, 1962
COVER BY BRILLHART

One of the enduring institutions of science fiction, Poul Anderson burst upon the scene in 1946 at the ripe age of twenty and never looked back. *After Doomsday* was one of his finest efforts, and the splendid Brillhart cover with its startling human-alien encounter adds to the collectibility of this fine PBO.

❧❧❧

## A CLOCKWORK ORANGE
### ANTHONY BURGESS
### BALLANTINE, CIRCA 1966

This early paperback captures the feeling of Burgess's terrifying cross between a futuristic dystopia, a JD novel, and a linguistic experiment. There was an MTI a few years later when Stanley Kubrick's film version was released.

## CHILDHOOD'S END
### ARTHUR C. CLARKE
### BALLANTINE, 1953
### COVER BY RICHARD POWERS

This magnificent novel marked Clarke's breakthrough from a talented pulp craftsman to an important novelist. It contains a few remnants of his pulp days and strong foreshadowing of the serious themes of *2001: A Space Odyssey*.

## A CONFEDERATE GENERAL FROM BIG SUR
### RICHARD BRAUTIGAN
### BALLANTINE BOOKS, CIRCA 1970

Prose laureate of his generation, Richard Brautigan was an astonishing talent and had begun a brilliant career when he ended his own life.

## DARE
**PHILIP JOSE FARMER**
BALLANTINE BOOKS, 1965
COVER BY ROBERT ABBETT

This is one of the prolific and popular Farmer's lesser-known works.

## DO IT!
**JERRY RUBIN**
BALLANTINE BOOKS, CIRCA 1970

Jerry Rubin, Eldridge Cleaver, "scenarios of the revolution." Yes, indeed. Hippy/counterculture literature has become meat for university library special collections and a topic for graduate theses. What a long, strange trip it's been!

## DAVY
**EDGAR PANGBORN**
BALLANTINE BOOKS, 1964
COVER BY FOSTER

A sensitive visionary and a fine stylist, Edgar Pangborn's few books are not heavily collected but remain readable. Foster's cover painting, a strange combination of dreamlike imagery and almost photorealistic technique, is outstanding.

## LA DOLCE VITA
**FEDERICO FELLINI**
BALLANTINE BOOKS, 1961

That's Anita Ekberg, onetime sex goddess, on the cover. Nearly one hundred pages of photos as well as the text make this MTI of interest to film students as well as collectors.

### EXECUTIVE SUITE
CAMERON HAWLEY
BALLANTINE BOOKS, 1952
COVER BY HARRY BENNETT

Is this a PBO? Simultaneously issued in hardcover by Houghton Mifflin and in paperback by Ballantine, *Executive Suite* is a window into the corporate world of the 1950s. All of those execs, and of course not a woman or minority among them! It's not a great novel but is a cornerstone of any Ballantine collection.

### ENGLAND UNDER HITLER
COMER CLARKE
BALLANTINE BOOKS, 1961

This is a sort of alternate-history nonfiction book. Nazi-era collectors go for this kind of thing.

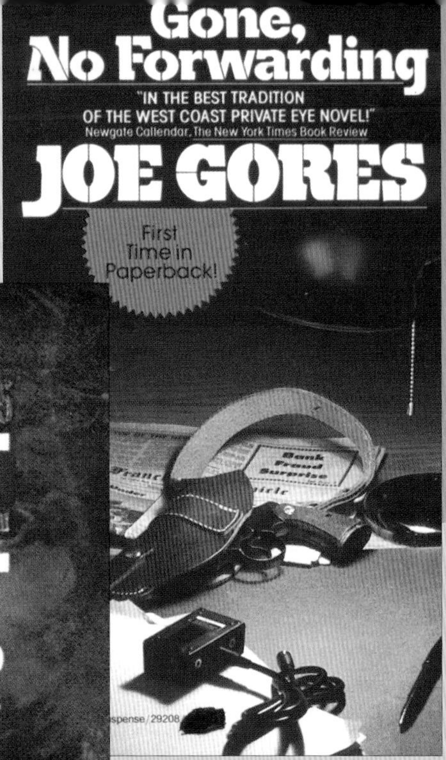

**Gone, No Forwarding**

"IN THE BEST TRADITION OF THE WEST COAST PRIVATE EYE NOVEL!"
Newgate Callendar, The New York Times Book Review

**JOE GORES**

First Time in Paperback!

F 731 **BB** BALLANTINE BOOKS 50¢

THE RISE AND FALL OF THE LUFTWAFFE: 1939-45

**THE FIRST AND THE LAST**

**ADOLF GALLAND**

GERMANY'S COMMANDER OF FIGHTER FORCES

**BB** $1.25

**A Fine and Private Place**

a novel by
**Peter S. Beagle**

---

## A FINE AND PRIVATE PLACE
PETER S. BEAGLE
BALLANTINE BOOKS
COVER BY GERVASIO GALLARDO

Anything by Beagle is worthwhile, but many readers still consider this amazing fantasy about death, by turns funny and heartbreaking, his best.

❝❝

## THE FIRST AND THE LAST
ADOLF GALLAND
BALLANTINE BOOKS, 1963
COVER BY ED VALIGURSKY

The authentic rendering of World War II combat aircraft in Valigursky's fine cover painting adds to the interest of this book. It's sought by military historians and airplane buffs.

❝❝

## GONE, NO FORWARDING
JOE GORES
BALLANTINE BOOKS, 1981

A living paradox, Joe Gores is both a Shakespeare scholar and tough-guy author. In the tradition of Dashiell Hammett, Gores is a private eye turned mystery writer. He brings to his books a sense of authenticity, especially as many of them are based on actual cases that he worked.

❝❝

## HARDROCK

**FRANK BONHAM**
**BALLANTINE BOOKS, 1958**
**COVER BY MEL CRAIR**

During the Depression of the 1930s, Frank Bonham
was an unsuccessful would-be mystery writer. He met
Ed Earl Repp, a prolific pulp veteran who alternated
westerns with science fiction stories. Repp was so successful that he needed ghosts to keep up his production,
and he hired Bonham. By 1948 Bonham was ready to
step out on his own.

## HOMBRE

**ELMORE LEONARD**
**BALLANTINE BOOKS, 1961**

Before switching to crime and caper novels, Elmore
Leonard wrote westerns, first for the pulps, then for
book publishers. His two careers overlapped for a full
decade, 1969-1979. His westerns, including this fine
PBO, were excellent.

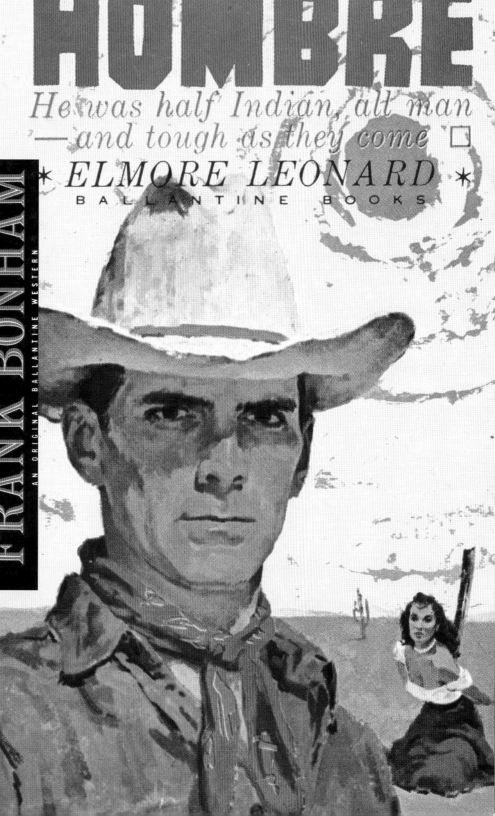

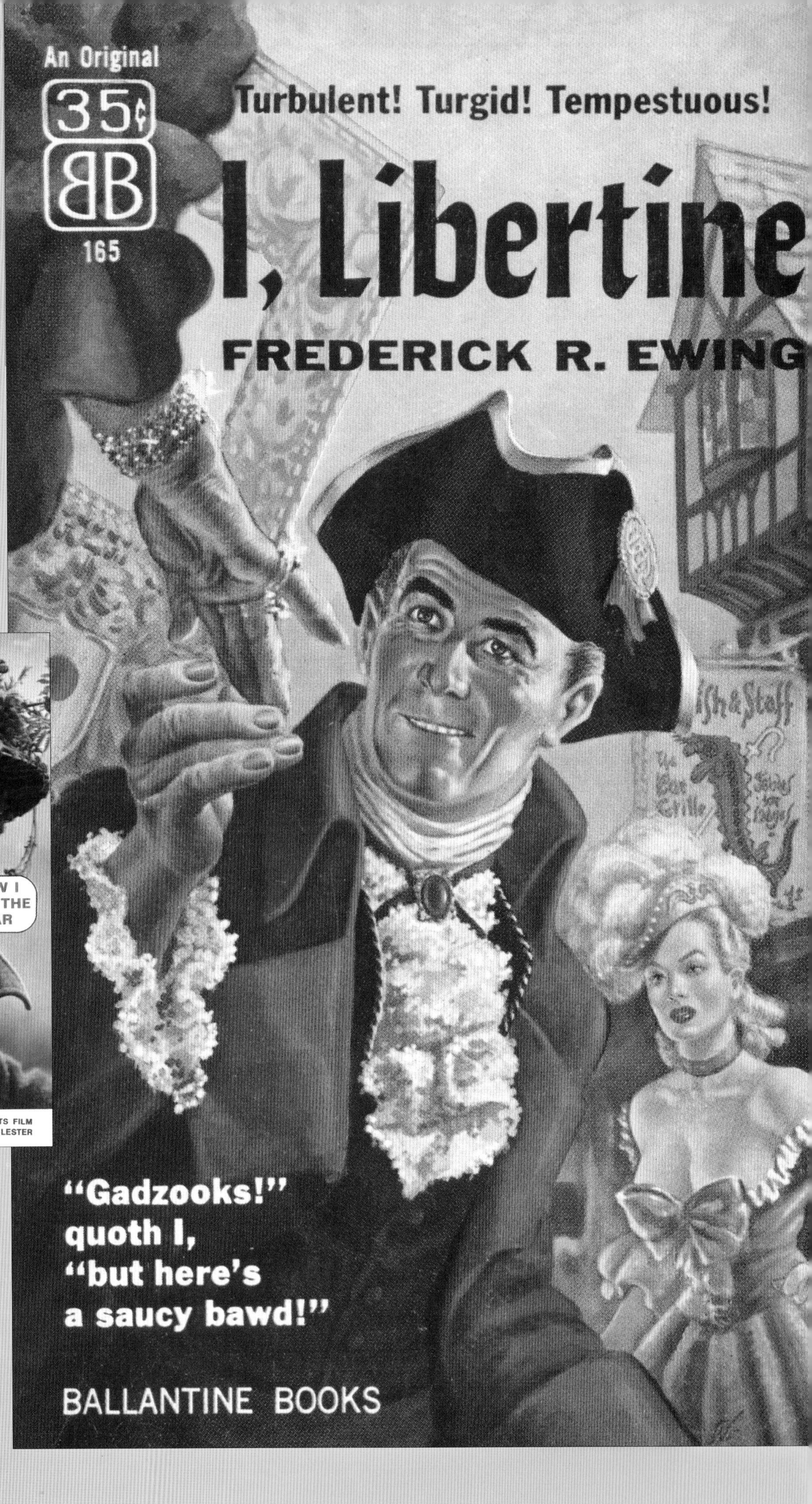

An Original
35¢
BB
165

Turbulent! Turgid! Tempestuous!

# I, Libertine

## FREDERICK R. EWING

"Gadzooks!"
quoth I,
"but here's
a saucy bawd!"

BALLANTINE BOOKS

A BALLANTINE BOOK

HOW I
WON THE
WAR

A NOVEL BY PATRICK RYAN • NOW A UNITED ARTISTS FILM
STARRING JOHN LENNON AND DIRECTED BY RICHARD LESTER

of hardbound and paperbound editions of the same title, but Ballantine announced that this would be the company's main publishing strategy.

Some titles, like *Executive Suite*, would be co-published by Ballantine and other companies. In other cases, Ballantine would produce both the hardcover and the paperback edition. The relatively expensive hardcover edition would reach the carriage trade through bookshops and garner reviews and publicity, while the paperback, distributed to newsstands and drugstores and racked alongside similarly priced periodicals, would appeal to the low-budget buyers.

The perceived peril was that the availability of the low-priced edition would draw potential customers away from the hardcover edition. By traditional paperback publishing methods, the hardbound edition would have had its run before the low-priced paperback ever saw the light of day. With Fawcett's publication of paperback originals, there was no hardcover at all. But the Ballantine plan looked risky, to say the least.

Would the new strategy work?

If *Executive Suite* were to be considered the test case, the answer was that the new strategy worked beautifully. The Houghton-Mifflin edition of the book reportedly sold in excess of 20,000 copies, a very respectable if less than spectacular number for a book by a new author completely lacking in track record, reputation, or credentials. Sales of the Ballantine paperback approached half a million copies.

What sort of books did Ballantine choose for its first releases? Among the first ten Ballantines were three westerns: *Saddle by Starlight* by Luke Short (Ballantine Number 4), *Blood on the Land* by Frank Bonham (Ballantine Number 7), and *Concannon* by Frank O'Rourke (Ballantine Number 10). *Concannon* was a PBO issued with a dust jacket. The actual book cover ("wraps") was painted by pulp magazine veteran Norman Saunders. The dust jacket featured a painting by Robert Maguire.

There were two novels of a grimly realistic nature that in a later era would have fallen somewhere between designations of juvenile delinquent and sleaze: *The Golden Spike* by Hal Ellson (Ballantine Number 2) and *Tides of Time* by Emile Danoen (Ballantine Number 6). The list was rounded out by three general novels and a humor-cartoon book, *The World of Li'l Abner* by Al Capp (Ballantine Number 8).

*The World of Li'l Abner* was Ballantine's first cartoon book but would be far from its last.

Not until Ballantine Number 16, *Star Science Fiction Stories*, edited by Frederik Pohl, did Ballantine enter the arena of science fiction, a realm in which it came to have success from the outset and for decades to follow.

Ian Ballantine would claim, many years later, that he had been a sympathetic supporter of science fiction all along. He claimed to have been the driving force behind Bantam's publication of *Shot in the Dark*, edited by Judith Merril, in 1950.

Merril's anthology was brilliant. Remember that the accumulated science fiction short stories of the past half century or longer had not

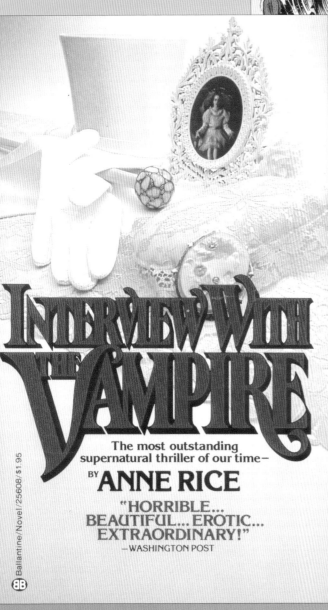

### INTERVIEW WITH THE VAMPIRE
ANNE RICE
BALLANTINE BOOKS, 1977

Sometime pornographer Rice is the
unquestioned queen of vampire novelists,
with occasional forays into mummy stories
and other such. This great cult writer is
equally at home on the shelves of first
edition collectors and read-'em-to-bits
paperback consumers.

### INSIDE MAD
BALLANTINE BOOKS, 1961

This collection from the brilliantly satiric
*Mad* has publisher William Gaines's name on
the cover, but editor Harvey Kurtzman might
have been a more appropriate credit line.
Latter-day readers who know *Mad* only from
its magazine-format issues are in for a treat
when they see the original.

### HARVEY KURTZMAN'S JUNGLE BOOK
BALLANTINE BOOKS, 1959
COVER BY HARVEY KURTZMAN

The original guiding talent of *Mad* magazine,
Kurtzman worked for other publications
ranging from *Humbug* to *Playboy*. This collection
is a work of sheer genius.

## JAMES DEAN
**WILLIAM BAST**
**BALLANTINE BOOKS, 1956**

Live fast, die young, and leave a pile of smoking rubble behind— James Dean was the hero of 1950s would-be rebels. This celeb bio PBO is typical of its breed.

▮▮▮

## JOHN CARTER OF MARS
**EDGAR RICE BURROUGHS**
**BALLANTINE BOOKS, 1965**
**COVER BY ROBERT ABBETT (?)**

This eleventh and final volume in Burroughs' Barsoomian series contains one novelette actually written by Burroughs and another ghosted in the 1940s by his son John Coleman Burroughs.

▮

## MARILYN MONROE AS THE GIRL
**SAM SHAW**
**BALLANTINE BOOKS, 1955**

A PBO/MTI in conjunction with Monroe's film *The Seven-Year Itch*, the photos in this volume make it a major target for Monroe cultists as well as MTI collectors.

▮▮▮

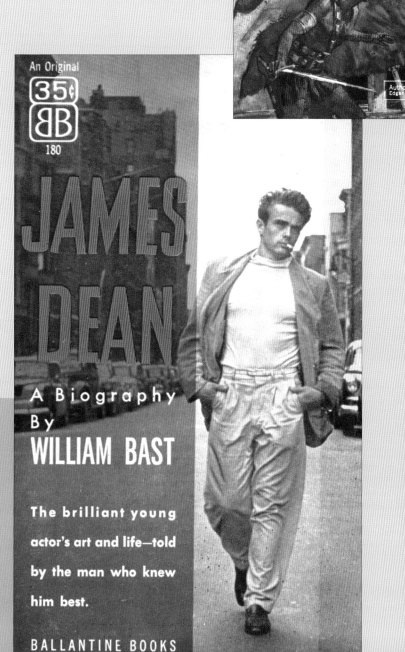

## MORE THAN HUMAN
**THEODORE STURGEON**
**BALLANTINE BOOKS, 1953**
**COVER BY RICHARD POWERS**

One of Ballantine's early "semi-PBOs,"
co-published with Farrar, Straus & Young,
*More than Human* is Sturgeon at his best:
visionary, humane, even profound.

📖📖📖

## THE OCTOBER COUNTRY
**RAY BRADBURY**
**BALLANTINE BOOKS, 1955**
**COVER BY JOE MUGNANI**

Here are some of Bradbury's earliest and most
original short stories, reprinted from an Arkham
House edition with many others added. A rare
Ballantine hardcover also exists.

📖📖📖📖

## MESSIAH
**GORE VIDAL**
**BALLANTINE BOOKS, 1954**
**COVER BY RICHARD POWERS**

This early science fiction novel is one of half a
dozen or more which Vidal has interspersed
among his historicals and other works. Vidal
tells the story of Ian Ballantine's introducing
him to L. Rob Hubbard. It's one of the
strangest literary encounters of all time.

📖📖

A REPRINT
50¢
**BB**
F139

# Ray Bradbury
author of FAHRENHEIT 451

# THE OCTOBER COUNTRY

BALLANTINE BOOKS

ORIGINALS
35¢
**BB**
46

the provocative story of six people who
became—together—a new kind of humanity
by THEODORE STURGEON

# more than human

FARRAR, STRAUS & YOUNG
with
BALLANTINE BOOKS

A REPRINT
35¢
**BB**
94

The brilliant satire of a world
that worshipped the Angel of Death

## MESSIAH
### Gore Vidal

A BALLANTINE REPRINT

REACH FOR TOMORROW

stories by the author of *Childhood's End*

**Arthur C. Clarke**

BALLANTINE BOOKS

AN ORIGINAL 35¢ BB 135

Ballantine/Novel                    24550/$1.95

THE SMASH **#1** COAST-TO-COAST
**BESTSELLER!**
THE
**SEVEN-PER-CENT
SOLUTION**
Being a Reprint from the Reminiscences of
**JOHN H. WATSON, M.D.** as edited by **NICHOLAS MEYER**

BB 95¢        01535                          3

THE AUTHORIZED EDITION
OF THE FAMOUS FANTASY TRILOGY
**"THE LORD OF THE RINGS"**
*Newly Revised, with a Special Foreword by the author*
**J.R.R. TOLKIEN**
*Part Three*
THE RETURN
OF THE KING

HOUGHTON
MIFFLIN
COMPANY

*Dolphin
Edition*

WITH
BALLANTINE BOOKS

BB   F 561  AN ORIGINAL                    50¢

THE SILVER
**EGGHEADS**
A HEADLONG RIOT OF HILARIOUS
SCIENCE FICTION SATIRE
**FRITZ LEIBER**

BALLANTINE BOOKS

---

**REACH FOR TOMORROW**
ARTHUR C. CLARKE
BALLANTINE BOOKS, 1956
COVER BY RICHARD POWERS

A rare "horizontal" PBO, to judge
by its cover, but the guts of the
book are printed in the usual
vertical format. It includes some
of Clarke's finest stories.

◧◧◧◧

**THE SEVEN-PER-CENT SOLUTION**
NICHOLAS MEYER
BALLANTINE BOOKS, 1975

The fix was in on this Sherlockian
jape. Meyer had a Hollywood deal,
and the publicity machinery went
into high gear, creating a bestseller
out of a rather lackluster pastiche.
Later editions included several
MTI printings.

◧

**THE RETURN OF THE KING**
J. R. R. TOLKIEN
BALLANTINE BOOKS, 1966
COVER BY BARBARA REMINGTON

This final volume of Tolkien's
great *Lord of the Rings* forms a
triptych when placed with the
other volumes. However, the
Ace editions, with covers by
Jack Gaughan, preceded the
Ballantines into print and are
the preferred collectibles.

◧◧

**THE SILVER EGGHEADS**
FRITZ LEIBER
BALLANTINE BOOKS, 1961
COVER BY RICHARD POWERS

Proof that Powers could be as
representational as he wanted to
be: that perplexed-looking fellow
in the robot's arms is none other
than Ian Ballantine himself! The
book is not really top-drawer
Leiber but it has its moments.

◧◧◧

been picked over by more than a handful of anthologists before Merril. Without the fear of utilizing over-familiar stories that later anthologists would encounter, Merril had very close to *carte blanche*. She assembled a selection of twenty-three stories by such authors as Theodore Sturgeon, Leigh Brackett, Fredric Brown, Gerald Kersh, Robert A. Heinlein, Stephen Vincent Benet, Margery Allingham, James Thurber, Edison Marshall, and Philip Wylie.

The book was a worthy successor to earlier efforts by Donald A. Wollheim, beginning with *The Pocket Book of Science Fiction* in 1943. He had faced opposition within Bantam, Ballantine said, and had been driven to the subterfuge of sneaking this groundbreaking anthology into print by disguising it as a detective novel. Three years later, and with his own company under his unquestioned control, Ballantine moved ahead.

Frederik Pohl, the editor of *Star Science Fiction*, was a veteran science fiction writer, magazine editor, and agent. For this anthology he drew on many of the authors in the stable of *Galaxy Science Fiction* magazine, with which he was closely associated both as a contributor and assistant to and eventually successor of editor Horace L. Gold. Pohl was also a former literary agent and an experienced anthologist with two prior science fiction anthologies to his credit: *Beyond the End of Time* (Permabooks, 1952) and *Shadow of Tomorrow* (Permabooks, 1953).

*Star Science Fiction* was a pioneering effort in that it did not mine the back issues of pulp magazines, as previous science fiction anthologies had, but instead commissioned new stories by leading authors of the day. The table of contents of *Star Science Fiction Stories* reads like a Who's Who of science fiction writers in 1953: William Morrison, C. M. Kornbluth, Lester del Rey, Fritz Leiber, Clifford D. Simak, John Wyndham, William Tenn, H. L. Gold, Judith Merril, Ray Bradbury, Isaac Asimov, Robert Sheckley, Henry Kuttner, C. L. Moore, Murray Leinster, and Arthur C. Clarke.

The book was received with great enthusiasm and led to a series of five more volumes, a spin-off *Star Short Novels*, a self-cannibalizing "best of" called *Star of Stars*, and a single issue of a digest-sized *Star Science Fiction* magazine.

In addition to its outstanding lineup of authors and stories (which would deteriorate in the late editions of the series), *Star Science Fiction* was notable for its cover art. Science fiction illustration as practiced in the pulp magazine era was almost always highly representational, literalistic, and more often than not sensational. Mighty machines, heroic spacemen, scantily clad spacewomen, bizarre alien creatures, remote and exotic landscapes, and astonishing weapons were favorite themes.

To create a cover illustration for *Star Science Fiction*, Ballantine selected painter Richard Powers. Powers' conception was a moody, semi-abstract composition that seemed to say to buyers and readers, "This is a science fiction book unlike other science fiction books." Hidebound traditionalists in the science fiction community reacted violently to the selection, but once again both sales and critical response approved of the book, and Ballantine's science fiction line was successfully launched.

**SLIDE RULE**
NEVIL SHUTE
BALLANTINE BOOKS, 1964
COVER BY ED VALIGURSKY (?)

Although the attribution is not confirmed, the fine authentic painting is most likely by Ed Valigursky, who was able to combine high drama with accurately-depicted technology in his work. Shute never let his readers down, whether writing fiction or history.

**SO CLOSE TO HOME**
JAMES BLISH
BALLANTINE BOOKS, 1961
COVER BY RICHARD POWERS

Sometimes austere, even dour, Blish may have been the most brilliant mind to emerge from the New York Futurian Society of the late 1930s —a group that included Frederik Pohl, Judith Merril, Donald Wollheim, and Damon Knight. His short stories were always excellent and thought-provoking.

**SONG OF THE AXE**
N. C. MCDONALD
BALLANTINE BOOKS, 1961
COVER BY SULLIVAN (?)

This novel and *Witch Doctor* (Ballantine, 1969) seem to be the only books of the elusive N. C. McDonald.

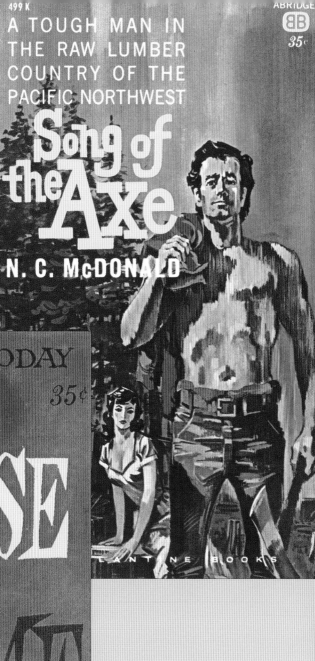

A TOUGH MAN IN
THE RAW LUMBER
COUNTRY OF THE
PACIFIC NORTHWEST

499 K

ABRIDGE

35¢

# SONG of the Axe

### N. C. McDONALD

NEVIL SHUTE
## SLIDE RULE
From the best-selling author of
On The Beach—a superb account
of the pioneer days of flying.

U5006 BALLANTINE BOOKS 60¢

DEADLINES FOR TODAY

35¢

# SO CLOSE TO HOME

### JAMES BLISH

BALLANTINE BOOKS

201

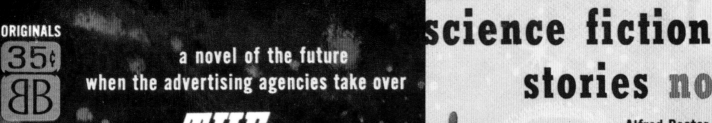

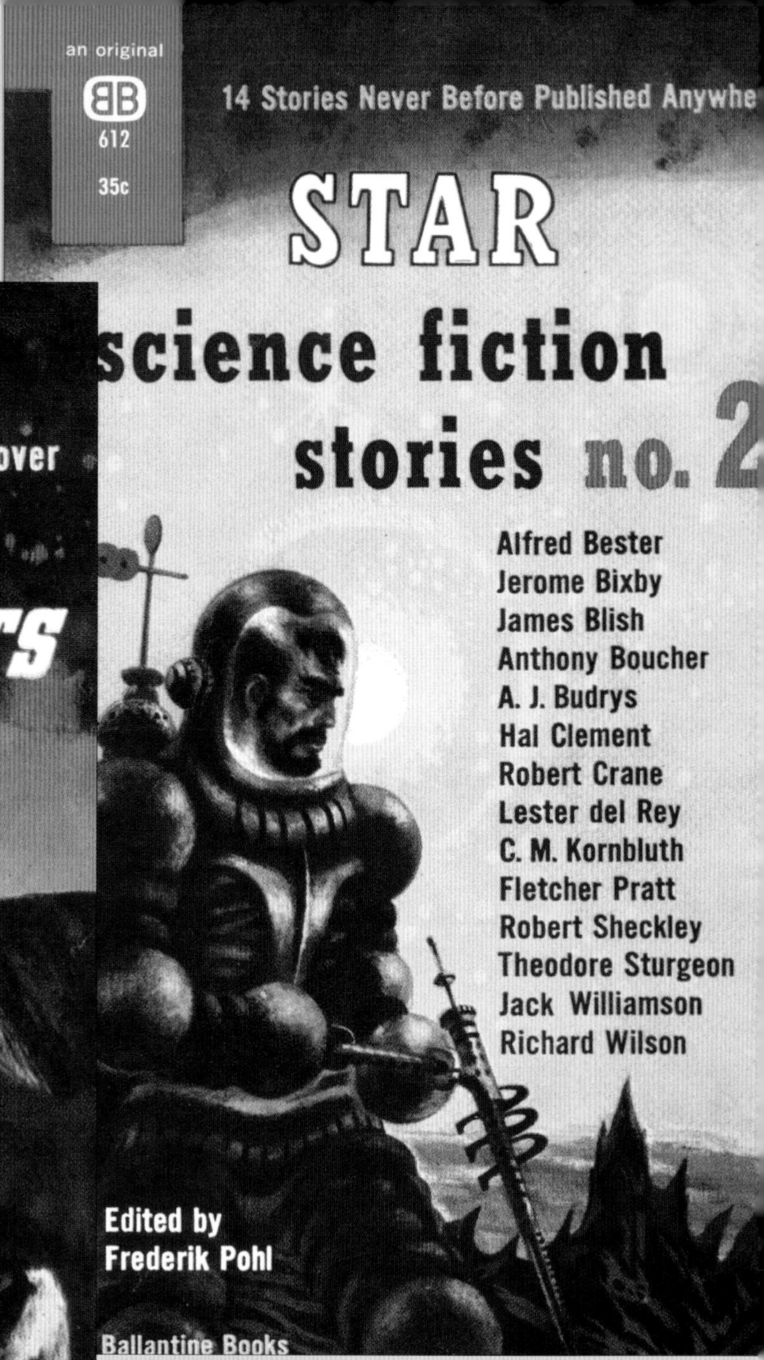

an original

**BB**
612
35c

14 Stories Never Before Published Anywhe

# STAR
## science fiction
## stories no. 2

Alfred Bester
Jerome Bixby
James Blish
Anthony Boucher
A. J. Budrys
Hal Clement
Robert Crane
Lester del Rey
C. M. Kornbluth
Fletcher Pratt
Robert Sheckley
Theodore Sturgeon
Jack Williamson
Richard Wilson

ORIGINALS

35¢

**BB**

21

a novel of the future
when the advertising agencies take over

# THE
# SPACE MERCHANTS

By Frederik Pohl
and C. M. Kornbluth

Edited by
Frederik Pohl

Ballantine Books

BALLANTINE BOOKS

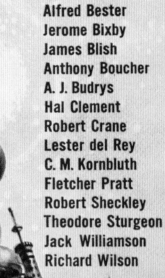

**THE SPACE MERCHANTS**
FREDERIK POHL AND C. M. KORNBLUTH
BALLANTINE BOOKS, 1953
COVER BY RICHARD POWERS

*The Space Merchants* was Ballantine's first science fiction novel, preceded only by the first *Star* anthology. Previously serialized in *Galaxy Science Fiction* magazine, the book was a hard/soft PBO that set a trend of satirical science fiction that ran for years and is still a major work. It is also highly collectible!

**STAR SCIENCE FICTION STORIES NO. 2**
EDITED BY FREDERIK POHL
BALLANTINE BOOKS, 1954
COVER BY RICHARD POWERS

This later edition of a PBO anthology first issued in 1954 retains the original striking cover art. The *Star* series ran down in its later numbers, but the first few were absolutely brilliant.

### THE TEACHINGS OF DON JUAN: A YAQUI WAY OF KNOWLEDGE
CARLOS CASTANEDA
BALLANTINE BOOKS, CIRCA 1977

Was Castaneda a genius, a spiritual guru, an overrated simpleton, or a fraud? Whatever he was, millions of readers seeking enlightenment took him very seriously.

### TALES FROM THE CRYPT
BALLANTINE BOOKS, 1964
COVER BY FRANK FRAZETTA

The cover artist found a unique way of dating and signing his work—he put it on a tombstone on this collection of horror comic book stories. The EC titles of the 1950s are legendary among comic collectors; the black-and-white paperback reprints only hint at their impact.

### TROUBLE IS MY BUSINESS
RAYMOND CHANDLER
BALLANTINE BOOKS, 1972
COVER BY TOM ADAMS

Chandler was of course one of the most influential of all mystery writers and one of the most reprinted. The Ballantine series of Chandlers with their hypnotic covers by Adams are treasures in themselves.

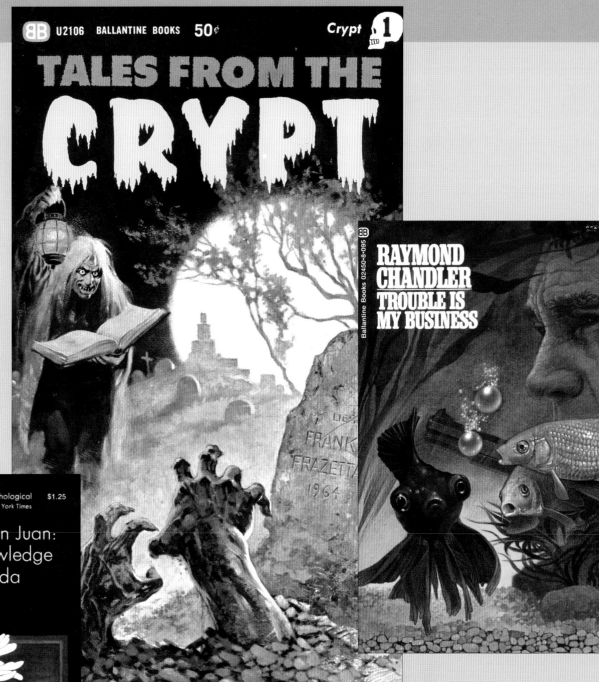

## U-BOATS AT WAR
**HARALD BUSCH**
**BALLANTINE BOOKS, 1962**
**COVER BY ED VALIGURSKY**

One of Ballantine's remarkable war books with their equally remarkable Valigursky covers, *U-Boats at War* actually bears the artist's signature.

📖📖

## WORLD OF PTAVVS
**LARRY NIVEN**
**BALLANTINE BOOKS, 1966**
**COVER BY RICHARD POWERS (?)**

The PBO first novel of this popular author's long career, and according to some, his best, is greatly sought-after by Niven fans.

📖📖📖

## WAR BONNET
**CLAY FISHER**
**BALLANTINE BOOKS, 1952**

Henry Wilson Allen wrote screenplays and westerns as Clay Fisher and Will Henry. Their quality varies greatly, and he is now largely out of print. Still, this Ballantine/Houghton Mifflin "semi-PBO" remains an important Ballantine "co-pub."

📖📖

**THE WIZARD OF OZ**
L. FRANK BAUM
BALLANTINE/DEL REY BOOKS, 1991

Assisted by her husband, science fiction writer Lester del Rey, editor Judy-Lynn Benjamin del Rey did such a fine job with Ballantine's science fiction line that she was rewarded with her own imprint. With Baum's fantasy classic series now in the public domain, many competing editions are available.

**THE MADAMS OF SAN FRANCISCO**
CURT GENTRY
COMSTOCK EDITIONS, 1964
COVER BY RICHARD AMSEL

Richard and Dori Gould ran Comstock but Ballantine put up the money, leading to many battles. Ballantine wanted books by Zane Gray. The Goulds preferred more serious history and authentic novels. They won.

If Ballantine Books, headed by Ian Ballantine, his wife, Betty, and editors Bernard Shir-Cliff and Stanley Kauffmann, was aiming for the high road of mass market publishing, a company that started at approximately the same time chose to take the low road. Ace Books was the creation of one of the legendary figures of popular (and populist) publishing. His name was Aaron A. Wynn. A veteran of the print wars with a background in periodicals, Wynn had published confession magazines, pulps, and a series of comic books, the familiar logo of an ace of spades marking his comics.

He decided to enter the book publishing world in 1945, creating Current Books, then merging that company with another and bringing forth Ace Books. At first he published hardcover books, one of the choicest and most collectible being a murder mystery by Samuel W. Taylor. A versatile writer, Taylor had started in the pulps, moved on to the slicks in the 1940s, and finally turned to nonfiction and became a leading Mormon historian.

Along the way Taylor found time to write two murder mysteries, both of which Wynn published in hardcover editions: *The Man with My Face* (1948) and *The Grinning Gismo* (1952). Aaron Wynn was often described as a sharp dealer with a difficult personality, but in later years Taylor described him otherwise.

"We always got along beautifully. Anything Aaron asked for, I said it was just fine with me, but he'd have to talk to my agent about it. He was the official bastard!"

Within months of the hardcover publication of *The Grinning Gismo*, Wynn launched a paperback line, Ace Books. An associate of Wynn's, Walter Zacharius, suggested an interesting gimmick for the new paperback marque.

The gimmick was to publish two novels (or a novel and a short story collection) in a single binding, using two "front covers" and flipping the page layout at midpoint so that each "book" was upside-down and backward relative to the other.

The Ace Doubles were not the first experiment in this kind of publishing. An earlier example was the "2-4-1" series issued by the English publisher, Harry Green Limited, but in their case the "books" simply followed each other like short stories in a collection. Zacharius's brilliant idea was the "upside-down, two-front-covers" design.

Wynn called on editor Donald A. Wollheim to run the Ace Doubles series. Wollheim was a near contemporary of Ian Ballantine's, born in 1914 to Ballantine's 1916. A lifetime New Yorker, Wollheim had been one of the pioneers of science fiction's fan publishing movement. He was a founding member of the New York Futurian Society, a group that combined enthusiasm for science fiction with a penchant for radical politics in the late 1930s and 1940s. Members included Frederik Pohl, Cyril Kornbluth, Judith Merril, Damon Knight, James Blish, Virginia Kidd, Richard Wilson, Robert W. Lowndes, and Isaac Asimov.

Having learned something about publishing in the fanzine world, Wollheim cut his professional teeth in 1941 as the editor of *Stirring Science Stories* and *Cosmic Stories*. Wollheim also learned something about low-end business operations. The publisher of these pulps claimed to have no money with which to pay for stories, but if authors donated their works to the first few issues of the magazines, they became favored contributors and would receive premium rates once the magazines became profitable.

Thanks to his Futurian connections, Wollheim was able to fill the pages of *Stirring* and *Cosmic* with the works of an unprecedented assemblage of brilliant young talent. However, the magazines went out of business before becoming profitable, and the authors were never paid.

Undaunted, Wollheim went on to edit two of the earliest and most significant anthologies in the history of science fiction. These were *The Pocket Book of Science Fiction*, 1943, and *Portable Novels of Science* (Viking), 1945.

Wollheim had worked as an editor at Avon Books, where his pulp sensibilities fit in well. Many of the books under his control sported lurid and sensationalistic covers, far more like the covers of pulp magazines than the dignified, subdued packages of most paperback books issued by Penguin or the early Pocket Books and Bantam Books. Although successful at Avon, Wollheim found himself torn between his enthusiasm for the company and his work there and his political convictions when the previously independent Avon was bought by the Hearst Corporation.

William Randolph Hearst was anathema to Wollheim. Wollheim saw Hearst as a reactionary, crypto-fascist apologist, and would have nothing to do with him, even to working for a company owned by Hearst. He resigned from Avon and went to work for Aaron Wynn at Ace Books.

Despite Wollheim's long association with science fiction, there were no science fiction or fantasy titles among the early Ace releases. Instead, the early Ace titles (all of them doubles) were divided evenly between crime and western fiction.

The very first Ace book (Ace D-1) featured Taylor's *The Grinning Gismo*, reprinted from the A. A. Wynn hardcover. It was paired with *Too Hot for Hell* by Keith Vining. As prominent an author as Taylor was, Vining was obscure. *Too Hot for Hell* was his first book. The second, *Keep Running*, was published by the largely forgotten Chicago Paperback House in 1962 (A-105).

The second Ace book (Ace D-2) was comprised of *Bad Man's Revenge* by William Colt MacDonald and *Bloody Hoofs* by J. E. Leithead.

All four "front" covers were painted for Ace by pulp veteran Norman Saunders. Saunders had long been known for his brawny, "he-man" images, and his paintings, coupled with dramatic title typography, made for eye-catching packages. They stood in dramatic contrast to Ballantine's more sedate presence. Remember that Saunders also worked for Ballantine—and all's fair in love and war and publishing.

The differing cover styles established distinct personae for the two entries into the paperback market which they would carry for many years.

Since the first Ace Double had been a mystery package and the second a pair of westerns, and since Wollheim and Ace maintained a rigid alternation of genres, Ace D-15 was due to be a crime-oriented double. It was, with a further appeal to the public's ongoing interest in the drug problem. The titles were *Junkie*, by William Lee, and *Narcotic Agent* by Maurice Helbrant (once again, an obscure author). Both covers were painted in a shadowy *noir* style by Al Rossi.

*Junkie* carried the cover blurb, "Confessions of an Unredeemed Drug Addict." The Rossi painting features a buxom sweater-clad blonde in a short skirt and bright red tights struggling with a male for a heroin fix.

*Junkie* and *Narcotic Agent* drew no more attention in 1953 than any number of other sensationally packaged novels and factual (or allegedly factual) exposés of the dangers of heroin, cocaine, opium, or marijuana. In that era LSD and other more exotic drugs were either totally unknown or arcane topics familiar to few readers; they would have their day during the "hippy" era of the 1960s and 70s.

Within a few years writer and counterculture guru William Burroughs came to public notice with the publication of such books as *Naked Lunch*, *Nova Express* and *The Ticket that Exploded*. Interest in Ace D-15 began to grow when it became known that "William Lee" was a pseudonym of Burroughs.' In time, the little thirty-five-cent paperback would be worth a thousand times its cover price, with its value still increasing.

Following *Junkie* / *Narcotic Agent*, Wollheim inserted a pair of translations into the Ace Double series (D-16), *Crime d'Amour* by Paul Bourget and *Germinie* by Edmond and Jules Goncourt. He then returned to the familiar pattern of alternating mysteries and westerns until Ace D-25, *The Code of the Woosters* and *Quick Service* by British humorist P. G. Wodehouse.

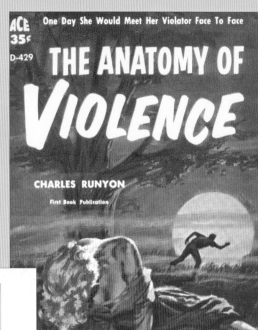

One Day She Would Meet Her Violator Face To Face

ACE 35¢
D-429

# THE ANATOMY OF VIOLENCE

**CHARLES RUNYON**

First Book Publication

ace SCIENCE FICTION CLASSIC F-282 40¢

EDGAR RICE BURROUGHS

## BEYOND THE FARTHEST STAR

A new interplanetary novel by the creator of Tar...

Complete & Unabrid...

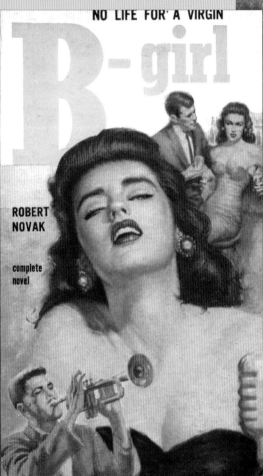

S-174
ACE
25¢
BOOKS

NO LIFE FOR A VIRGIN

# B-girl

**ROBERT NOVAK**

complete novel

ACE DOUBLE SIZE NOVEL D-191

FRANK G. SLAUGHTER

# APALACHEE Gold

"A REAL THRILLER"
—New York Herald-Tribune

35¢

AUTHOR OF "DIVINE MISTRESS"

complete and unabridged

## B-GIRL
**ROBERT NOVAK**
**ACE BOOKS, 1956**

Are you old enough to remember what a B-girl was? Bar owners would hire them to hang around and get suckers to buy them drinks. The "drinks" were tea. The sucker would pay for whiskey. The girl would get a cut of the profits.

📖📖

## THE ANATOMY OF VIOLENCE
**CHARLES RUNYON**
**ACE BOOKS, 1960**

An adaptable journeyman, Runyon wrote hardboiled crime and science fiction PBOs for Ace, Fawcett Gold Medal, and Lancer Books.

📖

## APALACHEE GOLD
**FRANK G. SLAUGHTER**
**ACE BOOKS, 1956**

Slaughter was a bestselling author of swashbucklers and other historical costume dramas.

📖

## BEYOND THE FARTHEST STAR
**EDGAR RICE BURROUGHS**
**ACE BOOKS, 1964**
**COVER BY FRANK FRAZETTA**

When Ace and Ballantine divvied up the Burroughs rights, Ace wound up with this intriguing interplanetary story from late in Burroughs' career. Burroughs collectors and Frazetta fans vie for copies.

📖📖

## CAPTAIN CROSSBONES
DONALD BARR CHIDSEY
ACE BOOKS, 1958

This PBO was a typical swashbuckler of the sort that Chidsey turned out for Ace, Avon, Dell, and other paperback houses. Avast, me hearties!

## THE BIG QUESTION
JOHN KENNETH
ACE BOOKS, 1960

This PBO by the probably pseudonymous John Kenneth was inspired by the 1950s' scandal over rigged television quiz shows. It is certainly an historical curiosity if not a great work of literature.

## CITY
CLIFFORD D. SIMAK
ACE BOOKS, 1958
COVER BY ED VALIGURSKY

Like so many fictioneers, Clifford D. Simak (1904-1988) started out as a journalist. Unlike many of his colleagues, he continued to work as a reporter and editor for the Minneapolis *Star* and *Tribune* for more than fifty years. His great story-cycle *City* won the International Fantasy Award, a forerunner of the Hugo and Nebula.

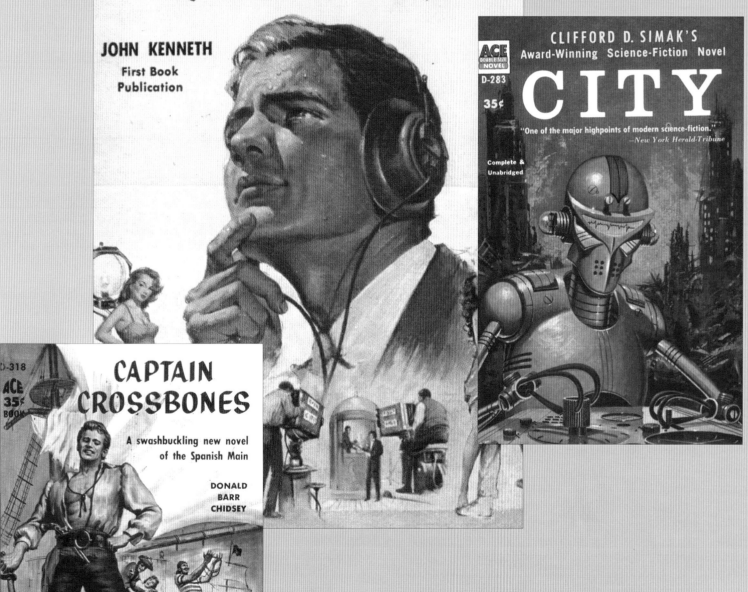

## THE CODE OF THE WOOSTERS
P. G. WODEHOUSE
ACE BOOKS, 1953
COVER BY NORMAN SAUNDERS

Few paperback houses, even those as deeply genre-oriented as Ace, failed to experiment with sometimes surprising choices. This early Ace Double featured two novels by British humorist P. G. Wodehouse, with delightful, lighthearted covers by pulp veteran Saunders.

❚❚❚

## THE COLOR OF HATE
JOE L. HENSLEY
ACE BOOKS, 1962
COVER BY GEORGE ZEAL

*The Color of Hate* (PBO) was Indiana journalist-turned-lawyer-turned-judge Hensley's first novel. Hensley specialized in suspense rather than conventional detection. The dangerous themes in this book almost certainly grew from actual cases that he dealt with. He also served as Harlan Ellison's attorney when Ellison was threatened with a court martial during his brief military career.

❚❚

## CONAN THE CONQUERER
ROBERT E. HOWARD
BACKED WITH

### THE SWORD OF RHIANNON (PBO)
LEIGH BRACKETT
ACE BOOKS, 1953
COVERS BY NORMAN SAUNDERS AND ROBERT SCHULZ

This early Ace Double is one of the great Ace collectibles. Howard (1906-1936) was a bizarre, unstable individual who committed suicide as his mother lay dying. Brackett (1915-1978) was as sane as Howard was crazy. She wrote science fiction, hardboiled mysteries, and fine screenplays in her long career. Her husband was Edmond Hamilton.

❚❚❚

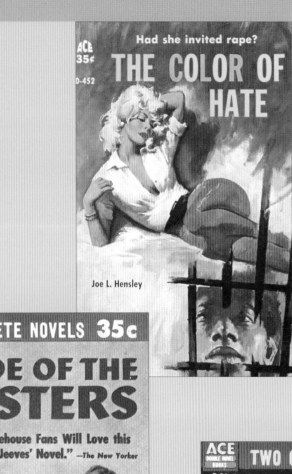

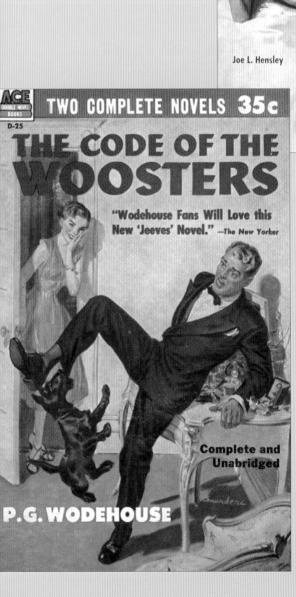

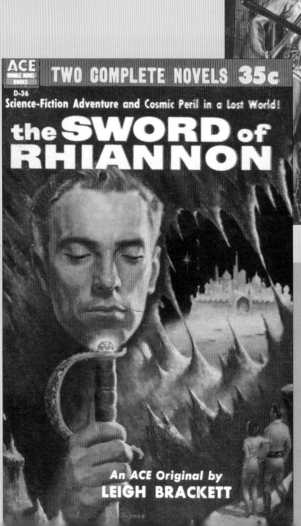

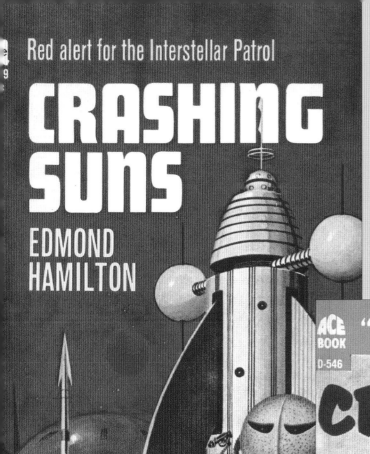

Red alert for the Interstellar Patrol

# CRASHING SUNS

### EDMOND HAMILTON

First Book Public...

ACE D-57 TWO COMPLETE NOVELS 35¢
DOUBLE NOVEL BOOKS

ON A THROUGH TRAIN TO TERROR!

## counterspy EXPRESS

ACE BOOK
D-546

"NOBODY CAN TOP NORTON"
—St. Louis Globe-Democrat

35¢

# THE CROSSROADS OF TIME

Complete and Unabridged

## A CHASE THROUGH ALTERNATE WORLDS

### ANDRE NORTON

---

**CRASHING SUNS**
EDMOND HAMILTON
ACE BOOKS, 1964
COVER BY VALIGURSKY (?)

Ed "World Wrecker" Hamilton (1904-1977) was
one of the three great space opera writers of the
pulp era, the others being Jack Williamson and
Edward Elmer Smith. *Crashing Suns* gets the title
as grandaddy of them all — it was originally serialized in *Weird Tales* in 1928 although the Ace edition
is a PBO. Hamilton's wife was Leigh Brackett.

❝❝

**THE CROSSROADS OF TIME**
ANDRE NORTON
ACE BOOKS, 1962

Alice Mary Norton wrote as Andre Norton,
Andrew North, and Allen Weston. A prolific
writer, she produced science fiction, fantasy,
historical novels, gothics, and children's books.
The clever cover painting on *Crossroads of Time*
(regrettably uncredited) is quite amazing when
split vertically and covered with a blank sheet
of paper.

❝❝

**COUNTERSPY EXPRESS**
A. S. FLEISCHMAN
ACE BOOKS, 1954

Backed with *Treachery in Trieste*, by Charles
L. Leonard, this Ace Double was a good solid
entry in the Cold War spy-versus-spy derby.

## D FOR DELINQUENT
**BUD CLIFTON**
**ACE BOOKS, 1958**

David Derek Stacton (1925-1968) wrote half a dozen JD and hard-boiled novels for Ace and Pyramid between 1958 and 1961 and then disappeared from the bookshelves. What became of him? The charming uncredited painting on this PBO offers an amazing collection of JD novel icons. How many can you count?

## DARK OF THE WOODS
**DEAN R. KOONTZ**
**ACE BOOKS, 1970**
**COVER BY JEFF JONES**

Doubled with a Koontz PBO (*Soft Come the Dragons*, cover by Jack Gaughan) this is one of the books that the author doesn't particularly care to see reprinted. Koontz was a competent but unremarkable science fiction writer in his early years, then found his *metier* in high tension suspense and borderline horror and leaped to the bestseller list.

## DEATH HITCHES A RIDE
**MARTIN L. WEISS**
**ACE BOOKS, 1954**
**COVER BY BARTON**

Martin L. Weiss seems to have written only two books, this Ace Double PBO and *Hate Alley*, Ace, 1957. The combination of good-natured GGA and impending violence is remarkably effective.

## FARE PREY
**LAINE FISHER**
**ACE BOOKS, 1959**
**COVER BY ROBERT MAGUIRE**

James A. Howard wrote ten books, nine of them under his own name and this PBO as Fisher. The reason is unclear, although he was closely identified with Popular Library and may not have wanted his editor there to know that he was working for Ace. Maguire's painting is fashionably *noir*-ish.

## THE GALAXY PRIMES

EDWARD E. SMITH
ACE BOOKS, 1965
COVER BY ED VALIGURSKY

Best known for his great "Skylark" and "Lensmen" series, "Doc" Smith wrote several other popular space operas. Valigursky's exciting space-tiger-leopard added a spectacular image to the PBO.

## THE GENERAL

KARLLUDWIG OPITZ
ACE BOOKS, 1957
COVER BY VERNE TOSSEY

A decade after the Nazi surrender, it had become possible to laugh at one of the most horrendous periods in history. At least for some people.

## THE GLASS TEAT

HARLAN ELLISON
ACE BOOKS, 1970
COVER BY LEO AND DIANE DILLON

Ellison proudly states that he was the art director as well as author of this PBO. Although often identified as a science fiction writer, Ellison has written JD novels and a wide variety of nonfiction including this volume of criticism by "the most outspoken columnist of the under-ground press."

## THE GOLDEN COUCH

HENRY LEWIS NIXON
ACE BOOKS, 1956

Henry Lewis Nixon (sometimes rendered "Henry Louis Nixon") was essentially a sleaze writer, published by Beacon, Intimate, Stallion, and Royal Giant Books. His greatest success was the often reprinted *Confessions of a Psychiatrist*. This PBO is about as close as Nixon ever came to mainstream publishing and about as close as Ace ever came to publishing sleaze.

First book publication of a great new novel by the author of THE SKYLARK OF SPACE

### the galaxy primes

...WARD E. SMITH

ace book
29350
$1.25

## HARLAN ELLISON
# the Glass Teat

A NOVEL OF THE PRIVATE LIVES AND LOVES OF PSYCHIATRISTS

S-190
ACE
25¢
BOOKS

THE GOLDEN COUCH

HENRY LEWIS NIXON

"Racy and colloquial . . . a real eye-catcher."
—Washington Post & Times-Herald

ACE
25¢
BOOKS
G-256

# THE GENERAL

KARLLUDWIG OPITZ
Complete & Unabridged

...HE BEVERLY HILLBIL...
...CHERY AT MY LAI, h...
...re seen through the...
...e most outspoken co...

## THE IMPOTENT GENERAL
**CHARLES PETTIT**
ACE BOOKS, 1953
COVER BY NORMAN SAUNDERS

Backed with *Love in a Junk and Other Exotic Tales*, this quixotic blend of militarism, eroticism, and satire may well be the most peculiar book Ace ever published. The Saunders cover is a gem!

## HOOTENANNY NURSE
**SUZANNE ROBERTS**
ACE BOOKS, 1963

Always ready to jump on a trend, Ace turned out a sizable body of nurse novels, including half a dozen PBO's by Suzanne Roberts. This author's nurses included cross-country, Vietnam, celebrity suite, and even rangeland. So why not a hootenanny nurse romancing a guitar-twanging young doc?

## THE DAY THEY H-BOMBED LOS ANGELES
**ROBERT MOORE WILLIAMS**
ACE BOOKS, 1960

Robert Moore Williams (1907-1977) contributed regularly to the science fiction pulps of the 1940s and to the paperback industry in the 1950s and 1960s, placing most of his works with Ace, Lancer, and Popular Library. His Jongor and Zanthar series are sometimes collected as associational items by fans of Edgar Rice Burroughs.

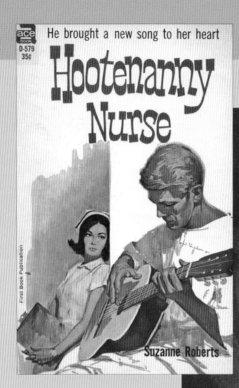

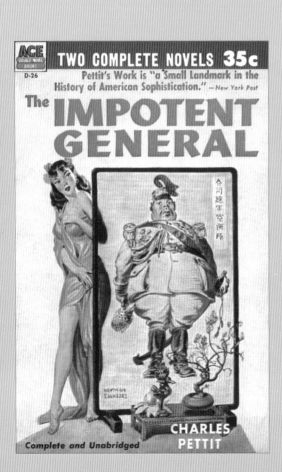

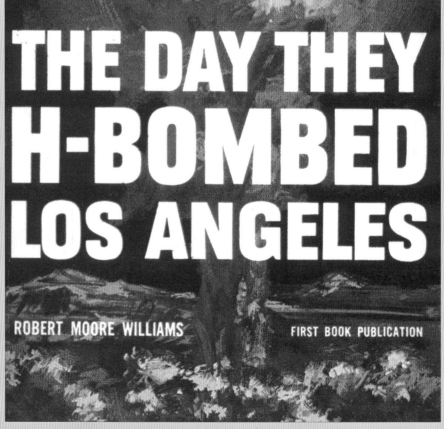

Even so, it was not until Ace D-31 that Wollheim finally got his freedom from Wynn, who had always shown a certain suspicion of science fiction. Ace was doing well and Wollheim ran with *Universe Maker* and *The World of Null-A*, both by popular science fiction writer A. E. Van Vogt.

Van Vogt seemed like a safe bet for Ace. By 1953 he had appeared frequently in the science fiction pulps for some fifteen years. A variety of publishers had brought out his novels in hardcovers, and NAL had introduced him to the mass paperback market in 1952 with *Mission: Interplanetary*, a retitling of his 1950 hardcover *Voyage of the Space Beagle*. This book would achieve renewed fame decades later when it was alleged that the film *Alien* had been plagiarized from its pages; the studio settled out of court.

The Van Vogt double was the first of hundreds of science fiction novels, anthologies, and single-author collections to be published by Ace. While Ballantine concentrated on new works, Ace benefited from Donald Wollheim's long association with the pulp magazine field, where vast numbers of science fiction novels had appeared either as serials or (in the case of somewhat shorter "novels"—actually novellas or long novelettes) complete in single editions.

Prior to this time, science fiction had been a scarce commodity in book form, with most stories appearing in pulp magazines and then disappearing into the files of collectors. In the 1940s a number of specialty houses, owned by long-time fans, began mining the back issues of the magazines for novels which were then published with loving care in small editions and distributed to devoted enthusiasts. But it was Wollheim who had the vision to produce large numbers of science fiction paperbacks for the mass market.

This is not to say that Ace was a science fiction publisher. Aaron Wynn and Donald Wollheim were businessmen, and Ace Books published a wide array of titles. Wynn, Wollheim, and the other editors at Ace were quick to react to ever-shifting public taste. When nurse romances were

in vogue, Ace published nurse romances. You could paper a room with cover images of winsome young women in white looking dedicated to the service of humanity or gazing limpidly at handsome, white-clad young doctors. When the neo-gothic craze of the 1960s and 1970s was in full howl, Ace produced a freshet of books with endless variations on the classic neo-gothic cover painting.

You know what these books looked like. A stormy night with the moon shrouded by scudding, dark clouds; a tall and foreboding mansion standing silhouetted against the eerie sky; a frightened young woman in a wind-whipped white gown racing across the lawn while a single candle flickers frighteningly in a tower window.

Ace published historicals, war novels, juvenile delinquent books, and borderline sleaze. They added a line of "singles" and the Ace Star series for larger and more expensive books, but they remained best known for their genre-oriented Ace Double Books.

They published a series of highly regarded "best of the year" science fiction volumes, edited by Wollheim and his brilliant protegé Terry Carr starting in 1965; Wollheim continued the series when he left Ace and founded DAW Books. This was not the first such annual series, but it was the first to appear as PBOs and was eagerly awaited each year.

Carr edited a series of Ace Specials, science fiction novels of unusual literary merit. Between Ace Doubles, Singles, and Specials, this publisher promoted an eye-popping array of science fiction authors: Samuel R. Delany, Ursula K. Le Guin, Philip K. Dick, Roger Zelazny, Robert Silverberg, Harlan Ellison, Andre Norton, Clifford D. Simak, Jack Williamson, Edmond Hamilton, Dean R. Koontz and many others.

Wollheim had long been fond of the works of Edgar Rice Burroughs, and had sought to obtain paperback rights to Burroughs' science fiction and jungle adventures. Following Burroughs' death in 1950, the administrator of his estate

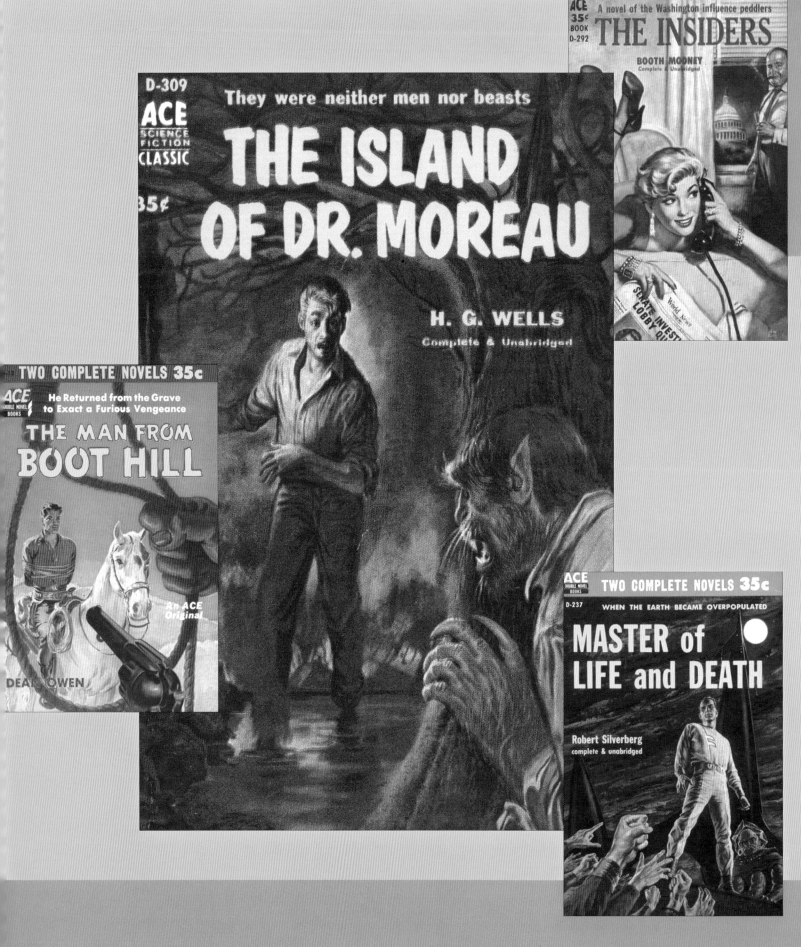

### THE MAN FROM BOOT HILL
**DEAN OWEN**
ACE BOOKS, 1953
COVER BY NORMAN SAUNDERS

Dean Owen's half of this western Ace Double was a PBO, backed with a reprint by Dan J. Stevens. Saunders' painting is a marvel of good design and clean, almost minimalist execution. Owen specialized in westerns but went as far afield as novelizing *The Brides of Dracula* for Monarch.

### THE ISLAND OF DR. MOREAU
**H. G. WELLS**
ACE BOOKS, 1958

Wells wrote his science fiction early in his career, and followed it with shelves full of "serious" books. What does anybody read any more? You got it!

### THE INSIDERS
**BOOTH MOONEY**
ACE BOOKS, 1958
COVER BY VERNE TOSSEY

In 1958 Ike was in the White House, Nixon was vice president. How much influence peddling went on in Washington? Mooney apparently fancied himself an insider. He wrote a biography of Lyndon Johnson for Avon and one other novel for Gold Medal.

## THE NURSE AND THE PIRATE

PEGGY GADDIS
ACE BOOKS, 1961

The hard-working and thoroughly professional Gaddis wrote all sorts of romantic novels, including this rather astonishing cross-genre hybrid.

## NEGATIVE OF A NUDE

CHARLES E. FRITCH
ACE BOOKS, 1959
COVER BY ROBERT MAGUIRE

A fine, moody Maguire serves for Fritch's PBO half of this Ace Double. Most of Fritch's work was science fiction, but he also wrote *Kim Novak: Goddess of Love* for Monarch in 1962.

## MIG ALLEY

ROBERT EUNSON
ACE BOOKS, 1959
COVER BY VERNE TOSSEY

A fine, realistic painting by Tossey graces this otherwise very standard novel of Men Who Risk Their Lives By Day And The Women Who Share Their Love At Night. This time, it's set in the Korean War, 1950-53.

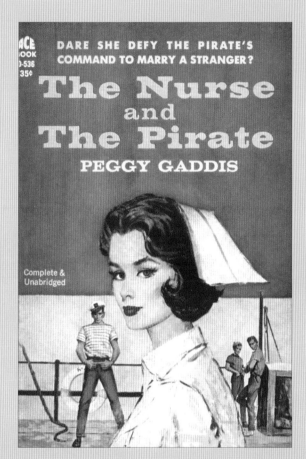

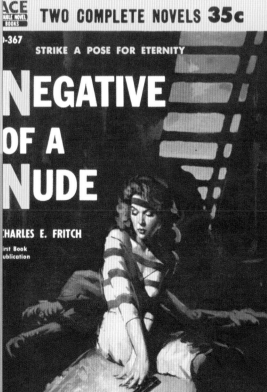

## MASTER OF LIFE AND DEATH

ROBERT SILVERBERG
ACE BOOKS, 1957
COVER BY ED EMSHWILLER

The amazingly versatile and productive Silverberg has written everything from juvenile adventure to the most sophisticated science fiction, biographies, travel guides, and even a good deal of sleaze (the latter, pseudonymously). To the credit of Ace Books during the Wollheim era, that company promoted the early works of many writers who went on to much greater things, Silverberg among them.

## QUANTRELL'S RAIDERS
FRANK GRUBER
ACE BOOKS, 1953
COVER BY NORMAN SAUNDERS

Equally at home writing hardboiled detective novels and solidly crafted westerns, Gruber wrote both sides of this Ace Double, one a reissue, one a PBO.

## THE PRISONER
THOMAS M. DISCH
ACE BOOKS, 1969

A writer of truly staggering brilliance and depth, Disch went from writing PBOs for Ace and Berkley to become one of the nation's leading novelists, poets, critics, and operatic librettists, both under his own name and several pseudonyms. Even this TVTI does not fail to surprise and impress, although it is obviously minor Disch.

## RETURN TO TOMORROW
L. RON HUBBARD
ACE BOOKS, 1954
COVER BY VALIGURSKY (?)

Before he invented Dianetics and Scientology, L. Rob Hubbard (1911-1986) was a versatile pulp writer, turning out westerns, South Sea adventures, science fiction, and fantasy stories by the ream. This PBO, based on a serial Hubbard had previously placed in *Astounding Science Fiction*, deals with the problems created by the time-dilation effect of very high-speed travel. It's very hard to come by, as devotees of Hubbard's religion scour available sources for copies of his early works.

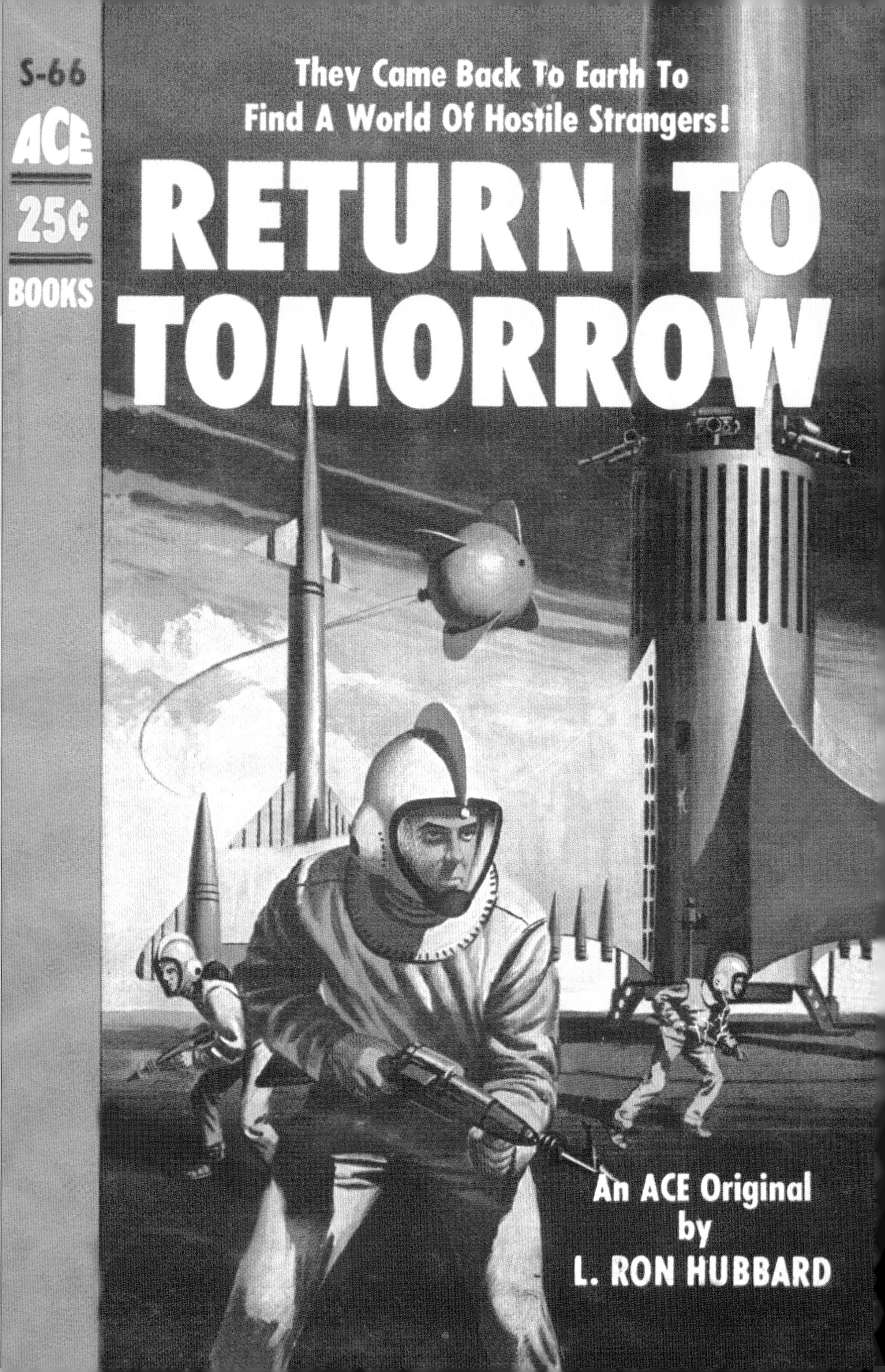

S-66

ACE

25¢

BOOKS

They Came Back To Earth To
Find A World Of Hostile Strangers!

# RETURN TO TOMORROW

An ACE Original
by
L. RON HUBBARD

had shown little interest in exploiting the literary rights, much more in a combination of film and comic book licenses and real estate investments.

Frustrated, Wollheim had packaged a series of novels by the late Otis Adelbert Kline (1891-1946) for Ace. Kline had been an admirer and emulator of Burroughs, and his interplanetary and jungle tales closely paralleled Burroughs' own.

In the early 1960's a flaw in the Burroughs copyrights was discovered, and several companies leaped to publish new editions of old Burroughs titles. Wollheim, at Ace, was quick to do so. He obtained a series of glorious cover paintings, many of them by artists who had cut their teeth in the comic-book industry. These included, most notably, Roy G. Krenkel and Frank Frazetta. These Ace singles are among the most beautiful and highly sought of 1960s paperbacks.

Caught sleeping at the switch, members of the Burroughs family finally took action. Hulbert Burroughs, a surviving son, came to New York to meet with various publishers. The result was an arrangement with Canaveral Press to produce hardcover editions of Burroughs' books. Paperback rights would be divided between Ace and Ballantine Books, with Ballantine getting the more desirable Tarzan and Martian series. Ace had to settle for Burroughs' "hollow earth" and Venusian series. Other one-offs were divided between the two.

Even so, bad blood now existed between Ballantine and Wollheim. With the Burroughs revival in full swing, a New York radio station devoted a popular all-night talk show to Burroughs. Among a round table of guests, both Ian Ballantine and Donald Wollheim were slated to appear. Each agreed until he heard that the other was included, and then both men cancelled.

Another bone of contention between Ace and Ballantine arose over J. R. R. Tolkien's great fantasy trilogy, *The Lord of the Rings*. Originally published in England, the Wagnerian adventure was available to American readers only in the form of imported copies. The American publisher

Houghton Mifflin obtained American rights to the books, and for its initial editions used sheets imported from England. These were then bound in the United States and issued under the Houghton Mifflin rubric.

Matters of copyright law have always been complex and contentious, and international copyrights especially so. It happened that a provision of the U.S. copyright law placed a limit on the number of copies of a foreign book that could be imported and sold in the U.S. Even unbound sheets counted as imported books. Beyond this number, the publisher was required to print the books in this country.

Houghton Mifflin had exceeded the limit on imported copies (sheets) of *The Lord of the Rings*. Consequently, the trilogy lost its copyright protection in the U.S.

Wollheim learned of this and under his direction Ace Books raced an edition of the three volumes into print in 1966, with striking cover paintings by Jack Gaughan (Ace Number A-4, 5, 6).

As if to repeat the sequence of events with the Edgar Rice Burroughs books, Ballantine struck a deal with Houghton Mifflin and with Tolkien himself to bring out an authorized edition of the books. Tolkien revised the text of his books just enough to create a "new" edition (not that any reader would notice the difference) and Ballantine issued the revised version of the books with genteel cover paintings by Barbara Remington.

Ballantine also experimented in other ways. The company was responsible for several regional lines of books, most notably Comstock Books. Comstock was an independently owned company but was backed by Ballantine. Its volumes of Western Americana—many of them with striking cover artwork—were produced in limited editions and distributed mainly in the West. Other Ballantine "regionals" operated in New England, in the Northeast, and in the South.

### RUMBLE AT THE HOUSING PROJECT
EDWARD DeROO
ACE BOOKS, 1960

Apparently DeROO wrote only one other book, *The Little Caesars*, also a JD for Ace. Note the grand collection of JD literature icons in the uncredited painting. Check out the TV antennas sprouting from the tenement roofs!

### RIVERBOAT GIRL
P. A. HOOVER
ACE BOOKS, 1956

What do you bet that P. A. Hoover's river runs smack through the middle of Erskine Caldwell country? Hoover wrote four novels, all about man-destroying women living on or near bodies of water.

### SLAVES OF THE KLAU
JACK VANCE
ACE BOOKS, 1958
COVER BY ED EMSHWILLER

This is the PBO side of a Vance Double, backed with his *Big Planet*. Vance is considered one of science fiction's finest stylists and most creative writers. It is a mystery that he hasn't been discovered by the rest of the literary world.

S-168
ACE
25¢
BOOKS

SHE SEPARATED THE MEN FROM THE BOYS

## RIVERBOAT GIRL

Complete Novel
**P. A. HOOVER**

ACE
35¢
BOOK

Old Terror In New Buildings

## RUMBLE AT THE HOUSING PROJECT

EDWARD DeROO
First Book Publication

ACE
TWO COMPLETE NOVELS 35¢
D-295

It was always open season on escaped Earthlings

## SLAVES OF THE KLAU

Jack Vance
Complete Novel

### TARZAN AND THE LION MAN
EDGAR RICE BURROUGHS
ACE BOOKS, 1963
COVER BY FRANK FRAZETTA

Before the settlement with Edgar Rice Burroughs, Inc., that parceled out rights to Ballantine and Ace, there was a mad scramble for titles. Ace's packages were superb and collectible in their own right, aside from their appeal to Burroughs completists.

### SPIDERWEB
ROBERT BLOCH
ACE BOOKS, 1954

With each passing year Robert Bloch (1917-1994) becomes more and more a favorite of collectors. For the sake of his half, this Ace Double has become a target.

### AND THEN THE TOWN TOOK OFF
RICHARD WILSON
ACE BOOKS, 1960

Wilson was a member of the New York Futurian group that included such luminaries as James Blish, Donald Wollheim, Judith Merril and Frederik Pohl. For most of his life, Wilson pursued an academic career, but he did write three novels, all PBOs, one for Ace and two for Ballantine. *And then the Town Took Off* is good fun but hard to find because it's back-to-back with Andre Norton's *The Sioux Spaceman*.

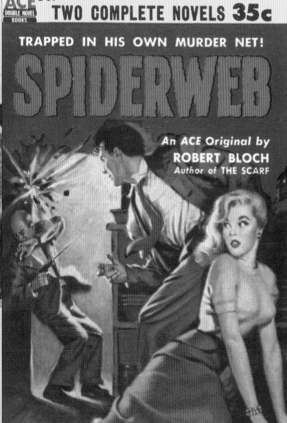

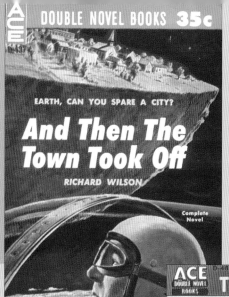

EARTH, CAN YOU SPARE A CITY?

## And Then The Town Took Off
RICHARD WILSON

Complete Novel

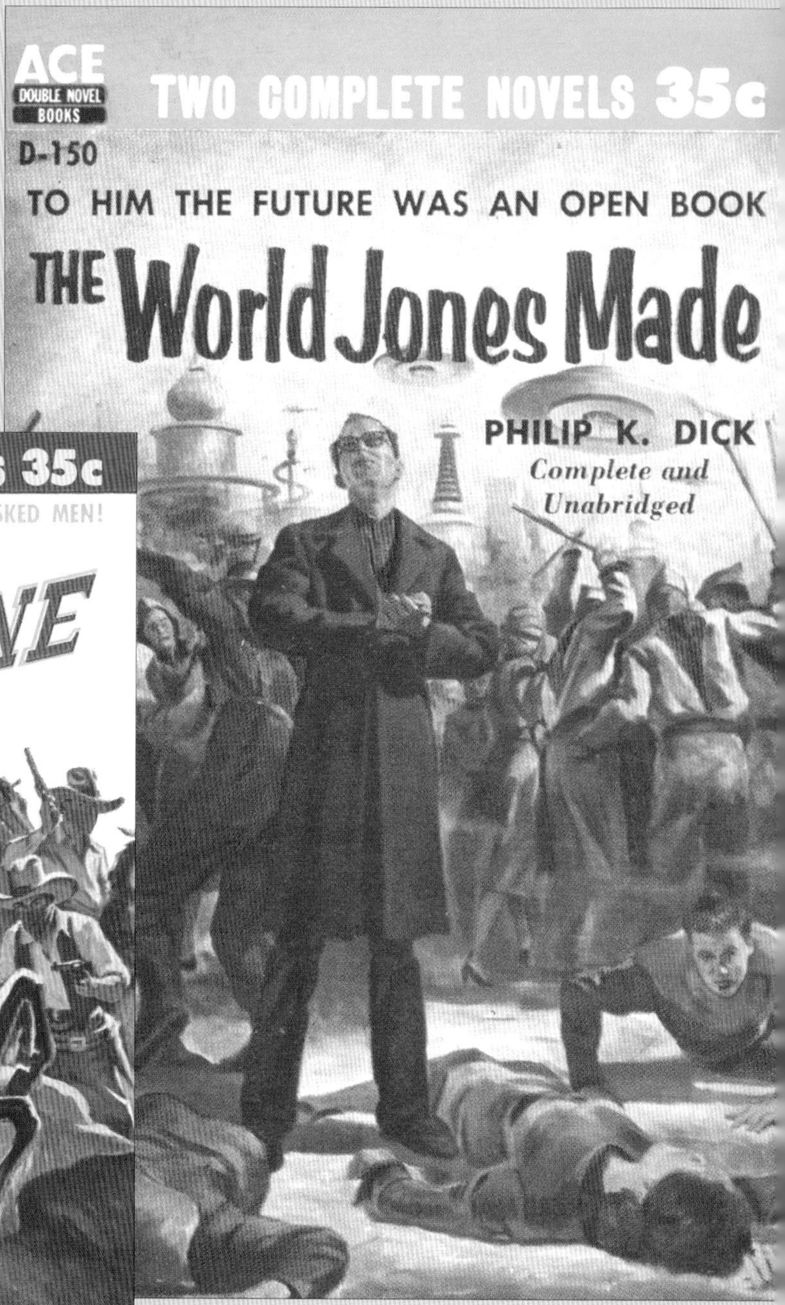

ACE
DOUBLE NOVEL BOOKS 35c
D-437

---

ACE
DOUBLE NOVEL
BOOKS
D-150

TWO COMPLETE NOVELS 35c

TO HIM THE FUTURE WAS AN OPEN BOOK

## THE World Jones Made
PHILIP K. DICK

*Complete and Unabridged*

---

ACE
DOUBLE NOVEL
BOOKS
D-48

TWO COMPLETE NOVELS 35c

LYNCH LAW RULED IN THIS VALLEY OF MASKED MEN!

## UTAH BLAINE

An ACE Original by JIM MAYO

---

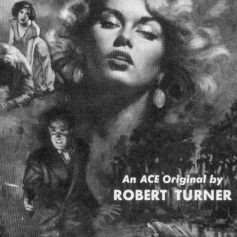

ACE
DOUBLE NOVEL
BOOKS
D-55

TWO COMPLETE NOVELS 35c

## The Tobacco Auction MURDERS

Death Was the Highest Bidder!

An ACE Original by
ROBERT TURNER

---

### THE TOBACCO AUCTION MURDERS
ROBERT TURNER
ACE BOOKS, 1954
COVER BY ROBERT MAGUIRE

Robert Turner (1915-1980) wrote half a dozen
mysteries and other novels plus a collection of
short stories under his own name and as Mercer
D. Cook and Don Romano. The fine Maguire
cover adds to the desirability of this Double.

### UTAH BLAINE
JIM MAYO
ACE BOOKS, 1954

Here's a real sleeper if you come across a
copy and the seller doesn't realize what he
has. Jim Mayo was Louis L'Amour.

### THE WORLD JONES MADE
PHILIP K. DICK
ACE BOOKS, 1956

One of Don Wollheim's great protégés, Philip
K. Dick (1928-1982) has supplanted Heinlein
as the science fiction writer most read on and
off campuses, in and out of the science fiction
community. He was just beginning to reap the
rewards of a lifetime of struggle when he died
at age fifty-three.

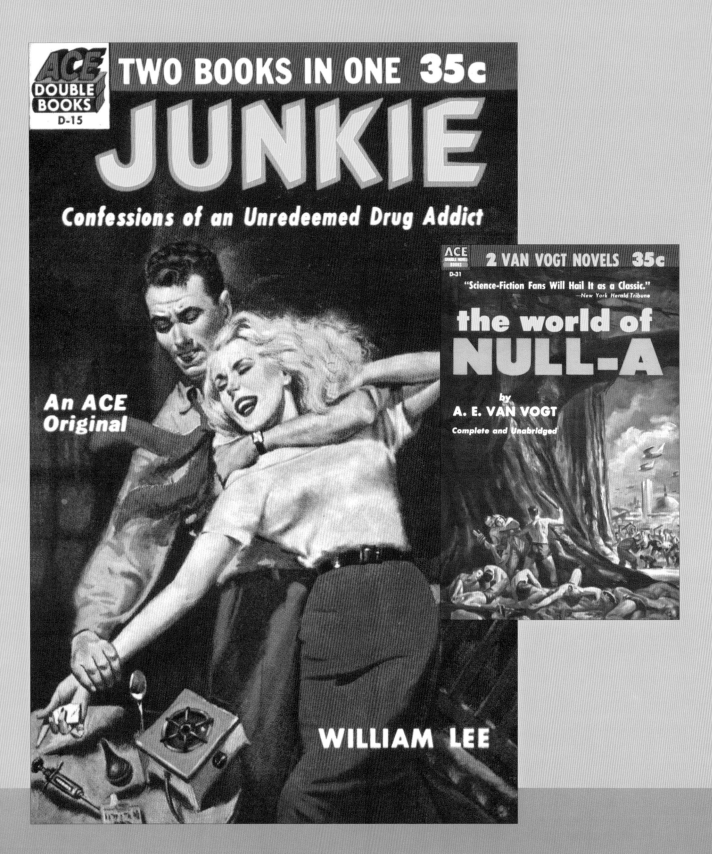

**JUNKIE**
WILLIAM LEE
ACE BOOKS, 1953

This PBO half of an Ace Double introduced a new author whose real name turned out to be William Burroughs. The book was regarded as just one more sensational drug "confession" when first published, but as Burroughs' literary stock soared, so did its value. It is almost impossible to find of course—but there might be a copy lurking in your great-uncle's attic!

**THE WORLD OF NULL-A**
A. E. VAN VOGT
ACE BOOKS, 1953

Van Vogt (1912-1999) exploded into the science fiction pulps in the late 1930s and became an instant star. In later years his eccentricities seemed to overtake his talent, and his later books are less highly regarded than the early ones.

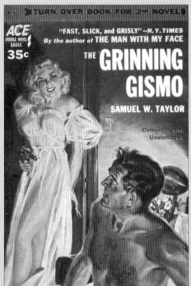

Another collected Ballantine line was Beagle Books. Created in the early 1970s in response to distribution problems, the Beagles are indistinguishable from Ballantine Books except for their logos and publisher's indicia. The Beagles included several novels by Ruth Rendell and others, but their greatest strength was in horror fiction. H. P. Lovecraft collectors in particular seek out the Beagle editions of 1970 through 1972.

Beagle Books are quite scarce. Designed to remedy Ballantine's distribution woes, the Beagles were themselves very badly distributed. For all anyone knows, cartons of them are moldering away in a warehouse somewhere.

Following Aaron Wynn's death, Ace Books was sold several times. Donald Wollheim left the company in 1972 to form DAW Books in partnership with his wife, the former Elsie Balter. Both Wollheims lived until the 1990s, and following their deaths DAW Books remained under the control of their daughter. Eventually Ace disappeared into the maw of a publishing conglomerate, becoming a mere marketing logo.

Ballantine Books was also sold several times, becoming part of another giant conglomerate but retaining more of an independent identity. Ian Ballantine returned to Bantam as an independent packager and remained active and remarkably creative and energetic until his death.

The Ballantine "regionals" were by now long gone, and the Beagle Books experiment was little more than a footnote to publishing history. The battle of titans is now a closed chapter and mostly forgotten.

THE GRINNING GISMO
SAMUEL S. TAYLOR
ACE BOOKS, 1952
TOO HOT FOR HELL
KEITH VINING
COVERS BY NORMAN SAUNDERS

The prize of prizes, though neither novel is a masterpiece and neither author is widely remembered (although Taylor's literary invention of flubber recurs in Disney films). This was Ace Double D1, the book that started it all.

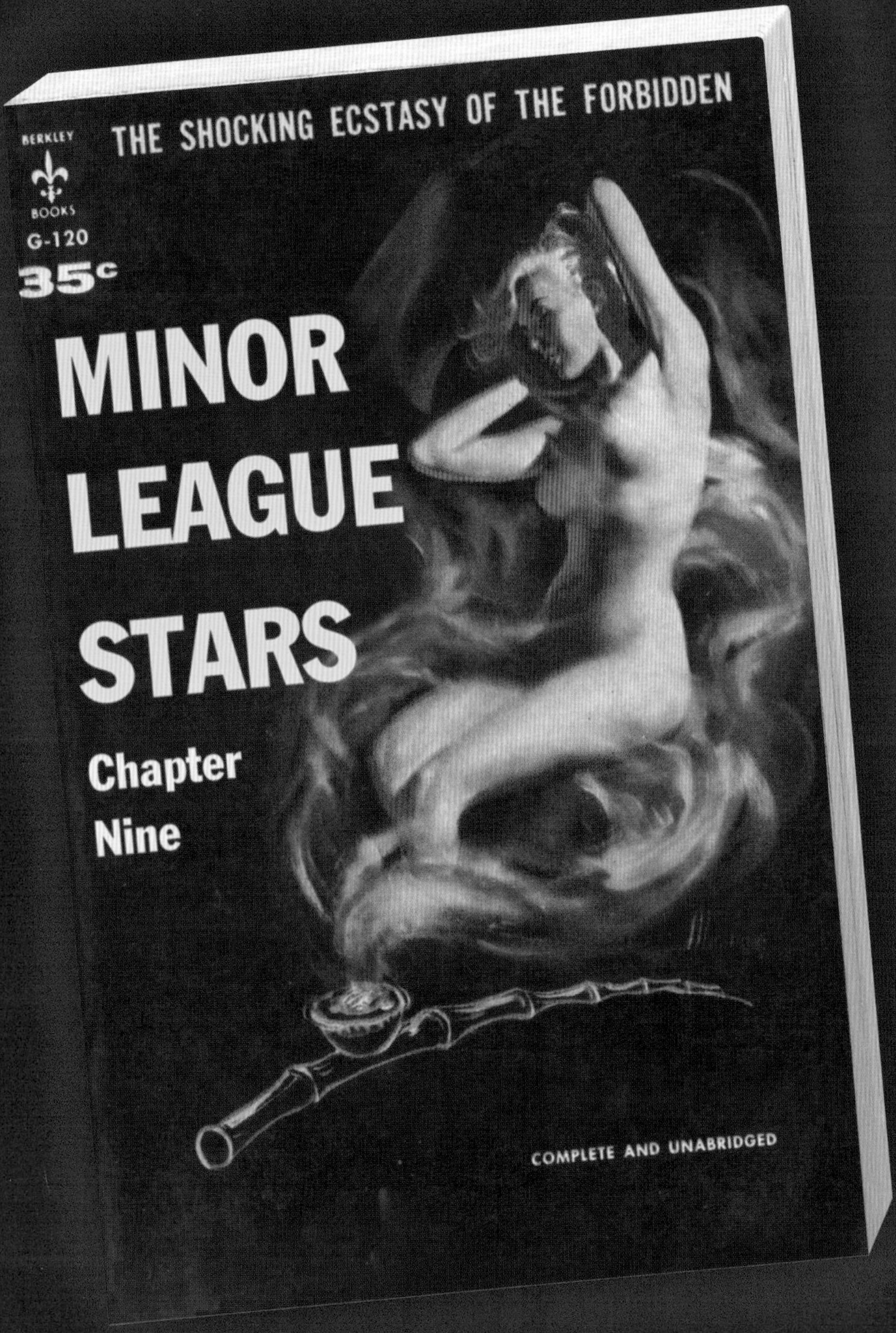
THE SHOCKING ECSTASY OF THE FORBIDDEN
BERKLEY BOOKS
G-120
35c
MINOR LEAGUE STARS
Chapter Nine
COMPLETE AND UNABRIDGED

From a running start in the 1930s, the paperback industry had grown to a gigantic enterprise. Within three decades of Robert de Graff and Ian Ballantine's race to reach the newsstands and bookshelves of the nation with their Pocket Books and American Penguins, there were no fewer than 585 different paperback imprints on the market. Between new issues and backlist titles, there were some 63,000 *different* paperbacks on sale.

Another thirty-odd years have passed, and the number of companies to try their luck at the paperback game is in the thousands—the total number of titles issued on the order of 250,000. That's a quarter million different books, not a quarter million copies.

Some publishers have existed barely long enough to produce one obscure book and then disappear without a trace. Others have endured for decades and issued thousands of different titles. Of the proverbial "nine majors," eight still survive although every one of them has been absorbed into a larger conglomerate: Ace, Avon, Ballantine, Bantam, Dell, Fawcett, Pocket, and Signet. Sometimes there are layers upon layers of conglomeration. The once mighty Fawcett has become an imprint of Ballantine, which has become an imprint of Random House. Only Popular Library seems to have disappeared utterly from the racks.

It's obviously impossible to cover the thousands of publishers that have come and gone from the paperback field, but let's try to touch on at least a few of the more important and more interesting of the "minors."

For instance, consider Red Arrow Books. From their headquarters in Milwaukee, Wisconsin, this company was actually an entry in the race to "get there first." Red Arrow followed the lead of Kurt Enoch's Albatross and Allen Lane's Penguin Books, color-coding its covers for easy identification by readers. Red covers meant mystery and crime fiction, green meant travel and adventure, and blue meant general fiction.

In 1939 and 1940, Red Arrow issued a dozen numbered books:

1. *Thirteen at Dinner* by Agatha Christie
2. *Murder on the Hudson* by Jennifer Jones
3. *Murders in Praed Street* by John Rhode
4. *Death in the Library* by Philip Ketchum
5. *Death Wears a White Gardenia* by Zelda Popkin
6. *My South Sea Island* by Eric Musprat
7. *Yankee Komisar* by Commander S. M. Riis
8. *Girl Hunt* by Laurence D. Smith
9. *The Seven Sleepers* by Francis Beeding
10. *Captain Nemesis* by F. Van Wyck Mason
11. *Windswept* by Olga Moore
12. *Pirate's Purchase* by Ben Ames Williams

There was even an unlucky thirteenth Red Arrow Book, *The Unspeakable Gentleman* by John P. Marquand.

This was certainly a good set of titles, and several of the authors remain in print after more than sixty years. Philip Ketchum's *Death in the Library* came back as Dell Book Number 1— surely a distinction for this otherwise nearly forgotten author. A number of the other Red Arrow titles have reappeared over the years, including Christie's *Thirteen at Dinner*, a 1933 Hercule Poirot novel published in England as *Lord Edgeware Dies*.

What went wrong? Why did Red Arrow disappear while both Pocket and American Penguin became major and enduring institutions? Was it the conservative design of the books? An inability to distribute them effectively? A shortage of operating capital? Could it have been the location of Red Arrow's headquarters, so distant from New York, the hub of the nation's publishing industry?

It is a mystery.

❧ ❧ ❧ ❧ ❧

Another very early entry was the Mercury Mystery series, published by Lawrence E. Spivak. A walking paradox, Spivak was a brilliant, articulate man who combined high literary and intellectual taste with a keen commercial sense. He had taken control of the old *American Mercury* magazine and then broadened his line

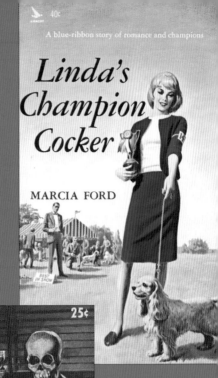

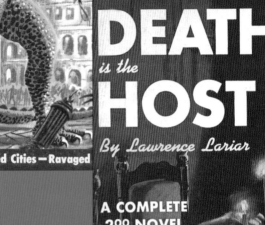

## THE WONDERFUL WIZARD OF OZ

L. FRANK BAUM
AIRMONT, 1960S
COVER BY ROY KRENKEL
AND FRANK FRAZETTA

This uncommon edition of
*The Wizard of Oz* has charming
illustrations by Roy Krenkel.
The striking cover painting is
allegedly mostly Krenkel's work,
with the assistance of Frank
Frazetta—a rare and wonderfully
successful collaboration!

## 20 MILLION MILES TO EARTH

HENRY SLESAR
AMAZING STORIES SCIENCE FICTION
NOVEL/ZIFF-DAVIS PUBLICATIONS, 1957

Possibly in emulation of the *Galaxy*
digest-size novels that made a companion series to *Galaxy* magazine
starting in 1950, *Amazing Stories*
tried out this MTI in 1957. The
author, Henry Slesar, was a productive and highly respected mystery
writer trying his hand at science
fiction. This was the only book in
the *Amazing* series.

## DEATH IS THE HOST

LAWRENCE LARIAR
ATLAS MYSTERY, 1940S

The Atlas Mystery digests are
among the most puzzling of all
short-lived paperback publications.
Approximately two dozen titles
appeared in 1944 and 1945, all
under the Atlas rubric, but claimed
by no fewer than eleven different
publishing companies. Lawrence
Lariar (1908-1981) wrote at least
ten crime novels.

## LINDA'S CHAMPION COCKER

MARCIA FORD
AIRMONT, CIRCA 1960
COVER BY ED RIEN (?)

Airmont was closely affiliated
with Avalon Books, a low-budget
line of science fiction hardcovers
edited by the talented Robert A.
W. Lowndes. The Airmont paperbacks were also heavily tilted
toward science fiction, but as this
charming bit of fluff indicates,
they published other titles as well.

## THE SINGING WIDOW
VERONICA PARKER JOHNS
ATLAS MYSTERY, 1945

Veronica Parker Johns (1907-1988) wrote five mystery novels, two of which were Atlas paperback editions. Little more is known about this author, but she certainly hit lucky when it came to the uncredited painting on *The Singing Widow*.

## GRAND HOTEL
VICKI BAUM
BART HOUSE, 1946

There were forty-one Bart House mass-size paperbacks and five digests, the latter published as Bartholomew House books. All are collectible. Vicki Baum's famous "crossroads" novel was first filmed in 1932 with an all-star cast, but this edition is not an MTI.

## THE WHISPERED SEX
KAY MARTIN
HILLMAN BOOKS, 1960
COVER BY DARCY

Hillman was a significant publisher with several paperback series, magazines, and comic books in its line. Author and critic Ann Bannon has theorized that Lesbian novels were packaged primarily to appeal to the voyeuristic interests of male readers.

## THE WEIRD SHADOW OVER INNSMOUTH
H. P. LOVECRAFT
BART HOUSE, 1944

This PBO is one of the two most sought-after Bart House titles; the other is Lovecraft's *The Dunwich Horror* (1945). More than sixty years after his death, Lovecraft has risen from pulp obscurity to both mass popularity and scholarly respect.

with new fiction-oriented, digest-sized periodicals. He was instrumental in the creation of *Ellery Queen's Mystery Magazine* in 1941 and *The Magazine of Fantasy* (which quickly evolved into *The Magazine of Fantasy and Science Fiction*) in 1949.

He also created the Mercury Mystery series, which would ultimately issue well over 200 titles. These were attractive, digest-sized books with modest cover designs, usually by the talented George Salter. Spivak's association with Salter was an enduring one. Salter would eventually design the title lettering and provide a number of cover paintings for *The Magazine of Fantasy and Science Fiction*.

Spivak's concept of what constituted a mystery novel was remarkably broad, and a list of Mercury Mystery authors is far from a list of the usual suspects. The first Mercury Mystery was *The Postman Always Rings Twice* by James M. Cain. Although he considered himself a serious novelist and not a mere genre writer, Cain is generally regarded by mystery critics as a leading pioneer of the "literate" hardboiled mystery, along with Dashiell Hammett and Raymond Chandler.

Many other standard mystery authors appeared in the series, but Spivak managed to include novels by the master of seagoing swashbucklers, C. S. Forester, and by Sinclair Lewis, Pearl S. Buck, John Steinbeck, and Rudyard Kipling.

After a while the list settled down, however, to such authors as Ellery Queen, Georges Simenon, Frederick Nebel, Dorothy Cameron Disney, Agatha Christie, Rex Stout, Frances and Richard Lockridge, Frank Gruber, and Anthony Boucher.

Mercury Mysteries are numbered from 1 to 209. After number 209 the series was rechristened as a magazine, although oddly there was a Mercury Mystery Number 233, *A Man Named Thin*, by Dashiell Hammett. Serious Hammett scholars know—and others should be apprised —that this book is a short story collection, its title deriving from a fictitious character, one Robin Thin. Don't confuse this book with Hammett's famous novel *The Thin Man*.

❧ ❧ ❧ ❧ ❧

If there were no other reason to remember Lion Books, a simple two-word phrase would suffice: *Jim Thompson*.

Lion was created by Martin Goodman, a publisher with the background we've come to expect. He was a pulp publisher starting in the 1930s. In the 1940s, operating under a variety of corporate facades, he was one of the most successful comic book publishers. His line included three great superheroes: Captain America, Human Torch, and Sub-Mariner. In the 1950s he broadened his magazine empire with a series of so-called "men's sweat" magazines; these were down-market alternatives to *Playboy* and its many imitators that burgeoned in that decade.

Goodman created a distribution company to move his magazines and comics and studied the newsstands in search of fresh ideas for product. He quickly spotted the trend to brightly-colored paperbacks and jumped on that bandwagon in 1949 with Red Circle Books. The name was borrowed from Goodman's pulp magazine line. After seven Red Circle paperbacks, Goodman changed the name to Lion Books. Numbers 8 through 11 were Lion Books, 12 and 13 were Red Circle again, and starting with number 14, it was back to Lion.

Lion had a good run. Numbering went through 233 (1955). A companion line, Lion Library, ran LL-1 through LL-174 (1957).

The earliest Red Circle and Lion Books offered a fairly undistinguished variety of westerns, general novels (with a distinctly sexy bent), and a couple of minor movie tie-ins. All Red Circle Books were reprints except for *Passion in the Dust*, a western by Paul Evan Lehman (6, 1949). With the switch to Lion Books, Goodman continued the reliance on reprints. In short, Goodman was operating a typical low-end paperback house, picking up titles ignored or rejected by publishers with bigger budgets and sprinkling his line with occasional PBOs. The packaging reflected Goodman's pulp background.

The most notable early Lion title was *The Lottery* by Shirley Jackson (15, 1949). How this book by the brilliant Jackson slipped past more prestigious (and higher-paying) houses is puzzling, but it did. Soon Lion added several more interesting titles: *To Keep or Kill* by Wilson Tucker (21, 1950), *Baseball Stars of 1950*, a PBO edited by Bruce Jacobs (23, 1950), *Twilight Men* by Andre Tellier (24, 1950), *The Indiscreet Confessions of a Nice Girl*, anonymous (30, 1950), and *We Too Are Drifting* by Gale Wilhelm (70, 1951).

Lion picked up occasional titles by authors generally associated with other publishers. They managed to snag a Richard Prather PBO, *Lie Down, Killer* (85, 1951) and a Bruno Fischer PBO, *The Lustful Ape* by "Russell Gray" (38, 1950).

Lion or Lion Library also published books by Robert Bloch, Richard Matheson, Cyril Kornbluth ("Jordan Park," "Simon Eisner"), John Dos Passos, David Karp, Damon Knight, Thomas Wolfe, Rex Stout, Fritz Leiber, Algis Budrys, and Graham Greene. Lion or Lion Library's anthologies included a couple of Judith Merril's best: *Human?* (205, 1954) and *Galaxy of Ghouls* (LL-25, 1955).

But Lion's immortality rests on the shoulders of James Myers Thompson (1906-1971). Early in his career Thompson wrote pulp short stories and "true detective" cases. Working as an oil-field worker in the 1930s, he then became a Communist. He was close friends with the young Louis L'Amour until Thompson's wife grew tired of L'Amour's mooching habits and threw him out of her kitchen and out of her house. During World War II, Thompson worked in an aircraft factory in San Diego. He drifted into burlesque, finding work as a small-time comedian, and was a steeplejack, a professional gambler, and an unsuccessful journalist.

He wrote three early hardcover novels published between 1942 and 1949. His career was going nowhere.

Then he met Arnold Hano and Jim Bryans, editors at Lion Books. Hano was an experienced paperback editor, cutting his teeth at Bantam Books. Thompson's biographer, Robert Polito, describes Thompson's first meeting with Hano and Bryans at Lion's office in the Empire State Building.

Thompson was a huge man, an Oklahoman by upbringing, soft-spoken, courtly, and melancholy.

Hano and Bryans had worked out a technique for developing original novels with their authors. The two editors would sketch out brief synopses of story lines, often based on sources in myth or classical literature. They would then arrange a "pitch conference" with a writer. It worked rather like a Hollywood pitch session, only in reverse. Instead of the writer pitching to a producer, the editors would pitch to the writer.

They might discuss as many as five or six synopses at one session. The writer would pick one or two and set to work.

Thompson's first two PBOs for Lion were *The Killer Inside Me* (99, 1952) and *Cropper's Cabin* (108, 1952). *Cropper's Cabin* was a "Southern trash" novel, rather in the mode of Erskine Caldwell's wildly successful Signets.

*The Killer Inside Me* was Thompson's masterpiece.

This book is narrated in first person by Deputy Sheriff Lou Ford, an apparently genial Southwestern lawman. Ford's town is sleepy and dusty, and Ford himself spouts clichés tirelessly.

Only gradually do we realize that Ford is a sadistic monster.

Only gradually do we learn that he is a multiple murderer.

Only gradually do we learn that he is insane.

In later years Hano would claim that the book was based on a synopsis that he created. Thompson, on the other hand, claimed that it

## BLACK OPIUM
**CLAUDE FARRÈRE**
**BERKLEY BOOKS, 1958, 1961**
**COVER BY ROBERT MAGUIRE**

This was apparently Farrère's only book, published twice by Berkley. Maguire's sensuous nude painting is regarded as one of the greatest of all paperback covers.

❚❚❚❚,❚❚❚

## LEAVE IT TO BEAVER
**BEVERLY CLEARY**
**BERKLEY BOOKS, 1960**

Famous children's author Beverly Cleary, creator of the beloved Ramona the Pest, turned out this TVTI and two sequels, *Here's Beaver* and *Beaver and Wally*, based on the popular sitcom. All are doubly collectible for the television connection and for Cleary herself.

❚❚

## LAUGHTER IN THE DARK
**VLADIMIR NABOKOV**
**BERKLEY BOOKS, 1958**
**COVER BY ROBERT MAGUIRE**

By the time this book was published, Nabokov's *Lolita* had become a *cause celebre* (although the film was still several years off), and Berkley was quick to cross-promote.

❚

A STRANGE WOMAN—A STRANGER LOVE

# PERVERSITY

5¢

BERKLEY BOOKS G-33

FRANCIS CARCO

COMPLETE AND UNABRIDGED

BERKLEY X1496 60¢

*High-voltage sex and spying by the author of "The Man from O.R.G.Y."*

# TED MARK

## I WAS A TEENY-BOPPER FOR THE CIA

25c
BERKLEY BOOKS 362

A NOVEL OF BLONDES AND VIOLENCE

# RICHARD S. PRATHER

Creator of SHELL SCOTT

# PATTERN for PANIC

COMPLETE AND UNABRIDGED

---

## PERVERSITY

**FRANCIS CARCO**
**BERKLEY BOOKS, 1956**
**COVER BY HARRY BARTON**

This is another example of the 1950s association of tobacco with sexuality, a strong suggestion of Lesbianism, and a fairly startling cover painting.

📖📖

## PATTERN FOR PANIC

**RICHARD S. PRATHER**
**BERKLEY BOOKS, 1956**
**COVER BY ROBERT MAGUIRE**

Most Prather paperbacks were Gold Medals or Pockets, with a few Tors late in Prather's career. His occasional appearances elsewhere, as in this Berkley reprint of a hardcover, are elusive. This book was written as a Shell Scott novel but was revised to change the hero's identity for the Abelard Schuman hardcover and later restored for a Gold Medal edition. The Berkley version follows the earlier, Abelard Schuman text, making it all the more collectible.

## I WAS A TEENY-BOPPER FOR THE CIA

**TED MARK**
**BERKLEY BOOKS, 1967**

When Lancer editor Larry Shaw's protégé Ted Mark decamped for greener pastures, the standard contract at Lancer was rewritten to strengthen the option clause. Mark was one of many Ian Fleming wanna-bes, his books now historical curiosities.

📖

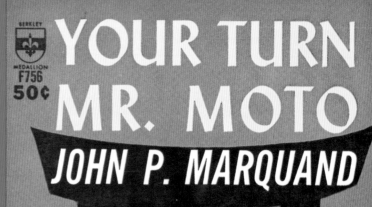

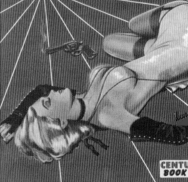

### THE BEAST MUST DIE

NICHOLAS BLAKE
BLACK CAT DETECTIVE, 1943
COVER BY H. LAWRENCE HOFFMAN

C. Day Lewis (1904-1972), Poet Laureate of the United Kingdom and author of many volumes of poetry and criticism, playwright, editor and academic, somehow found the time to write some twenty mysteries featuring the intellectual detective Nigel Strangeways. Sophisticated and literate, these fine novels have a modern counterpart in the works of Colin Dexter.

### YOUR TURN MR. MOTO

JOHN P. MARQUAND
BERKLEY BOOKS, 1963
COVER BY BARYE PHILLIPS

Essentially a mainstream writer, Marquand turned out half a dozen novels featuring his diminutive Japanese intelligence agent, Mr. I. O. Moto, in the late 1930s and early 1940s. Written with unblemished literary grace and powerful psychological depth, these books exceed all expectations of the form.

### HEADED FOR A HEARSE

JONATHAN LATIMER
CENTURY BOOKS, 1950
COVER BY "DUUR"

The talented Latimer (1906-1983) created one of mystery fiction's most off-beat private eyes in Bill Crane, who is featured in this novel. Equally able to write grim *noir* or madcap adventure, Latimer spent much of career writing "B" movies. He also contributed some fine scripts to the Perry Mason television series.

## THE LIVES AND TIMES OF JERRY CORNELIUS
**MICHAEL MOORCOCK**
**DALE BOOKS, CIRCA 1976**

Michael Moorcock got his start writing English-language speech balloons for Tarzan comics originally published in Italian. He moved on to a major career as novelist, short story writer, editor, publisher, screenwriter, musician, and lyricist. His best books may be *The Final Programme* (1968) and *Gloriana; or, The Unfulfill'd Queen* (1978) but that is a matter of opinion. This Dale book is hard to find.

📖📖

## THE X-RATED CORPSE
**MICHAEL AVALLONE**
**CURTIS BOOKS, 1973**

The incredibly prolific and versatile Avallone wrote mysteries, gothics, sex novels, and movie novelizations under a bewildering variety of pseudonyms, some of which also turned up as characters in Avallone's novels. Among them were both Ed Noon and Edwina Noon. This Ed Noon novel even features Avallone as a cover model—he's the fellow with the moustache.

📖

## TERRY AND THE PIRATES: THE JEWELS OF JADE
**EDWARD J. BOYLAN**
**JR., CHECKERBOOKS, 1949**
**COVER BY BILL WENZEL**

Multiply collectible, this PBO comic-strip tie-in was the first in Checkerbooks' experiment, publishing mass market paperbacks at fifteen cents. Adapted from Milton Caniff's classic comic strip, it is a true rarity.

📖📖📖

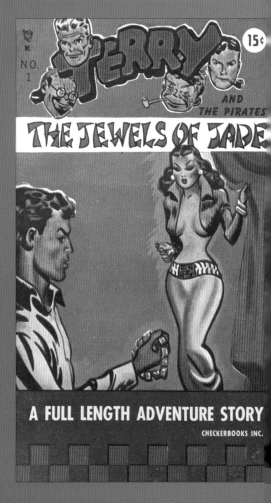

235

was based on reality, that Ford was a literal representation of a lawman Thompson had encountered while working in the oilfields of Texas and by whom Thompson was nearly murdered.

*The Killer Inside Me* led to a dozen PBOs, ten novels and two volumes of autobiography that Thompson wrote for Lion between 1952 and 1957. Almost all of Thompson's books are flawed, some of them very seriously flawed, but all are worth reading. And *The Killer Inside Me* is the exception to that description. It is completely brilliant. It is a perfect novel.

Thompson wrote books for Dell, Popular Library (one original novel, two screenplay novelizations), Regency, Fawcett, Lancer, and Sphere (UK).

In 1957 Lion and Lion Library were sold to NAL, and two more Thompson novels were issued as Signet PBOs.

In his later years, Thompson drifted into obscurity. He lived in Hollywood, picked up an occasional bit acting role, sponged off friends and acquaintances, and spent much of his time in an alcoholic fog. By the time of his death in 1977, he was very much a forgotten man. By 1980 he did not even rate an entry in the massive *Twentieth Century Crime and Mystery Writers*.

Enter Californian Barry Gifford, a talented *noir* writer himself. Gifford created a paperback line called Black Lizard Books. Under this imprint he brought a number of unjustly forgotten authors back into print, and the books were immensely popular. Most notable among them was Jim Thompson. Through Gifford's efforts a whole new generation of readers discovered this melancholy genius. National publications ran lengthy pieces both on Thompson as a writer and on the revival of interest in his books.

Two full-scale biographies of Thompson were published and the 1991 edition of *Twentieth Century Crime & Mystery Writers* devoted a full-scale entry to Thompson, including a glowing tribute by mystery writer Max Allan Collins.

❡❡❡❡❡

Fawcett Gold Medal, Lion, Pyramid and Graphic all got their start in 1949 in the United States, and Harlequin commenced publication in Canada. It was a banner year for the new paperback companies and all became important contributors to paperback history.

Pyramid was founded by Alfred Plaine and Matthew Huttner as Almat Publishing Company. Pyramid's proverbial "first ten" seem to have begun with Number 11—there is no record of Pyramid Books with lower numbers—nor was there a Pyramid 13. Maybe Plaine and Huttner were just superstitious. A single release of four titles reached the racks in 1949. Thereafter Pyramid kept up a steady pace of titles until the company…but that, as they say, is getting ahead of the story.

Pyramid's proverbial "first ten" showed a distinct leaning toward sex. Seven of the titles were suggestive, and the remaining three included two mysteries, one contemporary and one classic, and a suspense novel. Here's the list:

11. *Passionate Virgin* by "Perry Lindsay" (Peggy Gaddis)
12. *Reckless Passion* by Gordon Semple
14. *Blonde Mistress* by Hall Bennett
15. *Palm Beach Apartment* by Gail Jordan
16. *Set-up for Murder* by Peter Cheyney
17. *Tavern Girl* by Glen Watkins
18. *Shameless Honeymoon* by Thomas Stone
19. *The Moonstone* by Wilkie Collins
20. *Terror in Times Square* by Alan Handley
21. *Sin Street* by Doreen Manners

Not a very impressive selection. In fact, most of the early Pyramid books were reprints of the digest-size paperbacks of an earlier "sleaze" publisher, Knickerbocker Publications. The Collins was of course a public domain item—no royalty payments required. What about the others? Peggy Gaddis was a hugely prolific and accomplished author of risqué romances and medical novels with titles like *Reckless Virgin*, *Girl with No Past*, *Unfaithful*, *Backwoods Girl*, *Strangers in the Dark*, *Farmer's Wife*, *The Nurse and Pirate*, *Nurse Hilary*, *Betsy Moran, R.N.*, and *Young Doctor Talbot*. She was published by everyone from Ace to Venus Books.

Not to knock it—she provided an honest product for her paycheck, but you'd hardly call it great literature.

Peter Cheyney (1896-1951) was a member of an odd group of Englishmen who specialized in writing American-style hardboiled mysteries. Others included the talented James Hadley Chase and on at least one occasion E. C. Tubb, better known for his science fiction.

Cheyney was first rate. Hardworking and prolific, he created several successful series detectives including Slim Callahan, Lemmy Caution, and Everard Peter Quayle. He was influenced by the so-called Black Mask School including Carroll John Daly and Jonathan Latimer with occasional madcap influences from the American Robert Leslie Bellem and the so-English Leslie Charteris.

The result was a body of work that has dated only slightly and can still delight the modern reader.

Surely Cheyney's *Set-up for Murder* was the prize in the early days of Pyramid.

Pyramid succeeded and grew into a significant paperback house, seldom challenging the "majors" for high-priced books by top authors but developing a strong, versatile line of titles under a series of talented editors, most notably the dedicated, creative journeyman Donald R. Bensen.

One practice of Pyramid's that endeared them to authors was their sense of continuity. Of course many authors come to be associated with particular publishers: Erle Stanley Gardner with Pocket Books, John D. MacDonald with Gold Medal, Erskine Caldwell with Signet, and Jim Thompson with Lion. In other cases, the loyalty exists between author and editor or publisher.

Marion Zimmer Bradley and André Norton were both promoted and supported by Donald A. Wollheim when he edited for Ace Books and followed him to DAW Books when he left Ace.

Most authors prefer the stability of an ongoing relationship with an editor or publisher. As one writer expressed his attitude, "One-night stands are a lot of fun but after a while you've had enough of and you realize that you want to get married." The relationship helps to build a backlist, and it's a lot less nerve-wracking when the writer looks to the future.

This continuity wins favor with readers and collectors as well. Pyramid started publishing Vardis Fisher with *The Wild Ones* (G-57, 1952). In later years Fisher would produce a gigantic saga of prehistoric, historical, and pseudo-historical novels for Pyramid, winning a loyal following for himself and his publisher.

Under Bensen's sponsorship, Pyramid issued the space operas of Edward E. Smith, Ph.D.— *The Skylark of Space*, *Spacehounds of IPC*, *Skylark of Valeron*, and *Skylark DuQuesne*. Even more ambitious was Smith's modestly titled futuristic "History of Civilization." This series, originally published between 1948 and 1954, had become the center of a cult among science fiction fans and furnished (uncredited) inspiration for such varied productions as the 1970s revival of the Green Lantern comic book and George Lucas' *Star Wars* films.

The volumes were *Triplanetary*, *First Lensman*, *Galactic Patrol*, *Gray Lensman*, *Second Stage Lensmen*, and *Children of the Lens*. Mention the books to a science fiction fan of a certain age and prepare to lend him your handkerchief.

Pyramid also reissued the Fu Manchu novels of Sax Rohmer, sharing that author's popularity with Gold Medal, and a number of books by Rex Stout before Stout settled in at Bantam.

## PERILOUS DREAMS
**ANDRE NORTON**
**DAW BOOKS, 1976**
**COVER BY GEORGE BARR**

Norton collectors hunt for this book, of course. The splendid cover by Barr, whose use of color and light is both original and lovely, adds immensely to its appeal.

📖📖

## REFORM SCHOOL GIRL
**FELICE SWADOS**
**DIVERSEY ROMANCE NOVEL, 1948**

The ultimate sleaze cover and one of the most famous paperbacks of them all, this book was actually a retitling and repackaging of a book called *House of Fury*. The amazing photo cover was also used on a comic book version. Indescribable, unbelievable, incomparable.

📖📖📖📖📖

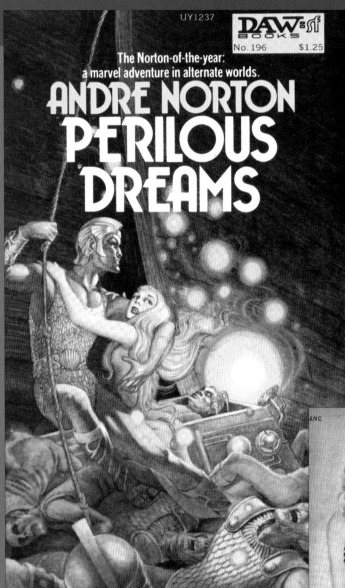

238

A SEQUEL TO THE IMAGE OF THE BEAST BY

PHILIP JOSÉ FARMER

BLOWN

$1 95

020139

AN ESSEX HOUSE ORIGINAL

FOR ENTERTAINMENT OF ADULTS ONLY
Sale to Minors Prohibited

"DAGGER OF FLESH"
is a brand new novel by your favorite author
RICHARD S. PRATHER

dagger of flesh!

HIS PLEASURE WAS WOMEN
HIS BUSINESS, VIOLENCE... HIS PARTNER—DEATH!

35¢

## DAGGER OF FLESH!
**RICHARD S. PRATHER**
**FALCON BOOKS, 1952**
**COVER BY RUDOLPH NAPPI (?)**

This extremely rare Prather digest PBO is probably
the most difficult of all Prather books to find.

◥◥◥◥

## BLOWN
**PHILIP JOSÉ FARMER**
**ESSEX HOUSE, 1967**

Essex House books feature an astonishing amalgam
of serious literature, artistic experimentation, and
pornography. All are collectible, most notably the
three by Philip José Farmer: A *Feast Unknown*, *Image
of the Beast*, and *Blown*.

◥◥◥◥◥

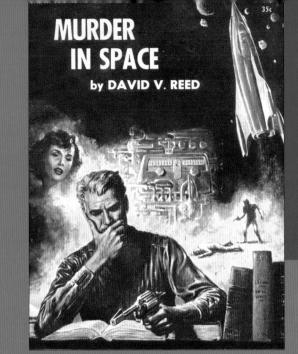

MURDER IN SPACE

by DAVID V. REED

THE NEW SERIES No. 2

TARZAN

AND THE CAVE CITY

*By Barton Werper*

Based on characters created by
Edgar Rice Burroughs

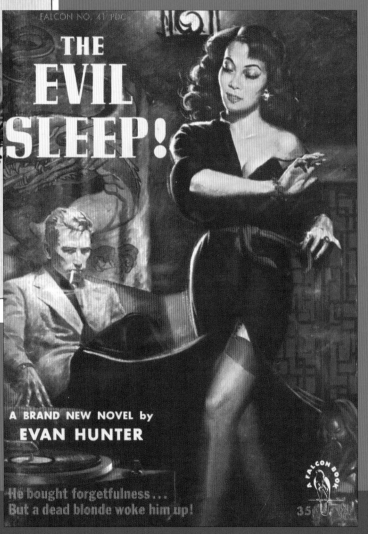

FALCON NO. 41 PBO

THE EVIL SLEEP!

A BRAND NEW NOVEL by
EVAN HUNTER

He bought forgetfulness...
But a dead blonde woke him up!

35

### TARZAN AND THE CAVE CITY
BARTON WERPER
GOLD STAR, 1964

When the Burroughs copyrights were in question, industrious Gold Star Books got five quickie Tarzan novels into
print. They were written by the pseudonymous Barton
Werper. The books were withdrawn on threat of lawsuit
and have become major collectibles for Tarzan fans.

### THE EVIL SLEEP
EVAN HUNTER
FALCON BOOKS, 1952

This early PBO is probably the toughest to find of all
books by Evan Hunter/Ed McBain.

## MURDER IN SPACE
**DAVID V. REED**
**GALAXY NOVELS, 1954**
**COVER BY ED EMSHWILLER**

David V. Reed wrote PBOs for Green Dragon Books, Uni Books, and World Fantasy Classics (U.K.). Two of his novels are well remembered for their titles if nothing else: *The Thing that Made Love* and *The Whispering Gorilla*. The Galaxy Novels series featured a number of fine books, including digest PBOs by Arthur C. Clarke, Raymond F. Jones, Clifford Simak, James Blish, Lewis Padgett, Malcolm Jameson, and Fritz Leiber.

## IF THE COFFIN FITS
**DAY KEENE**
**GRAPHIC, 1952**

Day Keene wrote scores of stories for the pulp magazines, then switched to books and produced almost fifty, most of them mystery PBOs. He also wrote radio scripts. Praised by Bill Pronzini for his sense of pacing and action, Keene always offers a good, entertaining read.

## MURDER BY SCHEDULE
**JULIAN HINCKLEY**
**GOLDEN WILLOW, 1946**

Only six Golden Willow Mysteries are known, numbered 51 through 56. While the publisher indicates that Hinckley's novel is abridged from one called *The Letter in His Throat*, no record of that book can be found—a mystery about a mystery.

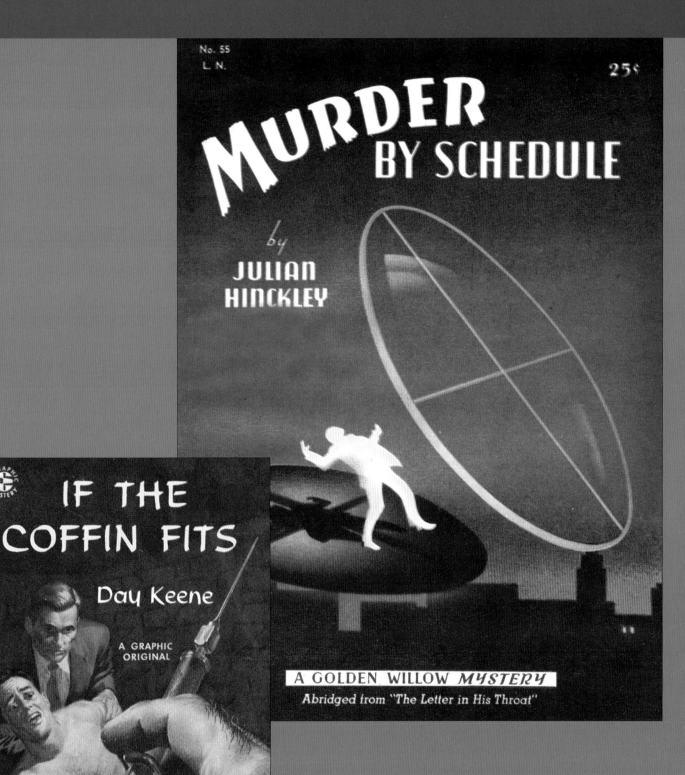

241

## HEADSMAN'S HOLIDAY
DEAN HAWKINS
GREEN DRAGON, 1946

Hawkins was a Southern regional writer who turned out four novels in the late 1930s and 1940s. *Headsman's Holiday* was his last known book.

## MODEL FOR MURDER
STEPHEN MARLOWE
GRAPHIC, 1955
COVER BY WALTER POPP

The tough-looking cutie on the cover of this early PBO by Stephen Marlowe (Milton Lesser) is actually the wife of the artist. Popp's covers were always excellent and have become collectible in their own right.

## THE LOVE LOTTERY
BERTIL SCHÜTT
GROVE, 1970'S

Ah, those good old hippie days—things like this are collected and studied by sociologists.

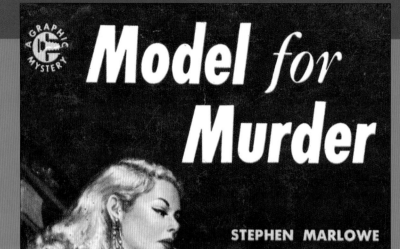

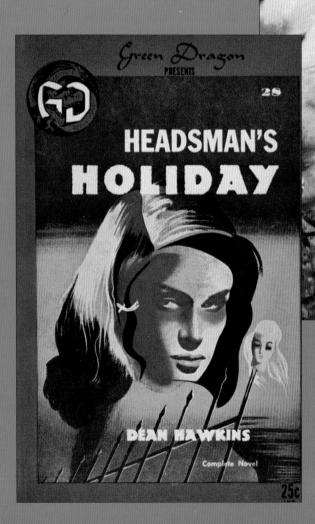

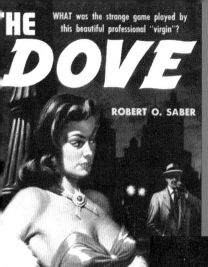

### THE DOVE
**ROBERT O. SABER**
**HANDI-BOOKS, 1951**
**COVER BY WALTER POPP (?)**
Robert O. Saber was a pseudonym of Chicagoan Milton K. Ozaki, who was a Handi-Books regular under both names. The cover offers startling possibilities.

📖

### THE CASE OF THE SHIVERING CHORUS GIRLS
**JAMES ATLEE PHILLIPS**
**HANDI-BOOKS, 1943**

This was the first published novel of James Atlee Phillips (1915-1991), a reprint of a 1942 hardcover, collectible mainly for its cute-silly cover. Writing as Philip Atlee, Phillips created a long-running series of PBOs for Gold Medal featuring intelligence agent Joe Gall. Critic Jeff Banks calls these books "the best American espionage series of the latter half of the twentieth century."

📖📖

### THE WINDOW WITH THE SLEEPING NUDE
**ROBERT LESLIE BELLEM**
**HANDI-BOOKS, 1950**

Cult author Robert Leslie Bellem produced hundreds if not thousands of pulp stories but very few books. *The Window with the Sleeping Nude* was a PBO for Handi-Books in 1950 and was reprinted by Harlequin the following year. Both editions are highly collectible.

📖📖📖📖,📖📖📖📖

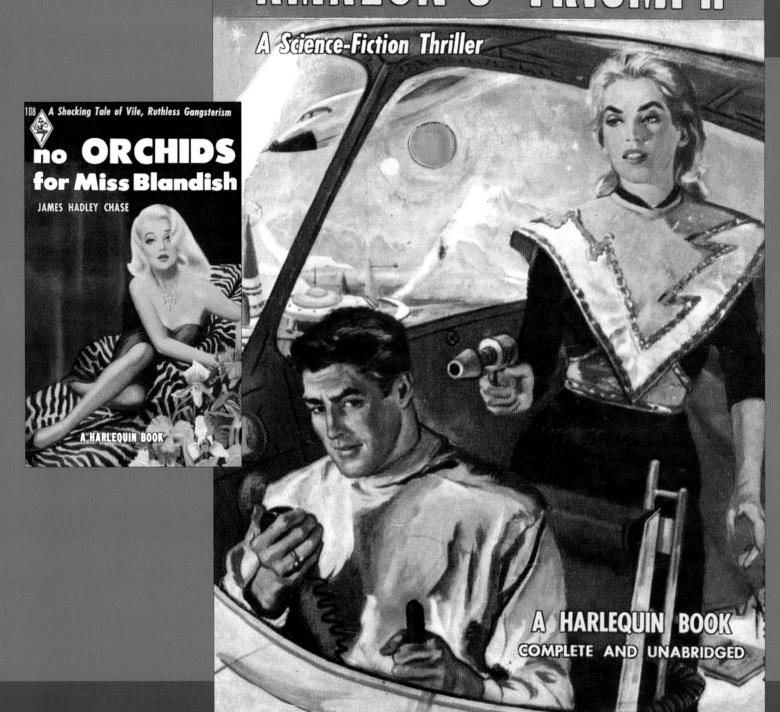

421    JOHN RUSSELL FEARN    35c

# THE GOLDEN AMAZON'S TRIUMPH

## A Science-Fiction Thriller

108 A Shocking Tale of Vile, Ruthless Gangsterism

# no ORCHIDS for Miss Blandish

JAMES HADLEY CHASE

A HARLEQUIN BOOK

A HARLEQUIN BOOK
COMPLETE AND UNABRIDGED

## NO ORCHIDS FOR MISS BLANDISH

JAMES HADLEY CHASE
HARLEQUIN, 1951

Englishman René Brabazon Raymond (1906-1985) wrote dozens of novels with American settings, American characters, and in American vernacular. He had the misfortune of achieving his greatest success with his first book, *No Orchids for Miss Blandish* (originally published in 1939), but virtually everything he wrote has merit.

◄◄◄◄

## THE GOLDEN AMAZON'S TRIUMPH

JOHN RUSSELL FEARN
HARLEQUIN, 1953

John Russell Fearn (1908-1960) was a major contributor to what Steve Holland calls "the mushroom jungle" of post-World War II British publishing. Under no fewer than thirty-three by-lines, he wrote hundreds of pulp stories and PBOs. His Golden Amazon series is highly collected in all editions, including the three volumes published by Harlequin. In the 1990s, Gryphon Books of Brooklyn, New York, began an ambitious program of reissuing Fearn's books in trade paperback format.

◄◄◄◄

### THE DYING EARTH
**JACK VANCE**
**HILLMAN BOOKS, 1947**

This PBO was Vance's first book and is an incredible rarity in this edition (although reissued in later years, so reading copies are not difficult to locate). If you ever come across a copy and you can make out the signature on the cover painting, you will win the gratitude of uncounted collectors.

### THE ELVIS PRESLEY STORY
**EDITED BY JAMES GREGORY**
**HILLMAN BOOKS, 1960**

If you're an Elvis collector you'll surely want this PBO. Make sure that the black-and-white photo section and the color pin-up of the King have not been removed. The editor of this potpourri was not the same James Gregory whose long, distinguished acting career included a stint as "Inspector Luger" on the *Barney Miller* television series.

### FATHER OF THE BRIDE
**EDWARD STREETER**
**HILLMAN BOOKS, 1950**

Spencer Tracy spanks Elizabeth Taylor on the cover of this MTI. Who could ask for anything more?

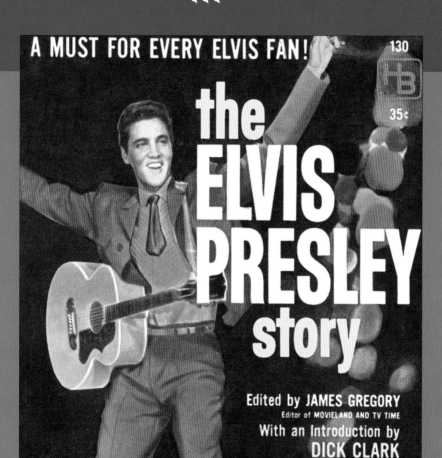

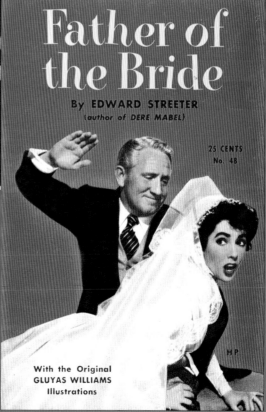

A HILLMAN 25¢ PUBLICATION

NO. 17

# Ed Earl Repp

# GUN HAWK

BH649 $1.95

# DONALD GOINES
## DADDY COOL

A deadly knife master—hit man swears to plug a youngblood pimp for the murder of his daughter, who's all that counts!

## DADDY COOL
**DONALD GOINES**
**HOLLOWAY HOUSE, 1974**

In the era of "blaxploitation films", a small industry of "blaxpoitation books" also flourished. Donald Goines (1937-1974), a self-described sometime pimp, numbers runner, bootlegger, thief, and convict, wrote with unquestioned authenticity. He turned out eleven books under his own name and five as Al C. Clark, within a period of five years before being gunned down on a Detroit street.

## GUN HAWK
**ED EARL REPP**
**HILLMAN BOOKS, 1949**

Prolific author Edward Earl Repp (1900-1979) wrote thirteen western novels and two volumes of science fiction stories as well as many western screenplays and scripts for several television series including *The Lone Ranger*.

John Jakes may have furnished Pyramid with its greatest success. Writing under such bylines as Alan Payne, Jay Scotland, and William Ard (an author who had died in midseries), as well has his own name, Jakes had built a long career as a prolific and versatile author.

He wrote more than a dozen science fiction novels for a variety of publishers. When Lancer's successful publication of Robert E. Howard's Conan series created a fad for "fur jockstrap" novels, Jakes created his own muscular adventurer, Brak the Barbarian, and ran him through a series of adventures for Paperback Library, Avon, Pocket Books, and Dell.

As Jay Scotland he wrote historical swashbucklers. As William Ard he wrote three "swinger" sex novels for Monarch Books. But his biggest hit was the so-called Kent Family Chronicles. Allegedly created by a book packager and farmed out to Jakes as little more than piecework, this series was the ultimate example of the right product in the right market at the right time.

The United States was revving up for Bicentennial Fever in 1974 when the first Kent volume, *The Bastard*, appeared. In rapid succession, Jakes followed with *The Rebels*, *The Seekers*, *The Furies*, *The Titans*, *The Warriors*, *The Lawless*, and *The Americans*. The books were fat, colorful, well researched, and written with the sure hand of the seasoned pro.

Pyramid couldn't print them fast enough to meet the demand. Readers loved them, and today a set of first printings in clean condition is worth a pretty penny—if and when you can find the books!

The late 1960s and early 1970s were the era of Flower Power, hippies, psychedelia, the Beatles, and the Grateful Dead. Publishers were quick to jump on the bandwagon and follow the *zeitgeist*, and Pyramid produced one of the oddest (and most collectible) short series of books in the genre.

Chester Anderson, a cultural gadfly and onetime editor of the counterculture journal *Crawdaddy*, wrote *The Butterfly Kid*. In it, two characters named Chester Anderson and Michael Kurland wander merrily through the Sixties world of peculiar chemicals, complaisant beauties, music, painting, poetry, and a little-noticed interplanetary invasion by a race of giant blue lobsters.

Anderson's book was a huge success for Pyramid in 1967 (another case of right product, right market, right time) and called for a sequel. But Anderson didn't write it. Instead, Anderson's fictitious sidekick, Michael Kurland, was the author.

It turns out that Kurland was a real person, a successful writer of mysteries and war and spy novels. Pyramid followed Anderson's *Butterfly Kid* with *The Unicorn Girl* by Kurland (1969) and scored a second success.

Then another friend of Anderson and Kurland's, Thomas Waters, contributed a third volume to the series, *The Probability Pad* (Pyramid, 1970). Perhaps the joke was wearing thin, or perhaps the times were changing. Whatever the reason, *The Probability Pad* didn't do as well as *The Butterfly Kid* or *The Unicorn Girl*. Three decades later, it is consequently the hardest to find.

In 1974, Pyramid was bought by Harcourt Brace Jovanovich. Corporate chairman William Jovanovich modestly renamed the company Jove Books. Once again, a successful independent publisher became a tentacle on a corporate octopus. By 1979 HBJ had lost interest in Jove and sold the company to MCA Putnam, where it became part of a paperback stew along with Ace and Berkley.

❧❧❧❧❧

Graphic Books was created in 1949 by Sam Tankel and Zane Bouregy. The company produced 147 books in its primary line (numbered 11 through 157), plus 23 Graphic Giants (numbered G-101 through G-123). Co-founder Bouregy would go on to a remarkable career in low-budget publishing, both hardcovers and paperbacks, with Bouregy and Curl, Mystery House, Avalon, and Airmont.

Never a major player, Graphic still turned out any number of attractive books. Graphic's chief strength, as with so many paperback houses of the era, was mysteries. Also, as was not unusual, westerns ran a respectable second. Even so, Graphic managed to get books from a number of collected authors. These "one-offs," sometimes scarce, sometimes hidden, can become treasures.

An example is Graphic's PBO *Pattern for Murder* by "David Knight" (48, 1952). Just another period detective novel, right? Unless you know that "Knight" was Richard Prather!

Graphic published Sax Rohmer's *Hangover House* (32, 1951)—a relatively minor Rohmer but a *must-have* for the Rohmer collector. Then there was *Stand Up and Die* by Richard and Frances Lockridge 82, 1954), and *Model for Murder* by Stephen Marlowe (94, 1955).

Every Cornell Woolrich collector knows of course that Woolrich was also "William Irish." Graphic did a series of Woolrich suspensers under that name: *Deadline at Dawn* (16, 1949), *Deadly Night Call* (31, 1951), and *Phantom Lady* (108, 1955).

They published an admirable Craig Rice true-crime anthology, *45 Murderers* (G-203, 1954). And they were the main publisher for Milton K. Ozaki both under his own name and as Robert O. Saber.

Milton Ozaki (1913-1989) was a pioneer, almost certainly the first Japanese-American mystery writer. In 1946 he sent his first novel, *The Cuckoo Clock*, to Howard Browne, who was then editing mystery pulp magazines for Ziff-Davis in Chicago. Browne found the manuscript too long even to consider for his magazines but sent it to Ziff-Davis's book division on an interoffice memo.

A harried editor there, apparently mistaking Browne's buck-slip for a positive recommendation, bought the book without reading it. Browne hadn't read it either. Thanks to this missed communication, Ozaki became a published novelist.

He was in fact a pretty good mystery writer. Over the next fifteen years he wrote some three dozen mysteries, many of them PBOs. They were scattered among a variety of publishers, some majors or "major minors," but others remarkably obscure and almost impossible to find. He was published by Ace, Berkley, Gold Medal, Handi-Books, Harlequin, Jubilee, Moring, Original Novels, Phantom, Pyramid, and Star.

Graphic Books disappeared after 1957, leaving behind a tidy legacy of interesting, attractive, collectible books.

**RED THREADS**
REX STOUT
BANTAM (LA), 1940

**THE SHADOW AND THE VOICE OF MURDER**
MAXWELL GRANT
BANTAM (LA), 1940

Any "L.A. Bantam" is a collector's prize, those with pictorial covers doubly so. In the case of these two titles, one by the perennially popular Rex Stout and the other featuring the collectible Shadow, the sky's the limit.

❧❧❧❧❧

# The Shadow

## AND THE VOICE OF MURDER

BANTAM BOOKS

15¢

# Red Threads

## by REX STOUT

A MYSTERY
NOVEL

192 PAGES
PACKED
WITH THRILLS
INTEREST
EXCITEMENT
BY
AMERICA'S
MASTER OF
THE MYSTERY
NOVEL

A BIG BOOK
IN A SMALL
PACKAGE

BANTAM
BOOKS

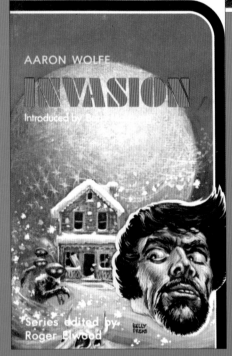

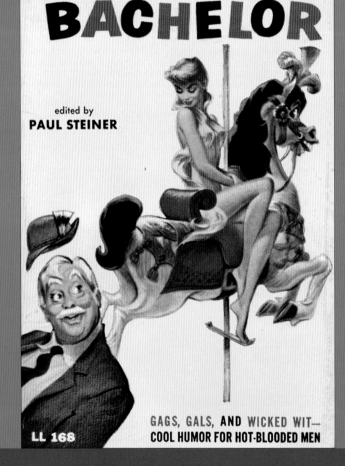

## INVASION
**AARON WOLFE**
**LASER BOOKS, 1975**
**COVER BY KELLY FREAS**

In the 1970s Harlequin attempted to replicate is success as a romance publisher with science fiction and mystery lines. Neither was successful and both were soon cancelled, but a number of collectibles came out of the experiment, including this pseudonymous novel by Dean R. Koontz.

## PHOENIX PRIME
**TED WHITE**
**LANCER BOOKS, 1966**
**COVER BY FRANK FRAZETTA**

This novel by the multi-talented Ted White was so successful that editor Larry Shaw sent messengers to White's home for chapters of the sequel. Unfortunately, the second Max Quest novel, *Sorceress of Qar*, didn't have a magical Frazetta cover and its sales were disappointing. White achieved great success as editor of *Amazing Stories* and *Heavy Metal* magazines.

## THE BEDSIDE BACHELOR
**EDITED BY PAUL STEINER**
**LION LIBRARY, 1957**
**COVER BY BUD HAWLEY**

Here's another entry in the Politically Incorrect derby, from the cheerful Lady Godiva and the happily startled elderly gentleman on the cover to the collected pin-up pics and risqué jokes inside.

## BACKWOODS SHACK
**HARRY WHITTINGTON**
## SPOTLIGHT ON SIN
**DOUG DUPPERAULT**
**LANCER DOUBLE, 1962**

Walter Zacharius claimed to have given A. A. Wynn the idea for his fabulously successful Ace Doubles. He tried it again at Lancer but used a split-cover design instead of the front-and-back format that had worked so well at Ace.

## THE BLONDE ON THE STREET CORNER
**DAVID GOODIS**
**LION BOOKS, 1954**

What a fine, evocative cover painting on this characteristically well-written but downbeat novel by Goodis.

## CAGE ME A PEACOCK
**NOEL LANGLEY**
**LION LIBRARY, 1956**
**COVER BY ROBERT MAGUIRE**

Noel Langley wrote a handful of mildly sexy, good-natured novels in the 1950s, then disappeared from the publishing world. The Maguire cover on *Cage Me a Peacock* captures just the right level of mild eroticism.

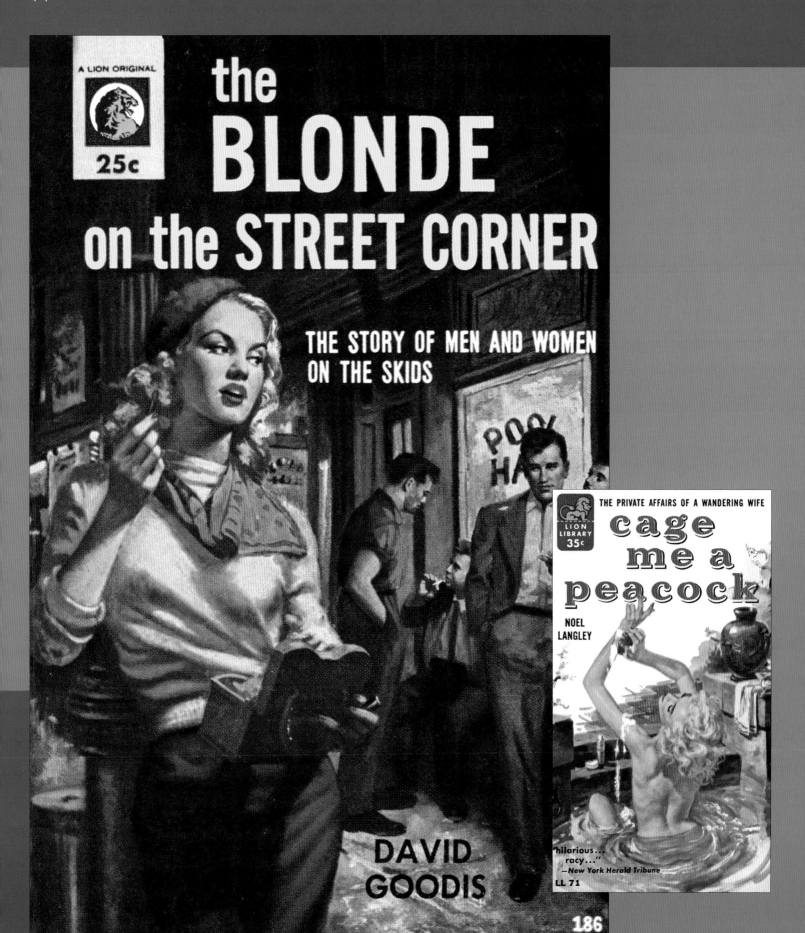

## THE KILLER INSIDE ME
JIM THOMPSON
LION BOOKS, 1952

A tortured, conflicted man, Thompson poured all of his pain and rage into the figure of Deputy Sheriff Lou Ford. The character is immortal, as is his creator.

📖📖📖📖📖

## A HELL OF A WOMAN
JIM THOMPSON
LION BOOKS, 1954

Any Jim Thompson PBO creates a rush of his fans and collectors. The Lion titles that he wrote under the sponsorship of Arnold Hano are especially desirable.

📖📖📖📖

## CONJURE WIFE
FRITZ LEIBER
LION BOOKS, 1953
COVER BY ROBERT MAGUIRE

Fritz Reuter Leiber, Jr. (1910-1992) was the son of an eminent Shakespearean, growing up backstage (and sometimes onstage) with the senior Leiber's touring company. The understanding of character and dramatic structure that he learned in the theater is clearly visible in his many fine novels and short stories.

📖📖📖

## THE KIDNAPER
ROBERT BLOCH
LION BOOKS, 1954

Robert Bloch specialized in psychological suspense, making even the most monstrous of criminal fiends into real, pitiable human beings. Norman Bates in *Psycho* is the best known, but similarly tortured figures appear in many of Bloch's books. Bloch's PBOs are increasingly in demand.

📖📖📖

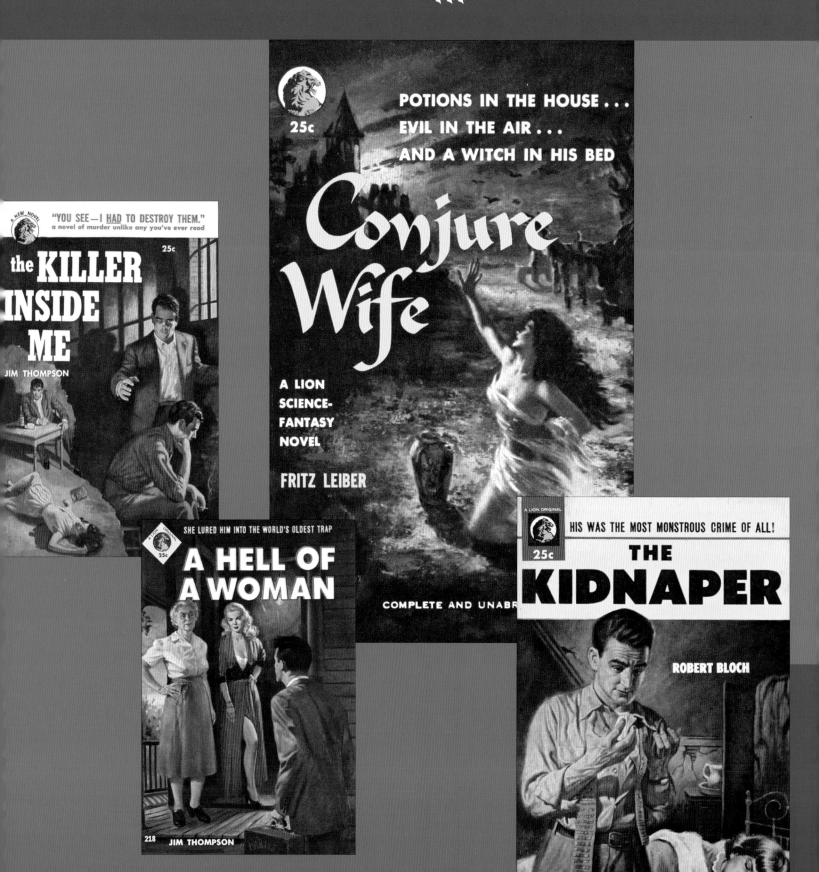

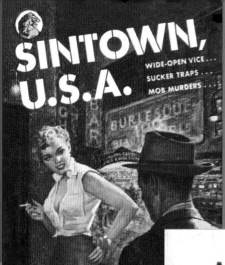

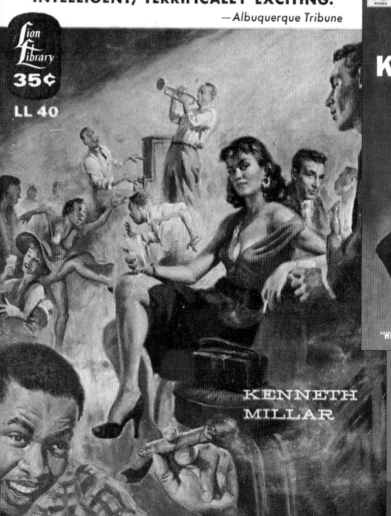

## SINTOWN, U.S.A.
**EDITED BY NOAH SARLAT**
**LION BOOKS, 1952**

A guided tour of the tenderloins of American cities at mid-century, this book is a virtual time machine of vice—or what passed for it in 1952.

## NIGHT TRAIN
**KENNETH MILLAR**
**LION LIBRARY, 1955**
**COVER BY SAMSON POLLEN**

Better known as Ross Macdonald, Ken Millar produced several fine novels under his own name. The stereotypical "jazz novel" cover correctly implies a world of alcohol, smoky nightclubs, music of raw power and beauty, and dangerous sexuality.

## THE DAY KHRUSHCHEV PANICKED
**GEORGE B. MAIR**
**MACFADDEN BOOKS, 1963**
**COVER BY STANLEY BORACK**

If Cold War paranoia were personified, this book is it. But in the era of the Hungarian Revolution, the Suez War, and the Cuban Missile Crisis, such books found an audience. The couple on the cover bear little resemblance to the Soviet Premier and his wife.

◥◥◥◥◥

And speaking of Harlequin…

Of course we all know of Harlequin as an immensely successful publisher of romance novels, but Harlequen was at one time a broad-spectrum paperback house and in later years made several forays into non-romance fields. Founded by Canadian publishing mogul Richard Bonneycastle in 1949 (still another product of that revolutionary year!), Harlequin was a general publisher well into the 1960s, producing nearly 700 books that included mysteries, westerns, spy capers, science fiction, and even cook books in both English and French!

Many of these early Harlequins are attractive books featuring colorful pictorial covers. Most of the authors were run-of-the-mill, but an occasional headliner appears in the Harlequin chronology, and a number of highly collectible books came across the border from Canada.

The first truly notable Harlequin was Ben Hecht's *Hollywood Mystery* (32, 1950). A famous and controversial writer in his day, Hecht has slipped into obscurity in recent years but still bears reading. Others include *The So Blue Marble* by Dorothy B. Hughes, *Night and the City* by Gerald Kersh, *Cardinal Rock* by Richard Sale, *Message from a Corpse* by Sam Merwin, Jr., *The Corpse Came Back* by Amelia Reynolds Long, *Spider House* by F. Van Wyck Mason, and *Convicted* by David Goodis.

In 1951 Harlequin brought out *The Window with the Sleeping Nude* by Robert Leslie Bellem. Primarily a pulp magazine writer best known for his flabbergasting stories of Dan Turner, Hollywood Detective, Bellem did manage to publish three novels under his own name and a couple pseudonymously, all of them highly collectible.

In 1952 Harlequin published a Canadian edition of English hardboiled writer James Hadley Chase's controversial *Twelve Chinks and a Woman*. But probably the most sought-after early Harlequins were their handful of forays into science fiction.

Stanley G. Weinbaum (1902-1935) was a resident of Milwaukee, Wisconsin, and a friend of authors Robert Bloch and Ralph Milne Farley. He broke into print with a short story, "A Martian Odyssey," in the July, 1934 issue of *Wonder Stories*. The story created a sensation and Weinbaum was suddenly in demand, but he was already fatally ill and would live only another year and half. In his short career he wrote three novels and enough short stories to fill several more volumes.

*The Black Flame* (Harlequin 205, 1953) was the first Weinbaum paperback. If you see it for less than the price of a house in San Francisco, grab it.

Prolific British writer John Russell Fearn created a proto-feminist superhero called the Golden Amazon. Fearn wrote some 26 novels about this fabulous character; Harlequin published three: *The Golden Amazon* (Harlequin 218, 1953), *The Deathless Amazon* (320, 1955), and *The Golden Amazon's Triumph* (421, 1958). As the Third Millennium dawns, Gryphon Books, an independent company with their headquarters in Brooklyn, New York, has launched a program to make the entire series available to a new generation of readers.

In the 1970s Harlequin created two significant spin-off lines, Raven House (mysteries) and Laser Books (science fiction). Neither was very successful. Harlequin had found its *métier*, romances, and soon dropped both Raven House and Laser Books. Neither line was especially distinguished, but both bear consideration for the occasional surprise such as Laser 9 by "Aaron Wolfe" (Dean Koontz) and first novels by several authors who went on to significant careers with other publishers.

Remember Walter Zacharius, the man who gave Aaron Wynn the idea for the Ace Doubles? In 1962 Zacharius and a partner, Irwin Stein, created Lancer Books. Lancer would last until 1973 at which time the partners separated. Stein retained what was left of Lancer, issuing a number of titles as Magnum Books or as "Magnum Easy-Eye" books. The latter were conventional paperbacks printed on green-tinted paper, the theory being that this would cause less eyestrain for the reader than the usual white or off-white paper.

Zacharius emerged as the publisher of Zebra Books, a new paperback house. After several years Zebra added a hardcover line, Kensington Books, (the name was still later applied to the paperbacks as well).

In its decade-plus of existence, Lancer was a prolific publisher, issuing more than 2000 titles. The numbering is difficult. There were series within series: "70s," "72-700s," "72-900s," "73-400s," and so forth. Most of the series contained one hundred titles, but some books seem to have vanished without a trace. Perhaps these were numbers reserved for planned titles that never appeared.

To produce that many books Lancer required a sizable staff. Zacharius and Stein were notorious for maintaining tight control over contracts and finances. Probably the most important of Lancer's editors was Larry T. Shaw. A onetime science fiction fan from upstate New York, Shaw was a journeyman editor who had worked on everything from large, slick hot-rod magazines to mystery and science fiction digests. After leaving Lancer he worked briefly for Regency Books in Chicago, returned to New York as an editor at Dell, and then moved to Los Angeles where he worked for a local publisher until shortly before his death.

Lancer Books are highly collectible, and this is due in part to the challenge of figuring out the numbering pattern and trying to fill in the gaps. But more to the point, Lancer published a remarkable number of significant books for a second-line operation. This can be credited largely to Shaw, whose knowledge was truly encyclopedic and connections myriad. His first love and area of greatest expertise was of course science fiction. But he knew mystery fiction as well, and was versed in military and naval history, aviation, and other fields.

He also managed to obtain a great many striking and desirable covers. Lancer published Frank Frazetta, Jim Steranko, Jack Gaughan, and Edward Emshwiller. Shaw also had a talent for picking the right book, putting it together with the right illustrator, and publishing it at the right time.

Perhaps his greatest success at Lancer was the Conan series. Created by pulp writer Robert E. Howard in the 1930s, Conan the Barbarian swaggered and sliced his way through a series of appearances in *Weird Tales* magazine. Howard was himself a bizarre, blustery character, so emotionally bound to his mother that he shot himself as she lay on her deathbed rather than face life without her.

In the 1950s L. Sprague de Camp assembled the Conan stories, rationalizing their chronology and internal content as much as he could. He added new material—some of it adapted from non-Conan stories by Howard, some of it by himself, and some of it by other admirers of Howard's. The result was a series of hardcover books, now highly treasured, published by the specialty house Gnome Press.

Donald Wollheim put Howard's *Conan the Barbarian* back-to-back with Leigh Brackett's *The Sword of Rhiannon* (D-36, 1953) but failed to follow through with additional volumes.

MANOR BOOKS    95¢ 95239

# Edward S. Aarons dark destiny

The stakes were high—but death could win the final pot

35-109   **MB**   The wonderful adventures of   35¢

# suzuki beane

## A lovable little hipster

my name is
suzuki beane
i have a pad
on bleeker street
with hugh
and marcia

"GO, SUZUKI, GO!...Suzuki Beane,
a second generation baby beatnik, is
in a class with Madeleine and Eloise"
*Denver Post*

written by sandra scoppettone

drawings by louise fitzhugh

## SUZUKI BEANE
**SANDRA SCOPPETTONE**
**MACFADDEN BOOKS, 1962**
**COVER BY LOUISE FITZHUGH**

Before emerging in the 1970s as a leading mystery
writer as both Sandra Scoppettone and Jack Early, this
talented writer turned out such marvelous bits of fluff
as the diary of young Miss Beane, daughter of a pair
of proto-hippies.

## DARK DESTINY
**EDWARD S. AARONS**
**MANOR BOOKS, 1970S**

Previously issued in paperback by Graphic, under
the byline Edward Ronns, the Manor version of this
novel is a leading candidate for the most bizarre
looking paperback of all time. If only the artist had
seen fit to sign the painting!

## WOMAN IN THE DARK
**DASHIELL HAMMETT**
JONATHAN PRESS MYSTERIES, 1951
COVER BY GEORGE SALTER

Still another Spivak series, the Jonathan Press Mysteries fit right in with Spivak's Bestseller and Mercury Mysteries. Reissued thirty years later to much fanfare as "Hammett's lost masterpiece," *Woman in the Dark* is a novelette, originally a magazine serial, and merely the title story in this fine collection.

📖📖📖📖

## DEATH OF A CHEAT
**JOHN M. ESHELMAN**
MERCURY MYSTERY, 1955
COVER BY GEORGE SALTER

Virtually interchangeable with Spivak's Bestseller Mystery line, Mercury Mysteries featured superb graphic design and some fine novels and collections in digest format.

📖📖

Mercury Mystery

Death of a Cheat
(THE LONG WINDOW)
by JOHN M. ESHLEMAN

*Salter*

"...action fine..."
THE SATURDAY REVIEW

A MERCURY PUBLICATION

COMPLETE AND UNABRIDGED          PUBLISHED AT $2.50

35 ¢

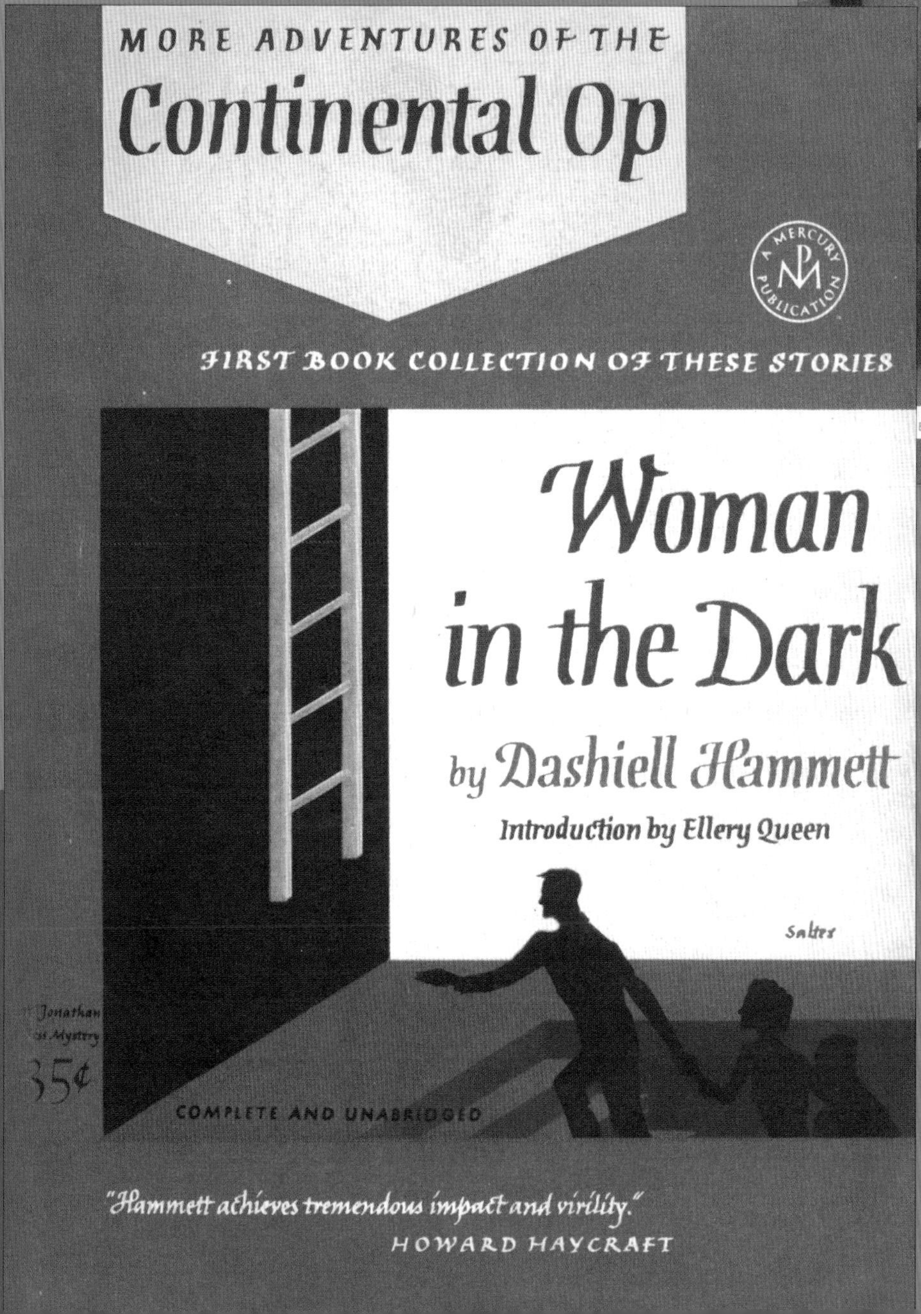

MORE ADVENTURES OF THE
# Continental Op

A MERCURY PUBLICATION

FIRST BOOK COLLECTION OF THESE STORIES

# Woman in the Dark
by *Dashiell Hammett*

Introduction by Ellery Queen

*Salter*

Jonathan Press Mystery

35¢

COMPLETE AND UNABRIDGED

*"Hammett achieves tremendous impact and virility."*
HOWARD HAYCRAFT

257

## WORLD OF IF
**ROG PHILLIPS**
**MERIT BOOKS, 1951**
**COVER BY MALCOLM SMITH**

Roger Phillips Graham (1909-1965) was a frequent contributor to pulp magazines, mostly working in shorter lengths, but he also published four science fiction novels between 1949 and 1959. Malcolm Smith's cover for *World of If* features a double dose of strategically placed laboratory equipment.

📖📖

## BLONDE BAGGAGE
**MARTY HOLLAND**
**NOVEL LIBRARY, 1950**

Novel Library specialized in risqué material that was considered at least borderline pornography at the time. There's nothing in these books that you couldn't show your grandmother today. Some of the covers were intriguing and the entire line is considered collectible.

📖

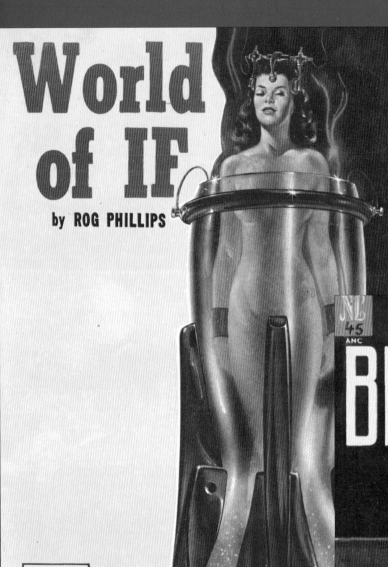

## PEEPING TOM
JACK WOODFORD
NOVEL LIBRARY, 1948

Josiah Pitts Woolfolk (1894-1971) contributed six of
the first seven Novel Library titles. He was a writer of
immense skill, scorned as an author of "dirty books," but
a man whose technique and practical advice on writing
bear study and respect.

❞❞

## NIGHT OF CRIME
ARMSTRONG LIVINGSTON
OMNIBUS, 1944
COVER BY CRAYATH

Born in 1885, Armstrong Livingston published thirteen
mystery novels between 1922 and 1945, most of them
set in New England or New York, and at least four of
them featuring Jimmy Traynor. Night of Crime, first published in 1938, is the only known Omnibus Mystery.

❞❞

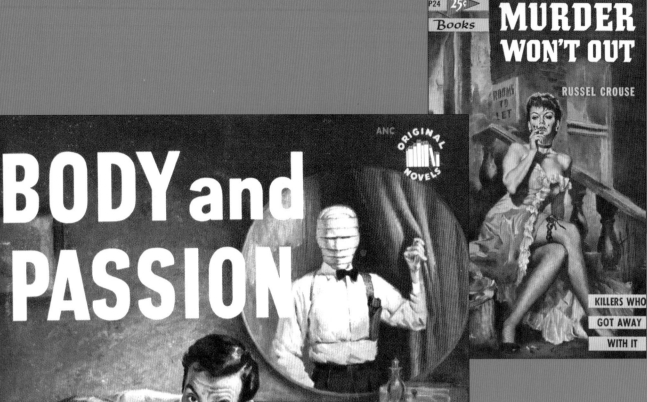

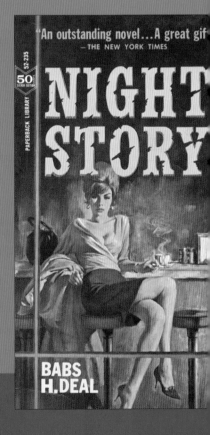

## BODY AND PASSION

**WHIT HARRISON (HARRY WHITTINGTON)**
**ORIGINAL NOVELS, 1952**

Despite its name, the Original line contained
a number of reprints, intermixed with its
PBOs. The skillful and always readable Harry
Whittington also wrote for Original Novels
as Hallam Whitney.

## MURDER WON'T OUT

**RUSSELL CROUSE**
**PENNANT BOOKS, 1952**
**COVER BY CHARLES BINGER**

True crime and unsolved mysteries are a perennial. Pennant was a secondary label for Bantam.

## NIGHT STORY

**BABS H. DEAL**
**PAPERBACK LIBRARY, 1963**

The cover looks like a piece of period
portraiture—slightly shabby elegance
from the beehive hair to the stiletto-
heeled, pointed-toe shoes. It's perfection
of its sort.

## FORTUNE TELLING FOR FUN AND POPULARITY
**PAUL SHOWERS**
**PERMA, 1948**

This is one of the early laminated "hardcover" Permas, collected more for the format experiment than for its content. On the other hand, if you really want to know the future…

📖

## THE OLD MAN'S PLACE
**JOHN B. SANFORD**
**PERMA (DOUBLEDAY), 1953**
**COVER BY JAMES B. MEESE**

All aboard for Caldwell Country! One other book, *Make My Bed in Hell*, is credited to John Sanford without the "B."

📖

## THE GOLDEN ISLE
**FRANK G. SLAUGHTER**
**PERMA, 1951**

This is another of Slaughter's lush costume dramas. If you were Canadian you had to pony up an extra four cents for a copy of this baby!

📖

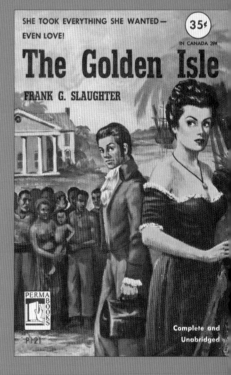

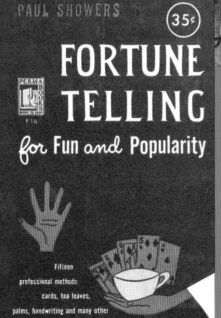

But in 1966 Shaw brought out *Conan the Adventurer* (Lancer 73-526) with a stunning cover painting by Frank Frazetta. This was followed by a new edition of *Conan the Conquerer* (73-572, 1967) with another spectacular Frazetta cover. The combination of Howard— or more accurately, of Conan—and Frazetta turned into a franchise series for Lancer.

In later years other publishers (notably Ace, Berkley, Dell and the relatively obscure Centaur Press) would reissue old Howard material and publish new Conan stories, especially after the release of several Conan films starring Arnold Schwarzenneger as the muscular hero.

Shaw also had a keen eye for new talent. Under his tutelage Lancer published several early works by Dean Koontz who would go on to a career as one of the world's best-selling (and best-paid) authors.

More to the point, Lancer was quick to respond to hot trends in publishing. When gothic novels were all the rage, Lancer published gothics; when nurse novels were the favorites of the moment, Lancer featured nurses. They took a fling with "double novels"—as did several other publishers—but Ace Books with their unique format was the only company to make much of a go of "doubles."

When Signet scored its huge success with Ian Fleming's James Bond series, light-hearted spy-capers became the rage. The books were boosted by the hugely successful motion picture series starring Sean Connery. A television series, *The Man from U.N.C.L.E.*, rode Bond's coattails from 1964 to 1968 and was so popular that a second series, *The Girl from U.N.C.L.E.*, was spun off.

Ace books captured the *U.N.C.L.E.* tie-in franchise, but Lancer countered with *The Man from O.R.G.Y.* (PBO, 72-918, 1965) by Ted Mark. Steve Victor, Mark's superspy, was described as "an unpredictable blend of James Bond, Casanova, and Dr. Kinsey." While nowhere near the writer that Ian Fleming was, Mark still managed to capture a Bondish air of sophisticated high-tech,

high-stakes adventure, spiced with more than a dash of sex. The result was a huge hit for Lancer and a series of sequels and spin-offs for Mark.

Lancer was outraged when Mark departed for a rival publisher in 1968. The result was a tightening of the option clause in Lancer's standard contract, but in this case the horse was already out of the barn. Steve Victor reappeared in *Back at the O.R.G.Y* (Berkley PBO X-1510, 1968).

🕮 🕮 🕮 🕮 🕮

Although the first Berkley Books appeared in 1955, the company was actually created the previous year by two veterans of Avon Books, Charles Byrne and Frederick Klein. (The name "Berkley" was formed from their respective last names and has no connection with Berkeley, California.) Berkley started life during the booming Eisenhower Era. The company featured a conventional mix of mysteries, westerns, and sexy novels. Later Berkley would develop a strong science fiction line which continued as a mainstay for Berkley after its purchase by G. P. Putnam's Sons in 1965. As Putnam continued a series of acquisitions and mergers, Berkley became one of several more-or-less interchangeable labels along with Ace and Jove (formerly Pyramid).

From the outset, however, Berkley interspersed its otherwise unremarkable line with surprising acquisitions. The first such was *S. S. San Pedro* by James Gould Cozzens (103, 1955). Cozzens was a highly regarded literary figure, a Pulitzer Prize winner for his novel *Guard of*

**ROCKET TO THE MORGUE**
H. H. HOLMES
PHANTOM MYSTERY, 1942
COVER BY SHAYN

Holmes was a pseudonym used by William Anthony Parker White (1911-1968) who was also Anthony Boucher and Theo Durrant. By any name, he was a most remarkable man, author, editor, and critic of crime fiction, science fiction and fantasy. He was also a broadcast personality and authority on opera. *Rocket to the Morgue* was apparently the only Phantom Mystery, although reading copies are readily available of later editions from other publishers.

🕮 🕮 🕮 🕮

# ROCKET
## to the MORGUE

A FULL LENGTH BOOK

# H. H. HOLMES
## Author of NINE TIMES NINE
### a *phantom* mystery

SHAYN

## THE POCKET PLAYBOY

**NUMBER FIVE**
**PLAYBOY PRESS, 1974**

Onetime *Playboy* staffer Frank M. Robinson has commented that this magazine wasn't published for guys who were cool but who wanted to think they were cool. Publisher Hugh Hefner's empire included its own paperback line before retrenchment set in.

## CELLINI SMITH DETECTIVE

**ROBERT REEVES**
**PONY BOOKS, 1946**
**COVER BY H. LAWRENCE HOFFMAN**

The talented Robert Reeves (1912-1945) was active in the theater, as is obvious from this book. He followed it with three more, all featuring Cellini Smith, prior to his death at a tragically early age.

## THE EXECUTIONER

**DON PENDLETON**
**PINNACLE BOOKS, 1969**
**COVER BY GIL COHEN (?)**

Critic George Kelley describes Don Pendleton's Executioner series as the first example of a new genre: "men's action-adventure novels starring a vigilante hero." With due respect to Mr. Kelley, the genre stretches back to Doc Savage, the Spider, the Shadow, and countless other 1930s series heroes. This is a new package for an old idea!

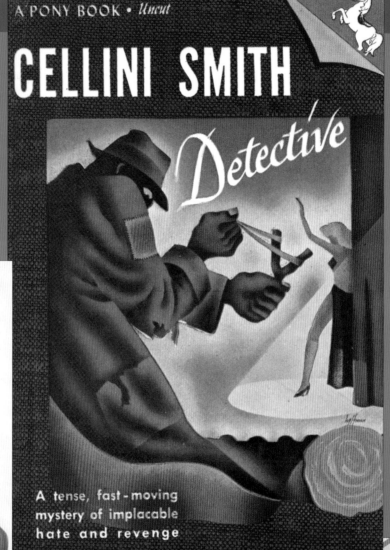

A PONY BOOK · *Uncut*

# CELLINI SMITH
## *Detective*

A tense, fast-moving mystery of implacable hate and revenge

# ROBERT REEVES

THE POCKET
16228 $1.95
# PLAYBOY
NUMBER FIVE

photos, facts, fiction, cartoons —with 16 full-color pages

FIRST THRILLING SERIES!

75¢

By Don Pendleton

# THE EXECUTIONER
## WAR AGAINST THE MAFIA!

Mack Bolan, Vietnam war hero, launches a bloody, one-man crusade against the most powerful gangster force in the history of the U.S.A.

14
Behind the walls of a girls' reformatory
5¢
BORN
INNOCENT
CREIGHTON BROWN BURNHAM

d in hell . . . We worked
, slept in chains, died
in chains!"
"So you won't work, eh?
Get your pants down!"
"I swore to God I'd kill myself before I went back to that hell-hole!"
"I am a fugitive
from a
CHAIN GANG!"
A Warner Brothers picture
starring PAUL MUNI
The grim and
brutal story of
our most shocking
prison system!
A PYRAMID BOOK
Printed in U.S.A.
45
I am a fugitive
from a CHAIN GANG!
One man's story of his
desperate fight for freedom!
25¢
ROBERT E. BURNS

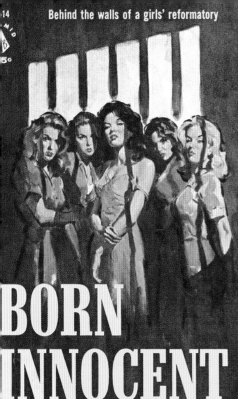

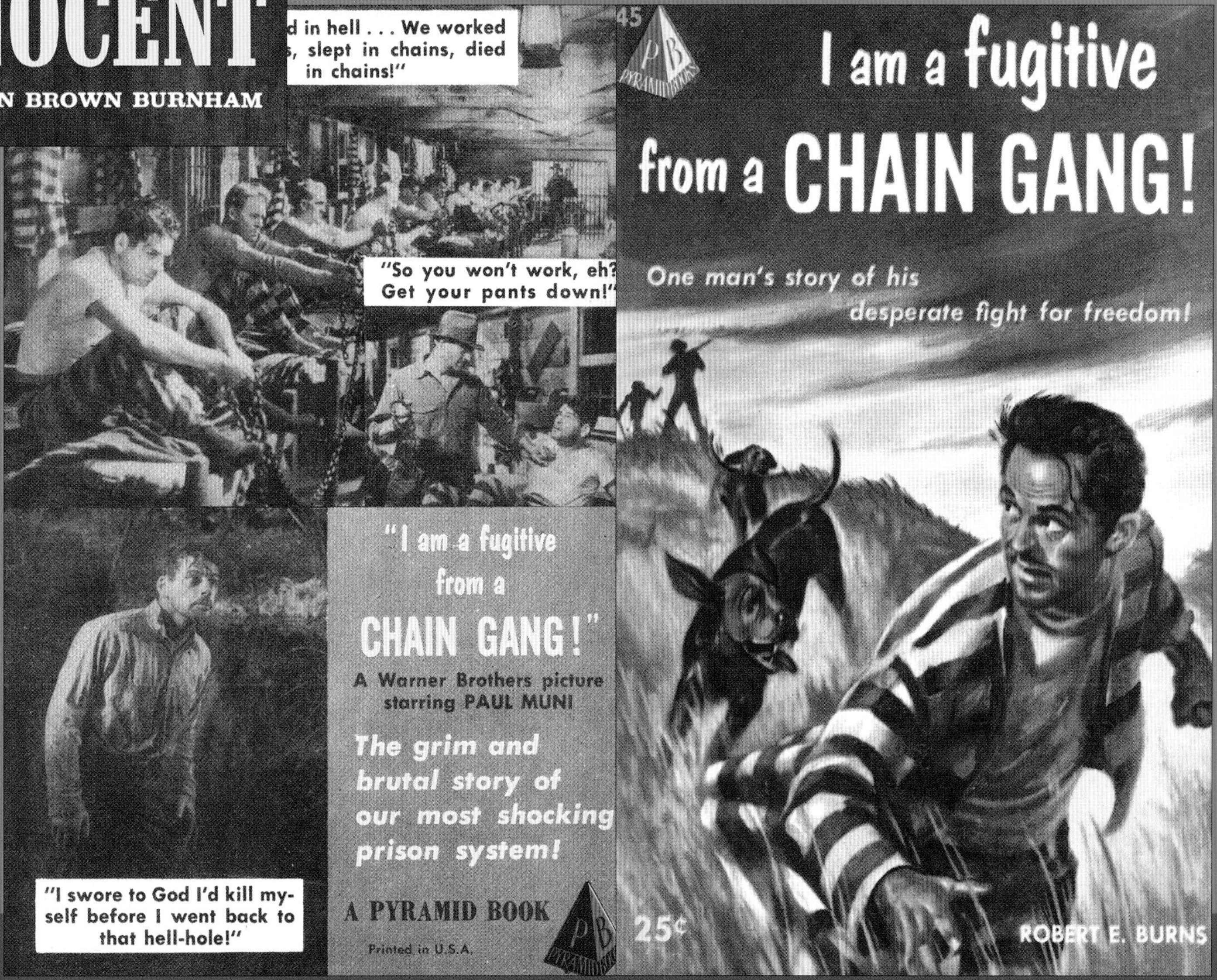

### BORN INNOCENT

CREIGHTON BROWN BURNHAM
PYRAMID BOOKS, 1959
COVER BY ROBERT MAGUIRE

Women-in-prison, girls-in-reform-school, women-in-the-Army—all have their suggestions of lesbian love and/or female-on-female violence, always salable commodities. This was apparently Burnham's only book.

### I AM A FUGITIVE FROM A CHAIN GANG

ROBERT E. BURNS
PYRAMID BOOKS, 1952
COVER BY HUNTER BARKER

On this unusual MTI the front cover painting makes no mention of the film, and the back cover is devoted entirely to the film. This is apparently the only book by this author.

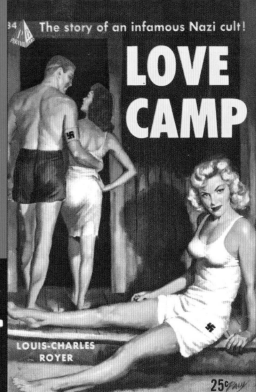

The story of an infamous Nazi cult!

# LOVE CAMP

LOUIS-CHARLES ROYER

25¢

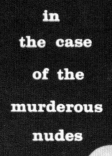

G520

PYRAMID
PB
35c

# HONEY WEST

in
the case
of the
murderous
nudes

# KISS for a KILLER

G. G. FICKLING
author of
GIRL ON THE PROWL

## KISS FOR A KILLER
G. G. FICKLING
PYRAMID BOOKS, 1960
COVER BY ROBERT MAGUIRE

The husband-wife team of Gloria and Forrest Fickling
wrote almost a dozen Honey West novels. Honey was
gorgeous and dangerous, one of many fictitious deadly
beauties inspired by the prototypes in Ian Fleming's
James Bond novels. Maguire's cover is irresistible.

## LOVE CAMP
LOUIS-CHARLES ROYER
PYRAMID BOOKS, 1953
COVER BY JULIAN PAUL

What corrupt fascination is there in everything
connected with the Nazi evil? The SS "love camps"
were especially vile, and they really existed. Royer's
other books include *The Harem*, *Unrepentant Sinners*,
*African Mistress*, *Where They Breed*, and *The Flesh*.

## RUMBLE
**HARLAN ELLISON**
**PYRAMID BOOKS, 1958**
**COVER BY RUDY DE REYNA**

This PBO is the first book by this highly collected author. Ellison allegedly joined a street gang for a time in order to get authentic details.

## THE REDHEAD FROM CHICAGO
**LOUIS-CHARLES ROYER**
**PYRAMID BOOKS, 1954**
**COVER BY JULIAN PAUL**

Julian Paul's montage painting is really quite striking.

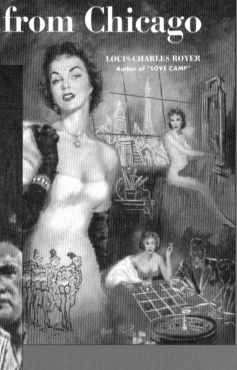

She was too rich to be good

# The Redhead from Chicago

LOUIS-CHARLES ROYER
Author of "LOVE CAMP"

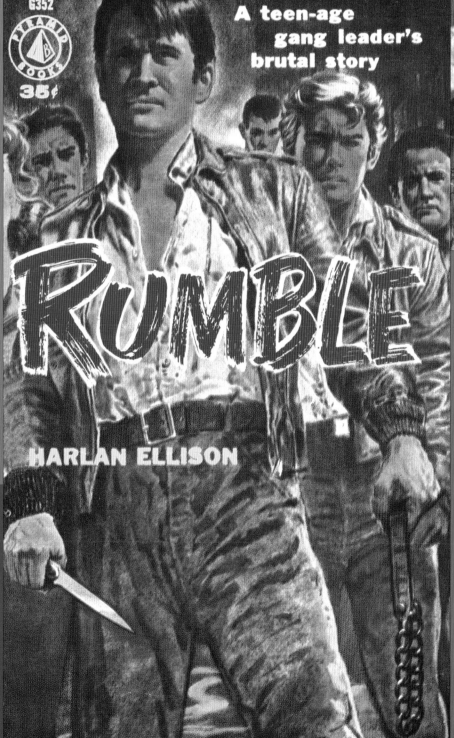

PYRAMID BOOKS
G352
35¢

A teen-age gang leader's brutal story

RUMBLE

HARLAN ELLISON

## TOMORROW AND TOMORROW
**HUNT COLLINS**
**PYRAMID BOOKS, 1956**
**COVER BY BOB LAVIN**

Collins is still another pseudonym of Salvatore A. Lombino, aka Ed McBain, Curt Cannon, Ezra Hannon, Richard Marston, and Evan Hunter. Whatever the by-line, this author has performed an amazing feat of production in many genres and formats (novels, short stories, screenplays) while maintaining an admirable level of quality.

## SIN STREET
**DORINE MANNERS**
**PYRAMID BOOKS, 1950**

H-e-y-y-y, another giant green hand cover! Now there's an idea for an aspiring specialty collector.

## BLUE STEEL
**SPIDER PAGE**
**PYTHON BOOKS, 1979**
**COVER BY GEORGE GROSS**

Here's an oddity. This book is copyright 1940 by a leading pulp magazine publisher, and we know that the pulp adventures of the Spider were written by Norvell W. Page. Put it all together and it spells a rare collectible.

268

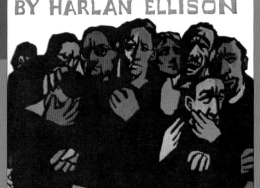

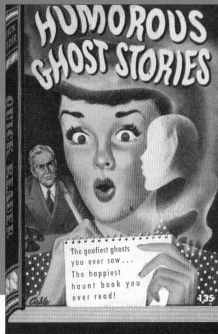

## GENTLEMAN JUNKIE
HARLAN ELLISON
REGENCY BOOKS, 1961
COVER BY LEO AND DIANE DILLON

Here is an early collection of short stories by
a highly collected author. Regency Books was a
superb company owned by William L. Hamling,
a onetime pulp and men's magazine editor and
publisher. Hamling was also involved in some
less savory publishing activities.

## THE GRIFTERS
JIM THOMPSON
REGENCY BOOKS, 1963
COVER BY ROSE

A collector's dream—or maybe nightmare!
The PBO is by the great Jim Thompson, and is
one of his better efforts, too. Part of a treasured
line of books in the rare horizontal format—
a dream if you have it, a nightmare if you're
looking for it.

## HUMOROUS GHOST STORIES
ANTHOLOGY
QUICK READER, 1945
COVER BY CIRKLE

An experiment in "subminiature" publishing,
Quick Readers issued forty-nine highly collectible little books between 1943 and 1945.

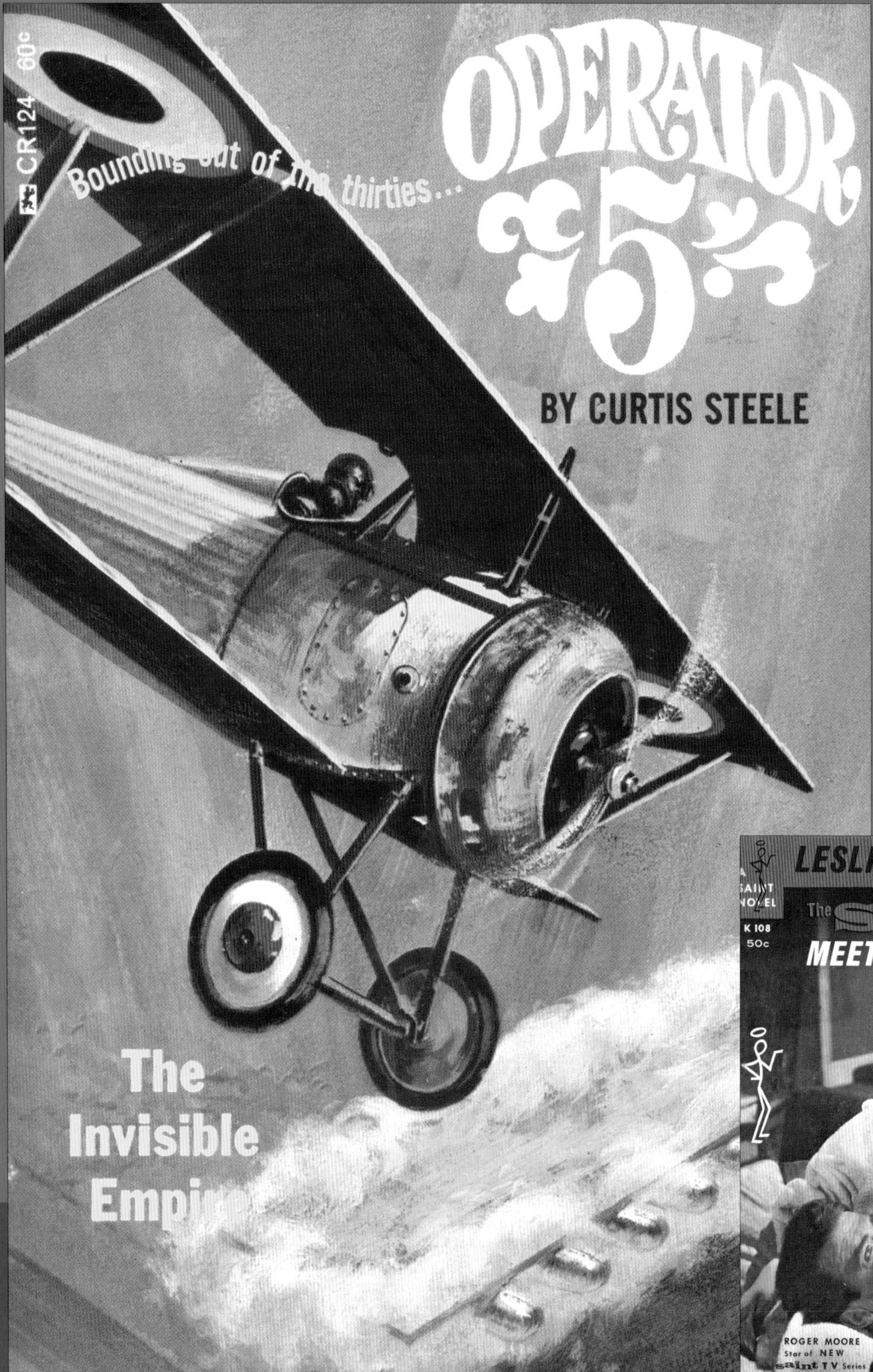

CR124 60c

Bounding out of the thirties...

# OPERATOR 5

## BY CURTIS STEELE

The
Invisible
Empire

A CORINTH SUSPENSE NOVEL • OPERATOR 5 BOOK NO. 3

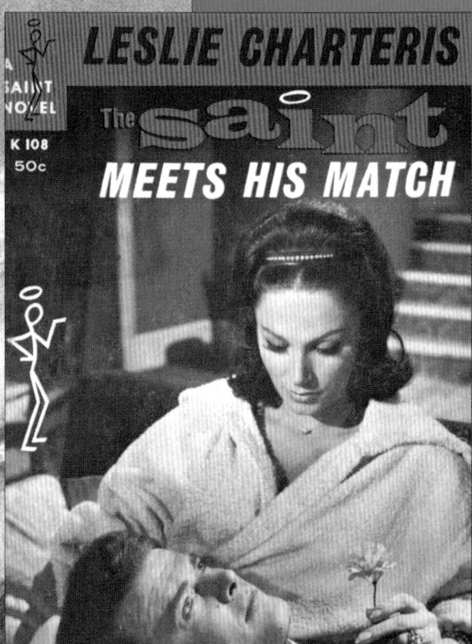

---

*Honor.* Cozzens' novels were selected no fewer than five times by the Book of the Month Club. And this was in an era when "BOMC" was a powerhouse in the literary world. In 1960 Cozzens' 1957 novel *By Love Possessed* won the Howells Medal of the American Academy of Arts and Letters, designating the book as the outstanding literary achievement of the preceding five years.

Another notable early Berkley Book was *Three-Day Pass to Kill* by James Wakefield Burke and Edward Grace (106, 1955). Burke was a former test pilot and war correspondent who found himself in Germany at the end of World War II. He wrote a series of novels and a volume of short stories that were published by local companies and sold primarily to American GIs serving in the Army of Occupation.

One of these, *The Big Rape*, described in chilling detail the battle of Berlin and its aftermath in which rioting Soviet soldiers ran rampant. *Three-Day Pass to Kill* was also set in occupied Germany in the late 1940s, as the tensions and paranoia of the Cold War settled in amongst the devastation and despair left by the just-ended hot war.

*The Man with My Face* by Samuel W. Taylor (Berkley 338, 1955) was another coup for the new publisher. Taylor is an icon among paperback collectors, thanks to *The Grinning Gismo*, the "front half" of the very first Ace Double. But *The Man with My Face* was actually a better novel.

It is the story of an everyman, a daily commuter who arrives home from work to be greeted at his front door by—himself. His double claims to be him, his wife insists that the other man is her husband. Even his dog expresses affection for the interloper and lunges at the protagonist.

What has happened?

You'll have to locate a copy of the book; I'm not going to tell you. *The Man with My Face* had previously been issued in paperback by Pocket Books (639, 1950) and was once again a success for Berkley.

Berkley issued Richard Prather's *Pattern for Panic* (316) in 1955 with a photo cover and again the following year with a striking Robert Maguire cover painting. Many of the early Berkleys featured splendid cover art; Maguire was the unquestioned star of the Berkley line, but Richard Powers contributed some noteworthy science fiction images as well.

As the years went by Berkley's list of authors came to reflect the "usual suspects" ranging from Poul Anderson to Robert A. Heinlein, from Carter Dickson to Harry Whittington, Helen McCoy, pulp veteran Lester Dent, Agatha Christie, Bruno Fischer, R. A. Lafferty, A. E. van Vogt, Simon Raven, and Ngaio Marsh.

The line still exists but, like so many other once-spunky independents, the little company created by Byrne and Klein is now just one more logo in the repertoire of a giant publishing conglomerate.

❦ ❦ ❦ ❦ ❦

When Donald A. Wollheim left Ace Books in 1972, he and his wife Elsie founded DAW Books, a pioneering company devoted entirely to science

**OPERATOR 5**
CURTIS STEELE
CORINTH REGENCY SUSPENSE NOVELS, 1966
COVER BY ROBERT BONFILS
Both publisher William L. Hamling and editor Earl Kemp had a strong background in the pulp world. The original Regency Books was a daring line of modern literature, mostly PBOs. The Corinth Regency line was a polar opposite, devoted entirely to PBO reprints of pulp magazine novels.
❦ ❦ ❦

**THE SAINT MEETS HIS MATCH**
LESLIE CHARTERIS
SAINT NOVELS, 1968
When the Saint came to television with Roger Moore in the title role, thirteen of Charteris's novels were reissued in this TVTI format. *The Saint Meets his Match* had first been published in 1931 as *She Was a Lady.*
❦

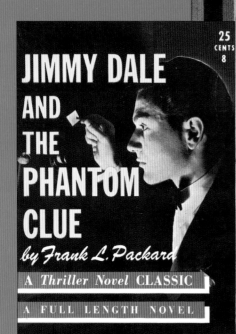

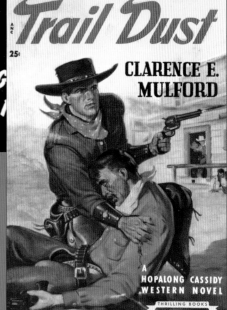

**JIMMY DALE AND
THE PHANTOM CLUE**
FRANK L. PACKARD
THRILLER NOVEL CLASSICS, 1941

An odd combination of old-fashioned melodrama and staccato
modernism, Packard still merits
reading. The thirty-nine Thriller
Novel Classics issued between
1941 and 1945, all in digest size
with photo covers, make a fascinating and desirable set.

📖📖

**POCKET DETECTIVE MAGAZINE**
TROJAN PUBLICATIONS, CIRCA 1950

Is it a magazine or a book? It is one
of many attempts to meld the two
formats.

📖📖📖

**TRAIL DUST**
CLARENCE E. MULFORD
THRILLING BOOKS, CIRCA 1955

Thrilling Books issued twenty
digest-size western novels,
starting with number 11, a
Hopalong Cassidy yarn by New
Yorker Clarence E. Mulford.

📖

**THE SPACE PIRATE**
JACK VANCE
TOBY PRESS, 1953

This PBO is the most sought-after
of the ten digests in this 1952-53
series. The cover painting on *The
Space Pirate* is uncredited but its
style suggests that of David Stone
Martin, who furnished covers
for several Galaxy Novels in the
same era.

📖📖📖📖

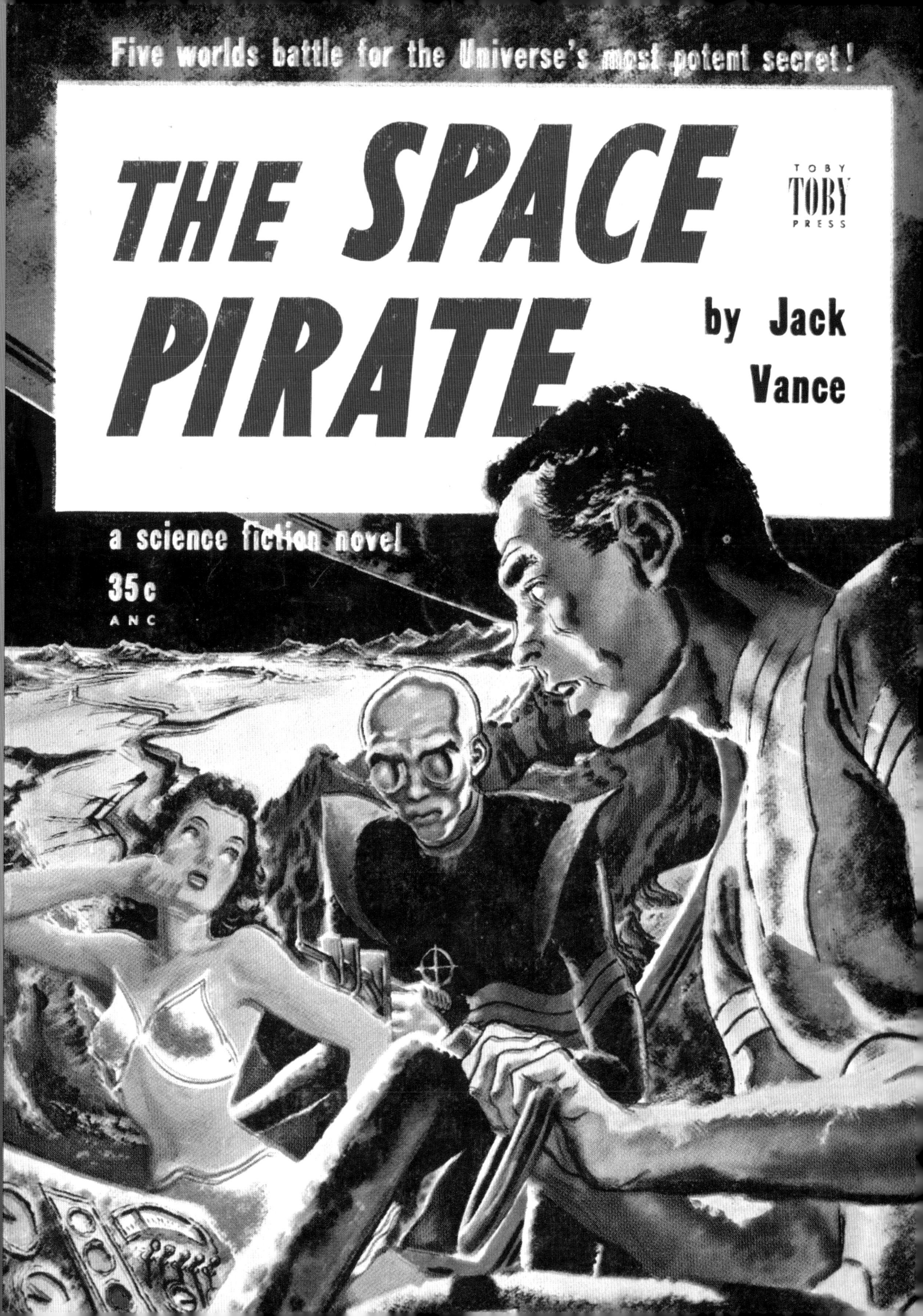

Five worlds battle for the Universe's most potent secret!

# THE SPACE PIRATE

TOBY
TOBY
PRESS

by Jack Vance

a science fiction novel

35c

ANC

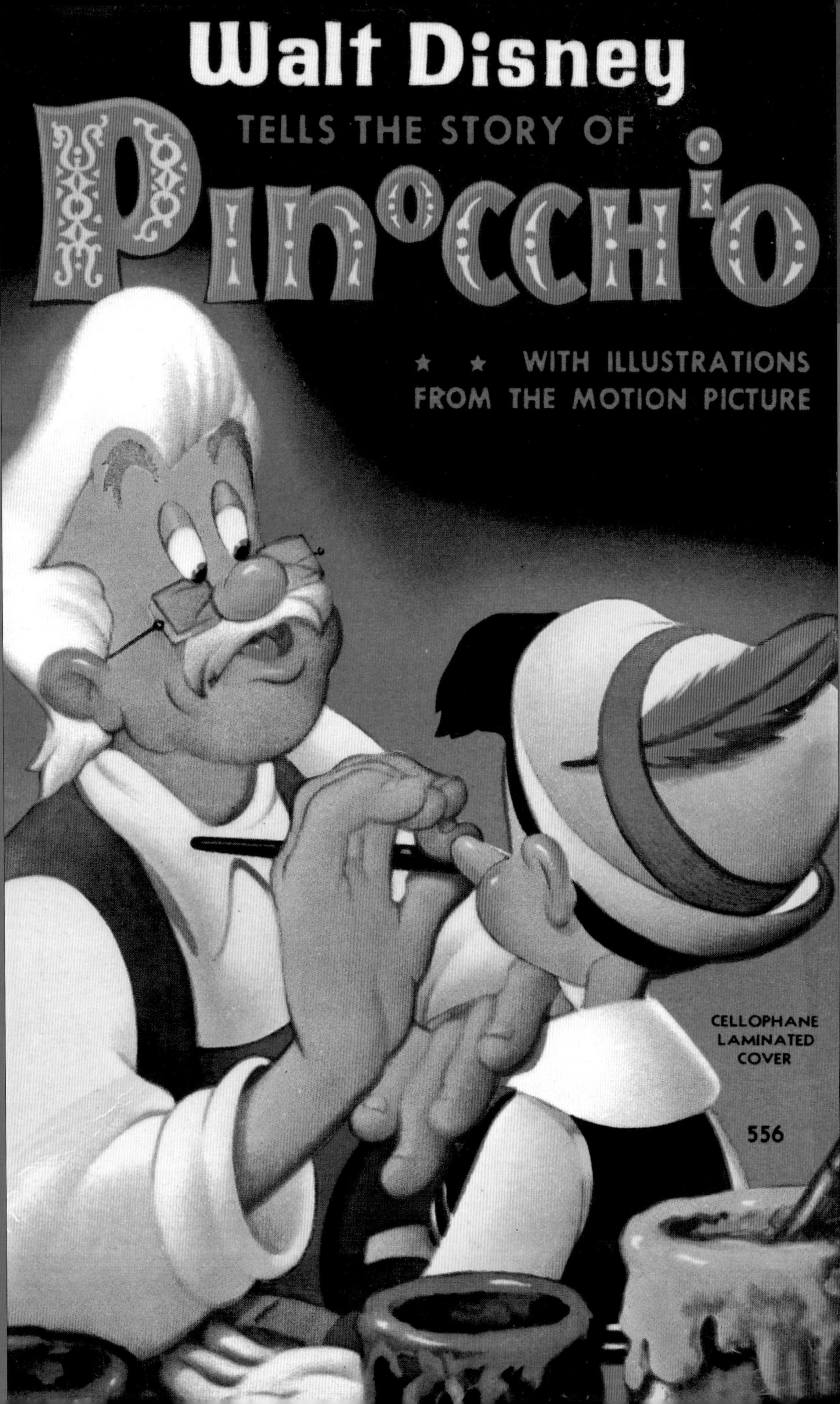

# Walt Disney

## TELLS THE STORY OF

# Pinocchio

★ ★ WITH ILLUSTRATIONS
FROM THE MOTION PICTURE

CELLOPHANE
LAMINATED
COVER

556

## WALT DISNEY TELLS THE STORY OF PINOCCHIO
**WHITMAN PUBLISHING COMPANY, 1939**

This MTI, with illustrations from the Disney film, is an extremely rare book. Disney collectors have been known to pay huge prices for a copy, which is simply outside the scope of most paperback collections.

📖📖📖📖📖

## REEFER CLUB
**LUKE ROBERTS**
**UNI BOOKS, 1953**
**COVER BY WARREN KING**

Yes, but did she inhale? *Reefer Club* is the most sought-after of the seventy-eight digest-size books in this series.

📖📖📖

## IN THE BEGINNING
**JOHN E. MULLER**
**VEGA SCIENCE FICTION LIBRARY, 1963**
**COVER BY FOX**

Vega Books was based in Clovis and Fresno, California. They issued eighty-two books in a sleaze line, one mystery, fourteen science fiction titles, and fourteen westerns between 1960 and 1970. And what in the world is V. I. Lenin doing on the cover of *In the Beginning*?

📖📖

## THE THING THAT MADE LOVE
**DAVID V. REED**
**UNI BOOKS, 1951**

The idea of a swamp-monster arising to menace innocent young womanhood was treated in an early Sturgeon short story and furnished the basis for at least two long-running comic book features, the Heap and Swamp Thing. Reed's version became the second most sought-after Uni Book.

📖📖

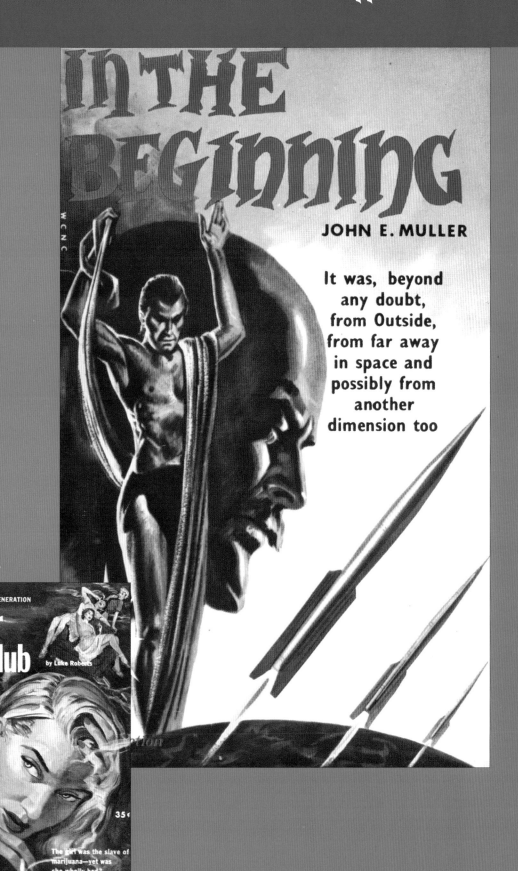

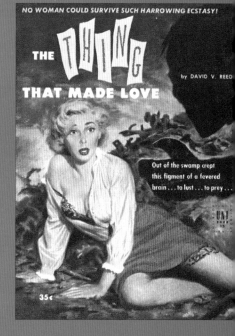

fiction and fantasy. Wollheim was a canny editor with long experience as a pulp magazine editor, anthologist, and book editor. He was also a dedicated collector who understood collectors. He knew that they could constitute a loyal core of customers for a publisher—certainly not enough to support a mass-market paperback house but nonetheless a valuable base upon which to build.

Known throughout the science fiction world and the publishing industry, Wollheim brought several of his popular authors and cover artists with him from Ace. He secured a favorable financing and distribution deal with NAL, whose own science fiction line was not extensive. Everything looked favorable for DAW, and for once the smart money was right—DAW was a success from the start.

The first ten DAW Books are:

1. *Spell of the Witch World* by Andre Norton
2. *The Mind Behind the Eye* by Joseph Green
3. *The Probability Man* by Brian N. Ball
4. *The Book of Van Vogt* by A. E. Van Vogt
5. *The 1972 Annual World's Best SF* edited by Wollheim
6. *The Day Star* by Mark S. Geston
7. *To Challenge Chaos* by Brian Stableford
8. *The Mindblocked Man* by Jeff Sutton
9. *Tactics of Mistake* by Gordon R. Dickson
10. *At the Seventh Level* by Suzette Haden Elgin

All DAW Books were numbered sequentially, and even after DAW followed the industry trend and began using ISBN (International Standard Book Number) designations, the company continued to place a sequential number on each title. Collectors were immensely grateful. A book might have an International Standard Book Number ten digits long (meaningful to computers but useless to collectors) but it would also be DAW Book Number 100, *Hadon of Ancient Opar*, by Philip José Farmer.

Major cover artists to work for DAW included Jack Gaughan, George Barr, Kelly Freas, Tim Kirk, Michael Whelan, Vincent di Fate, Karel Thole, and Roy Krenkel.

From the viewpoint of collectors, important DAW Books include *Old Doc Methuselah* by L. Ron Hubbard, *Flow My Tears, the Policeman Said* by Philip K. Dick, *Drinking Sapphire Wine* by Tanith Lee, *A Darkness in My Soul* by Dean R. Koontz, and *Downbelow Station* by C. J. Cherryh. DAW also took over the popular "Gor" series when author John Norman broke with Ballantine over editorial policy, and published popular series by E. C. Tubb, William L. Chester, and Marion Zimmer Bradley.

With the death of both Donald and Elsie Wollheim, control of DAW Books was assumed by their daughter, Betsy Wollheim. DAW Books thus remains that rarity of rarities in the modern publishing world, not only an independent but a family firm!

❡❡❡❡❡

Other "minor league stars" of the paperback world compete for the dollars of readers and the love of collectors. Some of the names conjure visions of familiar covers and beloved novels. Others draw only blank stares.

*All-Picture Mysteries.*

*Belmont Books.*

*Evening Reader.*

*Flagship Books.*

*Fotonovels.*

*Galaxy Science Fiction Novels.*

*Green Dragon Books.*

*Midwood Books.*

*Paperback Library.*

*Prize Westerns.*

*Three Star Books.*

*Thriller Novel Classics.*

*Yogi Mysteries.*

*Zenith Books.*

The list doesn't even begin to scratch the surface. These books are a cultural history of our times; they deserve to live.

## DEATH FROM NOWHERE
**STUART TOWNE**
YOGI MYSTERIES, CIRCA 1940

Stuart Towne was a pseudonym of Clayton Rawson, making this a highly collectible book. There was only one other Yogi Mystery, *Man about Broadway*, by Herbert Crooker.

## YOUNG SINNER
**ELISABETH GILL**
ZENITH BOOKS, 1959

Zenith Books issued forty-four titles between 1958 and 1960. They ranged as far afield as science fiction (Damon Knight), mysteries (Harry Whittington, William Campbell Gault), westerns (Tom Roan) and religion (Oral Roberts) in addition to borderline sleaze like *Young Sinner*.

More than a century ago our old friend Irvin S. Cobb was spanked by his parents for reading "nickul liburies." The incident doesn't seem to have harmed Cobb, as he went on to great fame and considerable fortune as a literary man.

Over the years uncounted school children have seen their favorite reading matter seized by stern-visaged school teachers, and there's little doubt that parents have a right—probably a duty—to monitor their children's cultural experiences and to direct their children to good books. This leaves open the question of which books are good and which are not. It also leaves open the question of how parents are to protect their children from exposure to bad books.

Any parent knows that placing a book, movie, television show, video game, or website in the realm of "forbidden fruit" is likely to make it more attractive rather than less to an inquisitive young mind.

Besides, it seldom works.

On a series of Sunday mornings in 1946, I found myself squirming on a hard pew in a fundamentalist church in a small town in New Jersey. Whatever religious impulse I might have felt was stifled rather than nurtured by the experience, and after a while I remember sneaking a copy of the *Avon Ghost Reader* into church with me. I hid the little paperback inside a larger hymnal and sat blissfully engrossed in the horror stories of H. P. Lovecraft, F. Scott Fitzgerald, Stephen Vincent Benet, and other luminaries while the preacher poured out his warnings of hellfire and brimstone.

The preacher didn't scare me; the stories in the book did. I know that if I'd been caught my punishment would have begun with the seizure of the book, and I don't know what else would have happened. Fortunately I was not caught, and I still own that precious little book with its lurid cover. It rests in a place of honor beside my computer and I gaze with pleasure at the cover painting of a gigantic, lurid green hand looming toward me!

It's delicious.

Most censorship is small-scale, local, and minor, but what starts small sometimes grows to frightening heights. To paraphrase that old hero of radio, pulp magazines, and paperbacks, the Shadow, "The weed of censorship bears bitter fruit."

It's important to distinguish between morality and legality. It's also important to be careful that in the interest of "protecting the children" we don't impose censorship universally. People have attempted to suppress literature that they didn't like for about as long as literature has existed. We don't need to trace the historical roots of censorship or detail the attempts of Adolf Hitler or Josef Stalin to control peoples' minds as well as their actions. We do need to note that our own Bill of Rights is deeply concerned with the issue.

The First Amendment states that, "Congress shall make no law respecting an establishment of religion, or prohibiting the free exercise thereof; or abridging the freedom of speech or of the press; or the right of the people peacefully to assemble, and to petition the government for a redress of grievances."

Over the years courts have debated endlessly about that sentence, some authorities asserting that only *political* expression is protected. But the First Amendment doesn't say that. It's pretty straightforward. And courts have generally rejected the argument.

Other authorities have argued that the First Amendment does not apply to pornography. Leaving aside for the moment the problem of defining pornography, I have to say that no matter how many times I read the First Amendment, I can't find such an exception in it.

"...no law... abridging freedom of speech or of the press..."

What is pornography? The word comes to us from the Greeks. It means literally "the writing of harlots." A handy definition is *the depiction of erotic behavior intended to cause sexual excitement*, or *material that depicts erotic behavior and is intended to cause sexual excitement.*

## AFFAIRS OF A BEAUTY QUEEN
**ORRIE HITT**
**BEACON BOOKS, 1958**

For the record, Orest "Orrie" Hitt is a man. Beacon was a prolific producer of softcore "sleaze" novels, and Hitt was one of the great, prolific producers.

## CONFESSIONS OF A PSYCHIATRIST
**HENRY LEWIS NIXON**
**BEACON BOOKS, 1954**

What does "A Beacon First Award Original Novel" mean? Probably that the author got paid for his efforts but not very much, you can be certain!

## HILL HOYDEN
**LON WILLIAMS**
**BEACON BOOKS, 1958**

From the Faulkner brothers to Erskine Caldwell to—Lon Williams? Why not?

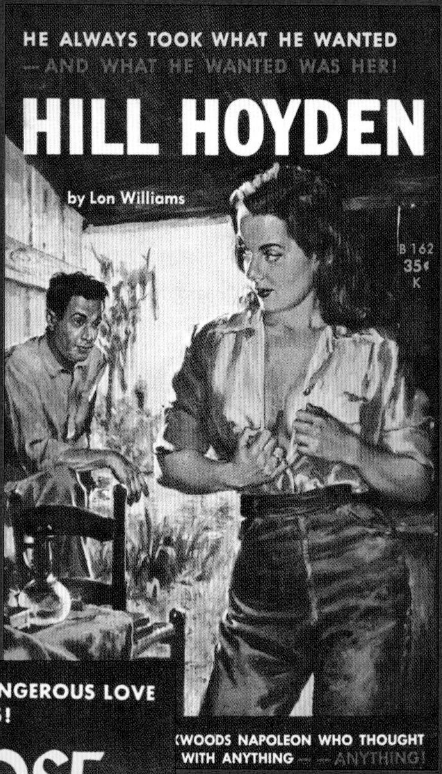

---

EVERY BOUDOIR WAS HIS OFFICE:
EVERY PATIENT HIS PLAYTHING —

# CONFESSIONS of a PSYCHIATRIST

by Henry Lewis Nixon

35¢
B-120

ON FIRST AWARD ORI

---

HE ALWAYS TOOK WHAT HE WANTED
— AND WHAT HE WANTED WAS HER!

# HILL HOYDEN

by Lon Williams

B 162
35¢
K

KWOODS NAPOLEON WHO THOUGHT
WITH ANYTHING — ANYTHING!

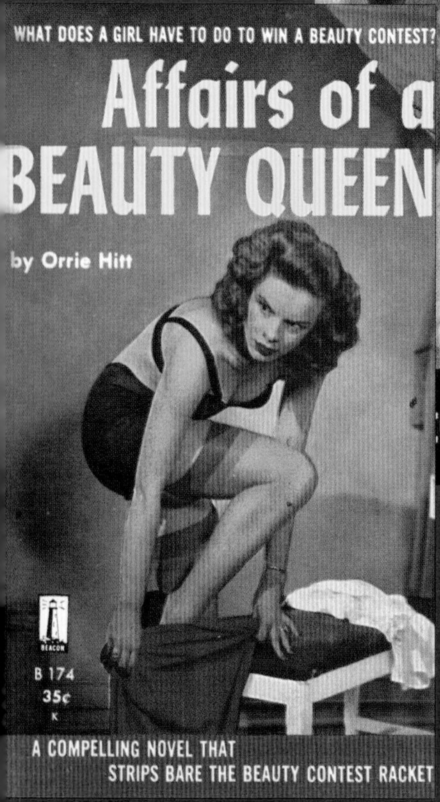

---

WHAT DOES A GIRL HAVE TO DO TO WIN A BEAUTY CONTEST?

# Affairs of a BEAUTY QUEEN

by Orrie Hitt

B 174
35¢
K

A COMPELLING NOVEL THAT
STRIPS BARE THE BEAUTY CONTEST RACKET

---

HE FOUND DANGEROUS LOVE
IN SOFT BLONDE ARMS!

# FOOTLOOSE FRAULEIN

(Walk In Darkness)

by Hans Habe
Author of
Off Limits

35¢
BB 147

THE STIRRING NOVEL OF
A DARK CONQUEROR—WHO
TASTED FORBIDDEN FRUIT!

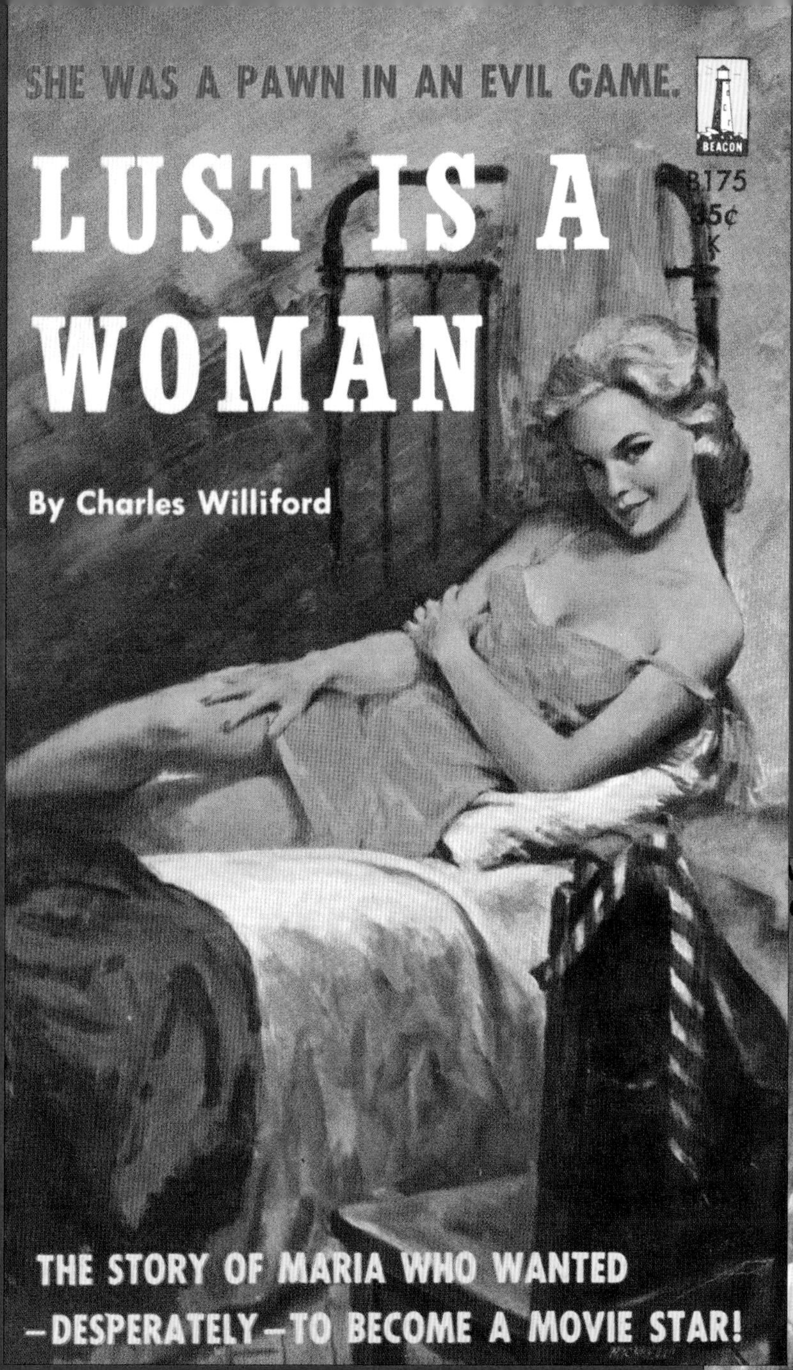

SHE WAS A PAWN IN AN EVIL GAME.

**LUST IS A WOMAN**

By Charles Williford

THE STORY OF MARIA WHO WANTED
—DESPERATELY—TO BECOME A MOVIE STAR!

BEACON
B175
35¢

world older than time, built
dope and vice, this was . . .

35c

**SIN IN SPACE**

by Cyril Judd

### FOOTLOOSE FRAULEIN
HANS HABE
BEACON BOOKS, 1957

As the Army of Occupation became transformed
into a Cold War tripwire, American G.I.'s stayed
on in Germany, providing inspiration for sleaze
authors.

### LUST IS A WOMAN
CHARLES WILLIFORD
BEACON BOOKS, 1958
COVER BY MICARELLI

Williford was a fine novelist, talented and serious,
whose publishing experiences and suffering were
comparable to those of the great Jim Thompson.
Late in life Williford finally achieved some
recognition, but if you stumble across one of
his early PBOs, grab it!

### SIN IN SPACE
CYRIL JUDD
BEACON BOOKS, 1961
COVER BY ROBERT STANLEY

Cyril Kornbluth and Judith Merril's fine
science fiction novel *Outpost Mars* (also known
as *Mars Child*) was reduced to a travesty for
this sleaze edition.

By that definition, at least half the motion pictures showing at your neighborhood multiplex are pornographic. So are about two-thirds of modern television shows and easily nine-tenths of the commercials.

If you'll permit this author to express his personal opinion, I have to say that I'm far more concerned over the publication of hate literature, the promotion of ethnic, religious, or gender-based animosities, and what is sometimes referred to as "the pornography of violence" than I am about sexy books.

But I would be even more concerned at either governmental or private attempts to prevent the publication of *any* book. At present there is little indication that our national government is trying to suppress books, but there are constant attempts by school boards, library committee, and self-appointed private groups to suppress books that they dislike.

If you think I'm off on a political diatribe here and you're wondering what this has to do with the history of paperback publishing, the answer is it has *everything* to do with the history of paperback publishing. If we didn't have a First Amendment and a free press, this would be a very different country.

The beginnings of what we think of as the free press can probably be traced to a heroic printer named John Peter Zenger. In 1753 this courageous journalist was tried for libel because he'd published a newspaper critical of the colonial government in New York. His defense attorney was Andrew Hamilton. Prior to this time, criticism of the government was considered libelous whether it was true or not, but Hamilton convinced the court to accept the truth as a defense against the charge of libel. Score one for the good guys!

Fastforward to 1868. A British judge, Alexander Cockburn, issued a ruling defining obscenity (not pornography) in terms of "the tendency of the matter . . . to deprave and corrupt those into whose hands a publication of this sort may fall." While Judge Cockburn's ruling had no direct affect in the U.S., it was widely influential. As Kenneth Davis points out, it tended to shift the spotlight from the book to the potential reader.

In the United States a moralist named Anthony Comstock founded the Committee for the Suppression of Vice and actually persuaded the Congress to pass a law effectively appointing him National Censor. To avoid the First Amendment protection of the press, the so-called Comstock Act was couched as a postal regulation, banning "every obscene, lewd, lascivious or filthy book, pamphlet, picture, paper, letter, writing, print or other publication of an indecent character" from passage through the mail.

The Comstock Act was wielded as a weapon by censors until 1933 when a federal judge, John Woolsey, ruled that James Joyce's novel *Ulysses* was "emetic, not aphrodisiac" and could therefore be imported into the United States and copies distributed by mail. Granted, this was a strange endorsement for the book, but since Judge Woolsey's ruling, the tide has generally run against censorship and in favor of free expression.

**TAWNY**
ORRIE HITT
BEACON BOOKS, 1959

There's a nice cover painting for this Orrie Hitt novel. Take another look at the object the model is holding—it is *not* a cell phone.

**ANYTHING GOES**
JOE WEISS AND RALPH DEAN
BEDSIDE BOOKS, CIRCA 1964

It's somewhat surprising that two male collaborators didn't choose a female pseudonym for an obvious Lesbian novel. *See page 288.*

**STREETS OF SIN**
MARK RYAN
BEDSIDE BOOKS, CIRCA 1960

A very nice JD cover serves for this sleaze novel—more proof that the genres overlap.

HE WAS A CHEAP TRAMP,
T SHE WAS A LUSCIOUS WOMAN...
D HE WANTED HER!

## TAWNY

rie Hitt

Take a voluptuous thrill-h
add one summer resort C
in a weakling of a husban
have the ingredients for o
Orrie Hitt's spiciest yarns

STREETS
OF
SIN

bq
BB
813
50¢

By Mark Ryan

A powerful novel
of wild delinquents
on the prowl...

The immoral story of a love-starved
temptress and her insatiable desires!

bq
BB
825

50¢

# ANYTHING GOES

By Joe Weiss
and Ralph Dean

aSn

Whatever Else He Was Giving Away, Sin Was
His Biggest Product!

## THE SIN DRIFTER
By ALAN MARSHALL

bq
BB

60c
1218

AN ORIGINAL
BEDSIDE BOOK

**THE SIN DRIFTER**
ALAN MARSHALL
BEDSIDE BOOKS

If only to save the author from dying
of sheer boredom, most sex novels,
whether softcore sleaze or outright
porn, had at least a modicum of a plot.
Here it's the old traveling-salesman-
meets-bored-housewife ploy. Alan
Marshall is alleged to have been a
pseudonym of Donald E. Westlake.

## TRAILER CAMP WOMAN
### By DOUG DUPERRAULT

bq
958

aSn
50¢

She tried to resist
the wild passions
that threatened to
wreck her troubled
marriage. She tried
to be good but
uncontrollable
desires ruled
her life!

BRANDON
75¢

# the hard sell girls
### BY DEL BRITT

## SADDLE SHOE Sex KiTTeN
### BY WAYNE WALLACE

BRANDON
75¢

She looked like a sweet nymphette,
but in his arms she was a tigress!

## ISLAND GIRL
(Island Ecstasy)

The spell of the tropics was in her smile, the lure of an island
goddess in her body. . . . and love was her favorite game!

By Amos Hatter

No. 364
35¢

---

**TRAILER CAMP WOMAN**
DOUG DUPPERRAULT
BEDSIDE BOOKS, 1959

Everybody knows that
mobile home parks are filled
with gorgeous loose women
in low blouses and tight shorts
and lecherous muscular men
in muscle-rippling t-shirts.

❏❏

**THE HARD SELL GIRLS**
DEL BRITT
BRANDON HOUSE, CIRCA 1960

Brandon House was associated
with Essex House, the publisher
of experimental literary novels.
Brandon House books were
closer to standard sleaze but
still managed to achieve a
definite level of class.

❏❏❏

**SADDLE SHOE SEX KITTEN**
WAYNE WALLACE
BRANDON HOUSE, CIRCA 1960

A classic!

❏❏❏

**ISLAND GIRL**
AMOS HATTER
CAMEO BOOKS, 1964

Any novel is designed, in
a sense, to evoke a sense of
fantasy in the reader. *Island
Girl* does it gorgeously: a sandy
beach, a swaying palm tree, a
surfer, a bathing beauty—and
not a hotdog wrapper or abandoned beer can in sight!

❏❏❏

## AGENT 0008 MEETS MODESTA BLAZE
**CLYDE ALLISON**
**LEISURE BOOKS, 1966**
**COVER BY ROBERT BONFILS (?)**

Really more a series of spoofs of the James Bond craze, the Agent 0008 books were good fun. Clyde Allison was a pseudonym of William Knowles.

📖📖📖

## THE MAN FROM C.A.M.P.
**DON HOLLIDAY**
**LEISURE BOOKS, 1966**
**COVER BY ROBERT BONFILS (?)**

Who was Don Holliday? A young author who would later achieve fame and fortune under another name? Or just a poor struggling fellow, desperate to pay the rent and buy some groceries?

📖📖

## THE DAY THE UNIVERSE CAME
**RAY KALNEN**
**NIGHTSTAND BOOKS, 1986**
**COVER BY ROBERT BONFILS (?)**

Nightstand Books, a Milwaukee based company, published a good many sleaze novels by Don Elliott (Robert Silverberg) and at least one by Paul Merchant (Harlan Ellison). These are in great demand and go for very high prices—especially the Merchant (*Sex Gang*). Alas, Ray Kalnen's identity is unknown. Maybe he was actually Ray Kalnen.

📖📖

## AFFAIRS OF A WARD NURSE
**MITCHELL COLEMAN**
**CARNIVAL BOOKS, 1953**
**COVER BY RAY PEASE**

The original title, *Born to be Bad*, had more zing to it, don't you think? Pease's cover is quite lovely and not at all sleazy looking.

📖📖

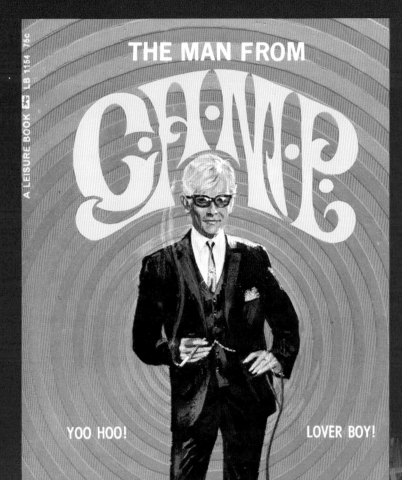

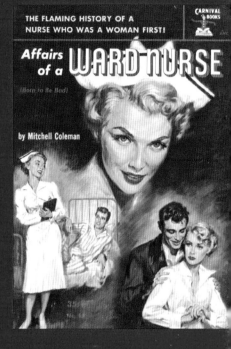

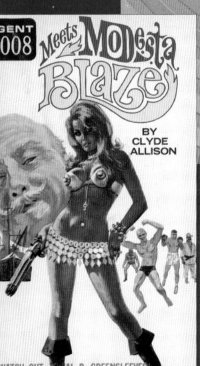

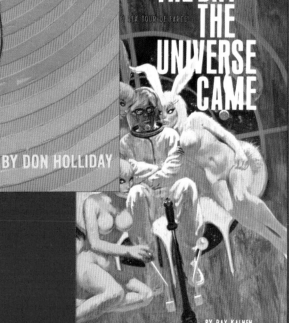

## THE HUNGRY ONES
CRAIG DOUGLAS
CRESCENT BOOKS, CIRCA 1962
COVER BY ELAINE

Even clowns have their needs, but don't you think he'd have a better chance if he switched to civvies?

📖📖

## BUY MY LOVE!
PERRY LINDSAY
EXOTIC NOVEL MAGAZINE, CIRCA 1952
COVER BY RODEWALD

Was this really a magazine or a digest-size book series? There were twenty issues, all published between 1949 and 1951, some seeming to be magazines and some books.

📖📖📖

## MOUNTAIN SIN CAMP
JOHN MITCHIE
DRAGON EDITIONS

Hands down, this is the silliest sleaze cover ever. What were they thinking?

📖📖

## TENEMENT GIRL
ALAN BENNETT
CROYDON BOOKS, 1955

Oh, you can tell that the hero's in trouble—collar open, tie pulled down, what degrading vice comes next?

📖📖📖

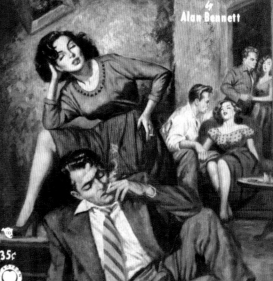

# CLEOPATRA'S
## Blonde SEX Rival

ANCIENT
ROME,
WHERE
ORGIES
WAS A
SPORT!

60¢

ADULTS ONLY

FRANCE

FIRST
AMERICAN
PRINTING

A GREENLEAF CLASSIC

GC205 75¢

# ORGY OF THE DEAD

MOVIE
NOW
SHOWING!

EDWARD D. WOOD, JR.

Special Introduction by Forrest J Ackerman

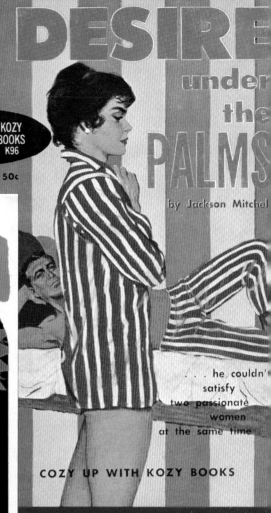

# DESIRE
## under the
## PALMS

KOZY
BOOKS
K96

50¢

by Jackson Mitchell

. . . he couldn'
satisfy
two passionate
women
at the same time

COZY UP WITH KOZY BOOKS

---

### CLEOPATRA'S BLONDE SEX RIVAL
**WALT VICKERY**
**"FRANCE", 1966**

In this case France was the name of the
publisher, not the country. It's an interesting
cross-genre novel, to say the least!

### ORGY OF THE DEAD
**EDWARD D. WOOD, JR.**
**GREENLEAF CLASSIC, 1966**
**COVER BY ROBERT BONFILS (?)**

Here is a true collector's prize—an MTI complete with photos, written by the man famed as
the worst director in Hollywood history, with an
introduction by screen-scream legend Forrest J.
Ackerman. It's an amazing item!

### DESIRE UNDER THE PALMS
**JACKSON MITCHELL**
**CIRCA 1960**
**KOZY BOOKS**

Nice touch there, with those pajama stripes
going in two directions!

## WOMAN'S DOCTOR
**LAURIS HANEY**
**MAGNET BOOKS, 1966**

How many times have we seen that pose, the model as seen from behind, her eyes apparently downcast, brassiere in one hand? Sometimes she's facing another woman, sometimes an alien from outer space, this time it's her doctor. *See page 283.*

📖📖

## CONFESSIONS OF A PARK AVENUE PLAYGIRL
**CARL STURDY**
**MAGAZINE VILLAGE, 1948**

You don't believe in an author named Carl Sturdy? He is credited with three novels. And isn't that a truly wonderful cover painting, whether you read the book or not?

📖📖📖

## LADY WRESTLER
**JAMES HARVEY**
**MIDWOOD BOOKS, 1962**
**COVER BY RADER**

There were all those doctor and nurse novels, secretary novels, soldier novels—why not a lady wrestler?

📖📖

## HORIZONTAL SECRETARY
**AMY HARRIS**
**MIDWOOD BOOKS, 1963**
**COVER BY RADER**

Of course this book was published before all those sexual harassment lawsuits made corporations start issuing code-of-conduct guidelines and sensitivity training sessions.

📖📖

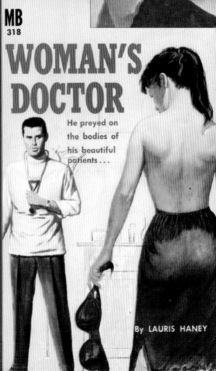

OULD SHE HAVE BEEN BORN A LESBIAN?

PERFUME AND PAIN

BY KIMBERLY KEMP

50¢
MIDWOOD
NO. F162

e knew no desire but
t for another woman.

Original Novel

MA301

MONARCH BOOKS 35¢

MONARCH AMERICANA SERIES

The Wild Days And Nights Of Belle Boyd—
The Notorious Confederate Spy

SHE WOULDN'T SURRENDER

James Kendricks

335

MONARCH BOOKS 40¢

The Dramatic Story Of A Woman Who Turned
Passion Into A Religion And Joy Into A Virtue

SPARE HER HEAVEN

MORGAN IVES

First Publication Anywhere

MEN CALLED HIM "PRETTY BOY" BUT ALL
THE GIRLS WANTED TO "STAR" WITH HIM

STAG MODEL

By JAMES HARVEY (an original novel)

35¢ MIDWOOD

### PERFUME AND PAIN
**KIMBERLY KEMP**
**MIDWOOD BOOKS, 1962**
**COVER BY ROBERT MAGUIRE**

Most sleaze books were PBOs, including this lesbian novel, but few of them warranted cover paintings by the likes of Maguire!

### SPARE HER HEAVEN
**MORGAN IVES**
**MONARCH BOOKS, 1963**
**COVER BY HARRY SCHAARE**

The immensely popular science fiction and fantasy author Marion Zimmer Bradley was Morgan Ives. She described this book, and others of its ilk, as "tepid romances." It is now desperately pursued by Bradley fans and collectors.

### SHE WOULDN'T SURRENDER
**JAMES KENDRICKS**
**MONARCH BOOKS, 1960**
**COVER BY ROBERT MAGUIRE**

Monarch was not strictly a sleaze publisher, mixing other kinds of novels and a great deal of nonfiction into its line. The Maguire painting for this Civil War sleaze novel is truly lovely.

### STAG MODEL
**JAMES HARVEY**
**MIDWOOD BOOKS, 1960**

An unusual simulated film-strip cover sets this sleaze book apart from most others.

Paperback publishers in the 1940s and 1950s opened themselves to criticism by packaging their books in sensational fashion. There's no denying that cover paintings exploiting sexuality, violence, and drug abuse were used to sell books.

The old struggle between Allen Lane and Ian Ballantine was just the beginning. Lane had thought that *any* illustrations on paperback covers were by definition trashy. The editors and art directors at the pulp-influenced houses of the Avon-Popular-Dell school soon left Pocket, American Penguin, and Bantam in the dust.

By 1952 Congress decided to look into the situation, and it seemed that a new round of Comstock-type legislation might be in the offing. The nation was in a state of confusion and paranoia. The Korean War was stalemated, tensions were high in Europe, and domestically, Senator Joseph McCarthy (Republican of Wisconsin) was stirring up anti-Communist hysteria. Senator Estes Kefauver (Democrat of Tennessee) had written a successful book called *Crime in America* and was conducting hearings on the subject. Dr. Fredric Wertham was publishing magazine articles about the evils of comic books; these would culminate two years later in his infamous book, *Seduction of the Innocent*.

The Speaker of the House of Representatives, Sam Rayburn (Democrat of Texas) appointed a Select Committee on Current Pornographic Materials. The committee was to be headed by Congressman Ezekiel Candler Gathings (Democrat of Arkansas, not Kansas, as is sometimes reported). Other members of the Select Committee included senior Republican and Democratic Representatives.

Congressman Gathings and his committee called a series of witnesses chosen to attack the publishing industry (emphatically including the paperback industry) for its alleged abuses. These abuses, the committee seemed determined to show, were leading the youth of the nation (and ultimately the entire nation) into a hopeless life of hedonism, corruption, and crime.

There was no pretense of impartiality. The very name of the Select Committee assumed that the materials in question were pornographic. Chairman Gathings described these publications as "the kind of filthy sex books sold at the corner store which are affecting the youth of our country."

Several representatives of the publishing industry were also called, but transcripts of the committee's hearing suggest that this was done less in the interests of fairness than in order to pillory them in the public spotlight. One witness was Ralph Daigh, a longtime Fawcett editor and executive, and a man highly respected for his decades of professional service to the publishing world.

The committee seemed especially fascinated by a Gold Medal book called *Women's Barracks* by Tereska Torres (132, 1950). Torres' books were published by Fawcett, Avon, and Signet. *Women's Barracks* was the most successful of her books, allegedly "the frank autobiography of a French girl soldier." The Barye Phillips cover painting was somewhat suggestive but far from pornographic.

Members of the committee and committee counsel engaged Daigh in an absurd ring-around-the-rosey exchange over the definition of the term "good books." Daigh insisted that the public decided which books were "good" by buying them, and rejected "bad books" by not buying them. Daigh capped his testimony with one of the few sensible statements to come out of the hearings, in response to a question asked by committee counsel Ralph B. Burton.

Burton: "Can you find anything in Shakespeare in equal number of pages, with as much obscene material as you find in *Women's Barracks* in the same number of pages?"

Daigh: "Well, frankly, I don't know. I go along with the chairman of the committee on the difficulty of defining the word 'obscene.' It is an extremely hard word to define, and it varies with individuals, and if I were to make such a listing it would differ from a listing made by someone else."

The list of books attacked by the Gathings committee illustrates the absurdity of the proceeding. Here are some of the titles that were specifically attacked by Gathings and his colleagues as obscene:

*Woman of Rome* by Alberto Moravia
*The Snow is Black* by George Simenon
*A World I Never Made* by James T. Farrell
*Young Lonigan* by James T. Farrell
*God's Little Acre* by Erskine Caldwell
*I Can Get It for You Wholesale* by Jerome Weidman
*The Amboy Dukes* by Irving Shulman
*The Wayward Bus* by John Steinbeck
*Dollar Cotton* by John Faulkner
*Tomboy* by Hal Ellson

At the end of its hearings, the committee recommended a package of legislation that would in effect have brought back the Comstock Act and might have led to the licensing of booksellers, perhaps of publishers. In the fight against tyranny, first against Hitler and Nazism and then against Stalinist Communism, the United States was treading dangerously close to adopting the same repressive policies that it had found so repugnant in those dictatorships.

Fortunately the Gathings committee's recommendations were quietly shelved.

In later years the threat of censorship has evolved but not disappeared. One change has been in the level and form of attacks on the freedom to publish and the freedom to read. The national Congress seems to have decided that there's no political profit in raking the publishing industry over the coals and attempting to restrict publication. In fact, it now gives official recognition to the American Library Association's annual Banned Book Week.

Under the rubric of regulating commerce, however, the government has restricted advertising of alcohol and tobacco products and has threatened to do the same to video games and other products. With these matters as precedent, some form of restriction on the production, distribution, and consumption of written material is still a dangerous possibility.

At local levels, school boards and library committees have taken on the role of moral guardian and censor of the nation's reading matter. The American Library Association publishes an annual list of banned books and "challenged books." The latter term refers to books which individuals or groups have attempted to have banned.

Topping the list in recent years have been the Harry Potter books by British writer J. K. Rowling. These charming fantasy novels have sold millions of copies and won huge popularity among both adults and children. The challenge to them has come mainly from religious fundamentalists who object to the books' supernatural themes of wizardry and magic. The fact that they are clearly identified as works of fiction seems to matter little if at all.

Also on the list are such important books as *I Know Why the Caged Bird Sings* by African American author Maya Angelou, the feminist social satire (or is it science fiction?) *The Handmaid's Tale* by Canadian author Margaret Atwood, the touching novel *The Color Purple* by Alice Walker, *Snow Falling on Cedars* by David Guterson, and even the classic *Of Mice and Men* by John Steinbeck!

The fact is that most "sleaze" books collected by hobbyists are primarily of interest for their covers. These are sometimes quite charming, occasionally sexy, but more often simply funny.

Can anyone take seriously a book like *Wild Wives*, "the autobiography of Linda Butler...as told to Con Sellers" (Novel Book 6022, 1962) with its brilliant blurb: *The true story of a beautiful female who committed every possible act of sexual perversity to fight the socialist menace!*

How about *Saddle Shoe Sex Kitten* by Wayne Wallace (Brandon House). Check out the cheerleader face, the big bow in the young lady's hair, and the bobby sox. The blurb: *She looked like a sweet nymphette but in his arms she was a tigress!*

**WILD TO POSSESS**

She Lit A Fuse Inside Men

GIL BREWER

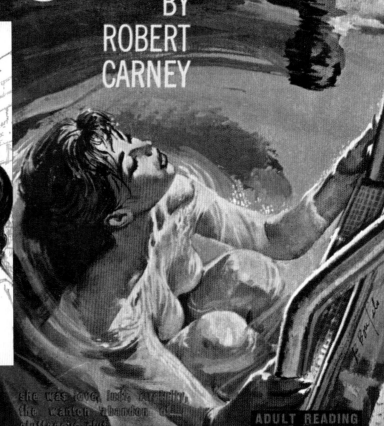

# anything goes

## BY ROBERT CARNEY

she was love, lust, virginity, the wanton abandon of gluttonous slut.

ADULT READING

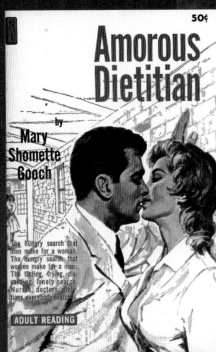

**Amorous Dietitian**

by Mary Shomette Gooch

The hungry search that men make for a woman. The hungry search that women make for a man: The tasting, trying, discarding, lonely search. Nurses, doctors, dietitians, everybody searches.

ADULT READING

---

### AMOROUS DIETITIAN

MARY SHOMETTE GOOCH
NEWSSTAND LIBRARY MAGENTA BOOKS, 1961
COVER BY BONFILS

"The hungry search that men make for a woman. The hungry search that women make for a man: The tasting, trying, discarding, lonely search. Nurses, doctors, dietitians, everybody searches." Ms. Gooch, meet Mr. Carney.

### ANYTHING GOES

ROBERT CARNEY
NEWSSTAND LIBRARY MAGENTA BOOKS, 1960
COVER BY BONFILS

"She was love lust, virginity, the wanton abandon of a gluttonous slut." Mr. Carney, meet Ms. Gooch.

### WILD TO POSSESS

GIL BREWER
MONARCH BOOKS, 1959
COVER BY ROBERT MAGUIRE

What's that old line about judging a book by its cover? Gil Brewer (1922-1983) was a prolific author of crime fiction, many of his novels appearing as PBOs. With a different blurb on the cover, *Wild to Possess* wouldn't even be considered sleaze!

## LIKE CRAZY, MAN
**RICHARD E. GEIS**
**NEWSSTAND LIBRARY MAGENTA BOOKS, CIRCA 1960**

A longtime science fiction fan, amateur publisher, sometime serious critic and frequent gadfly, Geis has also made a long career of writing sex books containing sly digs at contemporary culture. There's usually more to a Geis opus than meets the eye!

## WALL STREET WANTON
**DEAN HUDSON**
**NIGHTSTAND BOOKS, CIRCA 1960**

This is one of the many occupation-based sleaze books. Lady wrestlers, amorous dietitians— why not bigtime investment bankers?

## BAYOU BABE
**GEORGE H. SMITH**
**NOVEL BOOKS, 1960**
**COVER BY BILL WARD**

Novel Books used some of the wildest and most provocative covers of all sleaze publishers. *Bayou Babe* is an outstanding example. George H. Smith wrote a good deal of science fiction, sleaze, and cross-genre books including elements of both.

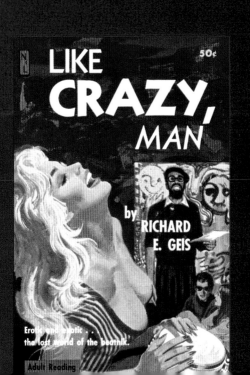

## DREAM CLUB
**ALBERT L. QUANDT**
**ORIGINAL NOVELS, 1952**

Albert L. Quandt was a JD/gang novelist of the
early 1950's, and far from the worst of that
breed. The decision to package this "sensational
novel of dope and twisted lives" as sleaze was
questionable. The prominent needle makes this
book a favorite of drug-book collectors.

## COME SIN WITH ME
**GAIL JORDAN**
**NOVELS INCORPORATED ROMANTIC SERIES, 1963**

This undated PBO digest certainly has the
look of the late 1940s or early 1950s. What
passed for sleaze in that era would probably
be considered teenage romance today. Gail
Jordan was Peggy Gaddis, an extremely hard-
working and talented writers who virtually
defined the neutral zone between romance
and sleaze.

## WILD WIVES
**CON SELLERS**
**NOVEL BOOKS, 1962**

Novel Books' entry in the Most Bizarre Blurb
Ever sweepstakes: "The autobiography of Linda
Butler—the true story of a female who committed every possible act of sexual perversity
to fight the socialist menace!"

What about *Lady Wrestler* by James Harvey (Midwood F193, 1962)? A double blurb here: *She wrestled with sin——and got pinned...Who are these beautiful girls who publicly use their bodies to entertain the fans and gratify themselves?*

As literature, most sleaze books are of little interest. It's the cover art and sometimes hilarious blurbs that make them entertaining. Many were written by bottom-feeder authors for bottom-feeder publishers and warrant little attention, but a sizable number were written by skillful and well-regarded authors seeking freedom from editorial restrictions, or simply because they were in financial straits and saw sleaze books as a quick and easy way to make a few dollars.

Sleaze collectors dote on the works of Charles Williford, Philip José Farmer, Marion Zimmer Bradley, and other truly talented authors who turned to sleaze at one time or another, for one reason or another.

And finally, there were the more legitimate novels that were repackaged as sleaze, with or without the knowledge or consent of their authors. An example was a fine and serious science fiction collaboration by Cyril Kornbluth and Judith Merril. Serialized in *Galaxy Science Fiction* magazine in 1952 as *Mars Child*, the book edition was retitled *Outpost Mars* (Dell 760, 1954), with a striking Richard Powers cover. Then it became *Sin in Space* (Beacon 312, 1961) with a few sex scenes added by an anonymous hand on Beacon's payroll, and a hilarious cover by Robert Stanley. (At least I hope it was supposed to be funny.)

Sleaze books cover every genre, from detective stories to westerns to exotic adventures. There are great numbers of "professional" sleaze books—those involving doctors, nurses, dieticians, librarians, secretaries, Wall Street investors, and lady wrestlers. They frequently cross genre boundaries with juvenile delinquent and gang novels, even on rare occasions with love stories.

Hardcore sex books are another matter. Whereas sleaze publishers have traditionally packaged their books for maximum visibility, hardcore publishers have generally tried to stay out of the spotlight, and most hardcore paperbacks are packaged in a way that not even Allen Lane would object to.

Gay literature is sometimes lumped with sleaze or pornography, depending on how explicit and lubricious the sex scenes are. A great many books dealing with homosexuality are of course serious literature of high quality and have been published accordingly. The works of James Baldwin—most notably *Giovanni's Room* (Signet S-1559, 1958)—immediately come to mind. Where the boundary lies between serious literature and pandering is a matter of opinion.

So is the intended audience, and in many cases even the identity of the authors. Ann Bannon, a respected academic and talented novelist, wrote numerous Lesbian novels in the 1950s and 1960s. In an essay written many years later she suggested that "It is true that many books were written and sold as 'Lesbian fiction' during the heyday of the pulps, that were, in fact, written by men using female pseudonyms. And male readers had no difficulty finding them. But by far the largest number was written by and for women."

With the growing acceptance of personal choice in lifestyles, there is today far less need for books to be sold "under the counter" and for their readers to spend their lives in the closet.

But there is a tendency by publishers to self-censor in the name of political correctness or perhaps out of fear of reprisals from offended pressure groups. The right to write, to publish, and to read, is not totally and permanently secure. Not by a very long shot.

## ROOM AND DAME
**GERALD FOSTER**
**QUARTER BOOKS, 1950**

What a charmer—multiple pictures-within-picture! Not only is there a girly calendar on the wall, the lovely titian-tressed mademoiselle is apparently reading a copy of *Exotic Novels Magazine*. Nice shoes, too!

📖📖📖

## SEX ALLEY
**RON GOLD**
**P.E.C., CIRCA 1966**

A sterling example of a not-quite-strategically-placed bowling ball, this book is a sure winner with your friend who specializes in sleaze books with a bowling alley theme.

📖📖

## OFF LIMITS!
**GEORGE L. BOTTARI**
**RAINBOW BOOKS, 1953**

This was the year that the Korean War ended in a bitter truce and military service was on the mind of every young man.

📖📖

## CONFESSIONS OF A CHINATOWN MOLL
**JEFF BOGAR**
**UNI-BOOKS, 1953**

Bogar apparently wrote only three books, *Confessions of a Chinatown Moll, Hillbilly in High Heels,* and *Tigress*, published by Lion in 1951. The Uni digest PBO shown sports one of the most striking covers of the era.

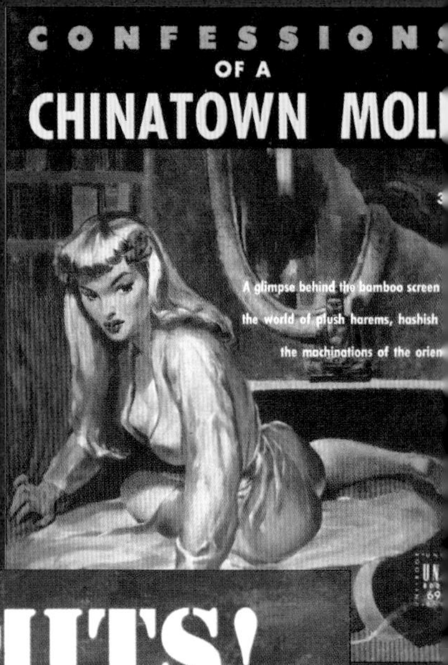

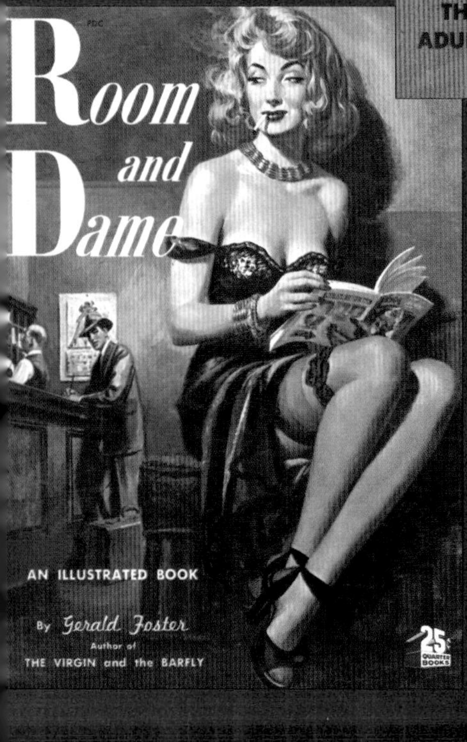

📖📖📖

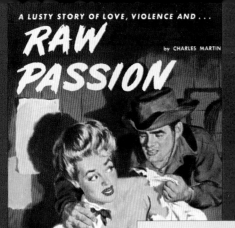

# RAW PASSION

A LUSTY STORY OF LOVE, VIOLENCE AND...

by CHARLES MARTIN

## VENUS BOOKS

An Exciting Story of Passion in the Hill Count

# Backwoods Girl

by Peggy Gaddis

35¢

### NO TIME FOR SLEEP

ANC

35c
No. 126

A BRAND-NEW NOVEL BY
*Amos Hatter*

VENUS BOOKS

A BLONDE, A BRUNETTE AND A MAN SPELL TROUBLE

---

### RAW PASSION
**CHARLES MARTIN**
**UNI-BOOKS, 1951**

Sleaze in the Old West. Well, why not? In later years there was at least one PBO western series that was a lot closer to serious, hardcore porn than this almost-innocent romance novel.

❝❝

### BACKWOODS GIRL
**PEGGY GADDIS**
**VENUS BOOKS, 1952**

Traveling man spies naked beauty in rural swimming hole —stop me if you've heard this one! Maybe Peggy Gaddis visits Caldwell Country would be more to the point.

❝❝❝

### NO TIME FOR SLEEP
**AMOS HATTER**
**VENUS BOOKS, 1951**

This was before the high-speed interstate freeway system was built. Motorists traveled rural highways and there was always a gorgeous hitchhiker with upraised thumb poised to offer an exciting adventure.

❝❝❝

On these pages you see eight covers of collectible paperbacks that could probably not be reissued today, at least in mass-market editions intended for a general readership. Scholarly editions would probably be permitted, but if any of these books turned up at most bookstores they would be returned to the publisher as unacceptable.

*Nigger Heaven* by Carl Van Vechten, despite its title, is not a racist attack on African Americans. In fact, Van Vechten (1880-1964) was a highly sympathetic chronicler of African-American culture, a highly-regarded music and drama critic, novelist, essayist, and photographer. He was the leading (perhaps the only) white man to be fully accepted as a member of the Harlem Renaissance, a hugely important cultural movement of the 1920s.

The very title *Nigger Heaven* was a generally understood term in the era when the book was first published (1926). It was still widely known in 1951, when the Avon edition was issued with its brilliant and regrettably uncredited cover painting.

A controversial but unquestionably important book, it could hardly be reprinted today.

*KKK* by Paul E. Walsh is also endangered. It's important to notice that the book does not glorify the Ku Klux Klan. On the contrary, it is a powerful attack on the Klan. The blurb alone tells the story: *The fearless novel that rips the mask off the hooded terrorists.* But just the letters, KKK, are enough to chill any thought of republication.

*12 Chinks and a Woman* by James Hadley Chase is another matter. Chase was a member of the British hardboiled school, a coterie of novelists who tried to imitate American writers in the genre. Chase could be very good at it. His best novel, *No Orchids for Miss Blandish*, is at least a minor classic of the form.

What is wrong with *12 Chinks and a Woman*? Obviously it *is* racist. It has the "C word" right there in the title, just as Van Vechten's book has the "N word." It is not an important book, and there is probably little reason to bring it back into print. But it should surely not be erased from history. As any number of readers, collectors, authors, editors, critics, and booksellers have commented, we must preserve our history, the ugly and evil parts of it as well as the beautiful and delightful. If we forget the abuses, they will happen again.

Lori Leigh Gieleghem, a high school English literature teacher in California, addressed the issue this way:

"With respect to book covers like *12 Chinks and a Woman* and *Nigger Heaven*, isn't it better to face up to our history of racism by looking it squarely in the face and not flinching? To do so is not to condone racist slurs, but instead to say, 'Look how outrageous and sleazy these covers were! Haven't we come a long way?'

"Alice Walker, a novelist and poet who has spent her life battling ignorance and racial prejudice, had this to say with respect to a show of pop culture items depicting racist stereotypes of black Americans: 'Inside each desperately grinning "Sambo" and each placid 300-pound "mammy," there is imprisoned a real person. We can liberate them by understanding this. And free ourselves.'"

## NIGGER HEAVEN
**CARL VAN VECHTEN**
**AVON, 1951**

Unpublishable today because of
its title, this book has always been
controversial. The brilliant painting depicts African Americans in
many roles, from working
women and men to nightclub
singer and *boulevardier*.

📖📖📖📖

## KKK
**PAUL E. WALSH**
**AVON PBO, 1956**

Whips, hoods, the burning
cross—a powerful exposé of
the Ku Klux Klan, issued several
years before the Civil Rights
movement of the 1960s.

📖

## UNDERGROUND ADS
**"EMILE NYTRATE"**
**POCKET PBO, 1970**

Even at the height of the sexual
revolution, who could possibly
find these headlines amusing?
Even the author of the book was
ashamed to put his (or her) real
name on it.

📖

## 12 CHINKS AND A WOMAN
**JAMES HADLEY CHASE**
**AVON, 1948**

Chase was a pretty good hardboiled writer and not known as
a racist. It's a sign of the times
that he thought nothing of using
such stereotypes and the
offensive title.

📖📖📖

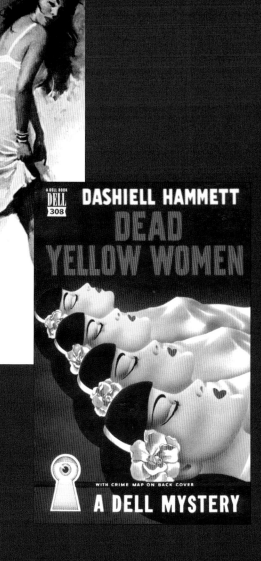

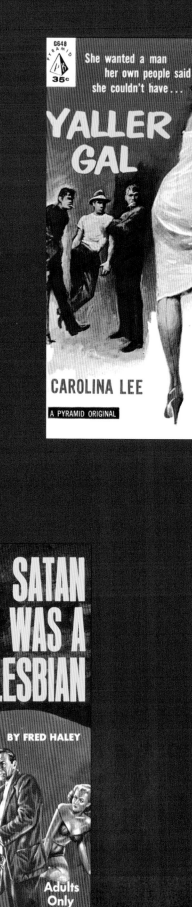

## THE DEVIL IS GAY
**FREDERICK COLSON**
**BRANDON, CIRCA 1968**

Something to offend everyone
—or maybe no one. Some publishers have treated the subject of
homosexuality with seriousness
and sensitivity, others as material
for blatant exploitation.

## SATAN WAS A LESBIAN
**FRED HALEY**
**P.E.C., CIRCA 1966**

P.E.C. was one of the most
enigmatic of sleaze publishers.
They did bring out a number
of intriguing books, including
this stew of diabolism, sadism,
and Lesbianism.

## YALLER GAL
**CAROLINA LEE**
**PYRAMID BOOKS, 1961**
**COVER BY GEORGE ZEAL**

This 1961 reissue of a 1958
PBO teases the reader with
the then-forbidden theme of
interracial sex.

## DEAD YELLOW WOMEN
**DASHIELL HAMMETT**
**DELL BOOKS, 1949**
**COVER BY GERALD GREGG**

Dell's (and Hammett's) entry in
the Politically Incorrect derby, this
striking mapback by a heavily collected author is very hard to find.

Perhaps the most shocking of the eight is *Underground Ads* compiled by "Emile Nytrate." Now there's a byline for you! It's the "I Dig Rape" headline that is both astonishing and grossly offensive. Any woman, and any man with an atom of decency in his body, would be outraged by this book.

As a product of the counterculture and the sexual revolution of the 1960s and 1970s, it is an appalling example of freedom gone wrong. Even more incredible, it was not issued by some low-grade exploitation publisher. It came from Pocket Books, the oldest and one of the most respected of American paperback houses!

From the viewpoint of the present day, Pocket Books should never have published this book or at the very least should have removed that outrageous box from the cover. But the fact is, Pocket *did* publish the book. It is part of history. It ought not be swept under the carpet.

Finally, note the book *The Devil is Gay* by Frederick Colson. Who would be offended? Homosexuals? Gay-bashers? Satanists? Fundamentalists? Who can say?

Just look at the uncredited cover painting on *Satan Was a Lesbian*, by Fred Haley. There's that short-haired, leather-covered, whip-wielding dominatrix, the business-suited male and the lingerie-clad female. The leering Lucifer in the background completes the picture.

There is a longstanding cultural association of what was considered illicit or deviant sexual behavior with sinfulness. If anything, extreme puritans would be expected to approve of these books. As for the people who actually bought them and took them home, what happened next is not pretty to contemplate.

*Dead Yellow Women*, by Dashiell Hammett, is a very different story. Hammett was one of the icons of the hardboiled school, still valid and widely read forty years after his death. *Dead Yellow Women* was a collection of Hammett's short stories, first published as a Jonathan Press digest. The Dell edition of 1949 features a fine, evocative painting of the victims.

Affiliated with progressive and even radical causes for most of his life, one would hardly expect to find Hammett using biased or racially stereotyped imagery, but the images of blacks, Asians, Jews, and various national "types" ranging from the drunken Irishman to the greasy, knife-wielding Mexican, to the wily Oriental were deeply ingrained in the national psyche. Along with many of his contemporaries, Hammett accepted these standard types with little or no question. The modern reader should really bear the original publication date of the stories in mind.

Then there's *Yaller Gal*, by Carolina Lee. Most Americans alive today have probably never come across this term. It referred to a woman of mixed-race heritage whose draw at the genetic roulette wheel gave her a light tan or "yellow" complexion and a suggestion of Asian facial features. Such women (and less often men), sometimes known as "high yellows," suffered in a racial wilderness, often rejected by both whites and blacks and unsure of their own identity. Lee's book bears reading in a later era for the insights it provides into the mores of the pre-Civil Rights Era.

The point is not that reproduction of this cover, or any of these covers, constitutes an endorsement of racism, sexual abuse, or any particular lifestyle. These covers and all the other hundreds of covers in *The Great American Paperback* are part of our development as a nation and a culture. In a very real and very important sense, they are part of us.

The good ones and the bad ones. The serious ones and the silly ones. The breathtakingly fine novels in incredibly lovely packages, the sleaze, and the garbage. They are all part of our history.

CHAPTER ELEVEN

No. 5
A HARVEST/
HBJ
ORIGINAL

# Where Do We Go From Here?

*Featuring*
DASHIELL
HAMMETT'S
ORIGINAL
STORY
"AFTER
THE
THIN MAN"

*Also* WILLIAM
HAGGARD ★ IRVIN
FAUST ★ JAMES
ELLROY ★ CHET
WILLIAMSON

JAMES LEE
SNYDER ★ ROBERT
SAMPSON ★ GEORGE
SIMS

It's been a long trail, from the Panic of 1837 to the dawning of the twenty-first century. It stretches from Rufus Griswold and Park Benjamin publishing *Brother Jonathan* in the United States and Baron Tauchnitz issuing his "traveler's companions" in Europe to the modern mass-market paperback.

But in a way, there's been remarkably little change. Publishers still strive to present an immense range of books, from great literature to vulgar entertainment, in colorful, handy, relatively inexpensive form.

In other ways, several major trends have become clear. Paperbacks (at least in the modern, post-1939 era) started out with dignity, descended into sensationalism, recovered to a degree and have maintained a precarious balance between elevation and pandering ever since.

These little books have achieved a degree of respectability as well that would warm the cockles of Allen Lane's and Robert de Graff's hearts. They are seen on university campuses, often as reading assigned by professors. They are stocked by libraries.

Even the PBO, once despised as a publishing format for second-rate books by second-rate authors, has come into its own. Ian Ballantine's 1950's dream of the simultaneous hardcover and paperback has not swept the publishing world, but it has survived. In many cases one company will issue the same book in three different formats: hardcover, trade paper, and mass paperback. The traditional distinction between haughty "publishers" and humble "reprinters" has blurred and in many cases simply disappeared.

A more disturbing trend is the slump in average sales per title. Remember those first books published by Robert de Graff's fledgling Pocket Books in 1938 and 1939. The unnumbered "test" edition of *The Good Earth* ran a mere 2,000 copies. The first ten numbered Pocket Books had printings of 10,000 copies each, and of course they sold extremely well.

De Graff's stated goal was to reach a first printing of 100,000 copies per title, and Pocket soon reached that level. De Graff also stated that for Pocket's most popular authors, like Erle Stanley Gardner, first printings as large as 400,000 copies became the norm. As the popularity of paperbacks continued to increase in the years following World War II, sales of top sellers like Mickey Spillane's Mike Hammer novels could reach to five or six *million* copies.

Of course, popularity of the degree attained by a Gardner or Spillane represented the pinnacle of paperback success. But even lesser publishers than Pocket or Signet could turn out sizable printings. Further, they could expect to sell virtually all the books that they printed—a factor that was potentially even more important than the raw number of copies sold.

Why was this so? In the earliest days of paperback publishing, relatively few titles appeared. Those which did tended to remain on display until they sold. A few were ruined by weather (those displayed outdoors) or by careless handling. On occasion, unsold copies were removed from sale, returned to the publisher, and reshipped to other outlets.

As late as 1960, two decades into the paperback revolution, Donald Wollheim told an interviewer about Ace Books' print runs and sales. Ace printed 90,000 copies of each book, Wollheim said, and sold virtually all of them.

Weren't there "hotter" Ace authors and "cooler" ones? Didn't the hot authors sell faster? Wouldn't that prompt Ace to adjust the print run?

No, Wollheim replied. "Hot authors" sold faster—Andre Norton and Philip José Farmer were Ace favorites at the time. "Cooler" authors like Tom Purdom and Kenneth Bulmer sold more slowly, but they all hit their 90,000 mark. It was Ace policy to let a printing become exhausted in this fashion, and if the publishers felt that the book had more potential, they would issue another printing, rather than vary the size of first printing.

A few years later, Ian Ballantine made a similar comment to the same interviewer. Ballantine spoke of issuing a title and letting it sell for a while, then "giving a book a rest" and later repackaging it and issuing a new edition.

Those days are long gone. As competition for display space on revolver racks and bookstore shelves grew ever more intense, books were no longer allowed to remain on sale until they sold. They had to sell fast (the industry term is "turn over") or they would be pulled in favor of other titles.

To make things worse, "pulled" books were no longer returned to the publisher to find their way to a warehouse and eventually be reshipped to a new seller. Instead, publishers began accepting "cover-only" returns. Retailers would simply tear the covers off pulled books and return them to the publishers for credit. The coverless books were supposedly destroyed but instead were sometimes donated to charity or sold (illegally) at huge discounts.

This latter policy caused dismay among both publishers who received no payment for the stripped-and-sold copies, and authors, whose royalty computations did not reflect these sales at all.

The result of the practice of pulling and stripping books was a drastic reduction in the "sell-through" rate of most paperbacks. From a rate of close to one hundred percent, average sell-through fell to sixty percent, fifty percent, or even less. Less attractively packaged or inefficiently distributed books could report a sell-through of as little as twenty-five percent.

This introduced a *huge* inefficiency to the industry and caused immense waste of paper, ink, press time, and shipping costs. It drove up the prices of those books which were sold. The cost of manufacturing, warehousing, and shipping two or three books had to be built into the retail price of one.

Along with comic books and television, paperback books were blamed for the demise of the pulp magazines in the 1950s and 1960s. Especially after the arrival of Avon, Popular Library and Dell, paperbacks did offer the same kind of reading matter that pulp magazines had provided and offered it in a compact version of the familiar pulp package. The development of PBOs exacerbated the problem.

Further, until the paperback publishing glut shortened the shelf-life of a typical title, these little books could remain on sale far longer than a magazine, which would be replaced by the next issue in a week or a month.

Now the wheel has turned; paperbacks are in trouble. In part they were the victims of their own success, with ever more publishers churning out titles until the market was flooded. Competition from videos and computers has also been blamed for some of the woes of the paperback publishers. It should be noted that comic books have suffered an even more precipitous decline in recent years, as rising costs and increased competition have decimated what was once a cultural icon.

So-called trade paperbacks have grown in popularity. These books use a larger format than the mass product, and their prices are pegged at a midpoint between those of the mass paperback and hardcover books. They are printed on better paper and are often bound better than typical mass paperbacks. Of course, in the early days of the paperback revolution, the little books were carefully designed, were printed on good paper (not newsprint), had sturdy covers and even end papers. It is altogether possible to find a sixty-year-old paperback, if has not been mistreated, with its cover still bright, its spine uncracked, its pages still white, its binding still tight, and its edges still smooth and sometimes lovingly stained red or gold.

The physical quality of the product has deteriorated, and it is hard to deny that this has hurt paperbacks in the marketplace. Probably the greatest change in paperback production was the switch to cheaper grades of wood-pulp based newsprint in place of traditional book paper. On a brand new book the difference is barely noticeable, although the paper tends to be slightly brownish, yellow, or gray. But within a few years—in extreme cases, even months—the paper often turns brown and, more seriously, may become brittle.

The increasing number of mergers and takeovers in the media community has led to ever fewer companies actually publishing books. This trend has proceeded much farther than is known by the casual bookstore browser because the corporate giants often retain multiple logos and book lines. It's a little bit like the automobile industry, where a giant corporation will market several brands of cars through several groups of dealers.

The biggest of the conglomerates is probably Bantam-Doubleday-Dell, which is in turn owned by a German media conglomerate. The British-based Pearson Group is not far behind. A handful of other conglomerates control the bulk of the publishing industry. Often editors are expected to turn out so many books that they can pay little attention to the manuscripts they handle. Agents and freelance editors or "book doctors" have taken on part of this burden, but its overall effect has been distinctly detrimental.

New trends in media may prove the final destruction of the mass paperback—or its salvation. One is Print-on-Demand (POD) publishing.

By traditional methods it was pretty expensive to publish a book. The cost of editing was substantial, typography could cost anywhere from many hundred to several thousand dollars for a single title, and making plates and setting up a print-run could run to many thousands. By the time the first copy of a book rolled off the press (or came back from the bindery), the cost could be terrifying. Of course, the *second* copy was practically free. It was just a matter of paper and ink and less than a minute of press time. What the publisher had to do was amortize the cost of that first copy across the entire print-run and potential sale of the book.

POD publishers often use authors' own computer files for typesetting. The grizzled veteran linotype operator in his green eye-shade and sleeve-garters has long since retired. The editorial staff is small or nonexistent, meaning that the author had better turn in clean, smooth copy. Smaller, cheaper presses and binding technology require minimal set-up. Warehouse and distribution costs are reduced because huge stocks of books need not be stored or shipped.

As a result, almost anybody can get almost anything published. Print-runs can be in the hundreds of copies or even fewer; costs are low. Distribution of POD books via traditional, commercial channels is almost impossible, but POD books are sold at book fairs, through specialty shops, or over the Internet.

Sell-through can be at least potentially close to the level of the 1940s and 1950s, eliminating the waste and inefficiency of the strip-and-return system.

Is this good? If you're an author who can't find a publisher, it's great. If you're a reader, it means that a greater variety of material will be available but also that an important filter has been removed between the army of writer wannabe's and the reader. This filter was traditionally provided by the publishing industry, which has a long history of turning away anywhere between ninety percent and ninety-nine percent of the manuscripts offered.

Early POD books tended to be pretty unattractive products. Most often, they were reissues of older, out-of-print volumes and were produced by simply photocopying an older edition. The quality of POD books has now improved greatly and some of them can compete with traditional books.

# Down the Badger Hole

## R. Lionel Fanthorpe: The Badger Years

## Debbie Cross

### STRANGE.WEIRD.EERIE

## Introduction by **David Langford**

full length feature story:

## *Curse of the Khan*

by R. Lionel Fanthorpe

A competing technology to POD is the "e-book." Several companies have tried to introduce e-books to the American market with limited success. One problem is the fact that a standard format and delivery system has yet to emerge.

Several authors including Stephen King have tried offering their works over the Internet. The reader pays a fee and downloads a file; he can then read the book on a computer screen or perhaps on a hand-held device.

He may want to print it out. There are still many paper junkies, and almost daily improvements in computer software and desktop printers are making this option more and more attractive. Binding such home-printed books remains problematical, but several options are available for dealing with the conundrum.

Collectors who feel strongly about first editions have expressed dismay at both POD and e-books. If the publisher runs off copies as few as twenty at a time, and if there is no indication on them as to *first printing*, *second printing*, and so on, how can you tell them apart? And as for e-books, it's conceivable that every copy will be different in some way, and the whole concept of "first edition" loses its meaning.

Publishers have also tried e-magazines with varying degrees of success. Some are supported by advertisers and are available free online; some sell subscriptions.

Other e-books are distributed in the form of small memory chips. The reader (human) owns a "reader" (electronic). Plug in the chip, turn on the device, and a page of type appears on the screen. The advantage here is that you can store a whole library of "books" on one chip and turn your book-size reader into any of them at will.

This much we know about the traditional book: it's several thousand years old. It has been one of humankind's greatest and most durable inventions. The only major difference between a first edition of Homer's *Odyssey* and the latest paperback version is that in Homer's day the pages of a book were pasted together end-to-end and spun between two rollers. For the past four hundred or so years we've been binding our books at the edge, which is both a clever concept and a real advance. The edge-bound volume is a random-access device, while the scroll-book was sequential.

Of course you'd have to be able to read classical Greek to get through that first edition *Odyssey*. Homer's disciples had to copy out books by hand; we now have printing presses. But even so…

Doomsayers to the contrary, it looks as if books are going to be with us for a very long time. And isn't that wonderful!

❡❡❡❡❡

Popular culture commentator Lee Server suggests, "There have probably been collectors of paperbacks since the appearance of the first paperback, more than five hundred years ago. As an organized pursuit, however, the collecting of softcover books is a quite recent development."

Kevin Hancer, a highly respected paperback scholar, collector, and dealer, takes a slightly more cautious position. "Anything that exists or was produced on this planet is undoubtedly collected

**DOWN THE BADGER HOLE**
DEBBIE CROSS
WRIGLEY CROSS BOOKS, 1995
A friend and admirer of British author R. Lionel Fanthorpe, Debbie Cross arranged for the publication of this tribute, with bibliography and excerpts from Fanthorpe's works.

**THE NEW BLACK MASK**
EDITED BY RICHARD LAYMAN AND MATTHEW J. BRUCCOLI
HARCOURT BRACE JOVANOVICH, 1985-1987
Published in digest format and distributed through bookstores rather than magazine outlets, NBM published eight truly splendid issues, then changed its title and format briefly before disappearing. Was it a magazine or a series of anthologies?

by someone, somewhere. Collecting is a peculiar passion that attracts many people in varying degrees and in many different ways." Hancer continues, "Book collecting has been a popular hobby for many years, and paperback book collecting often follows traditional patterns."

Jon Warren, another paperback scholar, collector, and dealer, gets more specific. "Collecting paperback books is not a new hobby… Indeed, collecting has been going on since the 1950s, when science fiction collectors began accumulating these new pocket-sized books by some of their favorite authors of the pulp era."

Piet Schreuders, one of the truly great names in the field, approaches the subject from another angle. "In the mid-1960s, comic books suddenly became 'in.' Learned articles were written for new magazines, shops specializing in comics were opened, and the comic books themselves, sometimes already 'antiques' three months after publication, disappeared behind plastic covers and were dealt in at shocking prices. The same thing happened to pulp magazines about five years later, and around 1975 it all started up again, this time with old paperbacks."

So take your pick. Is the hobby more than five hundred years old, or did it start in the 1950s, or in 1975?

In 1994, author and collector Frank M. Robinson stumbled across an intriguing classified ad in a San Francisco newspaper. Someone was offering a garage full of paper materials for sale in the suburban town of Concord.

Robinson dragooned a friend who had the good fortune to own a station wagon, and together they drove out into the suburbs. Would the garage doors be the entrance to Aladdin's cave, or would they lead only to mounds of five-year-old newspapers?

Happily for Robinson, the former was the case. The collection had been the property of the late P. J. Moran, who had started saving popular literature in his boyhood and pursued his hobby throughout a long lifetime. Unfortunately, the garage had caught fire at one time, and the fire had been extinguished with streams of water.

Much of the collection had been ruined by burning or soaking. In later years, insects had invaded the pages. Now Mr. Moran's heirs wanted to dispose of the material once and for all. And despite all the damage, the salvageable portion of the collection was still a treasure trove.

There were hundreds of nineteenth century "story papers." These publications *looked* like newspapers but they were full of exciting fiction about detectives, soldiers, cowboys, and spies. Shades of Griswold and Benjamin! There were dime and nickel novels, early pulp magazines, and early paperbacks.

The borrowed stationwagon was used at first to haul away the most precious of the precious lode. It took a rented truck to remove the rest of the materials. Robinson rented additional space near his San Francisco home and spent months sorting, cleaning, cataloging, and restoring the collection. Much of it now resides in the Stanford University Library at Palo Alto.

Moran is little known in the world of paperback collectors, but he may have been the first of the breed. In any case, his collection proved that paperback collecting was not a new phenomenon but a natural outgrowth of the collecting of earlier mass-oriented publications.

It's important to understand that most paperback collectors don't collect books in order to read them. At first this may seem strange, but in fact it is typical of antiquarians and collectors. Classic car collectors don't search out and refurbish 1920s Packards or 1930s Terraplanes or those so-rare 1947 Tucker Torpedoes in order to ferry the kids to soccer practice. Stamp collectors don't use their treasures to mail their payments to the local power and light company. Collectors of precious 78-rpm records may actually play them on rare occasions, but they are far more likely to transfer the music to tape or CDs and then store the fragile shellac original away.

The originals are preserved as cultural artifacts and are meant to be enjoyed for their beauty, character, and historic value.

If you want to read *The Maltese Falcon* and you happen to own a mint copy of Pocket Book number 268 in a brilliant dust jacket—don't read that copy! Hie yourself down to your local bookshop and buy a brand new copy for a few dollars, or scout up a reading copy at a paperback exchange, or try to score one at a flea market or a thrift store. But keep that gorgeous collectible copy in the best condition you can.

Paperback books are little treasures. Each one has a poster-like cover. The painting, the typography, and the blurb all combine to make a whole that is greater than the sum of the parts. Even the publisher's logo is a design feature which adds to the charm of the package.

Each collector has his or her own rationale for collecting a particular type or group of paperbacks. It might be possible to set out to acquire a copy of every paperback book ever published or at least every one ever published in the United States. It would surely be possible to try, but it would be impossible to achieve.

Instead, each collector sets his or her own set of goals. They may be as specific as trying to accumulate every title ever issued by a particular publisher, or as general as simply accumulating a collection of books that the individual finds interesting, pleasing, or amusing.

Collecting by publisher, or by series within publisher, is one of the most common venues of paperback collecting. Collectors have set out to acquire complete sets of Pocket Books or Bantam Books. It might be more appealing to some collectors to try and acquire a complete set of Ace Doubles, Dell mapbacks, Pyramid Green Door Mysteries, or Lancer Science Fiction Classics.

Others might seek out the products of an obscure or short-lived publisher. This would be easier to attempt; there would be fewer titles to search for. But it would also be far more difficult to achieve. The books just don't show up. Thus, if you're interested in Phantom Mysteries, your task looks easy: there was only one, *Rocket to the Morgue* by "H.H.Holmes" (a pseudonym of William Anthony Parker White, who also wrote as "Anthony Boucher"). But do you think you'll find a copy? Lots of luck!

Just two Yogi Mysteries, four "West in Action" westerns, five Red Dagger Mysteries, two Prize Science Fiction Novels, two Private Editions sleaze novels, three Metro Publications books and six assorted Merit Books.

There were apparently twenty-one Hangman's House mysteries, a single Bard digest, and twenty-nine of those holy of holies, the L.A. Bantams. Make a checklist of what you have and/or need and keep it with you. But also keep an eye out for the unexpected—completely unknown books still turn up from time to time.

There are probably other P. J. Morans out there, and you might turn out to be the next Frank M. Robinson!

From the earliest days of Pocket Books, most paperback publishers numbered their books sequentially. This made it easy for bibliographers and collectors to keep track of the titles. To this day, missing numbers in series leave room for debate as to whether totally "lost" books are lurking out there somewhere. They may have been numbers reserved for books that never appeared.

At varying times, mostly in the 1970s, almost every paperback publisher dropped its sequential numbering in favor of computer-based ISBNs (International Standard Book Numbers). Paperbacks issued since the switch may still be as beautiful or as silly, as outrageous or as important, but a great many collectors simply lost interest at that point and chose to concentrate on the earlier issues.

It's up to each collector to decide what appeals to him or to her.

**SUNGLASSES AFTER DARK**
NANCY A. COLLINS
ONYX (BALLANTINE), CIRCA 1989

This was an experiment that worked once. With vampire novels the latest craze to flood the shelves with their midnight imagery, Ballantine found a way to make its book stand out. A primarily white cover features a pale visage in extreme close-up, with no type whatever except for publisher's indicia.

ONYX
(CANADA $4.95)

STEPHEN
KING
UMNEY'S LAST CASE

penguin 60s

A common basis for collecting, perhaps second to publisher or series, is cover artist. Hundreds of artists have created cover paintings for these little books, and some of them have been true masters of the format. How can you capture the essence of a book in one image and project it in a manner that induces a browser to select *this* book out of the rows and rows of books that compete for his hard-earned money?

Some publishers credit the cover artist on the cover itself or inside the book. Sometimes the artists sign their work, sometimes they don't. Unsigned and uncredited paintings may be identified by style and by inference, and yet there are huge numbers of paperbacks that feature cover art by an unknown artist. Another field for the scholar and the researcher!

Every "artist-collector" has his own favorite, or group of favorites. It doesn't seem possible —or desirable—to collect every talented painter in the industry, but a list of collected cover artists would probably include the following: Robert K. Abbett, James Avati, James E. Bama, Rudolph Belarski, Earle K. Bergey, Ed Emshwiller, Frank Frazetta, H. L. Hoffman, Mitchell Hooks, Sol Immerman, Robert Jonas, Robert Maguire, Robert McGinnis, Leo Manso, Stanley Meltzoff, Barye Phillips, Richard Powers, George Salter, Norman Saunders, Robert Stanley, and Stanley Zuckerberg.

You may find an artist whose particular world vision and graphic style appeal to you more than any of these. Very likely you'll be happier catering to your own taste than following fashions.

Some collectors of course tailor their collecting to their reading preference. You may first have encountered a favorite book in a library copy or in a "reading copy" not of collectible nature. Later, you find a charming paperback edition of the book and add it fondly to your collection.

Thus there are mystery collectors, science fiction collectors, western collectors, and juvenile delinquent collectors. Of course if you have a favorite author, whether Agatha Christie, Ray Bradbury, Leigh Brackett, Ernest Hemingway, or Thomas Wolfe, you'll want to search out books by that author regardless of the publisher or cover artist.

There are collectors who specialize in paperbacks with "GGA" covers. GGA, or "good girl art," is an odd term the origins of which are much debated. The "girls" in good girl art are invariably gorgeous and sexy, often posed provocatively or in a partially unclothed state, and more often appearing "bad" than "good."

Other collectors favor all sorts of favorite cover themes: drugs (especially if the image features a hypodermic needle), monkeys and apes of all types (especially giant gorillas), costumed superheroes, pirates, gangsters, and cowboys. One of the world's great paperback collectors and authorities, Art Scott, specializes in putting together thematic slide shows. His greatest success may have been a solid hour of body-in-the-bathtub images, strategically placed foliage, brass beds, hypos, legs, gorillas, and other popular images, accompanied by knowledgeable commentary and hilarious asides.

Some collectors specialize in MTIs (movie tie-ins) or TVTI's (television tie-ins). Others specialize in superheroes, books with comic book or comic strip connections, cartoon books, or pulp character tie-ins.

A curiosity among collectibles, and not a particularly scare or "difficult" book, is *Double in Trouble*, the "crossover" novel by Richard Prather and Stephen Marlowe in which their respective private eyes collaborate. Sherlock Holmes collectors are a world unto themselves, and whole libraries are devoted to Holmesiana and Holmes-related materials.

One of the most difficult of all collecting categories is puzzle books. If the overwhelming majority of paperbacks ever published have been read and discarded, the highest percentage of all to bite the dust are surely puzzle books. Anyone who bought Popular Library or Dell crossword puzzle books would almost certainly work the puzzles and then discard the book.

Few such survive, and of those, a pristine copy (with "unworked" puzzles) is almost unknown. While puzzle books are generally of little intrinsic interest, their rarity makes them much sought after and expensive when found.

Where can you find vintage paperbacks? There are dealers who specialize in these little books. While a few choice items can run to hundreds or thousands of dollars, the great majority of paperbacks are still reasonably inexpensive. Compared to vintage pulp magazine or comic book collecting, paperback collecting is a hobby accessible to all and affordable by most.

There are a few shops that specialize in vintage paperbacks. On my first visit to the wonderful Rose Idlet's Black Ace Books in Los Angeles, I was literally stunned. The proverbial kid in the candy store or in Santa's Workshop had nothing on me.

Ron Blum's Kayo Books in San Francisco is equally delightful for the collector, as are other specialty shops scattered around the United States and in other countries.

Even more economical are paperback exchanges. Prices are low but condition is often poor. The overwhelming bulk of the books you'll find in such establishments are very recent and of little collecting interest unless you are willing to stash books away for several decades (in which case you can start an enviable collection for almost no expenditure).

Condition is one of the major factors that affect a book's collectibility. Look for either PBOs or first paperback editions of hardcover originals. They're sometimes hard to identify. You can pick up clues from publisher's indicia, copyright notices, or printing histories. If all else fails, a rule of thumb is that older paperbacks are more valuable than recent ones, and the lower the cover price (if all other identification efforts fail), the older the book probably is.

If you're buying a book simply because you like it, and if the price is reasonable, you needn't worry about collectibility and value. But if you are attempting to build a serious collection, and especially if you are paying a substantial price for the book, be careful.

Criteria for collectibility include image, age, "priority" (first printing), scarcity—and condition, condition, condition. Priority can be tricky. There have been many books published in paperback by one line and then transferred to another. The "new" publisher will usually start a new "printing history" for the book, omitting the paperback editions of the prior company.

Remember that a paperback in its dust jacket is worth many times the value of the identical book without the jacket. You can't tell if a book had a jacket just from looking at the book itself. Fortunately, several good paperback price guides have been published. The two best known are referred to by their authors' names: Warren and Hancer. Price listings become obsolete because market conditions change rapidly, but these guides are invaluable sources of bibliographic data, including indications of which paperbacks had jackets.

A paperback's value is reduced if the colors are faded, if the cover is torn or creased, if the pages are loose, if the spine is cracked, or if the paper is yellowed or brown (even more if it is brittle). If some former owner wrote in the book its value is *probably* lessened unless the former owner was a notable figure, in which case the value in increased. An Agatha Christie mystery with annotations by Erle Stanley Gardner would be a fabulous treasure.

Kevin Hancer has developed a useful scale for grading paperbacks, from mint down through near mint, very fine, fine, very good, good, fair, and poor. Paperback price guides usually simplify the scale. Dealers generally grade copies on a scale of G/VG/F—that is *Good*, *Very Good*, *Fine*. Obviously, the better the condition of the book, the greater its value.

Once again, if you are desperate for a book to complete a set or simply for your own pleasure, or if you fall in love with a book (it happens all the time!), you may be willing to settle for a lesser copy rather than do without. Besides, you can always keep an eye out for a better copy of a book you already own and upgrade when one comes along.

Reading copies are usually available for nominal amounts, and the joy of reading is the beginning of the love of books.

If you get a chance to attend a paperback collectors' "show", you should certainly seize the opportunity. You will be able to browse the stock of dozens or hundreds of dealers in a single day. You'll have the chance to meet authors and artists, to chat with fellow book-lovers and collectors, and to develop a network of connections.

You will find that most paperback collectors are friendly and generous, willing to share information on their hobby with one another and with the neophyte collector as well. If you come up against the occasional grouchy, competitive curmudgeon, just excuse yourself and go talk to somebody else.

Most cities have used bookstores, and these stores usually have paperback sections. Look for a dusty shop in a run-down neighborhood, run by an unshaven elderly man or a woman with her hair in a kerchief. Like paperback exchanges, these stores offer plenty of good reading copies for very reasonable prices. Occasionally you'll experience the thrill of finding a true collectible amid the dross. Thrift stores, yard sales, and library sales are all good places to hunt for good paperbacks. You'll have to wade through miles of trash, but you may be rewarded with a truly memorable find. Besides, one person's trash may be another's treasure.

Antique dealers occasionally take in collections of paperbacks and offer them for sale. Unfortunately, these otherwise admirable individuals seem to know very little about collectible paperbacks, and what they have to offer is seldom very interesting but all too often overpriced.

Will you ever find a treasure in a trash heap? Most collectors have stories of having done so. Tom Lesser bought a copy of the incredibly scarce "sideways binding" edition of *Halfway House* by Ellery Queen for ten dollars—it's worth hundreds. Art Scott found a copy of Robert Leslie Bellem's *Window with the Sleeping Nude*, complete with lengthy inscription by the author, in a thrift shop and bought it for ten cents. I once found a copy of the Armed Services Edition *Adventures of Superman* on a two-for-fifteen-cents table—an event I'll never forget. And then there are the "lost books." Study the price guides and bibliographies, run through the number sequences, and you'll notice missing numbers. What went wrong? Were these numbers reserved for books that never existed? Did the authors fail to deliver ther manuscripts? Did the publisher cancel the projects? Or are there still a few copies lurking in someone's attic or garage, tossed in the back of a dresser drawer, fallen behind a row of books in a personal library, stuck between two worthless volumes in a paperback exchange?

They might be anywhere, waiting to be discovered. You might be the one to discover them.

But the thrill that comes from making such a find is really a bonus. The real pleasure of paperback collecting lies in the warmth of the community and in the hours of pleasure that these small treasures, these artifacts of popular culture, history, and art, can provide.

# ACKNOWLEDGEMENTS

"Pigmies placed on the shoulders of giants see more than the giants themselves."
Lucan, 1st Century, Common Era

❦❦❦❦❦

Such a common sentiment and one so often paraphrased or repeated you'd almost think there was something to it. And of course there is.

I could never have put together a book like *The Great American Paperback* without the generosity and assistance of individuals far more knowledgeable in the field than I. My immeasurable gratitude for the information that they shared and for access to their precious collections (the source of most of the images in this book) goes to these noble women and men. They include Charles N. Brown, Lance Casebeer, Lloyd Currey, Rose Idlet, Thomas M. Lesser, Gary Lovisi, Dave Nee, Jan Murphy, Bill Pronzini, Robert Speray, and Tom Whitmore.

My special thanks to John Gunnison for computer processing of the images, to Michael Graziolo, the designer of this book, and to Richard and Lisa Perry, its publishers. They were patient with my tardiness, forgiving of my grumpiness, and diligent in their own efforts.

My thanks to family, friends, and colleagues who stood with me in times of travail. These include Patricia, Kenneth, and Thomas and Frances Lupoff, Crystal Reiss, Lloyd and Mary Stevens, James Reiss, Nicholas Jainschigg, Dave Nee, Lori Leigh Gieleghem, Frankie Y. Bailey, Charles L. Robinson, Eve Loring, Frank M. Robinson, Richard Wolinsky, Gary Turner, Benjamin Tamlyn, and Rod Richardson.

Special thanks to my literary agent and dear friend, Jack Scovil.

And above all, thanks to Art Scott, whose assistance in every imaginable regard has far exceeded the call of duty. Without Art's knowledge of these books, his patience with my obtuseness, his kindness, his technical expertise, and his selfless devotion, *The Great American Paperback* would never have got off the ground.

I willingly acknowledge the work done by others before me in the field of paperback scholarship. They are the giants on whose shoulders I stand. I refer the reader to the bibliography included in this book and recommend further reading in the publications listed, and beyond.

In addition, I should add that I have, myself, been part of the media world for more than fifty years. My books have been published by most of the major paperback houses and many of the minor ones — literally from *A* to *Z*, from Ace to Zebra. I have known and had dealings with many of the key figures in the history of the paperback field. These include Ian and Betty Ballantine, Donald and Elsie Wollheim, Betsy Wollheim, Helen Meyer, Jack Biblo, Jack Tannen, Hulbert Burroughs, Larry T. Shaw, Walter Zacharius, Robert Hoskins, Donald R. Bensen, Dori Gores (formerly Gould), and David G. Hartwell.

*The Great American Paperback* is as accurate as I could make it but as anyone who knows me can testify, I am the living exemplar of human imperfection. I take responsibility for such errors that may have found their way into these pages. In future editions of the book I will endeavor to correct any that are brought to my attention.

If I have omitted your favorite book, author, artist, or publisher, I offer my apologies. Even as sizable an effort as this one can barely scratch the surface of so huge a field. Space limitations were a factor, but other choices were purely judgment calls. Why is *Life on the Mississippi* included while *Huckleberry Finn* is omitted, when the latter is obviously the greater book? Answer: *Life on* the *Mississippi* is more important to the history of paperback publishing. Why is *Reform School Girl* included while *Moby Dick* is omitted? Answer: because the former is an icon to paperback collectors while the latter, masterpiece though it is and despite its many paperback editions, has had no great bearing on paperback publishing history.

Should I have given more attention to westerns and less to mysteries? More to love stories and less to science fiction? More to war books or sports biographies and less to "sleaze"? More to "serious" literature and less to popular entertainment?

All are judgment calls and all are my own. I take responsibility for them.

*Richard A. Lupoff*
Berkeley, California
November, 2000

# BIBLIOGRAPHY

Bonn, Thomas L. *UnderCover: An Illustrated History of American Mass Paperbacks*. Penguin Books, New York, NY, 1982. A pioneering attempt at a history of the field, with valuable information and color and black and white illustrations.

Corrick, James A. *Double Your Pleasure: the Ace SF Double*, Gryphon Books, Brooklyn, NY, 1989. A treasure trove of information for the specialist collector, listing not only Ace science fiction Doubles but prior (non-Ace) publication history and original publication data of anthology contents. Bonus is a brief memoir of Ace Doubles by their longtime editor, Donald A. Wollheim.

Crider, Allen B., editor. *Mass Market Publishing in America*, G. K. Hall, Boston, MA, 1982. Capsule surveys of 68 American paperback publishers, including many small and obscure houses not examined in other references. The generally excellent entries were prepared by an unusual mix of academic researchers, knowledgeable collectors, and fans.

Currey, L. W. *Science Fiction and Fantasy Authors: A Bibliography of First Printings of Their Fiction*, G.K. Hall, Boston, MA, 1979. Now dated but still useful reference work, especially with regard to PBOs by important science fiction writers.

Davis, Kenneth C. *Two-Bit Culture: The Paperbacking of America*. Houghton Mifflin, Boston, MA, 1984. A monumental achievement, the definitive book on paperback history in the modern era. Now badly dated, but a superb treatment of the era 1939-1984, with significant references to earlier periods.

Flanagan, Maurice. *British Gangster & Exploitation Paperbacks of the Postwar Years*. Zeon Books, Westbury, United Kingdom, 1997. Heavily illustrated (black and white) catalog and checklist of collectible British paperbacks. (See also Holland.)

Hancer, Kevin. *Hancer's Price Guide to Paperback Books* (third edition). Wallace-Homestead, Radnor, PA, 1990. Prices are badly out of date, but this book (or see Warren) can be an invaluable bibliographic resource for the collector.

Henderson, Leslie, editor. *Twentieth-Century Crime & Mystery Writers*, Third Edition. St. James Press, Chicago, IL, 1991. Major source of biographic and bibliographic data regarding hundreds of authors, with critical essays.

Holland, Steve. *The Mushroom Jungle: A History of Postwar Paperback Publishing.* Zeon Books, Westbury, United Kingdom, 1993. An excellent work on British paperback publishing, especially in the post-World War II era with important relevance to American authors and publishers. (See also Flanagan.)

Hubin, Allen J. *Crime Fiction III: A Comprehensive Bibliography*, Locus Press, Oakland, CA, 1999. Third edition of the classic mystery bibliography, now on CD-ROM. (Earlier editions in paper form remain useful.)

James, Roy G. *From the Pulps into Paperbacks: A Reference Document*. Gryphon Books, Brooklyn, NY, 1994, 1995. Thorough treatment of pulp characters and other pulp fiction reprinted or continued in paperback.

Lovisi, Gary. *Dashiell Hammett and Raymond Chandler: A Checklist and Bibliography of their Paperback Appearances*. Gryphon Books, Brooklyn, NY, 1994. Detailed illustrated bibliography of these writers in paperback.

Lovisi, Gary. *Science Fiction Detective Tales: A Brief overview of Futuristic Detective Fiction in Paperback*. Gryphon Books, Brooklyn, NY, 1986. Extended commentary and checklist of "genre-crossover" books.

Lovisi, Gary, editor. *Paperback Parade* (magazine). Gryphon Books, Brooklyn, NY, various dates. This magazine, originally a crude fannish production, has grown into an outstanding journal featuring cover reproductions, checklists, interviews with authors, editors, publishers and illustrators. A lynchpin for the paperback collecting community and a joy to the neophyte collector.

Lyles, William. *Putting Dell on the Map*, and *Dell Paperbacks 1942 to mid-1962*, Greenwood Press, New York, NY, 1983. Together the two volumes constitute a massive (700 pages) thoroughly researched history, analysis, and bibliography of Dell paperbacks. The books contain information gleaned from Dell and Western Publishing records as well as interviews with editors, writers, and artists.

Nye, Russell. *The Unembarrassed Muse*. Dial Press, New York, NY, 1970, 1973. Provides excellent information on "premodern" paperbacks and other mass publishing media.

O'Brien, Geoffrey. *Hardboiled America: The Lurid Years of Paperbacks*. Van Nostrand Reinhold, New York, NY, 1981. Thorough treatment of the more controversial aspects of paperback publishing, with excellent coverage of the Gathings investigation and other attempts at repression. Many color and black and white illustrations.

Peer, Kurt. *TV Tie-ins*. Neptune Publishing, Tucson, AZ, 1997. A comprehensive checklist of television tie-in paperbacks organized by TV show and extensively indexed.

Peterson, Clarence. *The Bantam Story: Twenty-Five Years of Paperback Publishing*, Bantam, New York, NY, 1970. Revised and expanded as *The Bantam Story: Thirty Years of Paperback Publishing*, 1975. A splendid treatment of the modern era of paperbacks, with valuable insights into the Lane-Ballantine-Enoch-Weybright relationship, creation of American Penguin and emergence of Bantam and NAL.

Reginald, R., and M. R. Burgess. *Cumulative Paperback Index, 1939-1959*. Gale Research, Detroit, 1973. A splendid research resource. Unlike Hancer or Warren, Reginald and Burgess sequence their book by author, providing a list of books by title, publisher, stock number, year and price. A new edition would be a blessing, but even the 1973 version is highly useful.

Reynolds, Quentin. *The Fiction Factory, from Pulp Row to Quality Street 100 Years of Publishing at Street & Smith*. Random House, New York, NY, 1955. Important "inside" history of this publisher, with information on dime novels and pre-modern paperback publishing.

Sallis, James. *Difficult Lives: Jim Thompson, David Goodis, Chester Himes*. Gryphon Books, Brooklyn, NY, 1993. Brief biographies of these writers, with insights into their relationships with editors and publishers.

Schreuders, Piet. *Paperbacks, U.S.A. A Graphic History, 1939-1959*. Blue Dolphin Enterprises, San Diego, CA, 1981. English-language edition of a book originally published in the Netherlands. The author is a brilliant and dedicated researcher and this book is a landmark of paperback scholarship with an emphasis on art and design rather than literary content or business.

Server, Lee. *Over My Dead Body, The Sensational Age of the American Paperback, 1945-1955*. Chronicle Books, San Francisco, CA, 1994. Highly readable cross between scholarly history and fannish love letter, lavishly illustrated in color.

Shatzkin, Leonard. *In Cold Type: Overcoming the Book Crisis*. Houghton Mifflin, Boston, MA, 1982. A rare exposure of the economics and difficulties of the publishing industry, including a strong chapter on the role of mass market paperbacks. Age has only made this book more poignant and relevant.

Smith, Curtis C., editor. *Twentieth-Century Science Fiction Writers*, Second Edition. St. James Press, Chicago, IL, 1986. Major source of biographic and bibliographic data regarding hundreds of authors with critical essays.

Tuska, John and Piekarski, Vicki, editors. *Encyclopedia of Frontier & Western Fiction*, McGraw Hill Book Company, New York, NY, 1983. Major source of biographic and bibliographic data regarding hundreds of authors with critical essays and photographs.

Wadle, Moe. *The Movie Tie-In Book: A Collector's Guide to Paperback Movie Editions*. Nostalgia Books, Coralville, IA, 1984. Thoroughly researched and highly useful checklist of MTI's.

Warren, Jon. *Official Price Guide to Paperbacks* (first edition). House of Collectibles, New York, NY, 1991. Prices are badly out of date, but this book (or see Hancer) can be an invaluable bibliographic resource for the collector.

Whiteside, Thomas. *The Blockbuster Complex: Conglomerates, Show Business, and Book Publishing*. Wesleyan University Press, Middletown, CT, 1981. A brilliant and explosive examination of publishing practices and abuses, originally serialized in *The New Yorker*.

Zimet, Jaye. *Strange Sisters: The Art of Lesbian Pulp Fiction, 1949-1969*. Penguin Studio, New York, NY, 1999. A gallery of lush paperback covers lovingly presented in color with brief accompanying text. Also contains a valuable memoir by Ann Bannon, a leading author of the genre.

# GLOSSARY OF TERMS

### ADVANCE

Payment from publisher to author prior to publication of the book. If the author delivers a complete manuscript, the advance may be paid in a single sum. If the author signs a contract for a work in progress, payments are usually divided—so much on signing, so much on delivery, so much on publication.

### ASE

Armed Services Edition. A book published for distribution to military personnel in wartime, usually without cost, differing from commercial editions sold to civilians.

### COVER-OUT, SPINE-OUT

Two means of displaying books. All publishers and authors want to see their wares displayed cover-out for maximum visibility to browsers and their rivals' books displayed spine-out—preferably in a dark corner and impossible to reach.

### DIGEST

A paperback book published in the format of such magazines as *Reader's Digest* (hence the term). Typically, these are about 5 1/8" X 7 5/8." Many, but not all, digests are saddle-stitched. Most Nineteenth Century paperbacks were digests but were side-stitched.

### DUST JACKET

Originally a folded sheet of paper placed over the binding of a book to protect the binding. Publishers soon learned that they could use "dj's" for advertising and promotional copy and illustrations. Most paperbacks are published without dust jackets; when a dj is present it greatly increases the value of the book.

### FPP

First Paperback Printing. This could be either a new paperback collection of previously published material or the initial paperback appearance of a book previously available in hardcover form. (See PBO.)

### GGA

Good Girl Art. A cover illustration depicting an attractive young woman, usually in skimpy or form-fitting clothing, and designed for erotic stimulation. The term does not apply to the morality of the "good girls," who is often a gun moll, tough cookie, or wicked temptress.

### GHOST

An author who writes under another author's name. This applies often in the case of celebrity autobiographies and novels. Some readers are crushed to learn that people like Margaret Truman, Chuck Yaeger, and George Sanders don't really write their own books. Some celebrity authors credit their ghosts with small by-lines, "with So-and-So." Others include little thank-you notes in the book.

### HOUSE NAME

A by-line belonging to a publisher. Any number of authors may write under this name, and sorting out who-wrote-what is a favorite sport of researchers.

### MASS

The most popular size for paperback books. Most paperbacks published in the early years of the modern era had dimensions of approximately 4 1/4" X 6 3/8." In the 1950's a slightly taller format (4 1/4" X 7") became the standard.

### JD

Juvenile Delinquent. JD novels concern teen-age gangs, often obsessed with hot-rods, marijuana, and illicit sex. Cover paintings are often striking, featuring a combination of gritty urban realism, GGA, and *noir*-ish lighting effects. These books are heavily collected.

### MTI

Movie Tie-In, a book issued in conjunction with a motion picture. This may be an already-existing book on which the movie was based, repackaged to exploit the popularity of the film, a novelization of the screenplay, or even an original novel based on the characters and "universe" of the movie.

### NOVELIZATION

A work of fiction derived from a motion picture, television, or play-script, or even from a comic book. Possibly the most bizarre novelization of all time was *The Bible*, based on a screenplay by John Huston, based on the Bible.

### ONE-OFF

A non-series novel by an author usually associated with a series character. Examples would be books like *The Deputy Sheriff of Comanche County*, by Edgar Rice Burroughs—no Tarzan, no John Carter—or *The Mountain Cat Murders*, by Rex Stout—no Nero Wolfe, no Tecumseh Fox.

### PACKAGER

An independent editorial-and-design service which contracts out writing to authors, then presents a final, publishable product, often including cover designs and illustrations, to the publisher. This is a classic case of the "middle man."

### PBO

Paperback Original. A book which appears first as a paperback, rather than being reprinted from a hardcover edition. Some (but not all) authorities limit this term to books containing material never previously published. This would exclude, for example, a novel that had been serialized in a magazine. (See FPP.)

## PSEUDONYM

A byline by an author, other than the author's real name. Some authors, like science fiction favorite Hal Clement (real name Harry Stubbs), enjoy full careers under pseudonyms. Others, like the versatile and prolific Evan Hunter, use multiple bylines to separate their work in different genres. Still others, sometimes respectable and very talented writers, use pseudonyms to pick up a quick paycheck turning out novelizations or sleaze books.

## RETURNS

Unsold books withdrawn from sale and returned to the publisher. These include "whole book returns," which can be placed back in stock and sold again if not damaged, and "stripped copies," from which the cover has been removed. Stripped copies are usually destroyed and only the cover physically returned. They sometimes find their way into circulation as reading copies, but are worthless as collectibles.

## ROYALTIES

Payments to authors based on sales of their books. These are usually computed on the basis of a percentage either of the cover price or the publisher's actual receipts. In most cases the author in fact owns the work and the publisher merely licenses it. Subsidiary income, such as from book club sales or motion pictures, is usually divided between author and publisher.

## SADDLE-STITCH

A form of binding in which all pages are laid flat and folded once, held together by staples. This form of binding produces a book with no spine, making display difficult.

## SELL-THROUGH

The percentage of a print run that actually makes it all the way through the distribution process and is bought by a consumer. Good sell-through makes for a profitable book, poor sell-through means money will be lost. In the early days of paperbacks books usually remained on sale until purchased, leading to great sell-through. With increased competition and reduced display-time, sell-through has shriveled to often alarming levels.

## SHARED UNIVERSE

A milieu created by one author, in which other authors may place their stories. The original author or packager then gets a slice of the "new" authors' earnings. Sometimes unauthorized works appear, leading to copyright disputes.

## SIDE-STITCH

A method of binding in which the pages are stacked, rather like a deck of playing cards, and then held in place by glue, staples, or thread (hence the term "stitch"). This gives the book a spine, useful in display and storage.

## SLEAZE

Sensationally-packaged, sexually-oriented books. Some of these contain marvelous inside jokes, puns, and covert references. Authors were typically paid very little, on a work-for-hire basis, and produced these books at lightning speed. They are not hardcore pornography, which is another category of fiction. Many sleaze books could have been published as hardboiled mysteries or as mainstream novels if the publishers had seen fit to do so.

## SPINE

The flat edge of side-stitched books, usually bearing title, author, and publisher's indicia. This permits books to be displayed "spine-out" in stores and collections, and eases browsing.

## SPINNER RACKS

Wire or wooden display devices, often mounted so as to rotate on a stationary base. The browser can look over the books mounted on one face of the spinner rack, then turn the rack to see another set of books.

## TVTI

Television Tie-In, a book issued in conjunction with a television series or other television feature. This may be an already-existing book on which the TV production was based, repackaged to exploit TV exposure. It may also be a novelization of one or more TV scripts, a behind-the-scenes puff book or exposé, or original fiction based on the characters and "universe" of a television program.

## WORK FOR HIRE

Writing for which the author receives a single lump payment rather than royalties. In such cases the publisher owns the work outright, and may license foreign editions, sell film rights, or otherwise profit from the work without further payment to the author.

## WRAPPER

Variant term for dust jacket or dust wrapper.

## WRAPS

The cover of a paperback.